Grotties Don't Kiss
A Prep School Memoir

by

Clinton Trowbridge

Qui Servire Est Regnare
(Whom To Serve Is To Rule)

--Groton motto

The Vineyard Press
Port Jefferson, NY

Also by Clinton Trowbridge

The Boat That Wouldn't Sink

Into the Remote Places (with Ian Hibell)

The Man Who Walked Around the World (with D.Kunst)

The Crow Island Journal

NOTES

Some names have been changed and some scenes slightly altered. "Cooper" and "Silly-Bee" are composite characters.

Portions of Chapters 3, 13, 17, 18, and 20 originally appeared as essays in *The Christian Science Monitor.*

Text references for quoted passages in chapter headings

Ashburn, Frank D., *Peabody of Groton*, New York, Coward McCann, Inc., 1944.

Biddle, George, "As I Remember Groton School." In *Views From the Circle*, edited by Louis Zahner and the trustees of Groton School, The Stinehour Press, 1960.

Duryee, Mary Ballard, "Etiquette," *The New Yorker Magazine*, New York, 1938.

Groton School, Vincent-Curtis, The Merrymount Press and the Meridan Gravure Company (promotional book about the school published by the trustees of Groton School in 1946).

Nichols, Acosta, *Forty Years More: A History of Groton School, 1934-1974*, the trustees of Groton School, The Stinehour Press, 1976.

3

First Edition

The Vineyard Press, Ltd
106 Vineyard Place
Port Jefferson, NY 11777

ISBN: 1-930067-13-5

This memoir is a purely subjective recollection of the author's days at Groton, and may not always correspond entirely to the memories of other students.

Cover Photo: *Groton Yearbook*, Class of 1946:

Fourt Row: Lathrop, Redfield, Powers, C. Gardiner, P.Kunhardt, B. Stevens, James.
Third Row: Train, Starring, M.Field,Trowbridge, J. Lawrence, G. Palmer, J. Gray, M. Morgan, G.Davison.
Second Row: Hutchins, Krumbhaar, D. Carter, Hart, Chandler, Stevenson. Wrenn, Hunnewell.
Front Row: Putnam, Peabody, S.Brown, P.Zabriskie, H. Welch, Hwoschinsky, H. Auchincloss.
Missing: Hooper.

To Elaine

Grotties Don't Kiss

Chapter One

Etiquette

When I get you home from Groton,
When I meet you at the station,
I remember not to kiss you,
We shake hands without elation.

I remember not to hug you,
I remember not to cry,
I remember not to give a
Little hitch-up to your tie.

I remember that detachment
Is a cue we give each other,
For a boy may have a father,
But he mustn't have a mother.

Mary Ballard Duryee (wife of Samuel S.Duryee,
Groton '13). *The New Yorker Magazine,* 1938.

At twelve, I was sent away to boarding school because, for one thing, it was cheaper than keeping me at home. My father was a minister, and a good friend of the headmaster, and therefore it was arranged that the fee would be only four hundred dollars a year. A gargantuan eater, I consumed that much in boiled potatoes alone. I would go to Groton, and "Uncle Jack" would see what he could do with me. It was his first year there, too. It would be my second attempt at the Seventh Grade.

Uncle Corny, who lived in Boston, dropped me off. I suppose I must have ridden up from Philadelphia by train. What I remember vividly was our standing together on the front steps of the main building, holding onto his hand while he talked with someone and waited for his chance to leave. I remember holding onto his hand tightly, not wanting to let it go; and when I finally put my face up to kiss him he held me away and shook my hand instead. "You're at Groton now," he said. "Grotties don't kiss." And then I scurried into the building, which smelled strongly of fresh varnish, and was marched off to where the rest of the new boys were, huddled around on the floor in the first form master's study.

The first thing Mr. Gallien, the form master, did, was explain the rules. Rule number one: no boy was ever to enter another boy's cubicle. A cubicle was a six foot by ten foot space with a curtain in front of it—bed, chest of drawers, chair, window. There were forty cubicles, twenty to each side of a long room: the master's study and bedroom at one end, a fire escape at the other. Two of the cubicles were occupied by prefects, sixth formers, whose job it was to help the master take care of us. There were other rules, a good many, but the cubicle rule was the most important. It was one of those rules that there are no exceptions to or real explanations for. Not only were you not allowed to enter someone else's cubicle uninvited, you were not to go into it even if he begged you to. No one could go into it, not even your parents, except for the

8

master and his two prefects. They could go in any time they wanted to.

After the explanation, we were assigned our cubicles and given half an hour to unpack. As soon as we were left alone, Robins and I grabbed Putnam by hands and feet and threw him into every cubicle of the dormitory—up one side and down the other. The noise eventually attracted the notice of the master and his prefects. "Take 6," several voices said, two words I would hear frequently in the years ahead.

"6" was six blackmarks, the heaviest penalty one could receive short of Black Death, which preceded suspension, which came before expulsion. Getting six blackmarks meant that you had to put in six hours on the following Saturday running around the Circle, a gravel track outside of which the buildings of the campus were situated. If you had more than six blackmarks in one week, you were a candidate for Black Death. In Black Death you were locked into a room for three days with nothing but bread and water and a Bible—oh, yes, and a piss pot. I remember that because Mike Dix got Black Death on November 10th, dumped his piss pot out the window onto the assistant headmaster's head on the morning of November 12th; and on that same day his sentence was changed to "expulsion" and we never saw him again.

My parents made their first trip up to see me on November 3rd—at the headmaster's request. I was failing in Latin and Mathematics, and barely passing in Sacred Studies, Social Studies and English. My attitude was not good. I had been on detention every Saturday since my

9

arrival and by my reckoning had put in a total of 143 miles around the Circle. Offenses included tardiness, messiness, talking in the study hall, laughing in same, participating in three minor disturbances after lights; and, worst of all, provoking laughter on the part of another student while he was being bawled out by one of the masters for another offense. The conference was with Mr. Regan, the assistant headmaster. Afterwards, my mother asked if they could take me out to lunch. "I'm afraid Clinton has some blackmarks to run off this afternoon," said Mr. Regan. "How many is it this week, boy?"

"Six, Sir."

"The usual number, I see."

"What about dinner then?"

"Saturday night dinners are generally taken at the school, Mrs. Trowbridge."

"So we can't see him at all today?"

"That is correct. Tomorrow between 2:00 and 4:00; that would be the only time."

"Then we'll see him then," my mother said and stormed out of the room.

My father joined me that afternoon on the Circle. "Thought I'd walk around with you for awhile," he said.

"You can't walk," I said. "You have to run," and I started to jog again. A funny look went across his face and then he smiled and pulled up next to me. We jogged along together, mostly in silence, for half an hour or so.

"Well, I'll see you tonight," he said and broke off. It wasn't much of a visit, but I appreciated the gesture. I still had about an hour to go.

The next afternoon my parents took Phil Kunhardt, my best friend, and me off in the car. I didn't tell them that I was not supposed to leave the campus, that I was "on bounds." "So what do you want to do?" my father asked.

"There's 'Bruce's, I suppose," I said. That was the local drug store.

"What about the movies, or bowling, or something like that?" my mother said. Phil and I exchanged glances. ".They're in Ayer," I said. So that's where we went.

We got in three games and had a hamburger and a chocolate milkshake each and it wasn't until we drove through the school gates again that I began to seriously contemplate the consequences.

"Mr. Regan wants to see you right away," we were told. It was as if the bowling ball I had just hurled with glee at the pins had unaccountably lodged in my stomach. I glanced over at Phil. His lips were a chalky white.

"I'll just go chat with Mary," my mother said.

"He said to bring you all," the boy mumbled nervously.

"Now?" my mother said. "What for?" The boy who delivered the message, who had been sent out to notify us as soon as we came in, did not elaborate but simply brought us into Mr. Regan's presence. He was in the headmaster's office this time.

One look at Mr. Regan was enough. I couldn't have spoken if spoken to, but then I wasn't. It was my parents he chewed out. Didn't they understand that the School had certain rules, that it was obligatory for the parents to uphold those rules, that it was incumbent upon

11

them to know what those rules were, that the boys could not, of course, be trusted to tell them, that they would naturally attempt to disobey or avoid obeying any and all rules, that...Mr. Regan's head, above its stiff collar, which was a half inch higher than anyone else's, was a tomato red.

"But how ridiculous," my mother said. "We only took them bowling. What's the matter with bowling?"

"Bowling is forbidden, Mrs. Trowbridge. Students are not permitted to go to Ayer for any reason whatever. Ayer is not a suitable place for young Grotonians."

"Ayer?" It's just a village, isn't it? Bowling's only a game."

"Not a gentleman's game, I'm afraid, not one that brings out the qualities that the school attempts to inculcate in its students."

My mother let out a sort of hoot. "And football, I suppose that is?"

"Football! Football, Mrs. Trowbridge, is a team sport that tests character. The wars of the British Empire were won—or lost—on the playing fields of Eton. Football, or Rugger as it used to be..."

The sinking sensation in my lower intestines had long since disappeared. My mother had a look on her face that threatened to explode into violence or laughter, either one unthinkable. Which would it be? What outrageous breach of behavior was to take place next? I stood there, with Phil next to me equally hypnotized, and wondered, almost idly, whether blood would be spilled.

Mr. Regan was a small man, a tiny man, I suddenly realized, with sloping shoulders, a prominent nose, and almost no hair. He looked very much like a bird, a flustered sparrow. My mother was taller than he was, and more powerful looking—a hawk, perhaps, an eagle, even. My father? He tried not to take part, stood grimly by: a soldier in the ranks, at attention, waiting for the battle to commence. And then, unable to expel, Mr. Regan dismissed. "That will be all," he said. "For the future, you know the rules."

We left the room, Phil and I hardly able to contain our grins. And it was never the same after that—Groton, that is. For from then on I understood, if only dimly, that Groton was a game. Staying at Groton was a kind of trick. It was unthinkable not to stay, of course: to get thrown out or quit. And you had to be infinitely clever, resourceful, brave and determined—as well as lucky—if you were to succeed. But succeed you must—one way or another. That was the point of being there.

Chapter Two

December 12, 1940

Dear Mammy and Daddy:

Be prepared for a terrible shock. In a few days you will get a
letter saying that I have been a very bad boy and that I have
gotten 11 blackmarks and 6 demerits accumulated in three
weeks. I guess that means no skiing trip and I don't think I
deserve it. I am very much ashamed of myself and I will
really make an attempt to be a better boy, but I'm afraid it's
not in my blood to be a good boy.

Your undeserving son,
Clinton Whiting Trowbridge

"Kunhardt!"
I skidded to a stop, tiptoed through the empty study hall,
and peeked around the corner to where Phil was standing
in the corridor being bawled out by Creeping Jesus
himself. I sneaked up until I was close enough to touch
Gallien on the back, and went into my silent convulsion
routine. Doubled over, holding my nose, I feigned
hysterical laughter. My face turned red, then purple.
Phil's mouth twitched.
"Kunhardt! Are you listening to me?"
"Yes, Sir!"
I gasped for breath, face contorted, and doubled over
again. Phil looked down at the floor.

14

"Well listen hard. And LOOK at me when I'm talking to you! It's one blackmark this time. If I catch you running down this hall again, it'll be two, then four, then six. You understand? Are you laughing at me?"

"No, Sir!" he exploded.

Gallien whipped around. "Trowbridge. What are you doing here?"

"Nothing, Sir."

Gallien knew something was up, but not quite what. "Well, go along now, both of you," he growled. "You mastered the collar stud yet, Trowbridge?"

"Yes, Sir. Almost, Sir."

"Half hour till supper. Think that'll be enough time?"

"Yes, Sir."

"Well, hurry then. DON'T RUN!"

Out of sight, we took the stairs two at a time. "You almost killed me," Phil hissed.

"What did I do?" He knuckled me twice on the arm.

"Here they come," said Applebee, the prefect. "Your bed's a mess, Trowbridge. Get it straight before dinner."

"Sir. Yes Sir, Sir."

"No lip, Stinky. Where you been?"

"Gallien just soaked Phil one for running." Applebee clamped his hand on Phil's neck and marched him to his cubicle.

"That hurts. Don't you know that hurts?"

I caught myself in the mirror. My hair was still wet but there was no sign of where I'd pushed in the pompadour. Applebee used Vitalis. Ritchie Simpkins had the best ears—flat against his head. Mine stuck out like flags. I held them back with my fingers. If I did that for half an hour every day...

"Get going, Trowbridge. You still have to get that collar on."

"Hey, Peter."

"Yeeesss."

"Someone's been in here."

"What d'ya mean?"

"Well, I didn't do this."

George Brewer came tearing down the hall, his shirt half off. "Maybe Brewer did it," said Applebee. "Or Robins. Hey, Robins! Or did you have somebody in mind?" Sam was greasing his hair back. He had his collar on and was knotting his tie. I put the stud into the back of the shirt and got it through the collar. Now for the front. The bell! "Peter!" He wasn't there. One more try. No good. I slipped on the tie, folded the collar back down. Another try with the stud. No good. The last bell was still ringing as I flew through the door, Brewer just behind me. I tore down the stairs, and lined up with the others. Gallien walked past us, checking, gave a nod to Whitridge, the senior prefect. The Sixth Form went in, then the Fifth, the Fourth, Third, Second, now us. I felt my collar burst loose, and put my hand up to cover it. Brewer smirked. We stood behind our chairs. Whitridge gave the blessing. We sat down. I pulled my napkin out of its ring and felt my collar pop out again. "Come here, Trowbridge," said Applebee from the head of the table. I pushed back my seat.

"Tell her to give me extra potatoes." I whispered to Brewer. I knew he wouldn't.

16

"I'm going to have to give you a lesson," said Applebee and snapped the stud through the collar hole. "That's one blackmark. One more and you're finished."

I nodded. That was six this week: four for the row we'd had in the gym, one last night for whispering during Gallien's reading; and now this one. And this was only Tuesday. There were no potatoes on my plate. I made a gesture to the maid. Hot dogs! Sauerkraut! Yuck. "Pass the bread."

"Please?"

"Come on. Butter!"

The maid came through the door from the kitchen with a steaming dish of potatoes. I heaped six onto my plate. They were flaky white and smashed but they smelled good. No butter. I held up the plate. The maid shook her head. I took another slice of bread. Maybe tomorrow afternoon I could go to the village and get some doughnuts—I'd lost twenty-two pounds since I'd been here and that was just over three months. At this rate I wouldn't make it until Christmas.

Brewer had started the row, accidentally, in the gym. He'd just finished proving he could recite the Lord's Prayer in one belch; and I was lighting farts for him, or trying to, when Billy Grant stormed in with some other Third Formers.

"Will you look at this?" he said. "This is how some people spend their precious Sunday afternoon." Grant and the others had been out in their hut, smoking. I could smell it.

"At least we're not breaking any rules," I said, sniffing the air meaningfully.

"Oh, we're not, are we? We're being goody, goody for a change." He came at me, undressed now. "Why don't we all take a shower, eh?" and grabbed me by the arm.

"Cut it out," I said. I still had my suit on.

"Cut what out?" he said, and started dragging me toward the door.

"Come on," I yelled. "Quit it!" I twisted like crazy but I couldn't shake him off.

"Sure, in a minute," he sneered, and yanked me through the door.

Simpkins was in the shower, but he moved out as soon as he saw us coming.

"Let go of me?" I yelled. "Let go." I swung as hard as I could and bounced one off his chest.

"Oh, you would, would you." He had me by both arms now, from behind. My shoes were slipping on the wet tiles. There was nothing I could do.

"You stinking rat, you..." I sputtered and twisted, but Grant held me tight. I could hardly breathe. And then he pushed himself away and held me where I was by the neck. I got my head out just enough to take a good breath, swung and missed, swung again and hit something, put my head down and... The pain practically knocked me out. Tears burned my eyes. I tried to get up but Grant had a vise grip on my neck and I couldn't move.

"There." He pushed himself away and I lunged toward him, swinging. Grant was laughing now and he caught my wrist and pushed me under the showerhead again, and all I could do was splutter and cry. I couldn't breathe. All of a sudden he let me go. I lay there for a minute, unable to move. I could hear voices shouting, and when I finally got the water out of my eyes and staggered to the edge of the shower there was Whitridge and Cowles and Hadden and Middendorf, all Sixth Formers, and looking very angry. Everybody, including Grant and myself, got four blackmarks. I tried to stop blubbering, but I couldn't. I slumped down onto a bench and tried to pull my clothes off, but I couldn't do that either. The sleeve to my coat was ripped at the shoulder, and I couldn't turn my neck; so I stayed bent over, breathing hard, trying to stop shaking.

"Hang those things up in your locker, Trowbridge," Whitridge said. I tried to look up but I couldn't; my neck hurt too much. Pretty soon they all left and I was able to get out of my suit, and after a while Palmer came in with my gray and white checked coat, my gray pants, and some other things

"Whitridge said he was going to report Grant to Crocker," Palmer said.

"Bastard," I grunted, calmer finally.

Grant was supposed to be my advisor. Some advisor. His father was a doctor in Philadelphia. They picked him, I guess, because we both came from Chestnut Hill. I shined his shoes and he always held back some of the money; the only advice he ever gave me was to shut up, for God's sake, and not bother him. He was a bully and everyone knew it; but the masters loved him, particularly Regan, so he never got into trouble. I almost didn't care about the blackmarks since he got four himself. Everybody got four, even Brewer, and he wasn't even in the room.

I almost wished that Whitridge hadn't come in, though. My suit would have dried out enough and then I wouldn't have stood out at chapel that evening—the only person in the whole school not in a blue suit. Grant whispered to me on our way back to Hundred House that he was going to pound me every chance he got while we were running around the Circle, and he pounded me one right there for good measure. Grant was very strong. He had curly brown hair, and his clothes always fit him exactly.

By the time I got my suit back from home, another two weeks had gone by and it was almost Thanksgiving.

"We're thrilled about your taking up the trombone," my mother wrote, "but next time you walk to the village in the rain, please wear your raincoat," and then she added something about a party I was supposed to go to. I'd been crossing off the days until Christmas vacation ever since September, but now I was looking forward to next term because if I practiced hard I had a good chance of making the band. I already practiced every chance I got, and I probably wouldn't have time to do anything else when I got home either. The only trouble was Billy Grant played the trombone too. I'd have to sit on the same row with him.

Chapter Three

"February 5, 1901 – Mr. Peabody spoke about renunciation. There are three kinds. First, renounce things which are absolutely wrong; then things which harm yourself; lastly things which harm others. He then spoke of the devil as a subtle spirit. His temptations are pride, irreverence, swearing, telling religious funny stories, and praying only with the lips."

Journal notation; George Biddle; in Biddle, "As I Remember Groton School," p. 122.

"My father's a banker," Jerry said.

"Mine's an alcoholic." I said, and we both laughed. Footsteps quickened on the boardwalk behind me.

"Clinton," said a familiar voice, and at the same time a hand pressed down on my shoulder. "Step back here for a minute, will you?"

I stopped and turned and there was Mr. Crocker looking very annoyed. Palmer walked on, as if he hadn't heard. When he was out of earshot, Mr. Crocker picked up the pace again and I fell into step. "Why did you say that?" he said. "Your father's a fine man."

"I know," I said. "I didn't mean anything," and I didn't really. It was a kind of joke, the sort of thing we said all the time. And yet it was true. I was just quoting my mother.

"It's a terrible thing to say. I don't ever want you saying that again, do you understand?"

"Yes, Sir."

"And tell Palmer you didn't mean it."

"Yes, Sir."

"Do you know what an alcoholic is?"

"Yes, Sir. I mean no, Sir. That is I'm not really sure."

"An alcoholic can't control his drinking. He has to drink. All the time. Your father's not an alcoholic."

"No, Sir."

"He may drink too much sometimes. But that's not the same thing. You understand?"

"Yes, Sir."

"Good." He smiled thinly. "Be sure to tell Palmer, now."

"Yes, Sir."

He reached into his pocket. "Life saver?"

"Sorry, Sir, but I can't. Gave them up for Lent."

Crocker looked puzzled. "But it's not even Christmas yet," he said.

"I know, but it's easier this way."

"Didn't I see you eating a candy bar the other day?"

"Yes, Sir. I only gave up hard candy." Mr. Crocker chuckled. "All right, Clintie," he said, and quickened his pace and walked off. This was the second time I'd been laughed at about this and I still didn't see what was so funny.

We had just finished Sunday dinner and my father, out of the blue, asked us all what we were planning to give up for Lent. He was going to give up drinking, he said.

22

The thought of giving up something for Lent had never occurred to me, so I looked around at Katharine and my mother to see what their reactions were. Katharine had her face in her plate. When she finished she excused herself, and my father let her go.

"All drinking?" my mother said, after awhile.

"Well, not sherry," my father said.

"Or wine, or beer or let's see what else?"

"No, just hard liquor. That's quite sacrifice enough."

All at once I understood. "I'll give up hard candy," I said and smiled. They looked at me, and then they both laughed, and my father said that would make his task much easier. My mother just laughed, and then laughed again. I wished I always had something to say that would make them laugh like that; but I couldn't imagine what was so funny. Giving up hard candy was nothing to laugh about. There were sourballs and lollypops, candy canes, lifesavers, butterscotch candies wrapped up in individual wrappers. Did jelly beans count, I wondered? It was not like giving up soft candy, I realized. It would take more than Lent for me to consider doing without Milky Ways, Chocolate Mints, Peppermint Patties, Forever Yours, chocolate bars with almonds, Babe Ruths... But the list was too long. As my father said, what we were doing was sacrifice enough.

My mother had called my father an alcoholic the previous summer. They were having a terrific fight, and she had said it so definitely and with such finality that I must have just accepted it as true, I realized. An alcoholic was someone who slurred his words when he'd had a drink, I'd supposed, for my father certainly did that. But he didn't drink all the time. In fact he made a big point of not starting to drink until an hour or so before dinner. If I wanted to talk to him seriously about something I planned to do it before then. If I wanted him to make sense that is. Sometimes it was more fun when he didn't make sense. But that drove Katharine crazy. She would pull away from him, and wriggle off his lap.

Drinking didn't seem to affect my mother at all. She never took more than two drinks together as far as I know and never slurred her words. When the phone rang after dinner, she would pick it up; and if we were in Chestnut Hill and it was a parishioner, she would do the talking. But she didn't like to do that. In fact, she hated it. And sometimes she'd refuse. The point of drinking seemed to be to make you feel better, and I didn't understand why she drank at all because it almost always made her feel worse. I saw her lying down once, after dinner, in Maine, on the lawn. She'd had too much to drink, she told me. She felt dizzy and was trying not to be sick. She lay there quite a long time.

I'd seen my father drunk, lots of times. If he and my mother had been fighting, for instance, quite often he would pour himself a hefty drink right after dinner, which he didn't usually do, and then he'd wander around outside, if it were summer; down to the shore maybe, if it were a pretty night and the mosquitoes weren't too bad. I found him down at the beach one time, skipping stones at the sailboat. "I can't hit it," he said. "It's too damn far out." He'd stopped slurring his words, but I knew he was drunk because that's the only time he ever swore. One night, when it was very warm, he took off all his clothes and went in for a swim. "Come on," he said. "Water's wonderful." And so I went in too. When we climbed back up the hill afterwards, he was laughing.

I'd seen Crocker drunk just that week, at early communion. I couldn't take communion because I wasn't confirmed. I was there because my grandmother had told me always to pray before I took exams. "God can't give you answers, Clinton. But he can give you a clear mind." I hadn't paid much attention when she'd said it, but as the exams got closer, I figured I'd give it a try.

There weren't many boys at early communion that Sunday, and Crocker had poured out too much wine. He'd blessed it so he had to drink it, and there was a lot of it. He filled the chalice up three times. When we walked back to Hundred House afterwards, I saw him stagger—a couple of times. He was drunk all right. He practically fell.

I didn't understand the whole business, frankly. Every time grown-ups had anything to celebrate out came the drinks. Champagne toasts at Grampa Whiting's birthday party; cocktails, highballs, hot rum punch for Christmas. Sherry after Church every Sunday. That was a ritual at Chestnut Hill. Drinking generally made people act childish, but I could act childish without drinking. If I didn't choose to drink when I got to the proper age, though, I'd be wasting something, it seemed. Nobody ever said so, but just as we looked down at Presbyterians for passing grape juice around in little paper cups instead of going to the rail and drinking wine from a silver cup; so we despised people who made a point of not drinking, like

25

my grandmother. What were they trying to prove? That they were better than the rest of us?

I looked forward to drinking but not the way I looked forward to my birthday or Christmas, or going to Maine in the summer. It was a sign of being grown up: like smoking, or going out with girls. What I was really looking forward to was learning how to drive the car.

Chapter Four

Silly-Bee took the long, ivory needle into his right hand, curled the second finger of his left over it, pulled the wool tight from off its needle, and looked up. "Simple what?" he said.

"Simple minded, I call it," said Cooper. "What's the point?"

"The point is to make blankets—nine inch squares, actually—to be sewn together into blankets. When the knitting machines come, you can make a pair of socks in twenty minutes, just by grinding a crank."

"Seems quite easy," said Train. "You just take the wool off one needle and put it on the other."

"Knitting for Britain," it was called. Cowles and Hadley in the sixth form had started it, either because Mrs. Nash had a relative in England or that Mrs. Irons was English; we didn't know which. No one would have taken it up, though, if Cowles hadn't been on the football team, and if Hollingsworth (left tackle), and Whitridge (the captain and senior prefect) hadn't joined in. By the time it got down to us, it was just a matter of learning how. At the big St. Marks's game at the end of the season, half the boys in the bleachers were knitting; and Cooper himself had made a ten foot scarf, which he wore every place but to bed and in chapel; and we felt honored rather than despised when the article in the Boston paper appeared with the headline: "Groton Knits While St. Mark's

Drills." By then knitting had become so popular that Crocker had to make an announcement disallowing it during classes 'cause of the noise.

Silly-Bee (or Silsby-Bassington as he preferred to be called) was one of the eleven English boys who came to Groton that fall, most of them in the upper forms. They were here to escape the bombings in London and because their parents wanted them to continue their educations. We were eleven over our one hundred and eighty-three as a result, but that was all right. There was a war on, at least in Britain; and lots of fifth and sixth formers were already talking about the possibility of a peacetime draft and what the age might be. We'd seen the pictures in *Life* that summer of Dunkirk and the Germans riding through Belgium and then France on their motorcycles and tanks. We'd seen the newsreels of the London streets with all the buildings down. So we were prepared to be a bit crowded in the dorms and in the dining room and have a few upsets. But we didn't like all the British boys. Silly-Bee was okay, though. We made fun of him for the way he talked, and of course we hated him for his prissy manners and his being able to put on a stiff collar in just five seconds. When he told us that his father was an earl and that he would be one someday, as well, we just laughed at him. But we loved to hear him tell stories about his school and the war. Silly-Bee had been sent off to Eton when he was five, so when we complained about the bullying we got from the upper formers, about compulsory chapel and blue suits on Sundays, and stiff collars and patent leather shoes for dinner, it was his turn to laugh. They had to wear top hats and tails all the time and never dress in

28

anything but black "for good old King George III" (He was a founder or patron or something.).

While he was in London waiting to come over, the swank hotel he was staying at was hit. "I was in the lobby, curled up on the floor," he said to a group of us in the gym locker one day. "Mother and Pater were there too. 'Here comes one!' someone shouted, but all I could hear was the sound of a motor car getting louder and louder. And then there was this terrific thud and things falling and people crying out. One man kept saying, 'Keep calm, now. Keep calm.' After a while the wardens came 'round with their torches and you could see great cracks in the ceiling and lots of plaster lying about, but no one was hurt to speak of." Buckingham Palace had been hit the night before, he said. "There they were, the King and the Queen, out in the street the next morning, inspecting the damage. 'You're a fine king!' someone shouted. 'You're a fine people!' called out the king. Queen Wilhelmena— She's the queen of Holland, you know—had a cot set up in the lobby right next to us. She didn't say anything at all. The rest of us slept on the floor. The bomb took off the top two floors. Nothing left of 'em. Everything just lying about in the street."

"Wouldn't you have been better off in the shelters?" Train said.

"Awfully crowded. All those babies. Pretty fetid down there, too," Silly-Bee said, wrinkling his nose. "Lots of people just stayed in their rooms. Later on, of course, we were queuing up in the afternoons to get the best seats, when Stan Lupino and the other comics started to do their routines. I miss that part. I do."

29

Gignoux, in the fifth form, was a terrific athlete, even better at baseball than at football, it was rumored; and Lawrence, in the sixth, not only got straight A's, but acted the female lead in the school play, and was friendly with everyone, even us. He never gave out a single blackmark, even when it was obvious the person deserved it. There were a couple of English boys, though, that we hated. Herrick in the third form was one. He was a bully, a worse one than Grant. His best friend was a very creepy boy named Edwards. I'd turn around in study hall and Edwards would be looking at me—his lips slightly open, flecks of spittle clinging to the corners—faintly smiling. There were a lot of boys like Herrick and Edwards at Eton, Silly-Bee said. We were lucky we had so few of them here. "But then the Rector hated fagging," he added. "Wouldn't have it in his school, he said."

"What's 'fagging'?" I said.

"It's when you have to do whatever an older boy tells you to. Or you get caned."

"Like shining his shoes?" I said.

"Like licking them," said Silly-Bee. There was a dead silence after that.

After a while Cooper said, "Where are these blankets going, anyway?"

"They'll probably be distributed in the East End," said Silly-Bee. "Conditions there are pretty appalling."
Still, knitting might not have been such a big thing if it hadn't been for all the brothers in the school. Cooper had Mathew in the fifth form, and Mathew was one of the first to take it up; so sooner or later, Cooper had to. Shep Brown, Bertie Wrenn, Bruce Chandler, and Miles Morgan

all had brothers in the third form who knitted, so they did, too. Of course it worked the other way. Johnny Gray had David in the third and Bill in the fifth, neither of whom knitted; so neither did Johnny. I never took up knitting, but that had nothing to do with British war relief.

Aunt Margaret, Grandpa Whiting's wife, was such a famous knitter that I never even thought of doing it. She could turn the heel of a sock in the movies, and every Christmas she loaded us down with argyles. If I started to knit, I'd be expected to match her. Grandpa Whiting wasn't much on British war relief, anyway. He kept saying that Roosevelt was going to get us into the war. Knitting was about the last thing he'd want me to do. He was head of his own coffee company (Private Estate Coffee, it was called.), and he wanted me to be a businessman like himself. He always called me "Pal." Aunt Margaret was his second wife. He'd met her in Florida someplace, after Granny Whiting had died. She was about my mother's age. She smoked cigarettes like a chimney and popped gum and called Grandpa Whiting "Boss." They had a big house in Englewood, New Jersey, and when we lived on West 81st Street, we went out to see them all the time.

That fall Grandpa Whiting sent me a whole box full of Willkie buttons. I didn't wear any myself. (Our whole family was for Roosevelt.), but I was glad to get them because they brought from five cents to fifty cents apiece. I sold the one that said "Dr. Jekyll of Hyde Park" to Cooper for seventy-five cents. We had a debate in social studies class about who would make the best President. No one but Phil and I put up our hands for the Roosevelt side. (You'd think he'd have more supporters since he went to the school himself.) So Irons picked Cooper and John Train to speak for Willkie and sent the four of us out of the room to prepare. We only had five minutes.

"We can say he's for the poor," said Phil.

"Right," I said. "What about the New Deal?"

"Definitely," said Phil. "We can start with that."

I led off. When it was Phil's turn, he couldn't think of anything else to say, so he just stood there turning red. Sit down, I kept thinking, but Irons wouldn't let him. He had his watch out and didn't even look at him, just kept calling out the time: forty-five seconds, thirty seconds, fifteen seconds. It was pretty mean, I thought. We lost the debate. I couldn't even explain what the New Deal was; but then Cooper tried to rub it in by saying that Roosevelt wasn't even worthy to stand up as a Presidential candidate; that he was practically a traitor to his country and certainly a traitor to his class. Irons didn't like that, you could tell, but a lot of boys did; and then someone said, "Good old Rosenfeld," and there were a lot of snickers, and Irons blew up and sent half the class out of the room.

When Roosevelt won the election, Crocker sent him a letter of congratulations from the whole school. A lot of boys, and some of the masters, were angry about that. They were opposed to some of the changes he'd made too: such as abolishing Black Death and "watching for squirrels." (That's when you get stood up at the window in the dining hall for the rest of the meal if you get caught talking too loud, or if you're rude or jiggle someone's elbow while they're eating or something. Mr. Regan introduced that punishment when he came to the school years and years ago, so he, for one, wasn't too pleased.) Most of the changes were popular, though, particularly the one that said we didn't have to wear our blue suits on Sunday afternoons, that we could change into our old clothes if we wanted to walk in the woods or play touch football or just mess around. Saved on the suits as well. A lot of people said that when the Rector and Mrs. Peabody got back from their vacation (They'd gone to Arizona for six months.), they'd be very upset about what the Crockers had done, but if they were, we never heard about it.

Some of the changes were because of the War. Blue flannel was needed for uniforms, so blue suits weren't as easy to replace any more. Just before Christmas, someone from the Army base in Fort Devens (just the other side of Ayer) asked the school if it would help with airplane spotting. There had been rumors that German planes had been seen over the East Coast, and even though there was probably nothing to that, still, in case things got worse, the whole Eastern Seaboard was being put on the alert. The top of the schoolhouse would make a perfect spot, they said, because it had such a great view. So the school agreed to help man the watches: masters and fifth and sixth formers. At night, men from the American Legion post in town took over. Fort Devens was a big base now. The War was in the air, all right; even though to us mostly what it meant was Charlie Chaplin in *The Great Dictator*, Stupnegel and Bud, and "Terry and the Pirates." The Führer and Mussolini were comic figures to us. But not to the English. There was one English boy in the sixth form

33

who'd come to Groton the previous year. He'd written a funny piece in *The Grotonian* about how normal everything was in his village thirty miles north of London when he'd returned to it that summer. He seemed to be pooh-poohing all the fuss. But when we came back from Christmas vacation, he wasn't with us any more. He'd joined the RAF and he was back in England being trained.

Chapter Five

I'd never gotten off the third Monadnocks in football, and I was in B sections in all my subjects, even Latin which was mostly a repeat; but when I got back to Groton after Christmas, I was surprised to find I was glad to be there. I'd stayed with Phil in Morristown over the vacation, and he was going to visit us in Maine this summer; and right away we got into a row in the bathroom, and Phil ended up shoving Jerry Palmer's toothbrush into the back of his jaw (accidentally, of course), and Jerry didn't even notice it until he got up the next morning and his face was all swollen up and he had to go to Pest House and Miss Winterbottom found out about it. So Phil got six blackmarks and a stern lecture from Gallien, and it all felt sort of normal. There were no organized athletics during the Winter Term, and I got in a lot of skiing. There was Big Pirate and Little Pirate to ski on, and I perfected my stem turn and got so I could do a pretty good herringbone up hill. When the snow wasn't good, I would box or practice the trombone. There was a lot more free time during the winter, and I liked that.

I thought the Spring Term would be even better, because I was crazy about baseball; and Phil and I had visions of going trout fishing and swimming in our spare time; but just after we got back from Easter Vacation something happened that was so awful that I couldn't even tell Phil about it. The worst thing was I thought it was probably my own fault. I'd been walking the knife-edge as far as being bad was concerned: taking a lot of chances. I thought I'd gotten away with it, but one day Edwards, in the third form, stopped me as we left morning chapel and said he'd been watching me, and that I was getting away with murder, and that he'd decided that since no one else was doing it, he was going to punish me. A week later he caught me running in Hundred House hall.

He was standing at the foot of the stairs to the first form dorm, his right foot placed casually on the first step, effectively blocking my way. He was fingering his bow tie, and he had that nasty smile on his face that made me want to look away. I tried to walk past him, up the stairs, but he vise-gripped my elbow, and forced his face practically into mine. "Follow me," he said. "We don't have much time."

We went out a back door of Hundred House and across a playing field and into the woods. I thought of turning around and running, but I knew he would catch me if I did, and that that would make it worse. There was no one else around. I'd been bad, I knew it. But I was sorry. I wouldn't be bad again. I'd learned my lesson, I really had.

"Don't!" I cried out. "I'll be good. I swear it." But Edwards just walked on.

After about a quarter of a mile he suddenly stopped. "This'll do," he said, turning to face me. "Now. Take your pants off." So that was it. He was going to beat me. "Take off your pants—and your underpants—and bend over: up against that tree." I was trembling now. He had no right to beat me. Beating was against the rules. But boys had been beaten. I knew that. Grant beat up on me all the time, though that was different. A metallic taste filled my mouth, as if I'd just licked the dust off a screen. Edwards was strong, stronger even than Grant. There wasn't anything I could do.

"Hurry up," said Edwards. "I told you we don't have much time." I undid my belt and let my trousers down, and took them off, carefully, so as not to get mud on them, and hung them up on a branch of the tree. I took off my underpants. Then I put my left arm across the trunk, pressed my forehead up against it, and waited. I was shivering. I could hear Edwards peeling the stick with his knife. I turned around. "Please," I said, starting to cry now. "Don't hit me."

"Turn around, Trowbridge! And don't turn back 'till I tell you to." He slashed me hard on the legs and I cried out and he grabbed my shoulder and hissed into my ear: "Stop that sniveling, you little prick. And don't you dare open your mouth, either." I waited, knees trembling, for the first blow. Instead, he put his hand on my bottom and then I cringed as I felt him push something up inside of me.

"Oh," I cried. I couldn't help it. I tried to straighten up, but that made it hurt worse; and he held me down.

"Don't move," he said, breathing the words into my right ear. And he held me down so I couldn't move and inserted the stick further up—slowly. Slowly. It was all I could do not to scream out. Finally he relaxed his hold a little and then I felt a searing pain as he pulled it out.

"Oh! Oh!" I moaned. I was sobbing now.

"Shut up," he said, in a very nasty voice. "It didn't hurt that much. You know it didn't."

37

"It did! It did!" I cried. But what I felt was shame. Shame. For what, I did not know. Or why I felt it. Vileness! Filth! Disgust! Shame!

Two weeks went by. I was hurrying back from the gym so as not to be late for the dinner bell when suddenly Edwards stepped out from behind one of the pillars at the entry to Hundred House.

"Tomorrow afternoon at the back door at four o'clock. Be there." I stumbled past him, all but fell. I felt so heavy, suddenly—so empty, so weak. I had been dreading just this, and now it had happened. For two weeks I had hardly spoken to anyone, despairing over what I should do. I had to tell someone. But who? Mr. Gallien? He was my form master. I was supposed to go to him if I had any problems. But I was a bad boy, wasn't I? And Edwards was one of his favorites. And Edwards was punishing me. What would he say if I told him? Would he even believe me? And how could I say it, put it into words? No, it was impossible. And then I would be squealing, wouldn't I? And if Gallien let out I was a squealer, then even Phil would stop being my friend. Not Phil but... There was nothing I could do. If I wasn't there tomorrow, Edwards would find me. There was no place I could hide. If only he would just beat me.

"What's the matter, Clinton? You look awful," said Train as he helped himself to some more mashed potatoes. "Lost your appetite?"

"Sort of," I said. I didn't think I was going to make it through the meal.

* * *

38

The Peabodys returned from Arizona on April 16 and there were big celebrations at the school. The Rector was a fine-looking old man, with an eye that pierced right through you and a grip of iron when he shook your hand. Mrs. Peabody was very elegant looking and beautiful, and I thought I'd never seen an expression that was so serene. She looked a little like Granny T., who ruled the big house in Maine; but Mrs. Peabody's voice was much sweeter, and she genuinely seemed to love everyone and everything: the boys, all of whom she knew by name (except for us new boys, of course); the masters, who kissed her on the cheek, even Mr. Regan (who blushed); the very buildings. If I could tell Mrs. Peabody, I thought, she would brush it away with her smile.

If I were in Maine or at home, I might be able to tell my father about Edwards; but it would have to come up very naturally; in a casual, joking sort of way; and probably that wouldn't happen; or if it did, I would realize the opportunity too late, and the moment would have gone by. Could I talk to Mrs. Crocker about it? (She was still Aunt Mary to me.) Tonight after prayers? "Good night, Clintie," she would say. Even when I'd been bad, she would always give me a warm smile.

"Good night, Mrs. Crocker," I would answer, and then very quickly, "Could I speak to you later, please?" Would she say, "Yes, of course." Would she look at me and understand? There would be no time for further talk. There were all of us to get through each night—the whole school—and she had to stop and say "good game," or "happy birthday," or "I do hope you're feeling better," to every third or fourth boy. But then, if I saw her, what would I say? That there was a boy who did something disgusting to me that I hated. That it hurt. That it made me feel so terrible that I thought, sometimes, I wanted to die.

"What is it, Clintie?"

I could not tell Aunt Mary about Edwards. How could I tell her that the boy she had talked with so cozily after chapel that Sunday had tortured me; the same boy who led the choir at the Christmas Service of Lights, who stood so tall and straight in his robes, holding that huge, shining cross out before him; whose mother and father were such good friends of the school?

"Edwards? It can't be. You can't mean Edwards, Clintie."

And if I said, "Yes, Edwards!" would she believe me or him?

No. I could not tell Aunt Mary—or anyone else—about Edwards. Not ever. So the torture and the dread would just go on.

The Peabodys stood in line with the Crockers that evening to say goodnight. "And who is this young man?" said the Rector when he came to me. Mrs. Crocker introduced me. "Clintie?" Wouldn't you prefer being called Clinton?" he said, looking me up and down with a kindly smile.

"Yes, Sir," I replied. How did he know?

"Something troubling that boy, Mary," the Rector murmured, lowering his voice from its accustomed boom. "Frowned all through that delicious meal."

40

"He's usually quite cheerful, Cottie. I'll speak to him." But she never did.

* * *

Edwards was there when I arrived. "You were whispering in study hall. I saw you," he said.

"No I wasn't," I said, quickly. And I hadn't been. I'd been on my best behavior for the past two weeks; hadn't received so much as one blackmark.

"That's a lie," he said. "Follow me." We crossed the field and went into the woods. "Take off your pants," he said, when we reached the tree. And when I was naked, he slashed me hard on my thighs. "That's for lying," he said. "Now get up against that tree." He'd peeled another stick and he was looking at me with that awful half smile.

"Couldn't you just beat me?" I said. "I won't tell." He gave a kind of laugh.

"Bend over," he said, flicking at my bottom with the end of his stick. And then he put his hand on my bare flesh and held me down, and I tightened my muscles and shivered and waited for the pain.

"I'll tell," I said, when it was over. I was sobbing.

"No you won't," he said. And I knew he was right.

* * *

In one of my dreams, I had Edwards by the neck and was banging his head up against a rock. The back of his head was beginning to turn into mush, but he continued to stare at me with those hard, cold eyes, making no sound.

41

In another dream, Phil, and Johnny Gray and I were swimming naked in a pond we'd found in the woods. We were splashing each other and having a great time when suddenly Edwards and two unfamiliar, older boys appeared. "I've got Trowbridge," cried Edwards in a loud voice and ran into the water with his clothes on and grabbed me by the waist, while the other two took off after Phil and Johnny. I managed to squirm away from Edwards, finally, but when I got back to the school I had to hide in the woods and hope that someone would come along and get some clothes for me. No one did and it began to rain, and then I woke up.

* * *

I was by myself even more now. Baseball didn't interest me any more and I never got off the third Monadnocks. Phil was on the second Wachusetts, and Johnny Gray was on the first; Cushing already had his eye on him as a pitcher. I spent my time walking alone in the woods, brooding over Edwards—wondering what I should do.

* * *

The bombing of London was at its most severe that spring. Westminster Abbey was practically leveled. Everyone was for England, now, and against the French who wanted us to pay no attention to the blockade. We were sending Britain arms as well as food, and everyone was saying that Lindbergh was wrong and that Britain really was our first line of defense. One night, instead of reading to us as he usually did, Gallien turned on the radio so we could hear Winston Churchill make a speech. It was great. No wonder Silly-Bee had been so excited. And for weeks afterwards John Train went around saying, "Give us the tools and we will finish the job." His accent was perfect, too. Even though it was more dangerous than ever there, three English boys went back for the duration, and two sixth formers were joining an American squadron attached to the RAF when they graduated, instead of going on to college. Even Roosevelt was getting more popular. We studied his speech about the Four Freedoms in social studies; and no one, not even Cooper, made fun of it.

We had a hot debate, though, about feeding Europe. I was pretty well up on that because it was practically all we had talked about at Christmas. The head of the movement *not* to break the blockade was a good friend of my father's: Pitney Van Dusen, another minister.

* * *

"Ministers opposed to feeding starving children," Grampa Whiting had growled, snipping the end off his cigar. "What next?"

"If we feed them, the Germans won't have to," my father had said, quite calmly.

. "And what about Mr. Hoover? Why don't you accept his plan?"

"Because it's naïve. The Poles and the French and the Spanish won't get the food. That's the whole point. The Germans will take it."

"Don't raise your voice, George," my mother had said. "Mr. Hoover thinks he's taken care of that." I remembered it all very well.

* * *

The War was getting closer, that was for sure. Twenty-one year olds were being drafted, and lots of factories had shifted over to defense work. There were huge strikes all the time; beetle-browed John L. Lewis was on the front page practically every day. Everyone seemed to hate him: my father, my grandfather; even some of the miners.

* * *

It was the end of May and hot already and only three weeks until we were out for the summer. I'd just left Pest House where I'd been down with a fever for the past two days when I saw Edwards standing by the back door to Hundred House. I knew instantly that he'd been waiting for me, and everything inside of me dropped.

"I haven't done anything," I said, but I knew it wouldn't do any good.

"You were whispering in study hall, Trowbridge. Be here tomorrow at four."

I hardly slept at all that night, and the next morning I felt so awful that even Gallien noticed. He pulled me aside after breakfast, and asked me if there was something wrong. "What is it, Trowbridge?"

"Nothing, Sir," I mumbled, and turned away.

"Have you been getting into trouble? Something I don't know about?"

"No, Sir."

"You've been awfully quiet lately."

"Yes, Sir."

"Nothing, eh?"

"No, Sir."

"If I find out there is something, it'll go much harder for you. Understand?"

"Yes, Sir. May I go now, Sir?" I was half way out the door when he gave his reluctant approval.

Edwards was there when I arrived and we walked off in silence. I felt so dead nothing much seemed to matter. When we got to the tree, I even stopped and took off my pants and underpants without being told to. I could hear him shut his knife after he peeled the stick, and I steeled myself and at the same time tried to relax. There was the initial pain but this time when he pushed the stick up he did so more gently: Slowly. Further. Further. It didn't hurt as much as usual. "There," he said, stopping at last. "It feels good doesn't it? Say it does." I grunted and held myself ready for when he would pull it out again. But he didn't. I heard him fumble with something, and then he began groaning, in a sort of whisper. "It feels good, doesn't it? Doesn't it?" he kept saying, as if to hide the noises he was making. His groans got louder and louder and finally he cried out and instantly was silent; and the woods rang with the sound that was gone. I felt his hand

45

relax on my tightened bottom; and then he pulled the stick out—very slowly, so that it hardly hurt at all. "All right," he said, in a calm, more natural voice. "You can get dressed now."

I turned my head and looked at him. "This won't happen again," he said.

"I don't understand," I said.

"Maybe you will when you're a third former," he said, and he turned and started back along the path, his head bowed.

Chapter Six

"Russia Declares War On Germany." My father put down the paper and looked across the table at my mother. "Thank God," he said. "Now it'll be over in no time." But it wasn't. In no time the Germans had reached Moscow, and they hadn't let up on England either. No one could believe it. Then one of our boats was sunk by a U-boat, and it seemed as if we might get into the war right then and there. Every day there was more bad news: another huge strike or some terrible catastrophe like all those Chinese suffocating in their own air raid shelter.

"Walter Lippmann says they ought to try Lindbergh as a traitor," said my mother one morning at the breakfast table.

"They will, if he keeps it up. America Firsters! Father Coughlin and his rotten crew," growled my father. Things were sure in a mess and getting worse, and even off trout fishing my father would come out with some remark about De Gaulle being his only hope, or something; and that would ruin the fun. We were supposed to be saving tinfoil and cheering each time the British bombed another city in Germany; but all I wanted to do was go sailing and play tennis and forget about all that. As far as having fun in Maine was concerned, we might just as well have stayed in Chestnut Hill.

Every morning my mother tutored me in English: ten spelling words a day and a composition a week. Plus rules. Then I'd go to my bedroom and work on turning English into Latin and Latin into English: ten sentences of each, to be handed in when I got back to school. I put the card table I used as a desk in front of the window, so at least I could look up every once in awhile and rest my eyes on the sailboat and the bay; but after a few days I moved it over against the wall again, and just did the sentences as fast as I could, so I'd be finished before lunch.

I was almost glad to get back to school. Regan had retired, for one thing. Wright had taken his place as senior master, and at least he was halfway human. We were in the Raj's dorm in Hundred House, and everything was a lot better than the year before. Pete Douglas was one of our prefects; and he let us listen to jazz records whenever the Raj wasn't around, and gave us feeds, and was generally a neat guy. I knew his sister, Sharman, from when we lived in New York—the Douglases were friends of my parents—and she'd already been up to the school a few times. She'd attracted a good deal of attention. Any girl would have, of course, but she was pretty, and knew it, and looked and acted a lot older than fourteen. There were thirteen new guys in our class, Phip Zabriskie among them, and I was the experienced one and could show him around. Best of all, I'd made the band.

My big trouble was Latin. I didn't pass my re-take exam, and the sentences I did over the summer were horrible. I wasn't good at any subject, really. My mind kept drifting. But in Latin I was hopeless. I couldn't have cared less how many parts Gaul was divided into; and why, I kept asking myself, were we studying a language that nobody spoke any more? Not that French was any better. I was in "B" Latin, and "B" French, and "B" everything else; and right away Phip was in Upper "A" in all his subjects; the quarterback of the first Wachusetts (and its star passer); and so far hadn't received a single blackmark. We didn't see much of each other.

Mr. Noble was my Latin teacher, and he also sat next to me in the band. I was at the bottom; then there was Mr. Noble, two other boys; and, at the other end, Billy Grant. Mr. and Mrs. Noble—particularly Mrs. Noble— were good friends of my parents. The main reason the Nobles were at Groton was so that Mr. Noble could coach football. He had been a big football star at Yale and was on the track team, too. He and my father, who went to Princeton, had gotten to know each other at meets. Out on the field, Mr. Noble always wore his Groton scarf and his old Groton football sweater; football pants, and football shoes. He was very good looking (a leaner jawed Dana Andrews), and the members of the football team worshipped him and imitated his bluff, hearty manner. He was not so terrific in the classroom. As for his trombone playing, I was pretty confident that he and I would be exchanging places before the term was out.

Mrs. Noble was the school sex bag. There were sixth and fifth and even fourth formers who drooled at the sight of her. She held herself like a movie queen; her clothes always looked both too tight and not tight enough; and the entire school followed the passage she made from the rear of the chapel to the communion rail and back again each Sunday morning with the kind of attention usually reserved for Dorothy Lamour.

49

Mrs. Noble's only competition was a kitchen maid we referred to, for the mystical extension of her bosom, as "The Shelf." There were "The Pigs," of course: "Blackie" and "Whitey," two other members of the kitchen staff; but they hardly counted. Anyone could kiss them—down in the Hundred House cellar among the shoe lockers. They smelled of dishwater and cabbage, and they giggled all the time, but the main thing was they were so ugly. The Shelf was built like Gypsy Rose Lee. The trouble with her was she had no face—no expression: a mannequin from Macy's; and she was as aloof as if she were a queen. She had terrific tits, though. You had to hand her that.

The first new boys I got to know were Jock Lawrence and Charlie Coster. Jock could sit down at the piano and rattle off "Begin the Beguine" without music, and Charlie played the drums. His heroes were Gene Krupa and Big Sid Catlett; and if he played something slow he would put a dreamy expression on his face that made him look like a dope fiend; and when he took a solo he chewed his lip and yelled and threw his hair around and bugged out his eyes and generally appeared completely crazed; and we would stomp our feet and shout out words of encouragement. And when it was all over and he was smiling, in a state of semi-recuperative collapse, we would clap and whistle. We were "hep," and he was "in the groove" and it was "yeah," and "dig it"—forever. Jock was cool: tall, restrained, and debonair. Charlie, or Chas, as he was called, was an animal; a sophisticated, modern animal who, if you believed him, had been pub-crawling for years; drank, smoked, played around with women; and knew the ways of the world, particularly the jazz world, inside out

50

as well as backwards. Chas was the first boy in the school to subscribe to *Metronome*. He smoked a very sweet-smelling Egyptian cigarette. He had pictures of glamorous looking girls in his wallet. Phil Kunhardt had a wind-up victrola—strictly forbidden—and a huge collection of records; and on warm days the four of us would go canoeing on the river, listen to records, and take in what Chas chose to reveal to us about "real life."

One of the big disappointments that fall was that they cancelled Bloody Sunday. Instead we had a "friendly" apple fight between the upper and lower schools. Bloody Sunday had been a tradition since the beginning of the school, but Mrs. Crocker thought it was barbaric and had it stopped. It was one of the worst things she could have done, and she lost a lot of her popularity because of it.

On Bloody Sunday there had always been a massive apple fight that involved the whole school and ranged over miles of ground. The official reason for getting rid of it was that the farmers were hard pressed that year because so many workers had taken jobs in defense plants. They needed pickers, not bands of hooligans destroying their apple crop. Gallien organized a group of volunteers to help harvest the apples; fifteen of us went with him several times; we'd even been willing to limit ourselves just to the apples that were already on the ground; but Mrs. Crocker was against it so they just cancelled Bloody Sunday and used the farmers' complaints as an excuse. At least Phil and I had experienced it. All Jock and Chas had were stories about it.

* * *

I'm puffing like an old work horse. My shoes are covered with mud; and my good, blue suit trousers are torn at the knees; but I've just clobbered Shurtleff in the back of the neck with an apple, and he's down. Clay and Carson, two other fifth formers, are bounding towards me; and I take one more throw, and miss; then Phil and I and Jerry Palmer and three guys from the third form take off, and our guys open the circle, and we're back behind the others, lying down on our bellies, panting like whales, and howling with glee. We've just made a raid on the enemy, and three fifth formers are down and five second formers. We'd trapped them up against the side of a barn and pummeled them good. Our side has won a major victory, and we feel like heroes.

It is later that day. Seven of us are on a suicide squad. There are forty or so of the enemy below us in an orchard gathering ammunition. We are to rush down upon them, whooping like Indians, while our main force creeps up on their rear. They attack. The enemy turns. And is destroyed. All we have to do is draw their fire. But when we charge down the hill, our main group isn't there. So we get killed. We're sitting ducks. Gignoux gets me one on the right ear and I go down in a heap. We're all captured and three of us have to be taken to the infirmary. Our main force comes up, finally; but they're too late, and the two sides have to call a truce so as to deal with the wounded. At first they thought my eardrum was burst, but it wasn't. I couldn't hear anything for a week, but that was all.

* * *

The "friendly" apple fight we had this year was pathetic. All we did was form two, long lines across the middle of the circle and lob apples at each other. There were masters patrolling, and no one was allowed to get closer than one hundred feet. The apples under the trees in the circle ran out practically right away (Most of the hard ones had either been eaten or used as missiles during the week before.), and the sides were so mismatched it was ridiculous. Plus it was Freshman Sunday and a lot of grads were back—about half of last year's sixth form—so it was more like old home week with a lot of joking going on, and people weren't paying that much attention to the "fight." That's how Silly-Bee got hurt. He was chattering away with Bill Dewert, who was on leave from the Scots Guards, and Goodyear, the first string pitcher, clobbered him one in the neck; Silly-Bee could hardly breathe for about five minutes. He was practically the only one even to get hit.

My biggest thrill that fall was listening to the World Series. I was a Yankees fan, naturally, having lived in New York City until I was eleven. So was my father. My mother and Grampa Whiting and Aunt Margaret were for the Dodgers, however; (My mother had been brought up in Brooklyn.) so the family competition was fierce. At the last minute Katharine decided she was a Dodger fan, too; so the sides were uneven. Granny T. didn't know what a baseball was.

It was the first time the Dodgers had won the pennant in years, and the whole city had gone crazy. It was called the Subway Series, 'cause for a nickel you could ride from Rockefeller Center to either Yankee Stadium or Ebbets Field; and I would have given anything to be there to help celebrate the return of the champs and win some money from Grampa Whiting. The Yanks were the clear favorites. After all, they'd won the Series four out of the last five years. Grampa Whiting had taken me to game four of the 1937 Series, the only one the Giants won, worse luck; and I still remembered the thrill of that homer by Lou Gehrig—and Lazzeri's hitting .400.

Grampa Whiting was sure the Dodgers would beat them this time, though. When they won game two, he called me up to crow. "Want to double our bet, pal?" he said.

"Sure," I replied, trying to keep cool. "A dollar it is, then." But I listened to game three as if my life depended on it. It was at Ebbets Field and the Bums would be sure to be screaming their lungs out the whole time.

Right up to the seventh when Russo hit a line drive that almost broke Freddie Fitzsimmons' knee, it looked as if the Dodgers might win; but Casey, the relief pitcher, couldn't hold the line and the Yanks won 2 to 1. The big game, though, was the next one. We heard the whole game on the Raj's radio. At the end of the third inning, the Yankees had three runs, the Dodgers nothing; but then the Dodgers picked up two runs, and another two in the next inning; and the fans went crazy. The cheering was unbelievable. Four to three in favor of the Dodgers and three innings to go. It was all up to Casey, but this time he held the Yankees down. It was the top of the ninth, two outs, no one on base. The crowd was completely wild.

And then Casey struck out Hendrich and the crowd started to pour onto the field, and Mickey Owen fumbled the catch in all the confusion and Hendrich sprinted to first; and the game wasn't over after all. What a moment. I could just picture Grampa Whiting's face. DiMaggio was up next. Well, Casey just slammed it in, apparently, and DiMaggio hit it for a single; and Casey kept throwing them straight and hard; and Keller doubled. The bases were loaded and Casey walked the next man, Dickey, bringing in a run, and then Gordon doubled and the Yankees had won.

I called up Grampa Whiting that night, just to rub it in. He could hardly talk. "Pal," he said, "you should have seen it. It was terrible."

"Want to double our bet?" I said, not thinking he would.

"Sure," he said, but he sounded as if he'd already lost. And, of course, he had. I almost felt sorry for the Dodgers.

* * *

Baseball was my game, not football. I was still on the third clubs and every time I hiked the ball I'd get pulled over on my face. I just couldn't seem to remember to brace myself. If I'd been a hot shot back, say, like Phip Zabriskie, or even an end, like Johnny Gray, it might have been different; but I wasn't very fast on my feet, and whenever I tried to catch the ball, it seemed to just spill out of my hands. Everyone had to play football, though, even Silly-Bee and Cooper; and it was embarrassing being on the same team with those guys—not to mention the first formers, some of whom were already better than you were.

Baseball was different. I'd pitched on the third clubs that past spring and hit well enough so that I'd been moved up to the seconds. You could take either crew or baseball in the spring. I wish I could have taken both. Crew was a terrific way to build up your muscles. You worked out all winter on the rowing machines, and by the time spring came your arms were like Popeye's. If you made it to the first clubs in baseball, you got to do practice hitting in the Cage. I hung around there last winter just to watch. You could tell by the sound of the bat, sometimes, when someone hit a homer.

* * *

The night before the St Mark's game we saw *Man Hunt*, with Walter Pidgeon. It was neat—all about a hunter who got Hitler in his sights and almost shot him, but then was hunted down himself. A French writer, André Maurois, spoke at the school a couple of weeks after that, all about how hard things were in France, and not just the no food but all the traitors. Mr. Moore, the Raj, ('cause his first name was Roger and he was dark skinned and looked sort of Indian) had him come back to the dorm afterwards so we could ask him questions, but not many of us did. It was getting toward the end of the term, and all most of us could think about was vacation coming up and final exams. The band was giving a concert in the Hall for the friends of the school and the staff on the last Tuesday of the term, and the trombones had a special piece where we all stood up in the balcony and played from memory. I was very nervous about that, as well as depressed at the thought of exams. Train asked a couple of questions but that was about it. I think the Raj was sort of sorry he'd asked Mr. Maurois back.

It was the first Sunday in December. Not quite two weeks to go. We'd walked back from the village where the choir had just given its Christmas carol concert. It was just getting dark and it was good to get into Hundred House and out of the cold. I hung my coat up and started toward the dorm when I noticed there was a big crowd of boys and masters milling about in the study hall. Bill Gray, the senior prefect—Johnny's oldest brother—was ringing the bells and people were quieting down, and I was standing with a bunch of others in the doorway, wondering what was going on, when Crocker came in. He walked straight to the platform. I could tell it was something pretty important from the expression on his face.

"Boys," he said, looking sternly around the room. "What you've heard is true. At 8:30 this morning, Japanese planes launched a surprise attack on Pearl Harbor. The United States and Japan are at war." There was a moment of silence and then everyone started talking at once.

Jock Lawrence was standing near me. "Where's Pearl Harbor?" I shouted into his ear.

"Hawaii," he said. "It's a big Navy base."

Boys were storming out into the hall now. We'd been told to go to our dormitories. "Why would they attack us?" I shouted to Jock, but in all the commotion, I guess he didn't hear me.

"I'll tell you what it means," said Silly-Bee, back in Raj's study. "It means you're going to get bombed, too. Invaded, probably." He seemed to be saying it almost in glee.

What I wanted was a map. Hong Kong, Singapore, the Philippines—where were they exactly? The Chinese had been fighting the Japanese for a long time. I knew that. But that wouldn't make the Japanese attack us, would it? It was hard to imagine a war with Japan. Japan was so tiny. Where would it be fought? In the air? On the sea? I could imagine the war in Europe pretty easily. Dunkirk. All the pictures and newsreels we'd seen. Tyrone Power and Betty Grable in *A Yank in the R.A.F.* That really put me there. But Japan and China were so far away. Even California was far enough away to seem slightly unreal.

Roosevelt announced it the next day. We were at war with Germany and Italy as well as Japan; and we were already fighting in the Philippines. He singled out Japan, though, specially. What she had done, no one else had ever done to us before. She had attacked us when our back was turned, when there were Japanese ambassadors in Washington discussing ways in which we might become involved in a Japanese, Chinese peace. And all the time she had a knife poised to stab into our back. America had been betrayed. "Yesterday, December 7, 1941—a date which will live in infamy—" It was a great speech. It made you proud and mad at the same time. It was exciting, too. The thought that we were actually at war.

Chapter Seven

"How do you tell the difference between a Chinaman and a Jap?" said John Train, who was sitting on the shoe locker next to mine. We were in the cellar of Hundred House, having an air raid drill, and it was so dark I could hardly see him.

"I don't know, John. Why don't you tell me?"

"For the phrase 'faultless fortress,' a Chinaman will say, ' faultless faultless,' " said John. "A Jap, 'fortress fortress.' "

"Velly intellesting," I said. "You have mo entetaining stolies?"

"Put out that flashlight," someone shouted.   It sounded like Douglas.

"How much longer do we have to stay down here?" a voice cried.

"Patience, boys," Mr. Moore said. He and Douglas and Lord, the other prefect, were checking the curtains. "That one over there, Peter. See if you can't get it pinned down tighter." Douglas went over to the window and fiddled with the material, then came back and joined the others. Their flashlights were covered over except for little slits, and they kept them pointed at the floor.

"You may sing, boys, if you wish. Lawrence! Why don't you lead them in something? How about 'The Road to Mandalay?' Without waiting for Jock to respond, the Raj started singing the song himself, in a rousing tenor

59

voice. We joined in, fitfully, "tum, te, tumming" on the second verse, but coming in with a bang on the dawn coming up like thunder part.

"Ivan Skavinski Skavar," someone yelled out when we'd come to the end, and Jock started it and we all sang lustily. It was like a sing song, though of course it would have been better if we'd had the books. Twice a month, during the winter term, the whole school got together in the library after supper and sang songs out of the Sing Song book. Even boys like Silly-Bee, who couldn't carry a tune, seemed to enjoy it.

Before we could get into anything else, though, the outside bell gave a tremendous blast, and then we could hear the inside bells being rung in the study hall up stairs.

"Forty-five minutes to go," said Train. "Think of it this way, Clinton old boy. Forty-five minutes less of doing homework. That should appeal to you."

"It does," I said. "Velly much."

"I don't think it's nice to make fun of the Chinese," said Vines, on the other side of me. "After all. They're our allies now."

"Confucius say..." Was that Train?

"Confucius say woman who fly upside down have clack up." Much laughter. It sounded like Brewer, or maybe Coster.

"Madame Chiang Kai-shek gave two pandas to the Bronx Zoo," said Putnam. "I'm going to see them as soon as I get home."

"Look here, you chaps," said Silly-Bee in a sharp, piercing voice. "You ought to be taking this more seriously. What if it were the real thing?"

"It's all ridiculous," said Putnam. "America can't be invaded. My father said so."

"Well, my father said Lindbergh was right. All the yellow races are the same, and we should lock them all up for the duration." This from George Cooper. Class reactionary.

"A slip of the lip may sink a ship," said Chas, in a perfect imitation of Jane Russell. General laughter.

Just then Douglas came running down the hall, opened the outside cellar door, and rushed out. A minute later Lord appeared and told us to sit tight, that there'd been a slight goof. Someone had left the lights on in the attic of Pest House and they were trying to find a ladder.

"Have we a spy in our midst?" said Train. "Perhaps someone ought to notify J. Edgar Hoover."

"It's just the sort of thing that *does* happen," said Silly-Bee. "The top of Pest House lit up would make a perfect beacon if bombers were looking for Fort Devens. You could be shot, you know, for so much as lighting a match during a blackout. And people were."

"Anybody want to talk about *Dumbo*? I thought it was swell," said Woolverton. General agreement about how funny *Dumbo* was.

Dumbo had been the school movie that night. We'd had to see the short before supper—a terrific thing about the RAF called 'Target for Tonight'—because of the blackout and air raid drill that started at nine. Tomorrow morning, early, we'd be leaving for Easter vacation; first the Boston bus at 7:25, and then the New York/Philadelphia bus at 7:30. We'd taken our last exams this morning.

The War made everything pretty exciting, that was for sure. To the upperclassmen the draft was the big thing, of course. At first everyone thought that they'd be taking eighteen-year-olds, but they finally decided not to. Twenty-one to forty-four. Those were the ages. You were 1A if you were unmarried and could pass the physical. Joe Lewis was one of the first to be drafted. There was a picture of him in *Life* standing in front of some Army building on Long Island looking very ordinary in a uniform even he couldn't quite fill.

Bob Metters, my father's curate, had joined the Navy. A lot of sixth formers were talking about signing up over vacation and not even coming back to graduate. Kromer, Crocker's assistant, was going in; and a bunch of other masters; the Raj, Iglehart, and Nicholls were joining up in June. Poor Kromer. Poor Army, I mean.

"Who would leave those lights on?" said Phil.

"What about that Jap sub shelling those oil tanks in Santa Barbara?" said Silly-Bee. "And everyone knows there're U-boats all along the East Coast."

"You *do* follow the news, don't you," said Putnam. "Jolly good."

"He's absolutely right," said Cooper. "We should pull back everything and defend our borders. The enemy is making plans right now to strike on both coasts, and up through Mexico. Did you know that a German torpedo washed up on a beach in Aruba just a few days ago? We almost went to Aruba over Christmas."

"If everyone saved their rubber bands," said Vines, "there wouldn't be a rubber shortage."

Someone farted.

The door opened and in came Douglas.

"They get the lights out?" said Phil.

"Not yet. They think it was the painters. No one can find a long enough ladder." The door opened again. It was the Raj and Lord.

"What time is it?" said someone. Lord's flashlight went to his wrist.

"9:22," he said.

It was getting stuffy; it smelled of shoes, and shoe polish, and damp earth; and every so often there'd be a whiff of coal gas from where the furnace was, or someone would let go with another fart. Someone sneezed.

I thought of Sarah, Sarah O'Kane, who had been our cook for four years, ever since we moved to Chestnut Hill. She'd gone to work in a defense plant. I missed her almost more than anyone. Just last week I gave the dorm a feed from a food package she sent me. There were a lot of sweet things this time, including a three-layer vanilla cake, my favorite, because, as she wrote me, sugar was certain to be rationed very soon. They were already rationing it here: only one teaspoonful in your coffee, and one and a half on your cereal. Cooper and Brewer had both been caught with socks full of sugar in their cubicles.

"Mr. Moore? I know a way up to the Pest House attic from the inside," said Phil.

"You do, do you? Well, you should have spoken up."

"Yes, Sir," said Phil, quickly, probably wishing he hadn't opened his mouth.

"They're sure to have found a ladder by now, Sir," said Douglas.

"Fifteen more minutes," Train said in a low voice, "I've been counting."

I tried to imagine what it would be like if this were a real air raid; but I couldn't, even from all the pictures I'd seen and all the things Silly-Bee had told us. He'd been in Winchester after the bombing. That was the worst, he said. Only the outside walls of the cathedral left standing. I tried to hear the bombers coming, the bombs sounding like approaching cars, Silly-Bee had said. I tried to imagine what would happen to us if a bomb hit Hundred House while we were all sitting here talking. We'd all be killed, wouldn't we? Everything would fall down on top of us. Then why were we here? Because it was safer down here than upstairs, say, if a bomb hit nearby—in the circle for instance.

What I'd do, I think, is run for the woods if it ever really happened. I'd get Phil and we'd go to the hut we dug that fall. It was only ten by ten feet, four feet deep— covered with boards and then dirt and sticks and things to hide it; but we had food stored there, and blankets, and Phil's victrola, and lots of records, and some candles and magazines. It would be safer there than here, it seemed to me. Who'd want to bomb the woods? A building was something you would aim at, even if it weren't all lit up.

It was a trap door Phil had found. He'd told me about it. He was a great one for crawling into things. He'd crawled through the whole heating system in the schoolhouse early that fall, before they turned the heat on. It was SCARY, he said. But fun. There was a drop at one point and he had to let go but luckily it wasn't far. That was the worst part. That and the dust. I'd guarded the

64

entrance for him: a grate in the ceiling of the hall on the second floor. I could hear him sneezing way before he got to me. When he came out, he was filthy but beaming. It was really neat, he said. Didn't I want to go too? He would stand guard for me. Not now, I said. Anyway, he had to get cleaned up before someone saw him. That wasn't my real reason, though. Crawling into strange, scary places wasn't my idea of a good time. I wasn't too keen on heights, either.

"Fifteen minutes are up," said Train. We counted off another minute and a half and finally the outside went off and the lights came on, and we all trouped up to our dormitory again. The Raj came around with both prefects and said good night to each one of us, which he didn't usually do; and when I looked out of the window after the lights were out, I noticed it was snowing. Not very hard, but if it kept up, by morning we would have a foot or so. No snow all winter, and now, just as we're about to go home, it starts. They'd have to call out the snow squads if it kept up, and the busses might be late, and then we'd miss our trains. The snow squads had been set up after Christmas—fourth and fifth formers, mostly—to help out the grounds people, now that so many of them had gone to war, or into defense.

Poor Mr. Cleary, I thought. He'd been one of the few left. He'd picked up some hitchhikers a few weeks before and they'd taken his money and then beaten him up so badly he almost died. He was blind in one eye now, and he might still lose his sight in the other. They caught them two days later, thank God, and we all hoped they'd get life. What a terrible thing to do. He'd only had a few dollars on him, and it was all because he'd been so nice.

I shut my eyes. "God bless Mammy and Daddy and Katharine and Gus, and Sarah, and Grampa Whiting and Aunt Margaret and Lem and Pinky—and Granny, too. And God bless Mr. Cleary and make him well."

Chapter Eight

It's Memorial Day and the Rector's eighty-fifth birthday. We are marching back to the school from the Groton cemetery, the trombone section leading the parade. It is my first uniform—white ducks, puttees, white shirt, school tie, blue blazer, overseas cap—and though I am steaming hot, I am wildly happy; for Mr. DeVoe has just told me I can move up to second place next year: between Semler and Grant. I'm full of Sousa marches and the glory of being in the front row. I am the youngest in the section. I have grown six inches in the last year and a half and lost thirty-two pounds. I am just Grant's height, though not yet his build.

And there's something else. I'm finished with Latin. No more Latin! There're four of us: Krumbhaar, Palmer, Brewer, and myself. We all failed French as well as Latin, so they've decided to concentrate on just one language for us. There'll be a special class. And if we don't pass... But French is a breeze compared to Latin. And just think. We're the first boys in the history of the school to get out of Latin. They've given up on us. We've won!

I'm going to visit Phil in Morristown next week. They've got a pool—a real mountain stream that feeds into a concrete lined pond in the woods—freezing cold. They have to clean it out every year, and they always find a dead rat or a woodchuck or some snakes stopping up the plug hole. Phil has the neatest house in the world. I've only been there once, this past Christmas, but we saw three deer in the field at the top of the hill behind their house. I liked Mr. Kunhardt a lot. He talks to you as if you were a grownup, and his eyes smile even when he tells you scary stories. He keeps a huge pipe in his mouth all the time and never wears a shirt, only shorts, all summer long; and even in the winter, in the house, he's so hot he walks around in bare feet all the time.

Phil has an older sister, Nancy, who is beautiful and very popular at dances; and a baby one, Dith, who slaves for him. Uncle Corny is the minister of the church in Morristown now; and when I was there we all went skating one night in the moonlight, and there were parties at the Lows, and Art Savage was there, and Aunt Serina, my mother's friend, who is always talking, and Pooch, Art's younger sister, who never says one word. How I would love to live in Morristown instead of stupid Chestnut Hill where there's nothing to do, only go walking in the Wissahickon.

As we march through the gates and past the Cage, four sixth formers—Carson, Gignoux, Billy Gray, and Holt—rush past us and surround the Rector, who is on his horse, next to Crocker, who has been leading the parade. At first I think something is wrong, but then a cheer goes up, and Crocker wheels around on his horse, all smiles; and we see that they've got the Rector up on their shoulders and are running toward Hundred House with him. Douglas, who has been behind Crocker, leading the marching, has turned toward us with his baton raised, and he yells out, "Company! Halt!" As soon as we come to a stop, a rather fumbling and unmilitary one, he dismisses us, and we race forward to see what's up.

Instead of stopping at Hundred House, they've put the Rector up on a chair and are parading him around the circle. The whole school stands around the steps waiting for them, and as they run past the Chapel, a cheer goes up and it gets louder and louder until by the time they've reached us it's deafening. We make a place for them to get through, and then close in on them again as they run to the top of the steps. They turn and face us, the Rector the only one with a straw hat on instead of an overseas cap, his face deeply flushed and smiling. They raise him higher and turn him slowly so all of us can see him, and then the Rector holds his arms out to quiet us—It's almost as if he's directing us at Sing Song—and when it's quiet, Crocker, who is standing on the top step, bellows out, "Three cheers for the Rector! Hip! Hip! Hooray!"

After the cheering subsides—the Rector has raised his hat about fifty times—when there is such quiet that you can hear yourself breathe—the Rector begins to talk. He is not known as a great speaker, but this is a great speech.

"When we first thought of founding a Christian school here," he says, "it seemed impossible that we would ever succeed." He goes on to tell how he and Mr. Gardner and Mr. Billings, all in their twenties, first got the land from the Lawrences, and how he got Phillips Brooks to put up the money for the first building (Brooks House). He tells us about the other buildings and all the people who gave money to the school. He seems to be talking to each one of us individually, as if it were important for each of us to know the school's history, because this is our school now.

He speaks about the teachers, too, way back to the beginning; and all the famous and fine men the school has graduated.

"During the Great War the circle was planted in wheat," he says. "We trained there, too: The Groton Battalion. Every man of us in uniform, each prepared to lay down his life for freedom." Just as they worked on farms in the summer during that war, so we should expect to make sacrifices now to help our country in its time of need. "Not that it wasn't jolly good fun, too, much of it," he says. "But don't get the wrong idea, boys. We are all soldiers. Soldiers in Christ. Soldiers in war when our country needs us. 'Onward Christian soldiers; marching as to war…' " He intones the first verse slowly and other voices join in, but then he stops.

He tells us about the fun, some of it; how the masters used to play along side the boys on the teams, how it really was like a large family, everyone pitching in to help. He speaks for about twenty minutes, I guess; and when he is finished I look over at Cooper, who is standing next to me, and tears are streaming down his cheeks. Cooper! I feel the same way. This is *my* school, I say to myself. My school too.

When we go trouping in for lunch, we're quiet for once. We're sitting at Kromer's table this year, and just last week we pinned him to the wall accidentally on purpose when we got up to leave. That same evening we set off three alarm clocks in the wastepaper basket while he was taking study hall. He turned red but pretended it wasn't happening, in spite of the laughter. Now all that behavior seems juvenile and faintly embarrassing. After

70

all, it's not his fault he speaks in that sweet-boy, Southern way. It's probably not even his fault that he talks all the time about how kind and sweet Jesus was; and how we should be kind and sweet too and try to live like him. He's going into the Army in two weeks as a chaplain. Poor Kromer. He's only been here for a year, and he's even more of a wreck now than when he came. The Army will kill him, for sure. The Raj, Nicholls, and the other masters, they'll survive. They're tough. But Kromer, milk-toast Kromer, will never make it back alive.

Anyway, all of this is beneath us now. Phil and Jerry Palmer, two of the worst offenders, are sitting on either side of Kromer, and they're chatting politely to him and passing the salt and pepper before he asks them, and I can tell everyone has a different attitude. It's the Rector's work. We've heard about it often enough from the older boys and the masters. He makes you feel you're good, deep down, and that you want to be even better. He's famous for it. He could probably straighten out Hitler himself if he could just talk to him privately for awhile.

Chapter Nine

The Rector complained a good deal about the vacations, especially the short vacations at Christmas and Easter. He said [the boys]... spent their time at the theater, and later discussed, not the merits of character portrayal, nor the problems presented, but 'the beauty of the actresses.'...
The vacations were too violent. The boys reacted from the cloistered existence at Groton like sailors getting shore leave; and though the damage was not permanent, it was unnecessary and exasperating.

George Martin, '06, in 1944; in Ashburn,
Peabody of Groton, p.250.

Marie not only broke my heart, she took a chip out of my father's as well. Who would believe that big, raw-boned Sarah O'Kane could have produced a niece so beautiful. Years later the mere mention of her name would bring either one of us to instant attention.

The very back of Marie's neck sent shivers down my spine. Upswept for the daily chores, her hair—the color of pale strawberry—would be piled into soft, glistening folds, and where it rose from the creamy smoothness of her neck, there were loose strands that fell back, that would not be caught, that arched over; almost, but not quite, touching the hollow of her skin. How many times did I look at that neck and ache to touch it, brush my lips against it, nuzzle into its fuzz.

"Marie?" I would say, and she would turn her head and look down at me from where she was standing on the stepladder putting plates away and smile.

"Away you go, you naughty boy. Can't you see I'm busy?" Then Sarah would yell at me from the kitchen, and I would leave, reluctantly, and Sarah would give me one of her looks, her piercing, gray eyes made all the more fierce by the wire-rimmed glasses caught up on the bridge of her nose.

"Ahh, get off w' ya now!" she would say, and toss her head; strands of steel-wool hair bobbing. Home from Groton at the end of my second form year, I looked at them from my window as they went to mass each morning across the street, Sarah's head covered with an ugly straw hat; Marie's russet hair curled under, bouncing on the shoulders of her navy blue coat, the fuzzy, light blue beret she wore framing it like a halo. Sarah O'Kane had an open, firm-jawed moon face; and though she smelt of garlic, tea and occasionally whiskey; and though she had a habit of pinching my arm when she was angry with me, and never spoke to me in anything under a yell; though she was always sweating, and had the largest feet and the most complaining corns of anyone; in spite of all these things, I loved her dearly and it was to her I went for comfort, or when I was in trouble.

I spied on Marie. I peeked at her through windows and from behind partly closed doors, the breath held in my throat. I followed her into the living room where she was dusting, from the pantry to the dining room as she carried the dishes. I followed her upstairs and into the bedrooms and down the back hall toward her room, but never further. That was her part of the house, hers and Sarah's; and even Sarah's room was off bounds to me. I glanced into Marie's room once when no one else was in the house and was surprised to see how plain it was: a crucifix on the wall, some holy pictures, the narrow bed— neatly made, nothing lying about—only brushes and pins and combs and a curling iron on the dresser. I didn't dare to go in.

Marie's uniform—pale green, her apron white—was always clean and slightly stiff form starch, and yet it fit her like a second skin. No evening dress, however plunged its neckline, however revealing or tightly fitted; no negligee however filmy or provocative; nothing she could have worn could have looked more wonderful on her than that plain, workmanlike uniform she wore every day except for her day off. I saw her in a sweater and skirt once, and almost lost my passion. She was sitting in a chair next to the stove, reading the paper, her hair tied back in a ribbon.

Marie didn't wear white stockings or nurse's shoes with her uniform, but bobby socks and saddle shoes like Marian Hutton; when she sat down at the kitchen table she would pull her skirt tight at the knees, and sometimes I would get a glimpse of her slip. When my parents had a dinner party, she would wear a shiny, black costume with a little white apron, black stockings, and black, shiny shoes with little heels, a starched white cap in her hair. She looked cute, but she wasn't the same. My Marie!

Marie had a wonderful smell. It wasn't perfume. It was a fresh, warm, buttery just-baked-bread sort of smell.

She would brush past and her delicate fragrance would linger, and I would be rooted to the spot, helplessly in love.

"Clinton. Time to get up." It was August, in Hancock Point. I lay there on my back—naked, aroused—waiting for her to come in, feigning sleep. She knocked again. I did not stir. The door handle turned in its latch and I could hear the sound of the door opening. And then there was a giggle and footsteps; and I felt myself redden, and I pulled the sheet up over me again, turned on my side, and waited. Sure enough. Galumph! galumph! The banging of size 12 shoes on bare boards.

"Get up, you terrible boy!" Sarah shouted. I grunted in reply. Downstairs, in the kitchen, I pretended not to know what they were tittering about. Sarah was gruff, but she had a twinkle in her eye. She never sent Marie to wake me again, however, and by the time I'd gotten back from Groton that Christmas, Marie was gone.

"Married, so young," my father said, and shook his head.

It took a good six months for my passion to cool; but there was a time there, when I was fourteen, that I though my love for Marie would never die.

Chapter Ten

"The quality of the replacement faculty was uneven.
There were some who would probably not have been engaged
under normal circumstances."

Acosta Nichols, *Forty Years More: A History of Groton
School, 1934-74.*

I was a day late getting back the next fall because the
train we were on was packed with soldiers, and it was
late; so we missed the bus and had to spend the night in
Worcester. I couldn't believe all the changes. I knew the
Raj and Kromer would be gone, but six other masters had
joined up as well, including Comstock, who was to have
been our third form dorm master in Brooks House. Taking
his place was a Mr. Urquehart, who had been discharged
from the Navy; no one seemed to know why. There were
six new masters besides him.

Third, fourth and fifth formers were waiting on table
now because so many of the help were working in defense
jobs; and we all had to sign up on various work squads,
make our own beds, and sweep out our cubicles, which
really bothered some boys. The best news was that
because the Navy wanted all the blue flannel there was,
we didn't have to wear blue suits any more; and they'd
decided to drop stiff collars and patent leather shoes as
well. Five new boys had joined our form, and one of them
was from Brazil.

Ebu, one of the new masters, was in charge of the waitering. Mr. Freiday was called "Ebu" because he taught French and that's exactly what he looked like—an owl. He had an owl's round face, and a Dutch bowl wig, which we knew all about from a fourth former seeing it half slide off his head when he was asleep one night; and, of course, glasses. He was practically blind, and so fat he waddled. He was one master we didn't have to worry about being drafted.

When we trouped in for supper, Ebu was standing inside the entrance to the dining room, looking from side to side and sweating heavily. He was flanked by two sixth formers: Kingsford and Gould, who served as his eyes. The waiters—two to a table—wore white mess jackets. So they wouldn't wreck their sport coats, I guess. Who was going to be the first to tip the soup tureen into someone's lap? I wondered, as I made my way to my seat. My turn came up next week. Perhaps it would be me.

* * *

It was two days later and Phil and I were getting into our football uniforms.

"Have you seen Fernandez?" I said, lowering my voice. He was the new boy from Brazil.

"Looks like a weasel."

"No, I mean have you *seen* him. Have you seen him in the shower?"

"No."

"He's got one that hangs to his knees."

77

"To his *knees*?" said Phil.

"Maybe a little below."

"No wonder he's so pale," Phil said, and we both laughed.

Everything about Ricardo Fernandez was long, and pale, and thin, except his eyes which were large and brown and sad. I had been in the locker room the day before with Brewer and Cooper and a few others when Fernandez walked in. He went way over to the other end of the room, took off his clothes, and sort of scuttled past us, but we had a good look.

"Jesus!" Brewer exclaimed. "Think what you could do with that."

"Belongs on a horse," said Cooper. "Or a donkey."

"Spencer's got a big one, and he's from the South, too," Palmer said.

"Brazil's not the South, stupid," said Cooper.

We had followed Fernandez into the shower room by this time. He was soaping his chest when we came in. It was smaller now, but not much.

The subject of Fernandez' humongous endowment occupied the whole school for more than a week. Every possible explanation for it was considered, from the unplumbed depths of the Latin temperament to the existence of a fertility plant of such potency that a drop too much would drive the taker mad, causing the holy vessel to shatter. He was a sort of hero at first, and then, gradually, his status declined; and we began looking at him with indifference, then pity, then contempt. It didn't help his case that he was shy to the point of silence, that when he did speak it was with a heavy accent, and that he

78

seemed to have no other particular talents to recommend him.

But by then we were obsessed by Urquehart. Everyone in the dorm hated him, including the two prefects: Kingsford and Nicodemus. He was tall and thin like Fernandez but not silent. He made us silent. That was something he was good at. There were no rows in his dorm, not after that first time.

* * *

"Trowbridge!" The dorm lights flashed on and there was Urquehart standing in the doorway to his study.

"Kunhardt!" "Train!" We scrambled down from the rafters where we'd been having a small feed and padded over to him, blinking from the lights. He fixed his left hand on my jaw and turned my face up to his.

"It was your food, wasn't it?" he said in a voice that made me shiver. "You were the ring leader, were you not? I've been warned about you."

"Yes, sir." I mumbled, scared, suddenly, by his ferocity. He released his grip on my jaw and told me to go into his study. "I'll see you one at a time," he said to Phil and John. "Wait here."

It wasn't so much what he said but how he said it. His voice was like a steel whip. Every word a blow. I could hardly walk back to my cubicle afterwards I felt so weak. He was a tall man, with even features, close-cropped, kinky brown hair, and a thin, dark mustache. It was partly the way he held himself, as if he were still in uniform. It wasn't just that he stood straight. It was as if he were made out of metal and couldn't stand any other way.

There were no rows after that, but there were the usual night time noises: feigned and unfeigned indications of sexual activity; pretend and not so pretend groans and grunts of masturbatory bliss, often accompanied by snippets of lusty narrative. And then one night we discovered that Urquehart had heard it all.

It was just before Halloween. Suddenly, without warning, a flashlight snapped on, there were sounds of a scuffle, and it turned out that Urquehart had dragged Fernandez out of bed and marched him into his study. Poor Fernandez. And he was one of the quiet ones. It was an hour before he returned. He wouldn't tell us what happened, or why, exactly, he'd been chosen as an example, but it didn't take much to figure it out. Standing there in the dark, spying on us, Urquehart must have seen or heard Fernandez "playing with himself." His cubicle was the one nearest the door. But he must have heard the rest of us then, too.

It was one of the unwritten rules that masters didn't look too deeply into our most private sex lives. Not even a prefect would drag a boy out of bed in the morning, for example, for fear of catching him with a boner. We were told by both masters and older boys, mostly with a good deal of tongue in cheek, that the sin of Onan, "who cast his seed upon the ground," was a deplorable one that would result in insanity or, at the very least, a forest growth of warts upon the hand, though most of us had left those ideas behind well before we'd entered the third

80

form. Urquehart's spying on us was not just unfair, however. To us it was darkly malicious.

The next night Fernandez was summoned to Urquehart's study again. And the night after that. And every night from then on for almost three weeks. If it hadn't been so horrible, it would have been funny. Why Fernandez, among all the others? We interrogated Fernandez, but still he refused to talk. Instead, he grew even more silent—and more pale.

It was close to Thanksgiving before anything more happened. And then it was two things at once: Fernandez and Urquehart both disappeared. It was awhile before the whole story came out. Urquehart had been discharged from the school by Crocker. And Fernandez had gone back to Brazil. The person who discovered the truth of what had been happening was Miss Winterbottom, the school nurse.

We had had our suspicions, of course. Silly-Bee was sure there was buggery involved. Unwelcome thoughts of Edwards haunted my mind. Silly-Bee wanted to go to Crocker and tell him what Urquehart was doing, but Phip, who was class president, talked him out of it. There was no proof that Urquehart was doing anything wrong, he said. We would do better to wait and see. Nor did we confide in Kingsford or Nicodemus, but then they weren't around much. None of us were, for that matter. Who wanted to spend any extra time in that dorm?

The truth was far worse than anyone had imagined. Apparently, Urquehart had forced Fernandez to confess that he had been "pleasuring himself," on a regular basis. After lecturing him on the vileness of his crime, he told him that as a punishment he must "pleasure himself," repeatedly, in Urquehart's presence, every night, until he was incapable of doing so any more. The purpose of this was to humiliate him, he said, to so fill him with self-loathing that thereafter he would never "pleasure himself" again. He must be broken of this loathsome practice, however painful the punishment was, for it was one that endangered his immortal soul. The sin of Onan could send Fernandez to hell.

Fernandez was a Catholic, one of the few at the school, and hell was very real to him. But Jock Lawrence, who was the only other Catholic in our form, was furious.

"It's only a venial sin, for heaven's sake. They can't send you to hell for that," he said.

"I didn't know it was a sin at all," said Silly-Bee, and most of the rest of us laughed.

After three weeks, however, Fernandez began to draw blood. In fear and trembling, he went to Pest House and told Winterbottom, and the whole truth came out.

Everyone was glad to see the end of Urquehart, and no one much minded that Fernandez was gone either. Things were tough enough without having our sexual privacy invaded.

Chapter Eleven

I coughed, twice, and all the students in Zahner's third form English class crossed their legs in perfect synchronization. Old Zu continued to fumble through the book. "Frost had been working on a long, narrative poem all night," he said. "Then, just at dawn, exhausted, he tossed off this one, one of his most famous." He looked around the room, noting nothing unusual in the fact that his twelve students all had their legs crossed from left to right, and continued, "Well, not exactly 'tossed off,' perhaps;" and he glanced up at the class, smiled, looked down again, and began to read. "Whose woods these are I think I know/ His house is in the village though." And so on. As he got toward the end, I readied myself. Just as Zu looked up from his book, The Rockettes of Groton School, as one man, uncrossed their legs and placed their right ankles over their left knees. "Stevens, what do you say? Is that Frost's best poem, or isn't it?" I coughed and in front of his face, in a semi-circle not ten feet away, the entire class, again as a man, uncrossed, then recrossed their legs. He looked baffled. "Is the period over?" he said. "Did you hear the bell?"

"Yes, Sir," Whitney said, quick as a flash, and Zu took off his glasses and pinched down on the inside corners of his eyes with the thumb and third finger of his right hand.

"Tomorrow, then. We'll discuss the poem some more tomorrow. My how quickly the time goes."

"Why did you do that," I hissed at Whitney as we surged down the stairs. "There was a good ten minutes left."

"He wouldn't have caught on if we'd done it a dozen times and farted in unison and taken our shoes off."

"Come on," I said. "He's not that far gone."

"Oh, no?" said Whitney.

"He's not half as old as Cushing."

"Cushing! Cushing would have killed us."

Cushing taught mathematics, and coached varsity baseball, and was the only master left, now that Regan had gone, from the days of the Rector. He was in his eighties, but if he thought you weren't paying attention in class, or, God forbid, sleeping, he would wing a piece of chalk at you or an eraser; and if he didn't hit you the first time, which he usually did, he would certainly get you the second.

The bell. We trouped out of the can and leisurely made our way into Study Hall, as if we'd just gotten out of class. Ebu was in charge. I was in his French class this year, which was very boring and hard. Ebu was ringing the bells and glancing around through his inch thick glasses trying to find the prefects, beads of sweat ringing his brow. Hawkes came in just then, another French teacher, and also new this year. He was short and fat and had a little Hitler mustache. It was not easy to get teachers these days we had been told. What with the war.

We trouped into dinner one night at the beginning of October, but after Crocker gave the blessing, he didn't sit down with the rest of us but instead stood there and introduced us to the Loewenbergs. Mr. and Mrs.

Loewenberg and their two small boys were Jewish refugees who had escaped from Germany. It was fortunate that the school had been able to take them in. Mr. Loewenberg, who had been a distinguished university professor, would be teaching German to a select group of students this year and French and German the following year, by which time he would be more proficient in our language. Mr. Loewenberg was dressed in a heavy, woolen suit that bagged out at the elbows. The boys wore shorts that came down over their knees; they stood there, stiffly, next to their parents, staring at the floor.

Mr. Loewenberg was thin and slightly stooped. He had wispy, grey hair combed straight back; and wore round, steel-rimmed spectacles that looked as if they'd been made out of wire. Mrs. Loewenberg, who was short and stocky, was also dressed in heavy, dark flannel. She had brown, very curly, close-cropped hair, and a wide, plain face with piercing eyes.

"...and so we welcome the Loewenbergs into the Groton family," finished Crocker. They sat down, to polite applause. It was meatless Tuesday, so no one had been in too big a hurry to eat.

There were some first formers at the next table laughing. They were pretending not to, of course, but Gallien had seen them and was glaring at them. One of them, Purvis, a fattish kid with stand-up, red hair, had turned purple in the face and for a minute I thought he might burst out laughing; but then he had the sense to get down on the floor and make believe he was looking for something, and when he came up again he was more or less in control. What a numbskull, I thought, just 'cause their clothes didn't look right. The guy next to him was worse. He was sort of sneering. Another Cooper, I thought—Cooper who wouldn't listen to Jack Benny on the radio 'cause he was Jewish. There weren't any Jews at Groton, of course, though Doc Irons who taught History said that some day there would be. "It's only right," he'd said. "Niggers, too, I suppose," Cooper had mumbled. Boy if Irons had heard that!

The only Jews I'd known were Louie Lowenstein from when we'd lived in New York and Billy Wasserman at Chestnut Hill Academy. Billy was hyperactive; he had wiry, blond-red hair that stuck out all over his head, and was at the top of the class in every subject. Louis, at nine, was dark and slow and immense, and slug-like. The Loewenbergs didn't fit into either category. They just looked poor, I thought. And unhappy. It was hard to imagine Mrs. Loewenberg as a faculty wife. Would she invite us over for tea, a few at a time, the way the others did? Probably she and Mrs. Noble wouldn't have much to talk about, even if she did learn some English.

"Whitney's Jewish," Jock said.

"How do you know?" I said.

"Look at those pointed shoes he wears."

"And that blue, pinstripe, double-breasted with the shark tooth lapels," smirked Coster. "And his hair's marcelled. That's a sure sign."

"Okay, okay," said Jock. "So he isn't. What do I know."

My parents had friends who were Jews. There was Aunt Rosie, who had been a roommate of my mother's at Smith; and Andy Teejan, who could play tunes on the

86

piano with a grapefruit. I'd heard my parents talk about the persecution of the Jews, about how Germany would be punished for that when the War was over. I'd seen pictures of refugees on *The March of Time*, and in *Life*, but the Loewenbergs didn't look anything like them either. Yet that's what they were. What would it be like, I wondered, to be uprooted like that; to walk out of your house one day with only the clothes on your back; to get on a train for another country, but with no place there to go; no money in your pocket; you and your wife and your children? I couldn't imagine it, hard as I tried.

Chapter Twelve

The Christian view of education begins with the assumption that reality includes not only nature and man but also God. Man is the middle term between the other two. Only as men relate themselves properly to both can they live constructive lives. In short, unless men learn to submit to what is above them, they cannot control themselves and what is below them... Although there is no aspect of the School which is not related to this objective, there are certain activities which can be more specifically defined as religious. First in importance is worship...

Groton, pp. 12-15.

I was never particularly religious, but during these pitiful years of adolescence, when my hopes, my convictions, the world itself, seemed shattering about me, I wanted something to which I could cling or drown myself in absolute faith and exaltation."

Biddle, "As I remember Groton School," p. 122.

I joined the Missionary Society that fall, not to please my grandmother, but because that got me to Ayer once a week. Nevertheless, she was moved to give me a Bible, with the inscription, "May Clinton always be a good boy," and later, when I presented her with a copy of the twelve page book of prayers that took me almost a year to assemble, and necessitated many trips to the printers in Ayer, she was so struck by my piety that, for the remaining few years of her life, I could do no wrong. "It's disgusting!" my sister would say after she had been corrected by our grandmother, and I had not. I could only smirk, and agree. In fact, I suffered more from duplicity than I let on.

At Groton, attendance at "church" was mandatory for everyone except the Catholics. They went to Ayer. "Church" meant the Groton School Chapel--every morning for a short spell right after breakfast, and twice on Sundays; Morning prayer with holy communion; and vespers. Jock was a Catholic and there were four or five others, each year. Catholics were considered both peculiar and favored. They were the escapees, the ones with the magic passes, the privileged few who jammed themselves into the Missionary Society station wagon each Sunday morning; and with much hilarity and enthusiasm and just-contained animal exuberance, drove out through the gates at high speed, by themselves; no masters, no supervisors, the oldest student driving. They would be back with us again for lunch – seemingly unchanged, but with an air about them. In my mind, of course, they had been indulging in all sorts of delicious sins. Had I thought about it much more, I might even have considered conversion. But in fact, I was far too busy trying to deal with my own religious life.

If all church had been vespers, I might be high up in the ranks of the clergy by now. I loved vespers. Warm and stuffed and sleepy from dinner and the afternoon's "free" activities—skiing, tennis—we would walk leisurely over to the Chapel in small groups while the bells intoned soothing, familiar hymns. There was none of the usual earnestness; instead, a relaxed, chummy, holiday atmosphere prevailed; almost as if we were all good friends, part of one family. Vespers was a quiet, meditative, peaceful time. "Holy" I would have said, did not the word carry such painful connotations.

> Now the day is o-ver
> Night is draw-ing nigh,
> Sha-dows of the eve-ning
> Steal a-cross the sky.

That hymn still brings tears to my eyes. It is impossible for me to sing it—to sink into those soft, slow cadences—without feeling benevolent. I was in the bass section of the choir, next to Mr. Cushing, and even he was mellow. During vespers I was so full of love and harmony and fellow feeling that I could look over at Billy Grant and forget that he had ever bullied me. Standing in the choir stalls, singing in joyous harmony, in our white robes, slightly elevated above the rest of the school—we felt like angels. Had there been a divine visitation then, we would simply have filed out and followed Him.

> A-bide with me; fast falls the e-ven-tide;
> The dark-ness dee-pens; Lord, with me a-bide:
> When oth-er hel-pers fail, and com-forts flee,
> Help of the help-less, O, a-bide with me.

As we did our best to bring out the harmonies of that serene and majestic hymn, I felt the flow of faith—was on the verge of rapture. Crocker's granite face looked as peaceful as George Washington's. There were smiles from the normally smileless and the expressions on the faces of the first formers in the front rows were positively cherubic. Then came the Bible readings—the lessons; the first by a master, the second by a sixth former. Paul's great words from First Corinthians: "Though I speak with the tongues of men and of angels, and have not charity..." Charity, love. It was real. It was a presence. It flowed and filled and satisfied. We left vespers brimming with love, overflowing with joy, uncomplaining for once as we sat in evening study hall, doing our homework or writing letters to our parents.

But vespers was the exception, not the rule. The morning services were short: two hymns, an exhortation or two, announcements, and a few prayers. Just a way to start the day. The essence of religion was saved up for morning prayer on Sundays and what followed it—the service of Holy Communion. Holy Communion would be enough in itself to instill a state of spiritual crisis in all but the hardest of souls; but to ensure that the essence lost not its savor, we had sacred studies classes which met three times a week; and the various collects and prayers and admonitions that were sprinkled through the service of morning prayer.

My preparation for all this was knowing something about the journeys of St. Paul from attending Sunday school in Chestnut Hill for a year and a half. We followed Paul's progress on the map and tried to imagine what his boats were like, what he and his men had to eat, how tough the going was—the sailors hampered in their movements by their flowing robes. Even there, there was the bit about Paul being bitten by the snake and miraculously recovering from it: a difficult item to explain, not that anyone attempted to do so. I was better prepared, actually, from having experienced the turmoil of Sundays at home. My father would have already held early morning Holy Communion before the rest of us were up. We would see him briefly at breakfast wordlessly cracking the top off his egg, his expression tense, and then not again until Sunday dinner—the traditional roast beef feast—when I would be raring to go, having been kept in bounds all morning. My father would still be touchy, though, as if the anxieties of the morning's worship had not quite worn off; and only later in the afternoon, when we might as a family all go for a walk together, would peace descend.

For the first year I was at Groton, I was not permitted to take communion, for in order to do that I had to be confirmed. Pre-confirmation instruction took up half of my second year, and it was not really until I was a third former that the words of the service began to sink in.

We do not presume to come to this thy Table, O merciful Lord, Trusting in our own righteousness, but in thy manifold and great Mercies. We are not worthy so much as to gather up the crumbs under thy Table....

Was I really less worthy than Smut—our ancient, farting, foul-smelling cocker spaniel—who lived under the dining room table and ate our scraps? "You crumb! You stupid little bastard!" I'd heard that often enough, but I didn't feel like a crumb, not most of the time. Or was it that we were not even as valuable to God as a servant? But a servant was valuable. Jesus washed his disciples'

92

feet. And he said we should be servants to each other, and to God. Then there was the general confession.

Almighty God, unto whom all hearts are open, all desires known and from whom no secrets are hid; cleanse the thoughts of our hearts by the inspiration of thy Holy Spirit, that we may perfectly love thee, and worthily magnify thy holy name; through Christ our Lord. *Amen.*

How could one feel guilt and love at the same time? And why confess to a Being who already knew what you were thinking and everything you did; who was even aware of your most secret desires? Crocker would be up at the altar. Acolytes—first formers—would bring out the chalice and the silver pitchers full of wine, and the silver trays covered with white linen napkins; and Crocker would wave his hands over it all, blessing it, transforming it; and then turn, and raise his arms into the air, and we would all sink to our knees and begin to feel, or resist feeling, or succumb to feeling, the leaden weight of our sins and the impossibility of ever ridding ourselves of them without the grace of Almighty God.

Minister – The Lord be with you.

Answer – And with thy spirit.

Minister – Let us pray.

For twenty-one and a half minutes!

After the misery, the abnegation, the confession, the request for absolution, the giving of absolution—one was meant to feel cleansed and joyful and at peace. I felt only confusion. The first time I filed back to my seat, the unfamiliar taste of red wine in my mouth, my tongue still sticky from the wafer, I wondered, was I now different?

Or would I be different later? There was the awful part about his body and blood, re-enacted in front of us by Crocker and others. "For in the night in which he was betrayed, (a) he took Bread; and when he had given thanks, (b) he brake it, and gave it to his disciples, saying – Take, eat, (c) this is my Body, which is given for you: Do this in remembrance of me..." It was all so vivid.

"Why, Sir? If Jesus knew that Judas was going to betray him...?" I never did get a satisfactory answer to that question—or to any others; not in sacred studies class or anywhere else... Not till college did the questions even make much sense.

"Don't worry about it so much," said Phil.

"The Mass is a mystery," said Jock. "That's why it's in Latin."

"Who knows?" said Chas. "The Shadow knows," and he would laugh evilly and then bang out something on his drums.

What I found out eventually was that most people went through the communion service with their ears closed and their eyes open, waiting for Mrs. Noble to make her way back from the communion rail. Sunday dinner afterwards was the best meal of the week, and the afternoon was free—apple fights in the fall; skiing in the winter; swimming, trout fishing in the spring. And then, after supper, came vespers, like a blessing, a soothing balm. The peace and quiet of evening prayers.

Chapter Thirteen

November 1941

Dear Mammy and Daddy,

…At Christmas the trombones, all five of us, have two neat solos in five part harmony, and it's neat. We play them off of the balcony in the hall. The things I want for Christmas are as follows:

1. Water-proof wrist watch
2. 2 or 3 kinds of mutes for my trombone
3. 3 really flashy ties
4. Money to buy swing records with
5. 1 good axe (with cover)
6. Boxing lessons for the rest of the fall and all of the winter term.

Love,
Clint

On January 14, 1943, to celebrate my fifteenth birthday and the fact that I had passed all my courses, my parents took me to the Café Rouge at the Hotel Pennsylvania in New York to hear the Glenn Miller band. We had come up from Philadelphia by train and spent the night. My mother liked jazz and swing and even be-bop, but my father was tone deaf and had only the tiniest ear for music of any kind. I should have been more grateful to them for extending themselves so, but the truth is I was far too excited.

We had reservations, but I was afraid if we were one minute late they'd give our table away to someone else. I pleaded with my parents at dinner to hurry up. But we burst in through the glass doors with minutes to spare, and followed the distant sounds of "In the Mood" into the Café Rouge. There they were, just as I had imagined them—casual, dark sports coats, matching pants—Bob Eberle, Billy May on trumpet, a couple of others; then Marion Hutton, sort of half-dancing, two more men (the Modernaires?), and on the end Tex Beneke. Behind that line was the band, "G M" emblazoned in huge, purple letters on the bandstands; Miller in the middle, looking modest, as if he were one of them; all of them beaming, as if they were just having fun; and all the while that smooth sound, that Miller sound. "Ooo, ahh. Ooo, ahh," went the brasses. "Ooooo, Ahhhh," echoed the reeds. And then Miller took up his trombone and his voice lifted above the rest; floated there, played, turned; dipped back down again to join the others; all in one motion, all one sound. And then they stopped. And we were shown to our table.

I had spent three evenings just the previous week sitting in the darkness of the Three Deuces listening to Benny Morton play. It was a small group and every time he broke out from the rest, he sent my goose flesh climbing. Benny Morton and J. C. Higginbotham were my true idols. But they were Negroes. I could never hope to play like them any more than a White pianist could sound like Count Basie, or anyone at all like Louis Armstrong.

My mother got my father onto the dance floor, but I could see that they weren't having a great time. My father wasn't much of a dancer. He could do an acceptable fox trot, but "Little Brown Jug" wasn't the sort of music you fox trotted to. I could see him looking around at the other couples dipping and twisting beside him, trying to get out of their way. I hated "Little Brown Jug." It was so corny. The next piece was "Pennsylvania 6-500." Tex Beneke and Bob Eberle and Marion Hutton and the Modernaires were all grinning like crazy and snapping their fingers. It was a show, that's all. It wasn't music. I sipped at my coke and took in the place instead. The room was about a third full—pretty good for so early in the evening. Everything was in red, of course, and very plush. There were a couple of other kids like myself with their parents, but mostly the place was filled with middle-aged couples—there for the dancing. The piece ended and Miller took up his trombone and went right into "Serenade in Blue." Now I leaned forward, listening. Miller's trombone was a brilliant gold, and it cast its reflections in dazzling beams around the room. The melody seemed to float there, above the band. How could he play for so long without taking a breath? His face wasn't even flushed. And when he finished, looking as if he'd done nothing unusual at all; he just stood there, smiling, leading the band.

At the intermission I walked over to where he was sitting. "Excuse me," I said, nervous but determined. "Excuse me, but could I just hold your trombone?" I play..."

"Sure, kid," said Glenn Miller, hardly looking up. Paralyzed by success, it took me a moment to react. Finally, I stepped onto the bandstand and in a daze picked up Miller's trombone; lifted it, slowly, as if about to play; and then held it there, and let myself imagine that his instrument was truly mine, that I was Glenn Miller, that I was running through the tricky part in "String of Pearls"—soaring, laughing with the music... How easy it was! I winked at the band, and Tex stood up and picked up the beat as I led with my left hand, allowing my smile to rest on the happy faces of the dancers below.

"Put down that trombone!" Slowly, I responded to the voice of the tough-looking man who was shouting at me from the table next to Glenn Miller's. He shouted again. The spell was broken. I felt myself turning red. As quickly as I could, I put the instrument back onto its stand. But then I heard another voice—Glenn Miller's.

"It's okay, Lou. I said he could." Lou looked surprised; and I picked the trombone up again, and with a little nod at the band, broke into "Moonlight Serenade;" and we were away, gone, in the groove, flying.

"How is it he let you do that?" my father said when I got back to the table.

"Did you get his autograph?' my mother asked me. I looked at them both with scorn. I was still up there, in the air above them, soaring on my wings.

If I couldn't be Benny Morton, perhaps someday I could be in a band; maybe even lead a band. I wouldn't play junk like "Little Brown Jug," or "Pennsylvania 6-5000" or "Chattanooga Choo Choo," which they were playing now. And I wouldn't dress my band up in corny saddle shoes and sport coats, either. But someday, maybe, it wouldn't be so bad to be in a place like this, entertaining the troops, grooving with the music, music of my making. And if some kid wanted to examine my trombone, maybe hold it for a minute and imagine he was me, why not?

"Sure, kid," I'd say, "Go ahead;" and let my manager be damned.

Chapter Fourteen

"Many masters, faculty, and boys gave service of one sort or another at Fort Devens, from teaching classes and leading discussions to providing concerts by the school band"

Nichols, *Forty Years More* p.44.

"How big a crowd do you think there'll be?" said Chas, as we sped out of the school grounds, Chas's drums rattling in the back of the Mish Station Wagon.

"I hope not too big," I said, already feeling sweaty with fear.

"All Moss told me," said Jock, who was driving, "was that the officer he talked to said the concert had been approved."

"You should have found out more," I said. "It could be the whole base, a command performance, all the top brass..."

"Wouldn't that be great?" said Chas.

"I don't think it'll be that big," said Jock.

Fort Devens, where we were headed, was just past Ayer. There were thousands of troops there now and an airfield and the town of Ayer had a dozen new bars in it and three new pool halls. That was the report, anyway. To us, of course, Ayer was more out of bounds now than ever. We happened to be driving toward it at the moment because Jock, being sixteen, had a license and Mr. Moss, the advisor to the Missionary Society, had persuaded the powers that be that Jock, at least, could be trusted and that anyway we deserved a reward after the concert we had just given at the school. "We" were The Three Shots of Rhythm, and our concert had been such a success that we were taking it on the road.

"We've been expecting you," said Sergeant Lyons, a beefy nurse who marched us toward a swinging door. "Ward 3" the sign read—not exactly what we had in mind.

The room contained about thirty beds and smelled like a public john. It looked like a barracks except that the soldiers were in hospital gowns, and most were bandaged. There were two in leg casts; others were sleeping, four were playing cards. A dozen chairs had been set up in the narrow aisle between the beds. Facing them was a small, upright piano.

Nurse Lyons pointed to a middle-aged man who was slumped over in one of the chairs. "Machine gun wounds in abdomen and upper left thigh. Progressing nicely. Wife, three children, Oklahoma City, auto mechanic. Here three months." Our presence was acknowledged by a faint smile. She went around the room. There was a young boy no more than eighteen who had been wounded in North Africa. His left ear was being restored by plastic surgery. When Nurse Lyons was about half through, one of the card players looked up. "Where's de punch?" he said, in a very tough-sounding, Brooklyn accent, "you said d'ed be punch."

101

"Later, Corporal Silvaro. First we're going to enjoy some music." She went on with her "introductions." Most of the men were young, in their twenties, but there were a few others, like "Anzio," who were practically my father's age. The older men were seated in the chairs.

"All right, now. Jamison! You and Wilbur bring up some more chairs." Reluctantly, slowly, the inmates of Ward 3 assembled themselves. When they were all seated, Nurse Lyons introduced us. "...so we're very fortunate to have them here with us today." Mild applause. And then she left. Corporal Silvaro rose from his chair, belched, "Up yours!" in a voice like a parrot's, and sat back down again. Much laughter.

"Come on, Silvaro. Give dese guys a chance." Another tough guy—or was he acting, too?

"What'ya got?" said a third voice.

"You got a theme song?" said another.

"'Song of India'," said Jock.

"Oh, yeah," said Silvaro, in mock seriousness. "I think I heard Tommy Dorsey play that once."

"Do your show," said one of the older men when the Ward was silent again.

"Sure. Do it," said Silvaro. "We got time."

"Song of India" went pretty well. I cracked on the high "D", but considering how nervous I was, that I got through it at all was a miracle. "Tuxedo Junction" was next and they liked that better, particularly Chas's solo. "String of Pearls" would have been good except that two of the notes on the piano were stuck. Then came "Marie," my favorite, We started it out at a good, fast clip, but Chas wasn't keeping the beat and I had to slow it down and then he dropped a stick in the last bar of his solo and out of the corner of my eye I saw that Silvaro and his buddies had started up their card game again.

"Three of spades. That's all you've got? A pair?" He threw down his hand in disgust. Just then the door swung open and in came Nurse Lyons bearing a pitcher. Behind her were two orderlies, one carrying a card table, the other a tray full of cookies and paper cups.

"Here comes de punch," yelled Silvaro and everyone got up and started milling around.

"So we've been enjoying ourselves, have we?" said Nurse Lyons, in her hearty-hearty voice.

"Put a shot in it, will ya, nurse?" said Silvaro.

"School days, the best days of my life," said 'Anzio,' his breath smelling of cherry Kool-Aide. "The teachers I had. I'll never forget..."

Our concert at the school the week before had been a wild success. The whole school was there, masters and everybody. Devoe even came backstage afterwards and congratulated us, something you had to be in the band to appreciate as he made no secret of what he thought of jazz. Crocker actually slapped me on the back. Finally, he had something to praise me for to my parents, he said, and croaked out his heartiest laugh. We were all pretty sure that it was Mrs. Crocker who had persuaded him to let us give the concert in the first place. It was a pretty big break from tradition. Not only was it the first jazz concert they'd ever had at the school, it was the first concert of any sort put on by students for the school as a whole. It was a full production, too; spot lights, a curtain that drew apart slowly to reveal the glittering slide of my

103

trombone. John Train had made stand-up posters with glossy blow-ups of each of us; "The Three Shots of Rhythm" on three inch, block lettering arching across the tops. And it all went without a hitch, practically. They made us come back for three encores—and we were slated to give another concert at graduation.

Nurse Lyons put out the last of the vanilla wafers and marched herself and the two orderlies over to the door. "Time for Part Two, everyone," she said. When the door shut after her this time, Silvaro made the whistling sound of a bomb falling; but at the end, instead of simulating an explosion, he farted, actually farted. The noise was so loud it echoed in Chas's drums. Brewer should have been there. He could have taken lessons.

We were ready to play but I noticed that very few of the soldiers were sitting down in the chairs. Many of the chairs had been removed, in fact, and about half the beds were occupied with figures in the prone position. "Moonlight Serenade," said Jock, apparently oblivious to what was happening. I noticed that some had pillows over their heads. When we were finished, only 'Anzio' clapped. "Ask them for a request," said Chas. "Maybe they don't want any more Jazz." Jock nodded and stood up.

"How about some requests?"

"Silence?" came a voice from the back of the room.

"We could sing camp songs," said Silvaro who was lying on his bunk reading a magazine.

"How about some Boogie Woogie?" said someone.

"Sure," said Jock, and he signaled us to get ready. We didn't have to discuss what we were going to play as we knew only one piece of Boogie Woogie. Jock started it off with his left hand, but with two of the notes stuck, there was definitely something missing. We got through the arrangement somehow, but I hoped they wouldn't ask us to play another. In the pause that followed, the same voice as before spoke up again a little louder, a little more insistently, and with unmistakable sarcasm: "What I said was how about some Boogie Woogie?" There was not even laughter this time.

"That's all we know," said Jock. In the silence that followed, Jock mumbled something about that being it then, and we packed up—as quickly as we could—and left.

After the school concert, the three of us had talked wildly about getting a date somewhere for the summer—in the Catskills, maybe. We had seen ourselves in lights and were already partially blinded. Driving back through Ayer, not even Chas speaking, we modified our goals. "How about a hamburger," Chas said. "Over there." We walked into the diner without even looking around first to see if we were being observed. "If Moss finds out we stopped, that's it," said Jock, in a dull voice. "No more Mish Wagon. No more trips."

"Who cares," I said.

We ordered hamburgers and fries and cokes, all around. The hamburgers came, and they tasted good. When we finished, we ordered another round. And when we got back into the car, we did feel better. Almost, though not quite, as if we'd been out on the town.

Chapter Fifteen

Miss Gash, longtime librarian at the school, tells of a conversation she had with one new boy a few weeks after the Fall term had begun. She was one of the few ladies he had seen at school, so he asked her who the lady who stood beside Mr. Crocker to say goodnight might be. Miss Gash said: "Who do you suppose she is?" The boy answered, "Why, I assume she must be his secretary."

Nichols *Forty Years More*, p. 125.

"Embrace me, my own embraceable you.
Embrace me, you irreplceable you."

Chas had the deeply serious look on his face of a drug addict enjoying a fix. Behind him, Phil was swaying back and forth with his eyes closed, a beatific smile on his lips. Jock was seated next to the phonograph dreamily gazing into the middle distance, a stack of records on the table nearby. I closed my own eyes and nestled back down into the velvet voice of Billie Holiday; caressed, comforted, cooled—yet warmed as well—by the images in my mind. I was making love to Gloria de Haven, or just about to. She was in my arms, her cheek pressed up against mine. I moved my head slightly; she looked up, smiling, and I reached for her lips... for her lips, for her lips... Like a flashbulb the light went on. Jock lifted the arm off the record and cursed, and Gloria de Haven was with me no more. Chas threw his pillow across the room and I dropped mine and Phil took a few more swaying steps and then quit, and we all stood around waiting for Jock to change the record, blinking in the light like convicts caught in the prison yard trying to make their escape.

It was two weeks to Washington's Birthday and the school dance but of course we weren't going. Fourth formers could go and serve on the stag line, but only fifth and sixth formers were allowed to invite girls. All the rest of us could do was ogle from a distance. That was plenty. We were out of our minds with excitement already. But if you thought about it it wasn't all that much. The presence of seventy or so girls on campus for the two days mainly just drove everyone crazy. Maybe it was just as well it happened only once a year. It was all we thought about for at least two weeks beforehand and all we talked about for a good two weeks afterwards. They might just as well have given us the month off for all the energy we had left over for anything else.

Parlor Night, the way Jock and Chas and Phil and I had it rigged up, was more satisfying, really. Dancing around with your pillows may not sound like much, but it was better than playing Old Maid or Rummy or Backgammon with the Crockers. Parlor Night was supposed to be social, polite, partyish; cokes and cookies and ping pong, too; home away from home, a tradition that went way back to the beginning of the school. Every night of the week a different form came over for an hour before bed. And it was fun: we'd enjoyed it. But dancing around to the music of Glenn Miller and Benny Goodman and imagining ourselves in the arms of Peggy Lee or Gloria de Haven was a lot more exciting. I don't know why they let us do it. Maybe they'd given up on us. Maybe jazz fiends were in a different category. It could have been a reward for the good work we did entertaining the troops. Phil was there, after all; 'cause he'd claimed he was our manager. Anyway, they gave us the room with the record player and though we didn't dare lock the door, we were pretty sure the Crockers wouldn't break in. As long as we kept the music down, we were safe. Still, it was scary. Mrs. Crocker probably would have had a fit, and Mr. Crocker, once he'd gotten the idea, would have thrown us out for sure. That was one reason we turned most of the lights off. The other was it was easier to imagine you were really dancing with someone that way.

But I was going to the dance. I was dying to tell the others about it, but naturally I couldn't.

* * *

Dave Krumbhaar and I had discovered the door that led from the cellar of the Schoolhouse to the space underneath the stage the week before. The trap door in the stage itself had been closed over by another floor, so the space underneath it was no longer used. It was the perfect place from which to watch the dance.

"Wwwhoowww!" said Shep. "All thththosssse ggggirls." Even Bruce Chandler allowed himself to smile.

It was David's idea to approach them. Phip and Shep were class officers. Neither one had ever had a blackmark. If we got caught, Crocker would never throw them out.

108

Bruce, too. Mr. Respectable. Plus his cubicle was the one next to the fire escape. The plan was simple. We were all in Brooks House in Hawkes' dorm. All we had to do was go down the fire escape and dash across to the cellar door of the Schoolhouse fifty yards away. We'd be in our pajamas. Shep walked in his sleep, sometimes, and that way the rest of us could pretend we were just trying to get him back, if we got caught. There was quite a bit of snow still around so we'd wear our slippers and bathrobes, too. Bruce wanted us to wear sweaters, under the bathrobes, but that wouldn't go with our story. We'd stuff our beds with clothes and make as little noise as possible and hope for the best. It was quite safe, really. After all, half the school and all the masters would be at the dance. Bates, the one prefect in charge, would be at the other end of the dorm in Hawkes' study, listening to the radio.

"Now!' I said. No one moved. "Quick!" I pushed Shep and he stumbled and would have fallen if I hadn't grabbed him. Phip ran out instead, zigzagging across the moon-drenched lawn. In his navy blue bathrobe, he was not only highly visible, but particularly suspicious looking.

"I can't," said Shep. "I'm t-t-too nervous." I turned to Bruce. He was poised as if to run, but in the wrong direction. I turned him.

"Go!" I hissed. And he went.

I grabbed Shep by the arm, and we started to run. Shep was trembling all right, but we made it. "I'm going back!" said Bruce, his voice breaking.

"Shhh!" Phip and I both spat out, and we steered him toward the shelter of some bushes and crept along until we reached the door to the cellar. Breathing hard, I opened it a crack and peered in to make sure Ralph, the janitor, was nowhere in sight. There was a bulb on in the hall, but his office was dark. The door to our part of the cellar was at the end of the hall on the right.

I'd known that Ralph would be upstairs because I'd asked him, quite casually, what he'd be doing that night, and he told me that he and Danny would be patrolling the upstairs halls in case any couples tried to sneak off. Just the same, it was a big relief to find he wasn't there.

"Let's go," said Phip, and we filed in and walked quickly down the hall, our hearts beating as if inside tin pails. We reached the door and went in. Flashlight. Where was it? I'd forgotten the damn thing. We stood there in the dark, everyone cursing and wondering what to do. Then Phip opened the door a crack and David ran over and removed the wood panel, letting in a blast of music, and a tiny bit of light. Phip shut the hall door and followed us through the opening to a stuffy, dusty place that was directly under the stage. The music was deafening. Not only drums thumping but feet stamping and the stage creaking like an old ship. Shep sneezed. Bruce knocked his head and groaned. But it didn't matter. We could have set off firecrackers in there and no one would have heard.

You could hardly see a thing. The only light came from a crack in the middle of the curtain. "We'll take turns," I said. Phip parted the curtain at the top about half an inch, looked out, then gingerly pulled it closed again, backing away.

"Romig," he shouted in my ear. "I could have touched him." He lit a match, beckoning the others to come over. How could I have forgotten the stupid flashlight? We lined up behind the crack, on our knees. It was dusty and dark and smelly and noisy and wildly exciting. "My turn," I said, pounding David on the shoulder.

The band was playing a corny version of "Jeepers Creepers." The singer sounded more like Lawrence Welk than Louis Armstrong. They had a violin, of all things. Bass, piano, drums, clarinet, trumpet and violin. Some sort of canned arrangement. The piece ended and there was an eerie calm, followed by muffled talk in the distance. "They're drinking punch," Phip whispered. "I see Robinson's girl."

"Where?" I said. "I want to see!"

"Shhh! Watch out!" Robinson was a shy, little English guy in the fifth form. He'd been sent over from London last year with a bunch of others to escape the blitz. When he turned up with a girl who looked like Hedy Lamarr, we could hardly believe it. He'd met her that fall at a concert. She went to Concord Academy and they were sitting in the same box with the other music students. Robinson played the organ—and the piano—and the harpsichord— and she played something too. Apparently, Robinson asked her to the dance as they were walking out after the concert was over. Just like that. We were impressed, all of us. But when we actually saw her we were bowled over. She was so beautiful you could hardly imagine speaking to her much less asking her out. He had to be tough, that guy, underneath it all. From the war.

I squinted through the crack with my right eye, holding my breath so as not to inhale the musty reek of those old curtains. Robinson's doll was nowhere in sight. Instead, a very thin girl in a yellow dress that came down off her bony shoulders was striding toward us. For a minute I thought she'd seen me. She came right up and stood there, not two inches away, an intense expression on her face. She looked from side to side and then down in her dress. Suddenly she reached inside. I couldn't figure out what she was doing, and then I saw that one of her tits was gone. She poked down her dress again and yanked and pulled, and stretched. When she finally straightened up, both her tits were there. Falsies! I'd danced with a girl at the Friday evening once who wore falsies. Unbelievable! The shock of looking down the front of a dress and instead of seeing something, there'd be this piece of rubber, her chest as flat as your own. I crawled back away from the crack in the curtain and let Shep take my place. Somebody's BO smelled so bad I was ready to leave, that and the falsies. The band had started up again and the noise was even more deafening then before. "Indian Love Song!" On the trumpet, for heaven's sake.

Phip lit another match and Bruce hobbled over and got in line. He hadn't had a real turn yet, and he was so excited he probably didn't care that the upper pocket was torn on his fancy bathrobe and that he was filthy and had lost a slipper. Shep wouldn't leave so he got down on his stomach and peeked out through the lower part of the crack. "It's neat!" he exclaimed, happy as could be.

* * *

I was just finishing my third turn at the crack. I'd been staring happily at Robinson's girl who had been cut in on by four different boys while I'd been there. I was about to turn and make room for Shep when I noticed a puddle of water about ten feet to my right. Oh, no! I thought, and then something fell out into the curtain above it, slipped down and slid out onto the dance floor: a broom handle. I squeezed over as fast as I could, banging into things, envisioning all sort of catastrophes. Phip lit a match. He and Bruce were huddled together over something. There were brooms and pails all around and one of the pails had turned over. Mop water.

"The broom!" I said, "Don't touch it!" I crawled back to the crack. Whoever noticed might think it had fallen over by itself. It could have spilled the water, too. The puddle was getting bigger, though—creeping right out there. The Nobles were dancing nearby and then... I shut my eyes. Mrs. Noble was shaking water off her skirt and two other couples had stopped to watch her. I pulled away from the curtain, my heart pounding like crazy. Get back! I thought, and motioned to Shep to follow me. A match flared and I could see the others already crouched by the wood panel.

We were just about to make our escape when the curtain flew up and a beam of light filled the space. The band had stopped playing.

"Ralph!" a voice bellowed. We glued ourselves to the back wall in silence. There was the clatter of buckets being moved, mops and brooms being pulled out. Finally, the curtain fell back down. We were just starting to crawl

113

through the opening to the cellar when the curtain jerked up again and Gallien's head appeared, framed in the light. "There's a slipper," he said. "Get Danny with the flashlight!" We took off. Fast. But we couldn't get past the cellar. The hall was bustling with activity. We would have to wait until the intermission was over. And by that time it would be too late.

"Damn slipper!" David said.

"What will they do to us?" said Bruce, his voice trembling.

"I don't know," said Phip. He looked grim.

* * *

The worst part was watching the buses leave. All at once the campus was so quiet. We went down to Ralph's office in the Schoolhouse, and he gave us each a familiar pail and some rags and then we went upstairs to the study hall and he put us to work washing windows. There were thousands of them. Great big windows along one whole side and two more at the end, each one divided into six inch panes. Bang, bang, bang, bang, wipe. Wipe again with a dry cloth. An hour later, our knuckles were bloody, our arms ached, and we'd hardly made a dent in the job. We complained bitterly to Ralph, who came to check on us about then, but he only smiled. "Mrs. Crocker sent you over something," he said. "Don't you want to see what it is?" We nodded our heads. Anything to keep from going back to work. He brought in a large tray with a napkin spread over part of it. "To keep your spirits up," he said, and unveiled the contents. There was a plate heaped with cinnamon donuts, a pitcher of lemonade, four cokes, a half dozen vanilla cupcakes, and a small chocolate cake already cut into slices. We dug right in. And two hours later we managed a good lunch as well. Mrs. Crocker herself came over to get us for lunch, and we were quite jovial by then and thanked her profusely.

From then on it was a sort of party. Oh, we worked. We worked all right. In three days we cleaned all the windows in the Schoolhouse, inside and out. But after a while we got the hang of it and it wasn't so bad. The trick was to let the rag do the work and not to spare the soap and water. And, of course, to go from top to bottom, not the other way around. And to take your time. When we got to the final polishing—one on the inside, the other on the outside—and we reached the point where you could hardly tell where the glass was, it was even fun. Satisfying. There were seven, huge windows along one side of the study hall, each one with forty-five panes. And when they were all clean, they sparkled in the sun. The whole room, in fact, became flooded with light.

I'd hated that room, I'd thought. I'd sat in it for three years, doing homework, or pinned down in detention. I was in my third desk now, half way back. Train was on my left, Walser on my right, as they had been for all three years; here and in chapel and in the study hall in Hundred House. The year after next I'd be in the last row. And the year after that, if and when I got there, I'd be standing in the rear—a sixth former: with the power to give out blackmarks. But next year, I'd be a fourth former and would be on the stag line at the school dance and allowed to cut in on anyone I wanted.

Would Robinson's girl be there, I wondered? I'd have to ask him, in a very casual way, if he were having her up. If so, I'd dance with her first thing. And I'd make such a terrific impression that by the time the dance was over, she'd be my girl, not Robinson's; and the following year she'd come up with me. I got very excited just thinking about it.

Chapter Sixteen

November 18, 1943

Dear Dad

You'll probably be rather surprised at what I'm about to tell you and I won't even try to make any excuses for myself. As you know I smoke, and I think you understand it. Yesterday Phil and I each bought a pack of cigarettes in Groton. We were not planning to smoke them here, but we bought them to have on Thanksgiving. This may seem stupid as we could get them at any drug store in Boston and there was no real reason for it except that we just wanted to have them in our study. Uncle Jack called us into his study today and told us how awful this was especially for the morale of the school and he put us on bounds so we can't go into Boston on Thanksgiving, and he's writing a letter to you about it.

We've also just had a long talk with Mr. Freiday about it and just things in general and he really made a lot of points clear to us. I'm not quite sure how you're going to take this and I know it's going to be an awful job pulling up our reputations but I think we can do it. I know for sure that I've definitely learned my lesson and there's never going to be any more trouble about that but all the masters are down on us terribly and things aren't too good. I know it's not too good a thing for boys our age to smoke but that's not anywhere's near the worst thing that some boys our age do. You can see that just by reading the paper. I just hope you'll see what I mean and when I get home I think it might be a good idea to have a talk on the subject....

I hope you get this letter before you get Mr. Crocker's, and I know how stupid it was.

Lots of Love,
Clint

I peeled back a corner of the pack of Luckies and pressed my nose up against the rich tobacco. "Ummmm!" I said, inhaling deeply. Phil did the same with his. For a while we inhaled in silence.

"One more week," Phil said and sighed. We had our pipes, but sucking on them was nothing compared to breathing in the aroma of fresh tobacco.

"Now we can light up as soon as the cab pulls out of the gates," I said.

"Six days, twelve hours and thirty-two minutes," said Phil, checking his watch. An hour later we were in Crocker's study getting blasted.

"I thought you two had reformed," he said. He was very pissed off. He got up from his chair and walked over to the fireplace. "And then you go and do a thing like this." His voice fell and he sounded weary. For a moment there was complete silence as he stared into the fire. Phil's face had turned white.

He was going to kick us out, I realized. Here it was a week before Thanksgiving and we were going to be expelled. Oh, my God! Already this fall my father had been up to talk to Uncle Jack about me. I'd been trying harder since then, too. I was passing in all my subjects, now, with an 85 in Sacred Studies. And here we'd gone and done it. Our lives were ruined. And for what? For buying two packs of cigarettes at Bruce's when we could just as easily have waited until we hit Boston. If only we hadn't opened them, if only...

118

"Your father and I were together here and at Harvard."
Crocker had turned to Phil and was speaking softly. "We
rowed in the same shell. What am I going to tell him? He
thinks the world of you. I know he does, because he's
told me so, many times. And what will your mother
say?" Phil looked on the verge of tears.

Two boys in our form had been kicked out just the
week before for smoking. They would probably return
after Christmas because they confessed right away and
otherwise they had pretty spotless records. The story
was that they'd seen some town boys standing in a group,
smoking; and they'd gone up and talked to them, and
while they were there they'd taken a cigarette and had a
few puffs. Some second formers had seen them, as well as
two sixth formers, so that when they were reported by
the sixth formers the fact that they had also served as a
bad example was a reason to be severe in their case. If
they hadn't readily admitted it and acted so upset about it
themselves, they would have been sent home for good.
Smoking was one of the big crimes. We all knew that.
Plenty of boys smoked, but they were very careful about
doing it in the privacy of their huts or some other place.

But we hadn't actually smoked any cigarettes, had
we? All we'd done was smell them. That couldn't be
such a crime. Why did Phil look as if he was about to die,
then?

"I'm going to have to make an example of you," said
Crocker, in a very stern voice. "You share a study. Mr.
Gallien didn't want you two to share a study, but you
persuaded us that you could behave, that you could be
trusted, were adults and could study together and would

119

not take advantage... Sucking on empty pipes is one thing. Having open packs of cigarettes in your desk drawers is another. How can you expect me to believe that you didn't intend to smoke them?"

"Sir, we did," I said, "but not until Thanksgiving, after we'd left the school."

"Well, you won't be leaving the school now," said Mr. Crocker. "You're on bounds for the rest of the term."

That night, before we went to bed, Mr. Freiday talked to us as well. "Stupid" was the word he stressed. You wanted to avoid doing stupid things. The boys last week had been very stupid. Of course someone would see them. Of course it would be reported. Naturally, no one could be perfect all the time. If you were being imperfect, however, you had better be imperfect in private. And as far as your public performance went, you had to avoid even the appearance of wrongdoing. It was amazing. Freiday came nearer to admitting what Groton was all about in that ten minute conversation than anyone else had since I'd been here. I hadn't liked being in Freiday's dorm; but now I saw in Freiday someone I might talk to. In spite of how much I hated his French class. And French. He might even understand.

"How did they find out?" said Phil later.

"Gallien," I said. "He searched our study."

"He's not allowed to do that," said Phil. "We're supposed to have some privacy now." I didn't say anything. I didn't have to. Gallien had found that catalogue in my bureau drawer first form year, hadn't he? And that was supposed to be private, too. Nothing was private to Gallien. That's why we called him Creeping

120

Jesus. That and because of how silently he walked; and what a model of behavior he made himself out to be. The catalogue had been for a whoopee cushion I'd wanted to send for. He made me write my parents for permission and then told me I wasn't to use it at the school. And I certainly wasn't to order itching powder or stink bombs or anything like that. It was decent of him not to just confiscate the catalogue, I had to admit. I ordered the whoopee cushion and the day we left for the summer Gallien handed it to me in a little bag. "Don't forget this, Trowbridge," he'd said, and gave me his I-know-all-about-you smile. There wasn't much that got past Gallien, that was true. But he also understood what it was within us that made us want to break the rules.

"What about the girls?" said Phil.

"We'll have to tell Richardson it's off." Richardson was my friend from last summer. We'd worked together at the Avon School farm in Avon, Connecticut, and he was planning to meet us in Boston with Liz and Beth from the farm and a blind date for Phil; and we were going to have twenty-four hours the likes of which no one had ever experienced before. Phil had worked up a fever pitch excitement about it.

It was Richardson who had taught me how to smoke. Of course I'd smoked before, but it was he who taught me style. He'd also explained the reason for smoking: to get girls. With a cigarette dangling from your lips you looked cool. If you looked cool, you were cool. And the girls loved you. They fell in your lap. He taught me how to hold a cigarette, how to knock it out of its pack, how to open the pack—just a little square tear at the corner. He taught me how to French inhale. How to inhale, period, without coughing. And Beth helped me to become a number one operating sex fiend like Richardson himself. Beth was in charge of the dairy. She was sixteen and had a terrific figure and what she liked to do better than anything in the world was neck. She made necking into an amateur sport. Hell, she could have gone professional. She could have gone a lot further than that, as a matter of fact and she would have, said Richardson, but she had a boyfriend right there on the farm—a great muscle bound brute named Gary. Gary was seventeen and he was our immediate boss in everything to do with the farm. He knew about Beth, but not only didn't he mind it, he egged her on. They egged each other on, for heaven's sake. They actually put on performances. But he drew the line at anything past necking for anyone else.

Liz was Richardson's girl. She was the daughter of one of the teachers at the school. He went to Avon and he knew all the ins and outs and one of the ins he'd gotten very familiar with was Liz. Liz went a good deal further than necking, though exactly how far I never found out, but she didn't mind doing some pretty heavy stuff with me as well, when Richardson wasn't available. Even when he was. But Richardson was a terrific guy. If you were his buddy, he shared. The girl he'd gotten for Phil was a friend of Beth's and she was sure to be a nympho too. Richardson had us lined up to go to Beth's on Friday and Saturday. Gary was in the Army now, so that much was out of the way. We would have Thanksgiving at Richardson's and we'd signed out for there for Friday as well. How exactly we were going to handle that night at

Beth's was going to have to be worked out. But knowing Richardson, it would be. But in fact nothing at all was going to happen now. We were on bounds.

Phil was furious. He would have hidden them more carefully if he'd thought that Gallien was going to sneak around in his desk drawer looking for things. "Maybe Mr. Krebs at Bruce's told them," I said. The idea of Krebs telling anybody anything was a joke and normally that would have gotten a laugh. But Phil didn't smile.

Ever since a year ago Christmas things had been hopping for us socially. Those New York dances! The Friday Evenings in Philadelphia were pathetic in comparison. The music in New York was real music, for one thing. Benny Goodman, not that Lester Lanin stuff. But the main thing was that the girls were better looking and more sophisticated. They danced up close to you and weren't embarrassed. There was one girl in particular I was planning to work on this coming vacation. The Saturday Evenings would be a whole lot better than the Friday Evenings, though, I'd heard; and if I wanted to I could go to both. And then there was Morristown. We were already set up for a string of parties there.

The thing was, though, that I'd had practice that past summer—a lot of practice—and Phil hadn't. So I was way ahead of him, and he was dying to catch up. Beth had really loosened me up as far as girls were concerned. She thought nothing of kissing you on the mouth—just like that, French kissing you too—and then pulling you down on the couch and going at it in earnest. She didn't care who saw or what they said. So after awhile you didn't care either. You laughed and teased back and

123

eventually learned how far you could go before she'd push you away. Roughly. So you'd get rough, too. And she loved that. And pretty soon you could put your arm around a girl's waist while you were outside waiting for the car to come up after some dance, and then just kiss her, as if it were the most natural thing in the world; and most of the time the girl wouldn't mind. Then in the car, on the way home... Or walking across a lawn in the moonlight... Beth didn't help you with your line, but she sure warmed you up for the passes.

It was Richardson who taught me how to string a line. Sometimes I was more successful than others. But he was such a pro that I hesitated to say anything when he was around. Phil choked up. That was his problem. He had red hair and wore glasses and when he was with girls he just turned red instead of talking. I tried to tell him a few things but he was pathetic. He needed a whole summer's worth of practice. Maybe two. And now we were on bounds till Christmas.

Thanksgiving came and half the school left. We ate stuffed turkey and the trimmings and consoled ourselves as best we could. All we could think about, though, was Richardson and the girls and everything we were missing. On Saturday night they were going to show *Random Harvest*, which I'd been dying to see. But I didn't care about that now. And what were we going to do for the rest of the weekend?

We'd just finished lunch on Saturday when Phil came running into the study. "We've got Blackie and Whitey for the afternoon!" he said, grinning broadly.

"What do you mean?" I said.

"They want to see our hut," Phil said, hardly able to contain himself. "I persuaded them."

"Boy," I said. "Pretty good."

We got to the hut half an hour ahead of time so as to clean it up a bit. We'd built it with Dave Krumbhaar the year before. The best thing about it was that nobody else knew where it was. It was about half a mile back into the woods from the ski trail and took a good twenty minutes to get to. We used it mainly to store food in and magazines and stuff. We'd go to it on half holidays or just when we felt like it. It was mainly just a place to get away from it all. Lots of boys had huts and most smoked in them, but we hadn't dared do that because the smoke stuck to your clothes. I certainly never thought we'd be entertaining girls there, even girls like Blackie and Whitey.

We'd necked with Blackie and Whitey a few times in the cellar of Hundred House, down behind the shoe lockers, but that was no great accomplishment. Blackie and Whitey would neck with anybody, even third formers. What was exciting though was their agreeing to meet us out here.

"It's foul down there," said Phil, emerging from the entry hole that was dug off to one side. We shook out the two blankets he'd brought up, and I went down with a flashlight and matches to light the candles and straighten things up. It smelled pretty rank, and there was a pile of dirt on the floor from where some animal had started to dig a hole. The tarpaper on the roof must have held up pretty well though, because the floor wasn't wet. I brushed off the mattresses, straightened out the magazines on the orange crates, and crawled back out, carrying a pail

125

full of dirt with me. Phil handed me the blankets and I threw them in. "We'd better go get them," Phil said, and we took off.

Blackie and Whitey were standing on the ski trail just where Phil had told them to when we arrived. "Hi," said Phil, who got there first.

"Where's your friend?" I heard Whitey say. I became aware of the sound of my heart beating.

Back at the hut we finally persuaded them to take their coats off and crawl down the bunny hole to where all the fun was. They were both pretty hefty, the heifer twins some boys called them, and I wasn't sure they were going to make it, but they did; Whitey did that is. We went down first.

Whitey had changed out of her kitchen uniform, all but the shoes, but underneath the perfume she'd put on lingered the vegetable soup we'd had for lunch. She had on a pale blue pullover, and her face was heavily made up with rouge and pink powder. Her lips were full and very red. I grabbed her hand and pulled her over to me and pinched her bottom.

"Fresh," she said and laughed and slapped my hand. I told her she looked like Betty Grable, and she did, if you took off thirty pounds or so, widened the space between her eyes and imagined there was something less lumpy under that red wool skirt. She had curly blond hair, too—very curly, very short. Her face was round and chubby and where the makeup didn't cover it, her skin was a pasty white.

"Aren't you going to offer a girl a drink?" she said, looking around.

"This is the bedroom," I said. "Come on. How about a kiss?" She giggled, but obliged. I reached up and put my arms around her, but she didn't move. "Ummm!" I moaned, feigning passion and pulled again, this time with more success. I let my left hand play over her shoulders. The back of her neck was damp with sweat. "Ummmm!" I moaned again, pressing with my tongue. She pulled away.

"Where's Roxanne?" she said, "and Philsie?"

"Don't worry about them," I said, "they're fine."

She bellowed out for Blackie, and I heard mumbles from above, but that was all. "You come down!" she yelled, "or I'm coming up!"

In a minute Blackie appeared, trailing Phil. Phil's face was all blotched with lipstick, and he was grinning like the proverbial cat. He snuffed out the candle on his side and I did the same. "Ummm!" I could hear him moan. I followed, ditto. It was a long time, it seemed, before I got my tongue past the barrier reef of Whitey's teeth.

"You gotta say you love me," she murmured, at one point.

"Sure," I said, trying to loosen her bra. The smell of vegetable soup was getting stronger. The temperature in the hut was rising. Phil sneezed. The bulls bellowed, the heifers snorted and groaned and circled. Big time stuff at the okay corral—though not exactly a performance.

What with *Random Harvest* that night and Blackie and Whitey all afternoon, we got through the weekend somehow. Beth and whoever the doll was Richardson had fixed up for Phil would be for some other time. Christmas maybe. In the meantime there was Blackie and Whitey. I agreed we should practice up all we could on them.

Chapter Seventeen

We had to play football and baseball no matter how thoroughly we disliked them and how indifferently we played, unless the doctor actually forbade it.

Biddle, "As I Remember Groton School," p. 293.

It was later that fall that we built our log cabin. There were three of us involved. Charles Gardiner, already translating Xenophon, was tall but frail. David Krumbhaar, with me in Freiday's French class, was short and wiry. I was roughly in between. We had each gotten out of football on medical excuses—all I had was a rash—and were signed up on Nash's woods crew. Maybe that's what gave us the idea. A fancy hut above ground—a better place to entertain whoever was around. We approached Mr. Nash and were surprised to find that he was enthusiastic. Amazingly, we were given permission. But first we had to be instructed. Instructed in the use of the axe.

Mr. Nash was a small, compact man with curly, dark hair, combed backwards; a trim mustache and the look about him of having been in the French Foreign Legion. The first thing he showed us was how to sharpen the axe. He took us to his shop and the sparks flew and the edge of his axe gleamed silver. And then he did something remarkable. He went outside to a large white pine, walked off six paces, lifted the axe up over his head and buried it in the tree. "Oooh!" we moaned. And for the next hour we were taught the rudiments of the axe throw.

There was the underhand, single flip, from two paces away. Holding the tip of the handle between thumb and forefinger, slowly swing the axe back and forth in a pendulum motion. On the third swing forward, just as the head reached the horizontal, release the axe, giving it a touch of spin. If correctly done, the axe turns in a graceful circle and thunks into the tree, handle upwards and parallel to the trunk. We all managed that one, on the second or third try. Next came the overhead, full turn: both hands on the handle, feet spread apart, axe held high. Then the throw. Harder this time. And with a decided flip at the end. David was the first to try. The butt of the axe handle splintered up against the tree. "Never mind," said Nash. And we returned to his shop. "Handle replacement," he said, placing the axe into a vise. "Essential to the woodsman's craft."

We got as far as the double overhead—in three afternoon sessions. Anything over that was pretty futile, Nash said, demonstrating the point by splintering a new handle into smithereens. There was much laughter, much wielding of weaponry; and from that first afternoon on we were Nash's men. Where he led, we cheerfully followed.

We each bought our own axes, with several spare handles; and during the second week, Nash taught us how to chop. I thought I knew, but I could soon see I didn't. In the first place, I had never chopped with a sharp axe before. "The cut should be a little wider than the diameter of the trunk," Nash said, and he proceeded to knock out a perfect ten-inch chip in four blows. "Angle your cuts, but not too much. See why the handle has to be straight?" Then with the admonition to "cut only dead trees," he left us to our own devices. How big to make the cabin, how to make it; we would learn all that by ourselves.

How to move the trees once we'd cut them down? Where to put up the hut to begin with? We finally decided on a place within sight of the ski trail, near a good supply of dead trees; and on a cabin that measured six feet by six feet on the inside, the logs to be between eight and ten inches thick.

Why so small a cabin? Because six feet on the inside translated to ten feet on the outside, and a ten-foot log that thick was as much as we could handle. We could have built a wigwam out of sticks. But this was Abe Lincoln stuff. We wanted our log cabin to look like one.

"Timberrr!" The tree fell and practically decapitated David who was standing underneath it.

"That was supposed to go the other way," he yelled out, much disturbed. Charlie and I grinned and watched him crawl out from among the branches.

Even more dangerous was the next step. While one of us worked on number two tree, the other two raced along opposite sides of the fallen trunk, lopping off the branches. If you hit a branch hard enough at exactly the point at which it was joined to the trunk, the branch parted from its surface with a pleasing "chunk"—cleanly and completely. Otherwise, it took a couple of strokes. Since we were keeping ferocious score, a couple of strokes over could lose you the game, so safety was frequently sacrificed to speed. If the axe didn't get you, a branch did;

and the miracle was that no eyes were put out, no human limbs lopped off, no stomachs or feet or livers impaled. Actually, our record was pretty good. Except for axe handles. Two that first afternoon.

As soon as the snow started to fly, it was much easier. Then we could attach ropes to the logs, and they would slip through the woods as if slathered in butter. We grasped the principle of the lever early in construction. And we learned that if we could raise the heavy butt end of the log onto its matching cut, we had a better chance of heaving the other, lighter, end up to horizontal.

I specialized in notches, David in planes, and Charlie in chinkings. David and I would confer on where to place the notches; and as I chopped he would kneel beneath me, as far to the other end as possible, and smooth away the knots and the high places, using his axe as a plane. When I finished, we would trade ends. The trick for me was to get the notches lined up on the same planes and cut to the right depth. Charlie gathered chips, and moss and bits of stick, and when he was done, even the cracks were invisible. How did they do it? we often wondered, contemplating our ancestors. The cabin improved as we went along.

We put in windows. One in each end wall. David wanted to "V" groove the logs, a task that would have taken weeks. Instead we borrowed a cross cut saw from Mr. Nash and some odd boards and nailed in frames. After much debate, we decided to make the roof out of boards too and cover them with tarpaper—though we had considered sod, and thatch, and even tightly bound-together spruce boughs. To finish things up, we put another, larger window on the side facing the ski trail; constructed a bed out of saplings along the other wall; and installed a wood stove.

The day after all was complete, we entertained Mr. Nash and various friends with bacon sandwiches and steaming cups of cocoa. Luxuriating like kings, we gloried in how hot it was with the stove roaring.

* * *

The group stopped and watched as I buried the head of my axe in a nearby tree.

"Let me try," said Phip, and unbuckled his skis. I handed him the axe. He held it above his head, and with a mighty swing let go. Smash. The axe handle splintered into kindling wood. Guffaws from all around. Phip reddened but retrieved the axe.

"I'll show you how to put in another one," I said lightly. "Stop on your way back."

"Didn't look hard," he said, and buckled up his skis.

The three of us stood there in formal, woodchopper poses in front of our cabin and watched them ski away. Phip was the second string quarter back on the football team. Next year he'd be first string and the captain, for sure. He was the varsity catcher on the baseball team. He was the best student in the fourth form, with the highest average of anyone in the school. He would be the senior prefect when we got to be sixth formers and would take all the prizes and would probably go on to become President of the United States; but for the moment, I was ahead of him.

I'd given him some lessons on the trombone that summer, though my mother had told me I was crazy. "He's already better than you at everything else," she'd said. But he didn't keep it up when we got back to Groton that fall. Would he go out and build a cabin twenty feet across and two stories high if I showed him how to put in a new axe handle? I didn't think so, though I heard my mother's voice warning me. I'd even teach him how to throw it. What the hell, I thought. I was feeling expansive.

Chapter Eighteen

Boys handed in all cash on their return to school, and throughout the term drew an allowance of twenty-five cents a week, of which a nickel was automatically put in the collection plate on Sunday. The remainder was usually spent in a weekly visit to Bruce's drug store, where a generous soda or sundae could be bought for fifteen cents, thus leaving a final five cents for a candy bar.

If some elements of the school were monastically severe, others were not. No boy waited on table, made his bed, or cleaned any area. All these duties were performed by janitors or maids, who maintained standards of neatness that the boy was unlikely ever to see again in life. For example, maids cleaned the dormitory lavatories three times a day. What in retrospect seems the most luxurious touch of all was the fact that boys might leave a pair of shoes at bedtime in boxes in the cellar marked with the appropriate cubicle numbers, and they would be shined during the night by the watchman.

Nicholas, *Forty Years More*, pp. 5-6. [Author's note: Though the above description is of life in 1934, all but the shoe shine were still current practices in 1940.]

"Come with me, Trowbridge. You get to shovel shit this afternoon." I followed Grant out of the gym and got into the back seat of the station wagon. Cooper was already there. I'd worked off three of my blackmarks that morning copying pages from the dictionary. At least this would be exercise, I thought, settling back for the ride. It was February. Two feet of snow and a crust you could skate on.

"Where are we going?" I said. No response. Grant was whistling, mindlessly; absorbed in his own crummy thoughts. I looked over at Frank. There were great, black rims around his eyes, his face was smudged with coal dust, and he was still wearing his old, sooty clothes. "You know where we're going?" I said. He shook his head and then shut his eyes. He'll never make it, I thought, and then I shut my own.

It was a dorm row, after lights. He and I had been caught with basins full of water coming back from the can. Lights. Action. "Take six!" Everyone else had made it into their cubicles. There was quite a bit of water already in the process of freezing on the floor.

Poor, old Frank, I thought. He was on the coal squad. I was on woods work. Each squad generally worked two or three afternoons a week, but what with all the snow, woods work was out, so I was shoveling shit this afternoon. But that was to work off my blackmarks. Shoveling coal was part of the war effort; so was woods work. I liked to work in the woods and I didn't like to shovel coal. I didn't know anyone who liked to shovel coal except Mr. Nash. Nash was head of both woods work and the coal squad.

"It's not fair," Cooper said. "I still have another three to work off."

"You should have joined maintenance," I said. Just then Grant stopped. We were there.

The barn was huge, as big as the baseball cage; and empty, at the moment, of cows. Grant got us a couple of

136

shovels and showed us where to start. The school had arranged it all with the farmer. Farmers or householders who needed help called the school and instead of running circles or copying pages out of the dictionary, we were sent out to help them. This particular farmer was about ninety, and the man who had been doing his heavy chores had recently joined up. All the old guy had managed to do was get enough of it out of the gutters so he and the cows could walk around. There were piles of it everywhere and a mountainous heap next to the big doors at the far end. "I quit," said Cooper, taking one look.

"You can't quit. You haven't started yet," said Grant, and then he left us. "I'll be back at five."

Cooper went over to a feed bin and sat down. I walked to the doors to see if I could open them. I undid a hook and pushed and the door slid along on a track until it was stopped by a post at the end. I saw that there was a big bucket hanging from a double track that ran back to where the cow stalls were. There were chains attached to the top of the bucket for lowering or raising it and a trip handle on one side. So why hadn't the old geezer dumped the bucket out a little further, into the wagon, for instance, that was just outside the double doors? No track. Wagon would have to be brought in. But wagon was three feet deep in snow, ice crusted snow that made a nice, shiny dome over it. Wagon was almost invisible, in fact. First job would be to shovel snow and ice out of wagon. Then fill wagon with manure. When wagon was full... When wagon was full it would be Spring. It was a big wagon.

I walked back to Cooper and sat down. "Big job," I said.

"Too big," said Cooper.

"We better get started," I said. "It's two o'clock."

"Why not just sit here till five?"

"And then what?'

"I don't know."

"I do," I said. We got our shovels and went out to examine the wagon.

An hour later we'd cleared the wagon of snow and made a path from it to the manure pile. Now we were sitting down again resting before starting on Phase Two.

I was just about to get up when Cooper said, "You know. I'm thinking seriously of quitting."

"You said that before. Frankly, I wouldn't advise it."

"I mean the school. I think I've about had it."

"Really?" I said. This was interesting. I'd thought of doing the same thing hundreds of times, "But look at it this way. We've only got two more years."

"Our parents pay good money and they put us on these work details and then we're too bushed to study..."

"It's the war," I said.

"First we had to make our beds. Then we had to clean out our cubicles. That's maid's work! Then they make us wait on table. And the next year we're out there in the kitchen loading up the stinking dishwasher. And now look what we're doing. What kind of a school is this anyway?"

"I don't know," I said. "It's..."

"It's farmer's work," Cooper practically shouted. "What am I, some kind of peasant? I might as well be living in Ireland on some stupid farm."

"Come on, Frank, I said. "Get going!"

Cooper started to pound on me and I smashed him back, and we got up and he chased me over to the open door. "All right." I said, brandishing a shovelful. "Come get me." So we started loading up the wagon. Phase Two.

One thing, though, old Frank was right about: it wasn't exactly fair. Shoveling cow manure was basically the same thing as shoveling coal. And they were both part of the war effort, really. Yet one got blackmark credit and the other didn't. Why? To me, shoveling cow manure seemed less bad than shoveling coal. So, why didn't you get blackmark credits for being on the coal squad? Four hours a week. Four blackmarks worth of credit. But what if you never did anything bad? Well, then you'd have them, just is case. But if the coal squad got blackmark credits, what about woods work? That was six, maybe eight hours a week. In the fall, anyway. Even I wouldn't be able to use up that many credits. Maybe you should be able to sell them, then? For how much? You could bargain. Say your parents were coming up for the weekend... But what if you were rich? It wouldn't matter what you had to pay. You could be as bad as you liked. And if you were poor? Well, you'd better be good, that's all.

How about maintenance? Helping Ralph and Danny dump wastebaskets, mop floors. Only sissies and weaklings did that. So what was that worth? Nothing. Well, something, I guess. One third credit? How about the other stuff: waiting on table, making beds. No. You didn't get paid for doing chores at home. When I brought in a load of firewood, I didn't hold my hand out for a tip. I shook my head. It was too confusing. The main thing, obviously, was to try to do what you liked to do, whatever anybody else called it.

I was beginning to enjoy shoveling cow manure. It was satisfying—watching the pile build up in the wagon. I even liked its smell. I liked it here in the barn, too; a whole lot better than sitting at a desk copying pages out of the dictionary. I'd rather be doing this any day than sitting in an office working at some boring job. I'd rather shovel manure than do a lot of things I could think of. They'd put this stuff on the fields and that would make the crops grow. Maybe I'd be a farmer when I grew up. That way I could do a little of everything and be my own boss. And in the winter, when there wasn't much going on, I could ski or chop wood.

"Come on," said Cooper. "There's Grant."

I leaned down and packed a shit ball and slipped it in the pocket of my jacket. When we got back to school I would wrap it up and leave it in my locker and when I got the chance... So I got caught. The worst Grant could do was give me six. Six hours of shoveling. I was already looking forward to being back.

Chapter Nineteen

Next to this intense religious drive should come Arnold's [Thomas Arnold of Rugby, Peabody's mentor] determination to make the boys themselves vicars of righteousness. It was not enough for a boy to be a scholar, he had to be a personal force for good in the society of which he was a part.

Ashburn, *Peabody of Groton.* p. 25.

Mr. Niehaus, one of the new teachers, wasn't like any of the others. He'd sneak up behind you when you were jiggling something around in a test tube and smash your arm to the bone with a knuckle sandwich. He was a small, stocky man whose hair stood almost straight up on either side of a central part, and the suits he wore looked as if he were in the process of bursting out of them. He taught with violence, hurling chemicals from one test tube to another, making fierce fires on his sofa-size, green lab table, the smoke billowing out, everyone coughing. Not everybody liked him.

Cushing threw chalk and erasers and smashed at our elbows with serving spoons when he found them resting on the table; but Mr. Niehaus wrestled with us. On days when he was feeling particularly charged up, he would sneak up behind Monster Bob, say, his prize pupil, a two hundred pound tackle on the football team— grab him in a full Nelson and, whooping, hurl him to the floor. Monster Bob—who was as strong as he was large—would twist up and around, not saying a word, and they would flop back and forth until, eventually, Fats Powers, Robins, myself and a few others would pile onto them; and Mr. Niehaus would end up buried in fourth formers. You could hear him at the bottom of the pile—laughing. It took that many of us, for he was strong.

I liked him and so did Phil and Jock and Chas and David Krumbhaar. Cooper hated his guts. One reason I liked him is that I could understand him. "Take this and pour it into that and then write down what you did and what happened." "Nope." "Stupid." "Jerk." "Duck." "Gotcha." These were his favorite words. Charlie said he wasn't a gentleman, which was true but irrelevant. Those of us who took his side also liked him because he kept lambasting Latin and History and even English and telling us that in contrast the sciences were practical, damn it, as well as useful. What would the world be without them? Best of all, he made chemistry into magic. Monster Bob worshiped him and stayed after class all the time and was clearly going to follow in Niehaus' footsteps.

Sometimes Niehaus would come in mad, though. A bunch of us would jump him and he'd shake us off as if we were fleas, march up to the lab table, set up the experiment and tell us curtly to write it all down in our notebooks. Later he would come around and give us hell if we didn't do it exactly right. "Poor Mr. Niehaus. The Mrs. must have locked it up on him again," Chas might whisper, and we'd try not to laugh. Niehaus brought on this kind of talk himself, for often he'd come bouncing in, grinning like one of us. "Sometimes you can't live with them. Other times you can't live without them. We just had one of those *other* times," he'd say. And then he'd strut around with his chest out, just daring us to take him on.

Mr. Niehaus didn't always notice what we were doing, either. He'd be going over an experiment with someone at the big table, and he'd get so involved, half of us could have left and he wouldn't have seen us go. Sometimes you could even catch up on your sleep, though you might be woken abruptly, if you weren't careful, by a horse bite that would pull you straight up in your seat, yelling.

Mr. Niehaus loved to give out advice; like where to park your gum if you were in a pay toilet and were going to brush your teeth (behind your ear, of course). Or he would criticize Gallien for making us read a book like *Lord Jim*. How many of us, for heaven's sake, were ever going to get into a situation like that one? Sometimes you couldn't tell whether he was joking or not. You'd react seriously, start defending Conrad, or the study of history, or something, and smash, he'd give you one in the arm and bust out laughing. One day he was on the subject of girls. He liked to give man to man advice, like when you kiss a girl, breathe in. Stuff like that. "You know what I go by?" he said, and someone obliged with, "No. What?" "The four Fs: Find 'em. Feel 'em. Fuck 'em. And forget 'em." He laughed but no one else did, and he must have realized right then that he'd gone too far 'cause right away he grabbed Monster Bob and wrestled him to the floor and knelt down on top of him. But when no one else did anything, he stood up and said, "OK, boys. Back to your desks. Write it up! Move it, now! I said, hurry!"

After class we had a meeting. "He's disgusting," someone said.

"He definitely shouldn't say things like that, not to us."

"Not to anyone."

"We should tell Crocker."

"Squeal on him?"

"It wouldn't be squealing. He's a master. Even if he doesn't behave like one."

"Well I'm not going to."

"He didn't mean anything."

"Oh, yeah?"

Finally it was decided that the Form officers, Phip and Shep Brown and Harry Welsh, would go to Crocker and tell him what Mr. Niehaus had said; mention that probably he hadn't really meant it the way it came out; argue for mercy, in other words; but go there anyway. Turn him in.

I was wildly opposed to it. So was Chas and so was Phil. Others were torn different ways. You could tell it had upset Monster Bob. Harry was furious. Shep was somewhat indignant. Phip, the head of the Form, didn't say anything but he looked grim. No one liked doing it. But Phip and Shep and Harry went to see Mr. Crocker that evening, and Mr. Niehaus was called in and the rumor was that he was almost thrown out on his ear but that he promised Crocker that he would mend his ways, and so he had been given another chance—for the sake of his family and because there was a war on.

Whatever happened between Mr. Niehaus and Mr. Crocker, or for that matter between Phip and Shep and Harry and Mr. Crocker; Mr. Niehaus was no fun at all from then on. He clammed up tight. He even looked different, as if he'd bought a new suit. There was no more wrestling, no more jokes, no more flashy experiments, even. Just hard work and everyone hating it and most of us feeling guilty about it all. I tried to loosen things back up a week or so later by grabbing him around the arms from the rear when he wasn't looking; but he threw me off as if I were poison, and with great but controlled anger spit out, "The next time you do that, Trowbridge, you'll get six."

Some boys were glad he'd changed and said so. But Phil and Chas and David and I apologized to him. We stopped him in the hall after class and managed to tell him how sorry we were. For a moment he looked like his old self. A tiny gleam came into his eyes. I waited for him to laugh or slug one of us. But then it was gone and all he did was thank us very politely and walk away. I wanted him to attack us, even if in hate. I wanted him to knock us down and beat us unmercifully and have it then turn into a free for all from which he would rise, roaring, and flailing around. I wanted to feel his knuckle up against my arm bone and hear his laugh of triumph as he broke free. I wanted to have his class return to being that crazy free for all it had been before. But it didn't happen. Mr. Niehaus was tamed and we had tamed him.

Chapter Twenty

The intramural club system is the backbone of the organized athletics. Boys learn to play team games and are pitted in keen rivalry against their equals. In football and in baseball, in addition, there is a first school team that plays a schedule against other schools... In the winter, fives, boxing, wrestling, skating, and skiing are popular. Less formal still are the walks through the woods and fields, perhaps looking for birds, perhaps just looking or just walking; and the canoeing on the Nashua, or "shooting" the Squannacook.

Groton. p. 27.

The way of the non-athlete at Groton was not so much hard as inconsequential.

Ashburn, *Peabody of Groton*, p. 101.

"Try him at third," said Cushing and I jogged out to third base, hunched over, in what I thought of as my professional run, and waited for a grounder to come my way.

"Crack!" The ball came zinging along and I got down in front of it, but it popped over my glove and bounced through my legs. I fumbled one catch, causing a run to come in, and missed a throw to first.

"Try him in left field," said Cushing after two innings of this. I wasn't too concerned. After all, I'd hit a two bagger my first time up and my second hit would have been a homer if it hadn't gone foul. One two base hit and one pop up, plus that would-be home run. Pretty impressive, I thought.

All that spring I'd been slamming balls for homers in the Cage. I was a lefty, like Babe Ruth. I took the hide off the ball every time it was pitched to me. I don't know if it was my newly acquired height or what, but suddenly I was a slugger and had a big reputation. Cushing had looked skeptical, as I'd never done anything before, but after my almost home run, he seemed pleased. "That kid can hit!" I could almost hear him saying it. Phip thought I had a good chance of making the varsity. He was the catcher and a good hitter too; and so did Johnny Gray—who had also grown a lot that year—and was Cushing's prize pitcher.

"Crack!" A pop fly, an easy one, coming right to me. I shaded my eyes and ran in a bit. No. It was going the other way. I loped off to the right and backwards, losing it in the sun. Ah. There it was. I ran, hard this time. The ball plopped down twenty feet away between me and second base.

All afternoon it went like this until Cushing finally took me out. I don't think I caught one. The trouble was I couldn't judge where the damn ball was going. Or if by some miracle I'd get my mitt on it, it would bounce out. I could hear the groans all the way out from the bench when that happened for the second time. Two runners got home, though I made an acceptable throw to the plate, stopping the third. And the next day I couldn't hit. Or the day after that. And then it was over. The beginning and end of my big baseball career.

It didn't happen in football. But I had never taken to football in the first place. It happened in boxing, in fives, and in tennis, however. Phil had been up to Maine the summer of the Joe Lewis, Max Schmelling fight and after that we had both taken up the sport. Sarah O'Kane kept rooting for Schmelling but Phil and I hung on Lewis' every slug and went wild when he won. "Good old Cho," I remember us shouting, as we pounded each other on the back. I got as far as beating "Fats" Powers, who was taller than I was; but then, suddenly, I couldn't seem to do it any more. I'd get tensed up and the next thing I knew I'd be on the mat.

Tennis was even worse. I had a big serve but it either went in for an ace or completely out. There was no middle ground. Sometimes I'd play singles with my father and actually beat him a set. Other times even Katherine could beat me. Phil and I came out about the same on the average; but everyone, including my mother, was steadier than I was.

I had just started to play fives that winter. I think I hadn't tried it before because Grant was on the team, and it was bad enough sitting next to him in the band. Fives was like squash, only you played it with miniature baseball gloves. The trouble was I kept hitting the ball with the fleshy part of my thumbs and then they swelled so badly I couldn't play. No eye/hand coordination. That was about it. Or only sometimes, when it didn't matter. It was a miracle, I guess, that I hadn't already lopped off

Gardiner's head with my axe. Skiing, sailing, trout fishing, chopping wood: those were my sports.

It had snowed a lot that past winter and after the cabin was done, I went out on the slopes almost every day. Paul Hwoschinsky and some others would already be there, packing the snow, and I would take a section of hill and side step carefully up and down until it was smooth of ridges; and then take another; and then, if it hadn't snowed too much, we'd get some runs in.

Hwoschinsky was always the first down the slope. Skiing was what he lived for, and he was the best in the school. He was a small boy with a thin nose and very bright eyes whom no one in the form knew very well. He'd come with Phip and Chas and Jock and the others in the second form, but for some reason he hadn't made many friends. I don't know why, exactly, but maybe it was because all he really seemed to care about was skiing. In the fall he cut trails with Mr. Nash and his crew; or by himself. Some of us would have been glad to help him, but he never asked anybody. He cut trails and built jumps and from the time of the first snow, usually just after Thanksgiving, until the thaws of spring, Paul Hwoschinsky would be out every afternoon on his skis.

Even at a distance, he was unmistakable. You might have just crossed the road between the Fives Courts, and Hundred House, and be putting on your skis; and you'd look up and there, at the far edge of the field, just before the trail went into the woods, would be a figure on skis gliding along at about twice the usual rate and you'd think: "Hwoschinsky!" On the slopes it was his grace that set him apart from the rest.

I was not in a class with Hwoschinsky nor did I aim to be. It wasn't even the skiing itself that interested me. What I loved was moving through the woods on skis; the way the spruces were capped in snow, the swirl of flakes on my cheek, the warmth of sun on my skin when it ricocheted up off the snow; even the cold, bitter wind that blew across the field and lashed tears from my eyes, even when I kept my head down and my eyes all but closed. I loved skiing the way I loved sailing. It was the same easy motion, and the air you breathed was the same nose-tingling fresh—spray in the face, sun, the sense of oneness with the natural world.

Nevertheless, I would have given anything to be good at baseball. I didn't mind failing at Latin or French or getting bad marks in other subjects; but to fail at baseball after my performance in The Cage was a disgrace. What was the matter with me that I couldn't perform? I pretended, of course, not to care. But inside I was miserable. I couldn't even watch the games. It was too painful knowing that by rights I should be belting out homers to the cheers of the crowd. "Trowbridge! Trowbridge! Trowbridge!" At least I could have been a pinch hitter. Even if it wasn't until the end of the eighth, still I could have come in and saved the day. I wouldn't have minded sitting on the bench.

Chapter Twenty-One

The summer of '44 was pretty much dominated by the war. Jock and I were working on a farm in Connecticut that belonged to his father, and even there we spent most of our free time listening to the news of the war on the radio. Before the invasion there was the anticipation of something big coming, and after June 6th, it was the progress of the war, the battle accounts, the liberations, the sweeping victories that held us glued. Patton was our hero, the way he charged ahead, mindful only of victory. Patton versus Montgomery, Patton versus the general staff. He was a real hero, the stuff that myths are made of, and we loved his contemptuous ways, the ramrod stiffness of his bearing, his fearlessness under fire. We never thought of him as a person. He was a force, an unstoppable one we hoped, who would bring the war to its conclusion.

But the war wasn't real. Reality was rocks and steaming Connecticut heat; long, filthy, backbreaking days in the fields. The farmer who served as our torturer was a stolid, red-fleshed fiend who sat in his tractor pulling a stone sledge and calculating with perfect cunning just how fast to go so as to keep us steadily at work. We prayed for huge boulders, ones he would have to haul to the edge with a chain, giving us some rest. When we hit one, we would call out, and he would turn in his seat and squint down at us with his suspicious, rat-like eyes; then reluctantly bring the tractor to a halt. If the boulder was obviously too large for us to manage, he would nod and we would release the chains on the stone sledge, let him pull around into position, fasten the chain around the rock, and give him the go ahead sign. Nine times out of ten the chain would pull off. He would turn his head, hoping to catch us in a smile; and either he would get off and arrange the chain more securely, or he would signal for us to try again. The trick was to gauge how many times we could get him to pull the chain off the boulder before getting down. Usually he would let us try again two or three times. If it was near the end of the afternoon, he might sit there for five or six, muttering gutturally, the dark sweat mark creeping up the side of his brown, felt hat. We would make a great show of wrapping the chain, taking as long as we could, of course. Often we would have to use the shovel and dig around the boulder, searching for a hold. Finding one, we would pull the chain tight and holler out for him to go. Then, as he took up the slack, Jock or I would lift the chain off the hump in the rock with a quick motion of the toe; and off old farmer Moeller would drive, while we composed our faces and waited for his fuming return.

There was nothing to do on the farm except work and listen to the radio; no town in the vicinity, no way to get there had there been one, no energy left to get there with anyway. Mrs. Moeller fed us and then we collapsed on our beds and listened to the war news on the radio. For me it was quite a contrast to the summer before, as I frequently told Jock. The farm job, which lasted from July 1 through the middle of August, was a move of desperation for both of us, more exciting plans having failed. Until the last minute, I had thought that Richardson, my buddy from the Avon farm, and I would be working at a girls' camp. When that fell through, it was either this or Maine, and I was too old and antsy to loaf about there all summer. For Jock it was the same. So here we were, battling the Moellers in the heat; manhandling huge boulders out of the rock-choked fields, and imagining what it would be like to be sweeping across Europe on the top of a tank.

Jock was more resigned than I was. Even this, he said, was better than working in his father's defense plant in Cleveland. He had spent most of the preceding summer standing at a conveyor belt, raising and lowering a lever with his right hand. It was hot and dusty and boring beyond belief. "Weren't there any pretty girls?" I asked him. He gave me a scornful look. It was better, he said to be out in the field fighting Moeller and the rocks all day than cooped up with a lot of people you had nothing in common with. "You didn't meet anybody you liked? Nobody interesting at all?" Jock shook his head. I figured he'd missed an opportunity.

In Avon, the summer before, I'd done a lot of hitchhiking. Richardson and I went into Hartford all the time and down to New Canaan once, for a weekend at the beach. When I left, I hitchhiked to Maine. Hitchhiking with Richardson was a lark. He wouldn't take just any ride. When a convertible would go by and then stop and back up and there were two not bad-looking girls inside, just dying to get to know us apparently, I would ask him how he did it; and he would grin and say, "Watch me." I followed his every move, but I never saw what he did that was so special. He had the know-how, that's all; and finally I just accepted that and enjoyed the fruits of his labor.

Hitchhiking alone was more an adventure, a casting of myself into the unknown. Going north, outside of Hartford, a furniture truck had stopped for me. It was early afternoon, my fourth ride. He wasn't supposed to pick me up, the driver said, but he wanted the company and besides he needed someone to help him unload. Not only would he pay me, but he would buy me dinner and breakfast and I could sleep in the back of the van.

As the delivery was only in Worcester, I wondered why we couldn't drop the stuff off that afternoon; but Jeff, the driver, gave me a knowing look and told me he had his reasons. It seemed odd, but I said okay. Around five we stopped at Mabel's Diner, so Jeff could fool around with Mabel, I gathered. She was the waitress as well as the owner, and clearly an old friend of his. She kept flirting with me, though, I noticed. She was about forty and kind of tough looking, but she had a warm smile and a pretty good figure. She was at the other end of the counter getting us some coffee when Jeff whispered to me, "You want her? She's yours. You can use the van." I almost choked on some pie. "Look kid," he said, when I'd recovered, "She's hot for you. What d'you say?" I couldn't say anything, literally. Each time I tried to I started to cough. "Okay," he said, "I'll set it up. You go outside."

I was standing by the van wondering what to do, when Jeff joined me. He was beaming. "She can hardly wait," he said. "She'll be out later, soon as she can." He walked over to the back of the van and slid up the door. "You can use that sofa there," he said, motioning with his arm. "But get some sleep too, okay? Got to roll out early."

Now was the time to leave, I thought, as I watched him go back into the diner. But instead, I stood there, unable to move. Finally, I climbed up into the back of the van, slid the door down most of the way, got onto the sofa, and tried to think. I could pretend to be asleep. I could hide behind the furniture. I could just take off.

Coward! Here it was, the perfect opportunity, and I was looking for ways to avoid it. I grabbed a blanket off one of the tables, spread it out on the sofa, took off my shoes and crawled in underneath. Lying there in the dark, furniture piled up all around me, the air fetid and hot, I thought of how wildly jealous Richardson would be when I told him about this; and of how calmly, how coolly, he would behave. I lay there on my back with my eyes on the slit of light underneath the door, my thoughts rocketing between desire and despair. A thousand times I thought I heard her coming. Would she knock, coyly, leaving it for me to jump up and let her in? Or would she send the door crashing up with one shove of her arm and come at me with her fur flying? I wished, vaguely, she was younger. I wished...

* * *

Jeff's shout woke me up. This was the house, he said. We were there. Where had the night gone? What had happened? I stumbled out of the back of the van, rubbing the sleep from my eyes. "So how did it go, soldier?" he leered.

"Great!" I said.

"She told me. She's nuts about you. Any time..." Had something happened after all? No. That much I knew. It was someone's idea of a joke.

We parked in a neighborhood of one story, stucco houses. Jeff walked up to one of them and pressed the buzzer. It was barely light out. In a couple of minutes a sleepy looking woman in a barely concealing negligee opened the door and asked us what we wanted. Jeff told her we were the moving van and were ready to bring in her furniture, apologizing for the early hour. "Sign here, please," he said very politely. "It just means you've accepted delivery," he added, seeing her hesitate. She signed and we started bringing things in. One of the first items was a coffee table, the kind with the sides that lift up so you can carry it like a tray.

"It's scratched!" she said, fully awake now.

Jeff stared at it as if he'd never seen it before. "That wasn't there?" he said, all innocence and concern.

"Certainly not!" she said.

"I'm sorry. I can't imagine what happened."

"Well, your company will pay for it."

Jeff didn't say anything. We just kept carrying in the furniture. Nothing else was damaged, and when we were all done and the woman had checked everything, she said she wanted full replacement cost for the table. It was new, she said, the scratch was deep and would never come out.

And then Jeff broke her the news. She'd signed a release. While she began to react, we left.

"Dirty trick, eh?" Jeff said. "You think that table was new? Woman took a knife to her own sofa once, slashed up the upholstery right in front of me; then asked for the insurance papers so she could file for damages. What a nerve. The sofa was leaking stuffing even before she slashed it. Ever since then, I get them to sign first, while they're still half asleep."

"But you can't make all your drops at five in the morning." I said.

"I can pick the tough ones," he said. "After a while you get to know."

I arrived in Hancock Point two days later. One of my rides was in a lobster bait truck. "Talk to me," the man said. "I'm asleep." I breathed through my mouth until the next light and then jumped out.

I stayed in the Wiscasset jail that night. I could have gone to a motel, but I didn't want to spend the money and so I tried sleeping on the grass in a little park. Two policemen came up to me—one old guy, the other young. I told them I was out of money and headed for Hancock Point, above Ellsworth. "You hungry?" the old one said. I was, as a matter of fact, and said so. So they took me to a restaurant and bought me soup and coffee. I felt bad about it, caught up in my own story, but I didn't know how to get out of it. Afterwards, they suggested the jail themselves. It was empty. Might as well use it.

I got to Hancock Point about four in the afternoon. Sarah O'Kane greeted me at the door. "So you've turned into a tramp, have you?" she said when I told her about my trip. "And you the son of a minister. Born to the cloth."

* * *

This summer's hitchhiking experience was very different. Old Moeller drove us to the bus station and I picked up a ride right away and made it to Hancock Point in sixteen hours, most of which I spent sleeping in the back of a pick-up.

My mother and father and Katherine had just come in from sailing when I arrived; and with them was my Godmother, Aunty Bee, and her daughter Kate. They had rented the Haskins house, on the other side of the Zabriskie's. I adored Aunty Bee who had been my mother's roommate at Smith College. I hadn't seen Kate for about five years. Her hair was blown out in the wind and she stood tall and straight, and when she smiled I realized she was beautiful. John and Helen were there too. They were roughly Katherine's and Gus's ages, respectively. Uncle George was in Italy with the Army. The Foxes lived in Gainesville, Florida, where Uncle George was a philosophy professor at the University, on leave for the next two years. "Treetops" was for sale, they said, the old Hawes place, just beyond the Haskins'. They'd only been here a couple of weeks, but Kate was dying for them to buy it.

We played tennis the next day; my mother and Aunty Bee and Kate and I. Kate was very good, with a strong, level forehand, but the tennis kept turning into Irish joke time; reminiscence time; the good old days at Smith.

For the next week Kate and I played tennis almost every day. She had never been in such a beautiful place, she said. And then they were gone, maybe to return the next summer, maybe not. A week later we had left too. I was a fifth former that year, with certain privileges, but the cloistered atmosphere of the school seemed more painful to me when I returned than ever before.

Chapter Twenty-Two

When one graduate was sent to prison for embezzlement, the Rector immediately went to see him at Sing Sing. This visit occasioned some controversy, but to the Rector the matter was very simple: one of his boys was in trouble. As his friend and his pastor, the Rector had to go to him. And that was that.

Nichols, *Forty Years More*, p. 30.

The boys wanted to live dangerously and see life. The Rector wanted them to be pure in heart, and keep unspotted from the world.

George Martin, '06, in 1944; in Ashburn, *Peabody of Groton*, p. 249.

Chas was dying to join the Marines. He had a brother with Patton's army who kept sending him war souvenirs; and he said that if he didn't do it over Christmas, he would sign up for sure in June. "Make that August," he said. "Might as well have the summer." None of us took him very seriously. The war was all we talked about, practically, but if you were seventeen you had to have your parents' permission and there was no chance any of us would get that. Jock would be eighteen that spring, but he wasn't about to enlist and skip his senior year.

It seemed as if every weekend all that fall the campus was flooded with graduates milling about in uniform, come back to say goodbye before going over, or just to pay a visit, to show us what we were missing. Every one of them looked terrific, even a short, little guy like Howe. In fact, Howe looked particularly good. He was in the cavalry and his boots shone like brass. The visor of his cap made his hawk-like nose look as if it were planed, and the little whip he carried was made of tightly braided leather. You could just see him, perched on top of a horse charging across a field, even though he probably spent most of his time in a tank. Curtis Poillon was in the Marines, but what made his uniform special was the braid that hung down in a loop from his left shoulder, which meant he carried the flag.

We'd all seen *For Whom The Bell Tolls*, of course, and Poillon, more than anyone, made us think of Robert Jordan—determined, heroic, and just a touch sad. We saw a movie almost every week, usually something to do with the war: *Watch on the Rhine, Stage Door Canteen*. They weren't usually the brand new ones. *Lifeboat* was an exception. After *For Whom the Bell Tolls* that was my favorite. The way they all kept so cool, jammed together in that boat, Tallulah Bankhead in particular; and how they dealt with the U-boat captain who sank their ship. We cheered our troops during the newsreels. And booed and hissed when the Japs came on, or Hitler and the Germans; and every evening before bed we'd listen to the radio and follow the course of the war across France as well as in the Pacific. The war continued to be exciting, the most interesting thing in our world; yet also far removed from us—unreal, like a movie.

Around Halloween, a man named Stapleton gave a talk to the school about a privately funded ambulance corps in France and the need they had for money and drivers. I'd gotten my license that summer and as he talked I could imagine myself driving across bomb-shattered fields, around craters; I could smell the gunpowder, hear the whistle of the shells; could see myself lifting the end of a stretcher, staggering with it to the rear of the ambulance, sliding it in. The blood. The cries. As he spoke I saw it all and when he was finished I asked him if I could join up. He didn't want to encourage boys to leave school, he said. Would I be willing to collect money for him? That's what they desperately needed help with. Of course. I was burning with enthusiasm. Phil and I both volunteered. We divided the school up between us. It would be easy, I said. How could anyone refuse to give to a cause like that?

The first person I spoke to said he was sorry but he couldn't help us. His money was all committed. He was lying, of course. Everyone knew he was one of the richest boys in the school. I sneered, privately, but I didn't say anything. Hwoschinsky gave me $5, which I thought was pretty good. Together Phil and I collected $104.32 from the form. "We've got to work harder," Phil said. "Make them dig in."

"How much are you going to give?" I said.

"$50. I've got to save some for Christmas." I'd already decided to give everything I had, $63.00, most of which I 'd earned from peddling packets of cocoa for Grampa Whiting.

"We'll tell 'em what we're giving," I said. "That'll shame 'em into it."

We made the rounds of the form again, this time with more success; $278.32 total, not counting our own contributions. Then we went after the masters. Gallien came across with $25 but not without a little speech. He'd heard we were lying about the amounts of money we'd given and then boasting about it, and advised us to cease and desist. We protested our innocence vehemently, but it was clear he believed his informant, not us. "If you really gave so much, how will you give to the next cause?" he said, smiling his little smile.

"I don't know," I said. "We didn't think about that."

"Well, think about it," he said.

Mrs. Crocker thought we were very good to be raising money for Mr. Stapleton's cause but warned us that some boys, some masters even, couldn't contribute and shouldn't be pressured. "Why not?" I said. "They can afford to go to Bruce's!"

"Some of them can't," she said.

"What about Gandhi?" Phil said. Phil was writing a paper on Gandhi. "Gandhi took a vow of poverty."

"Gandhi is a fine man," she said, "but you can't expect everyone to act the way he does."

"It says in the Bible…"

"It says in the Bible to show charity," she said, cutting me off quite fiercely. "It is not respectful to use pressure to make someone feel badly if he doesn't do things your way."

"It says in the Bible to give all you have to the poor and follow Him," I said to Phil in the hall as we left.

"She's right," said Phil. "We should just tell them what Stapleton's group is doing and ask for their help."

"Is that what Alyosha would do?"

"Who's Alyosha?"

"In *The Brothers Karamazov*." I'd been reading *The Brothers K* since August. It was practically the first real book I'd ever read and certainly the best.

"Alyosha is a sort of saint," I said.

"I don't know," said Phil. "I'm going over to nick Miss Winterbottom." And he left.

Alyosha would probably have been too shy to ask anyone for money, I thought, as I walked over to Brooks House to put the squeeze on Mommsen. I knew just what I was going to say. I would tell him all about Mr. Stapleton's work and what a fine job the volunteers were doing and how badly they needed gas for their ambulances and things like that; and if he didn't come across with a good, hefty sum, I would say, fine, it was entirely up to him, of course, and what, by the way, did those English cigarettes he chain-smoked cost? Were they terribly expensive or what?

Alyosha would probably have just wandered off to Ayer or someplace and given his coat to someone or had a long, serious conversation with a prostitute or a criminal, or some bum. I quit trying to imagine what Alyosha would do. In fact, I decided to give up Mommsen, go to the gym, get my double-bitted axe out of my locker, find Charlie and see if he wanted to chop some wood.

In the end we collected over a thousand dollars. Mr. Stapleton wrote us that we'd done better than anyone at any other school, and he sent a copy of his letter to Mr.

Crocker and we were called in and praised to the sky. Mr. Crocker told us how proud he was of us and that he would write our parents and tell them so.

Phil had collected from more people than I, but I had ended up with slightly more money. That was because I was a better salesman than he was as a result of selling cocoa for Grampa Whiting—since September. The cocoa came in little packets. The boxes Grampa Whiting sent me from his office on Fulton Street held ten smaller boxes with one hundred packages in each one, "Private Estate Cocoa" printed in bold letters on each package. All you had to do was dump the cocoa into a cup and fill it with hot water from the faucet. I sold the packets for five cents each and out of that I got a penny. Ten dollars commission on each big box. So far I'd sold five boxes. Mostly I sold them to fourth, fifth, and sixth formers in Hundred House. I'd go around to their studies after dinner at night. If the guy was a really hard sell, I'd wander in with a cup of steaming cocoa in my hand and pretend that I just wanted to chat, or borrow a book or something. Usually that would do the trick, but if it didn't I'd resort to other methods. I'd offer a discount, or maybe leave a sample or two. "It helps with studying, you know," I'd say sometimes. "There's a special ingredient in it that..."

There were a lot of surprises when it came to asking people for money, though. Mr. Cushing, for instance, wouldn't give me a cent. He was a pacifist, he said, and wouldn't give money for anything to do with the war— not even the Red Cross. I knew Cushing wasn't just trying to get out of giving money, but I couldn't picture him as a pacifist either. I'd heard him talk about the Japs and how they had given up their rights as a civilized nation when they attacked us at Pearl Harbor. He didn't exactly love Hitler, either; or Mussolini. I couldn't picture him letting the Germans into his house or blessing his enemies, or turning the other cheek. He'd be standing there with his shotgun barring the door. If he didn't have a gun he'd throw chalk at them or erasers, or books, or something.

When I finished *The Brothers K*, I went to John Train to talk about it. "Try this next," he said, handing me *A Portrait of the Artist as a Young Man.* "Father Zossima's the saint," he said. "Not Alyosha. Personally, I identify with Ivan."

"Ivan," I said. "He's the villain. He and his father."

"His father, yes. Ivan, no. Ivan is simply an intellectual."

John was that, all right. He was on the board of *The Grotonian* and wrote half the material and you didn't want to get in the way of his wit. His father was a famous writer and John would probably be a writer, too. He was small and nonathletic, but he was a relief pitcher on the varsity. He had a weird but very accurate side arm pitch which he got from throwing rocks at birds. The trouble was he couldn't throw the ball any other way. He'd been a cockswain on the crew his first form year and was on the fencing team. For a nonathlete, he did pretty well. He had a strange face, an old man's face on the body of a boy, an American Indian's face; an ageless, Roman senator's sort of face—the aquiline nose, the curled lip— also a pronounced cow lick which he emphasized in the

166

way he combed his hair; he had a high forehead and piercing brown eyes. At his summer home in Bar Harbor, where I visited him occasionally, he would lie on his stomach at the edge of a high cliff and shoot at the seagulls soaring below him with his high powered BB gun. He almost never missed.

John was like Ivan in one way. He said everything with great authority. He could be clever, or pompous, or cutting; and sometimes wise. "The fact that everyone likes Beethoven's 5th doesn't mean it's bad." That remark, delivered at the age of fourteen with his characteristic smirk, stayed with me for years.

Phil went off with Johnny Gray for Thanksgiving and when he got back I asked him what was wrong.

"We went to see Val Hollingsworth," he said, "you remember him?"

I nodded my head. When we were second formers, Hollingsworth, as a sixth former, had been one of the stars on the football team. He was a friend of Johnny's older brother, and he had a big reputation as a ladies man. He had looked particularly dashing in his uniform when he'd been back two years before, the last time I'd seen him.

"He was sitting up, by the window in his room." Said Phil. "He showed us where they'd cut off his leg. I almost got sick."

I tried to imagine it, but I couldn't. "God!" I said.

"It was his right leg. All there was was a stump. It happened in Italy. He was with Patton. He didn't say much else."

"God!" I repeated. I didn't know what else to say. I could hardly remember him actually. All I could picture, really, was his hair which was always perfectly combed and looked wet. It was parted fairly high on the right and was short and very straight. He had an incredibly square jaw. And then I remembered when he and Bill Gray and Douglas surprised us one time when we were having a snowball fight behind Hundred House. They could have soaked us six blackmarks each, but instead they joined in, or rather they caught us one by one and buried our heads in the snow. There wasn't much contact between younger and older boys at Groton, particularly not with sixth formers. Probably they fooled around with us because Johnny Gray was with us. It was Hollingsworth who rubbed the snow in my face while the others held me. He got it down my neck and in my ears and then he pushed me into the snow and the three of them sprawled all over me in a great, whooping pile up.

I could see Hollingsworth, now, sitting up very straight by the window, his face pale, a blanket over his knees. I couldn't picture his being wounded, what the leg had looked like before they'd cut it off; any of that. But I could see him folding the blanket to one side. I could see his left leg with its polished shoe and the stump of his right leg, with his trouser pinned up neatly around it. I could even see the pained, faintly weary expression on his face as if he were showing them something that had happened in football—a knee injury, perhaps. He had already learned to use his crutches, Phil said. And eventually they would fit him with a false leg, something he could get around on with the aid of a cane.

Suddenly the war was very real to me and I was glad I was at school and did not have to be in it.

Chapter Twenty-Three

"It is the aim of the school to be widely representative as possible."

Groton, p. 43

"Believing as I do in Kidd's Theory that the Anglo-Saxon race should be the predominant one for the good of the world..."

Endicott Peabody, Diary Notation, January 5, 1896.
Ashburn, *Peabody of Groton*, p.116.

Jackie Robinson was signed up by the Brooklyn Dodgers that year, and I got actively involved in civil rights. Chestnut Hill was an all white community; at least the congregation at St. Paul's was. Early in his ministry there, my father helped found the Philadelphia Fellowship Commission, which was aimed principally at promoting better relations between races, religions and ethnic groups. This was early in the days of the civil rights movement and the Fellowship Commission was idealistic and fraternal. It wanted to change peoples' hearts. I remember my father lecturing us that past spring, just before we were to go to Maine for the summer, about how spoiled we all were. Maury Fagen, one of the Commission's fellow founders and a good friend, had just told him that he wasn't going to be able to take his usual two weeks at the Jersey shore that summer because his son was starting college in the fall and they needed that money for his books, "We don't even know what that means," said my father, his lips pressed together and his eyes glaring. When had we ever felt the pinch? When had we ever had to do without? He was right, of course. But what were we supposed to do about it? It was like being reminded of all the starving people in Armenia when you couldn't finish the food on your plate. "Think of all the starving people in Armenia," someone would say, and if you did, the only result was that you felt vaguely guilty. My mother wasn't there, and neither Gus nor Katherine nor I said anything.

One of the things I eventually did about it was agree to be roped into serving as a member of a Fellowship team. A Fellowship Team was composed of a white Protestant, a Jew (he could be orthodox or reformed), and a Negro. The Negro could be of any religion, but in most cases he was Baptist. Fellowship Teams went around to groups and talked about brotherhood and things like that, but the main thing was that they were examples of people from different religions and backgrounds and races visibly getting along. I didn't serve for long, but I remember one occasion when I visited a Black, Pentecostal Church in South Philadelphia as part of a Fellowship Team. Each of us was supposed to give a short speech—who we were, where we were from, how we would bring about fellowship in the world. I'd written, with much pain, what I thought of as a brotherhood sermon. My mother had heard it and seemed to think it would do. I was the first to speak. I was giving it all I had when a voice cried,

"Praise the Lord!" I stumbled, though I did not stop, and then another voice, even louder, joined in.

"Praise Jesus!" And then the whole church began to rock.

"Amen!"

"Amen, brother!"

"Hallelujah!"

"Thank you Jesus!"

I stopped, in mid-sentence. The voices stopped. I started up again. So did they. It took awhile, but I finally realized it was a form of applause.

My hero in the civil rights movement was Walter White, the President of the NAACP. Kaplan, the Jew in our Fellowship Team, had given me some literature about the NAACP that Christmas and I'd become all hyped up about what they were doing. What I admired was their no nonsense attitude. They were interested in equal rights. Period. Equality before the law. Negroes should have the same opportunity to advance themselves in society as Whites. They should not be denied anything because of the color of their skin. Why were there no Negroes at Groton, I wondered? I spoke to Mr. Moss, the faculty advisor to the Missionary Society, about it. There was no good reason, he said. He supposed none had applied. I vowed I would do everything I could to change that situation.

I had read *Young Man with a Horn*, the life of Bix Beiderbecke. The whole history of jazz, of course, was tied into Negro history, the history of the South, Basin Street, New Orleans, the Blues. Without the Negro there would have been none of this; not only no Dixieland but no Tommy Dorsey or Glenn Miller or swing. Jazz musicians didn't show prejudice toward each other. They were a true fraternity, tied together by their common love of music. Gene Krupa and Big Sid Catlett; Harry James and Louis Armstrong. Benny Goodman had as many Negroes in his band as Whites. Actually, white musicians like Benny Goodman and Woody Herman and Jack Teagarden all acknowledged their dependency on Negro masters: Pee Wee Russell on the clarinet; J.C. Higginbotham on the trombone. Some of the best groups were all Negro: the King Cole Trio, the Duke Ellington Orchestra, the Count Basie Band. Of course jazz wasn't the real world. I realized that.

The thing to do, said Mr. Moss, was to get a prominent Negro to come to Groton and give a speech. Walter White, I thought. He would be ideal. And Mr. Moss agreed. The only trouble was that he didn't look like a Negro. He looked like a White man except that his hair was a little kinky, though not much more so than Whitney's. But Moss said that was actually an advantage. That he looked White but was thought of, and declared himself to be, a Negro showed the absurdity of the definition of what a Negro was. It also made it easier for him to get his points across to the Groton audience. After all, he not only looked White, except for a few drops of Negro blood, he was. We should approach Mrs. Crocker with the idea, Mr. Moss said. And he was right about that, too. She was very enthusiastic.

We formed a committee: Phip, Phil, Jock and I. Mr. Crocker was surprisingly receptive. I was commissioned to write Walter White and ask him to come. Much to our

172

surprise, he said he would. We arranged a date: the last Saturday in February. He arrived just before dinner and he spoke right afterwards. He looked even whiter in person than he did in his pictures. He was a small man, mild and polite in manner. He was not a particularly fiery speaker. What he said was good, but he didn't do much to put it across. He was sort of boring, actually; more like a lawyer talking about a case than a man in the throes of a passionate crusade. He hurried off right after his speech as there hadn't been many questions. It didn't seem to me to have been a great success. I had even seen a couple of students nodding off.

But Monday, in Doc Irons's current events class, it was different. We practically came to blows.

"You can't allow them to vote if they can't read."

"Read according to whom? Read what?"

"I thought you had to own property to vote."

"If I lived in Mississippi..."

"We have a Negro cook and when she leaves, my mother goes around and wipes off all the door knobs."

"Its true. There're lots of diseases."

"They like to be with their own kind. They don't want to mix with us any more than we want to mix with them."

"How would you like it if you had to drink from a separate water fountain?"

"It's medieval."

Irons spoke to me after class. "See what a good thing it was getting him up here? It has to be talked about, argued. And it's not such a simple matter. There are deep feelings to be overcome, roots..."

I read *Black Boy* and *Native Son.* I joined the
NAACP. I subscribed to *The Negro Digest.* We tried to
get Mr. Crocker to seek out a qualified Negro to apply to
Groton but he wouldn't.

"How many Negroes do you know?" he said. None,
we had to admit. "When they're your friends, they'll be
here." But what did it matter that I didn't know any
Negroes. I didn't know any Chinese either. It was a
question of policy. If Walter White knew that Groton
would accept a qualified Negro, he could get us one, I was
sure. "That's not the way to go about it," said Crocker.

"We don't even have any Jews," Jock said. Moss and
Irons and Crocker all agreed. The first step was to
educate. "Prepare the soil and then plant the seed." That
sounded good but that wasn't how Walter White had done
it. Law. Equality before the law. Justice. You challenged
the authority and if you were strong enough, it gave in. It
didn't change of its own accord. You didn't appeal to its
better nature. You had to make it change. Making it
change was dangerous, yes. But so was living in the South
if you were a Negro and challenged the system.
Lynchings. The Ku Klux Klan. Making it change here
would be easy. If Crocker turned down a qualified Negro
applicant, it was a simple matter of taking the school to
court, demonstrating to a jury that the school was guilty
of discrimination. No, said Irons. Groton was private. It
could discriminate as much as it wanted to. A private
school was like a club. And clubs were immune. They
could keep out anyone. And you had to let them. Even
the Klan.

I went to talk to Moss. Loewenberg happened to be there. "Vas a gut ting, Valter Vite, unt Robert tells me vas your idea." He clapped me on the back and smiled. I mumbled something, embarrassed, and turned to go.

"Sit down," said Moss. "We should discuss how we're going to follow this up."

"Ya, ya," said Loewenberg. "You mus no shtop mit dis."

I didn't know what to say with Loewenberg there. After all, as Jock said, we didn't even have any Jews.

"Ernest and I have just been talking," said Moss. "What would you think of a group of us going to visit some Negro leaders in Harlem, over the spring vacation? There's Adam Clayton Powell and..." Moss sketched out a plan that would involve himself and Loewenberg and the four of us and maybe one or two others. It sounded interesting. We would talk to some notable Negroes and get them to help us plan further events.

"If Jesus were alive," I said, "Don't you think..."

"Clinton! There is no need for that. Please do me the kindness of not being profane."

"I'm sorry. I didn't mean to..." I'd forgotten that Moss was a minister, too, though he never officiated in the chapel.

"Zee boy has a point, Robert," Loewenberg said with a smile. "Your Master vas a revolutionary—much more far dan Gandhi, he vent. Lazarus, zee money changers, his vords to zee rich man."

" 'My kingdom is not of this world.' He also said that," said Moss rather primly. And Loewenberg, though he looked as if he wanted to say more, apparently decided not to, and there was a moment of silence.

"About this trip to New York," said Moss. And we talked about that for a while but with less enthusiasm.

A revolutionary. I'd never thought of Jesus like that before. But, of course, everything he said and did was opposed to what was going on at his time. And as for treating people the same, just take the story of the Good Samaritan. Or how about that woman they caught in adultery? "In the very act," it said. He just told them to let her go, that they'd sinned too, hadn't they, so who were they... I reached down and packed a snowball. It was cold out and the stars were shining brightly. I could feel the cold pull my nostrils together when I took a breath. Maybe someone would come along before I got to Hundred House. Maybe I'd carry it in with me...

Maybe I'd go talk to Loewenberg sometime. I'd never seen him in the chapel, I realized. He probably went to a synagogue. I'd never been to a synagogue. Why not? What did I know about other religions? Nothing. And I was prejudiced myself. Loewenberg wore funny looking clothes and didn't speak very well and believed different things from the rest of us. So? He was different, that's all. He was a Jew. But I hadn't thought of him as being of a different religion, for some reason. Naturally, as a Jew, he wouldn't think about Jesus the way a Christian did.

I had known only one Negro in my life: Charlie, our janitor at All Angels Church in New York. It was certainly very hard to imagine Charlie at Groton. It was hard enough to imagine Charlie as a boy. Of course, any

Negro who came to Groton wouldn't be the least like Charlie. He'd be very well educated already, for one thing. Otherwise he wouldn't get in. What about friends? I would certainly go out of my way... Would I, though? He might be so well educated I wouldn't like him. And I certainly couldn't picture someone like Cooper, say, making friends with him. I could just imagine how someone like Cooper would react to the news that there would be a Negro at Groton in the fall. Still, even if he had no friends, a Negro at Groton would be a victory for the cause. It would break the ice. It would mean that other Negroes might eventually come and some day they'd be accepted, learn how to fit in.

Gene Krupa wouldn't fit into Groton, not to mention Big Sid Catlett. Jack Teagarden would hate it here. Certainly Bix Beiderbecke would have loathed it in a school like this. And how about Benny Morton? None of them would have come to begin with or stayed for more than two seconds if they had.

Up the stairs of Hundred House. Past the study hall. Into our study. There was Phil, bent over his desk, writing. I packed the snowball in my hands for one, last time and then I stuffed it down his neck.

Chapter Twenty-Four

"Lord, who shall dwell in they tabernacl
Or who shall rest upon thy holy hill?
Even he that leadeth an uncorrupt life,
And doeth the thing which is right,
And speaketh the truth from his heart..."

Psalm 15—spoken at the Rector's funeral,
November 20, 1944

President Roosevelt died that spring, and a week later so did my Great Uncle Rob, and I found myself consoling my parents with the thought that "It's sad he had to die, only I don't suppose it really is sad if we believe in a life after death." How could I have written that? In the first place I had no idea what I believed about life after death. It couldn't just be an extension of this life, because of course you didn't have a body. You could be alive in your mind, I supposed, but the idea of existing only in your mind—a brain thinking thoughts; no, not a brain, just thoughts thinking themselves—was not only incomprehensible to me but more than a little repugnant. The nearest I could get was to imagine a sort of daydreaming state that never ended. If I tried to go beyond that I was lost. What would you be daydreaming of, for instance? The Catholics had it all worked out: heaven, hell and purgatory; but they described those states in such a physical way that you

178

had to be hopelessly ignorant to believe in their existence. Yet in *A Portrait of the Artist*, Joyce had painted hell so vividly that even I could be moved to terror just reading about it. You had to take it all literally, though, for it to affect you. Try to make sense of it in purely mental terms and it all seemed ridiculous.

What was really stupid was that I knew perfectly well that Uncle Rob wasn't even a Christian. He was a follower of Gandhi, though not a Hindu. He was a socialist. He admired Gandhi for his social message. He didn't believe in life after death at all.

Uncle Rob lived with the Wetters in his three-story house on Washington Square. Pierce Wetter was Uncle Rob's adopted son. He'd been put in jail for being an anarchist, or something, and Uncle Rob had gotten him out. Uncle Rob had given a lot of money for the defense of Sacco and Vanzetti and Pierce Wetter was connected with them in some way. The Wetters were a little creepy, I'd always thought. They seemed so completely different from Uncle Rob.

Uncle Rob looked kind of like Gandhi. He was very small and because one leg was shorter than the other, he walked with a cane. He had Gandhi's great, hooked nose and bald head and bugged out eyes. He had the same receding chin, pursed lips, and frail body. He even had the same fierce light in his eyes, though dimmed by a monocle, as his upper lip was softened by a small, square, mustache. His body was robed in the elegantly cut clothes of a wealthy, Victorian gentleman. He always wore a morning coat, striped pants, spats, a wing collar with a pearl headed stickpin in his tie; and his straight, black cane was topped with gold.

I was very fond of Uncle Rob. Perhaps I had unconsciously wished him immortality for that reason. When I was a child, going to see Uncle Rob was always a joyous event, and one that I never came away from empty handed; for at parting he always pressed a silver dollar into my hand. His house matched his costume. Visiting him was like going to a museum. Leather bound books gleamed dully from the tall shelves; and priceless oil paintings hung on the walls, each illuminated by its own brass lamp. Uncle Rob was a bibliophile, my father said, which meant he loved books and collected them. He had written one himself, about his days as a New York dandy, and had known Henry James. It was hard to imagine him as ever having been a dashing ladies man, but then it was hard to imagine anyone old as young.

Uncle Rob had his share of adventures, too. There was the thrilling story of Grampa Trowbridge and Uncle Rob traveling in France on bicycles when they were young men. Without knowing it, they had put up at an inn that was notorious for its robbers. Hearing a noise in the middle of the night, my grandfather had gotten quietly out of bed, pistol in hand, just in time to confront a figure about to step through the window. With great presence of mind he pushed the barrel of his pistol into the man's chest and the would-be robber fell crashing to the ground. They pushed the bed against the door to guard against further visitors and in the process discovered a trap door which opened onto an oubliette containing the bones of previous guests the innkeepers had robbed. Uncle Rob loved to tell this story. Grampa T came out as a true hero: a dashing Ronald Coleman figure that I had some difficulty in putting together with the elderly patriarch I barely remembered—propped up in his bed, smelling of cigarette smoke.

My father was more influenced by the Uncle Rob who so vigorously supported Sacco and Vanzetti. He always claimed, in fact, that Uncle Rob's example was one of the reasons he himself had gone into the ministry. That a very wealthy, socialist dandy could be passionately concerned about justice for the poor and the dispossessed, and spend a significant portion of his life and wealth advancing the most liberal social causes was something that always struck me as odd. Odd, but also marvelous.

I had been toying with the ministry myself, strange as that sounds. The social gospel appealed to me deeply. What bothered me was the theology. We'd been reading *The Children of Light and the Children of Darkness* in Doc Irons's special Sacred Studies class. That socialism and Christianity were not incompatible was no surprise to me, nor that democracy was surrounded by pitfalls. I already knew that the ideal of human brotherhood— Willkie's One World—was the highest one of all. How to deal with the rest, though? The question of eternal life was just one of many.

I talked to Moss about it some, but he wasn't much help; and there didn't seem to be anybody else. Maybe I'd bring up the subject when I got home. Maybe I could discuss it with Claud Williams.

Claud Williams was a white minister who was very active in the South battling segregation. My parents had gotten to know him earlier that year and during Christmas vacation he had been to our house and I had met him. What he did was very dangerous. Crosses had been burnt on his lawn. His life had been threatened many times. But he seemed to thrive on that. Threats to his life only made life itself more precious, he said; and certainly he seemed to live with an extra degree of exuberance. When he talked he gave you his whole attention, unlike most people; and he could make the most difficult things plain. He was also a person who could always see the other side.

My mother was very prejudiced against the South. How could anyone live there with all its narrow mindedness and bigotry and raw hate for the Negro? The South was cursed with heat and ugliness and the pride of race. It was disgusting. Even Jefferson had owned slaves. In spirit the South still lived in the days of slavery. Two drinking fountains, two sets of schools, undoubtedly both of them inferior. It was absurd. Uncle Claud, as we called him, just laughed. Most Southerners were perfectly decent people, he said. The problem was basically an economic one. The real bigots came from the poorest of the whites, "the poor whites" or "red necks" as they were called. It was a question of self-esteem. They were on the bottom, but if they could believe that no matter how low they sank they were still better than any Negro, they could strut in their pride and incidentally feel it unnecessary to do anything to improve their own condition. Basically, it was sad. Sad for everyone. A waste. Tragic really.

Uncle Claud also wrote books. If I couldn't talk to him, I could at least read what he had to say. My father referred to him as a brilliant thinker. And my mother, who didn't like to be disagreed with, thought he was wonderful.

But how could I be a minister and not know what I believed? On my knees in the chapel, during that endlessly long, meaningless, but still depressing communion service, I asked God to help me—at least give me a clear mind. Then if that happened, I would present the question: How could anyone be raised from the dead? I'd place the idea of resurrection on the table, so to speak. Just put it there, as if it were a roast turkey, say, still hot from the oven. Would God just look at it? Or would he peel off a bit of the crisp skin? The idea of the turkey helped a lot. If I could see the turkey sitting there, steam rising from it, if I could actually see it there—not smell it—that was too physical; then all I had to do was watch, watch unblinking, for something to happen. I was actually waiting for a voice. Once I thought I heard something; but, if anything, it was no more than a trembling, a tremor, as if a very small earthquake had momentarily surrounded me. What I wanted was a revelation like Saint Paul's. Could that happen to ordinary people, though? The concept of a revelation, of course, was one of those mysteries I wanted clarification about.

One day I asked Cooper what he thought happened after you died. "Nothing," he said. "You just lie there."

"Conscious or unconscious?"

"Unconscious, like when you're asleep."

"No dreams?"

"Definitely no dreams."

"How do you know?"

"Nothing else makes any sense."

Was the alternative to complete belief no belief at all? Would I grow up into a skeptic? Cooper seemed to be a skeptic already. If the skeptics were right, though, everyone had wasted an awful lot of time, including Niebuhr. And if they were right, why were they afraid to die? Maybe not all of them, but certainly Cooper.

I wanted to go to Uncle Rob's funeral, but the school wouldn't let me. He wasn't a close enough relative. I'd missed my grandmother's funeral, which I could have attended but decided not to. Actually, the only funeral I'd ever been to was the Rector's here at Groton in the fall. Graduates from all over the world came to it and the campus was in a state of bedlam for two days. It was quite impressive. We sang special hymns and there were four visiting clergymen participating, including the Rector's son—Malcolm Peabody, my father's predecessor at St. Paul's—and the Bishop of Massachusetts. There was such a crowd that if I hadn't been in the choir, I might not have gotten in. What I couldn't get over was how joyous it was. Here someone very important and well-beloved had died, and instead of everyone being filled with sorrow, there were glorious statements made, and people wore proud, defiant smiles. I had never heard "Onward, Christian Soldiers" sung with such power.

"I am the resurrection and the life, saith the Lord; he that believeth in me..." But, of course. That was it. The Rector was in heaven, wasn't he? A cause for rejoicing. You embraced a religion because of its beliefs. You joined a particular church—the way you might a club—for the sake of your soul. You didn't want to lie in a grave looking at nothing for ever and ever, did you? Aware or not aware. Religion was a way of outwitting death.

Was there any other way? I wanted to go to Uncle Rob's funeral because I thought that he might have discovered one. I'd look at him in his coffin, all dressed up. Maybe he'd give me a sign—not a wink, of course, or a smile. But maybe something in the way his face was set would speak to me; maybe something in the folding of his hands.

Chapter Twenty-Five

"A man does not want to marry a doll, it is true, so it used to be said in old times; no, neither does he want to marry a tomboy.

"A Being breathing thoughtful breath,
A traveller between life and death;
The reason firm, the temperate will,
Endurance, foresight, strength and skill;
And yet a Spirit still, and bright
With something of an angel light."

That is the kind of person that a man hopes for in his wife. One on whose judgement he can rely, and who can understand the depths of his nature."

From a talk to undergraduates by Mr. Peabody in about 1910; in Ashburn, *Peabody of Groton*, p. 126.

Nothing was right. Here I was a sixth former and all I could think about was Kate and the summer we'd spent together. The War was over. I was in Abry's dorm with Charlie Gardiner; only twelve second formers to police. All the goodies I could eat, and blackmarks to hand out any time I felt like it. And I was miserable. I didn't see how I could get through the day, much less until Thanksgiving. All I had to do was stare out the window for a few seconds and scene after scene would come before my eyes, just as if I were really there. I couldn't work. I couldn't talk. I couldn't think. I was helplessly, hopelessly, entirely in love.

"You don't know anything about it," I said to Phil, who'd been needling me all evening.

"Tell me about it then. Maybe that'll relieve your mind."

"I'll relieve you of something else if you don't shut up," I said. As if you could talk about it. As if there were words. The way her hair blew. The way she looked out into the wind, like the figurehead of a boat. That firm, sure smile. The day we brought the *White Seal* over from Sorrento. When we heeled over, and I held it there, not luffing, the rail just not under, she got further up on the high side and leaned way back.

"This is wonderful," she said. "I love it."

The one other girl I'd taken out sailing had hated it when it tipped like that. She'd screamed. Turned white. Wouldn't go the next time I asked her. But Kate liked it just the way I did. The more it tipped the better.

"Want to try it?" I said.

"Not now."

"Tomorrow, then." We started the very next day.

The *White Seal* was our 19' sloop, very tender, and slim, and fast, and tippy; but it had a heavy keel, so it couldn't turn over. The further over it tipped, the more wind spilled from the sail. As soon as it started shipping water, the boat would begin to right itself. You allowed her nose to come up into the wind and then, just before she flapped to a stop, you pulled the tiller toward you and let her fall off, gently, luffing a little until you got up speed. I'd never been able to explain all this to anyone before. But Kate was fascinated. In a week she'd mastered it all; could lie along the raised deck and steer with her foot; could steer down wind with the jib out one way, the main the other—wing and wing—looking backwards at the wake; and keep on like that for as long as I said, without letting the main slip over into a jibe. The only time I ever saw her nervous was when we were running before a big sea, planing down about every fourth crest, and the tip of the mast began to whip back and forth. "What do I do now?" she said with remarkable calmness.

"Pull the jib in tight." When the wind came up even more and it started to happen again, I didn't even have to tell her. She trimmed the main 15° and things quieted right down.

"Only trouble is there's more danger of a jibe."

I nodded and smiled. She knew as much as I did, and was just as good. I wished we had two boats so we could race. But not really. I enjoyed being with her too much for that.

By early July we were almost never out of each other's sight. I would appear at her door in the evening and she or Aunty Bee or John or Helen would let me in. I loved the whole family, especially Aunty Bee.

"Listen to this," Aunty Bee would say, and she would read me a passage from Wodehouse or Shakespeare or Niebuhr or Emily Dickinson. Kate could recite Gussie Finknottle's speech from *Right, Ho, Jeeves*, drunken slurs and British accent and everything. She'd written it out on vellum in a stylish hand as a Christmas present for her parents the preceding year. The Foxes were all very bright and musical and interesting. John was a physics nut, anything to do with science. Helen was theatrical, fey. She and Gus and Mary Forrest Zabriskie (My brother grew up at the mercy of two adoring girls, poor boy.) gave such an elaborate burial one summer to a dead bird—making use of my father's surplice and stole and gold cross—that my grandmother called my father in and let him know how vehemently she objected to the blasphemy. Sometimes we'd play a game—chess, monopoly, charades; or someone would read aloud, or we'd get involved in a discussion. Who was the greater poet—Keats or Blake? Kate or Aunty Bee might play the piano, or they might teach me a new round. But whatever happened, afterwards—and often instead of—Kate and I would escape into the night and hand in hand go to one of our favorite hiding places.

Best of all was the field where the roses bloomed behind the cellar hole of the old Haskins house. The long, uncut grass billowed there in a perfect couch, and if the moon were out we could lie down and follow its track across the tops of the spruce trees and watch as it lit with lambent fire the holy glade between us and the tall trees. This was a mystic place, where it was easy to imagine the wee folk at play, to conjure up spirits of the past. Often we would lie there in one another's arms and imagine what it must have been like when this was a working farm; or before that, when Indians walked through these woods in silent, moccasined feet—hunting or, like us, engaged in trysts of love. We would talk or would lie silently and think each other's thoughts. Sometimes we sang together softly. We kissed or we didn't kiss. We lay next to each other and touched, or we didn't touch. We were outside of

189

time; poised, prepared to act; ready, yet not ready, to play the chosen parts. And then the moon would sink, or the evening chill would come, and we would rise, with a sigh, and I would take her home. Our parting kiss was always the most intense.

I saw Kate every day that summer. My father wanted me to go with him as crew on a huge yawl a friend was sailing down to Long Island. Normally I would have given anything for such an opportunity, but it would involve more than a week; and a week was composed of seven days and each day had in it twenty-four precious hours, and there were only two and a half of these weeks before Groton began. And so I said no, I couldn't go, I had to be with Kate. He was disappointed, and I'm not sure he understood. My mother understood only too well. Kate was her Goddaughter and the apple of her eye.

"Darling..." I'd read the letter over a hundred times. Smith was fine but she missed me so she could hardly stand it. The summer... Oh, what was the use. Thanksgiving. But that was ages off. What I must do, I saw, was leave that very day and go to her. But I didn't. We quoted poetry to each other instead. "Bright star, would I were steadfast as thou art." Keats. Edna St. Vincent Millay:

"O world. I cannot hold thee close enough!
Thy winds, thy wide grey skies!
Thy mists, that roll and rise!"

Shelley—"I fall upon the thorns of life! I bleed." Gradually, life became more bearable. I began to appreciate the fact that I was a sixth former, and that this was my last year.

"Take six!" I barked, catching the little snot-nose red-handed. Was he going to try to weasel out of it? I hoped he would. No. He looked away and walked stiffly out of Butler's cubicle and over to his own. I suppressed a grin. I didn't give many blackmarks, but it was good to have the power. Being in Abry's dorm was one of the real plusses. Paul Abry was more like a friend than a teacher. Of course I'd known him for years. Paul Abry had been our favorite tutor; mainly, I think, because he was so easygoing, so quick to laugh, so hard to ruffle. And he'd followed, for the most part, where we'd planned.

Abry was Crocker's assistant and he also taught Sacred Studies. He had a weakness for peanut butter and cinnamon toast and cider and doughnuts. He would grill bacon and cheese sandwiches for us after the dorm had gone to bed and play our favorite records. We had the best dorm. Everyone said so. Nothing but peace and harmony. I told Paul Abry about Kate and how perfect she was and how much I loved her, and he was sympathetic but at the same time he smiled. "What's the matter?" I said. "You think I'm exaggerating?"

"No, No," he shook his head. He didn't say anything more. I don't think he fully believed me. Perhaps he didn't really take it in. Why had he never married? I asked him.

"The right girl never came along," he said.

I mentioned I was in love to John Train and he questioned me about it and then pronounced his verdict; "Propinquity. Propinquity is all."

There was no one I could talk to. It was too private to share. One lives alone, I thought mournfully. Happiness would not be mine again till we were married.

We met at the Parker House for Thanksgiving dinner. I walked into the lobby and saw her and my knees melted. We hardly spoke, we were so shy. Was it the unfamiliar surroundings? The fact that we were in a city and dressed up? It was odd after all this time of intimate letter writing, baring our souls, that we should seem almost strangers, with nothing to say. After dinner we went to a pirate movie, *The Spanish Main*: and in the dark of the theatre we laughed and chattered and played with each other's hands. Afterwards in the Commons we talked about it, as if it had happened to two other people.

"Well, of course. That happens. We've been away from each other." Kate said, very seriously.

"It's all these clothes," I said. "I want to take them off and go swimming or something, don't you?"

Kate laughed. We walked around for an hour or more arm in arm, still not saying much, but more relaxed now. We sat down on a bench and I kissed her, clumsily. We got up and moved on. The clock was ticking, the day was fading fast. We had only until we went to sleep that night—in Needham, at a friend's house—for Kate had to take the train back to Smith at seven the next morning. We had hoped for two days, but we would not get them. She had too much to do.

"College is killing. You have no idea."

"I know."

"They expect so much more of you. I could spend all my time on Philosophy alone and still not get it all done."

"We're reading *The Federalist Papers*," I said, "in History. They're pretty good."

"Emmanuel Kant is about the most difficult writer I've ever encountered," she said. "My father says..."

Oh, hell, I thought. " Shall we go eat?" I said. "Get a beer?"

We finally found a place that would serve us—a fairly dingy hotel but with a pretty good band. And after a couple of beers we relaxed a bit and then we danced and had some more beer and danced again.

"I love you so," she murmured, and her eyes were as soft and moist as a deer's. I kissed her ear and then her mouth, and for a moment we held each other without moving in the dark of the half-empty dance floor.

When we sat down, I looked at my watch—11:30. The last train to Needham was at 12:00. We ran most of the way to the station, arriving just in time. In the empty car we kissed and snuggled and pretended this was the Siberian Railway and there were days and days ahead of us, instead of no time at all. We were each in bed by 2:00. In the morning we were shy again, but in the taxi we held each other tightly and kissed more passionately than we ever had before. When her train pulled out I followed her along the platform, running hard at the end. She had her handkerchief to her nose and her eyes were red. The memory of her crying!

For the next week I was a zombie again. Love was hell, I realized. That was the simple and final truth about it. Over Christmas I would hardly see Kate at all. And worse that that, she couldn't come up for the school dance. Dental appointments that could not be changed. She was miserable about it. I was miserable about it. But misery, by then, had become almost a way of life. And what about the summer? Congress had just voted through peacetime conscription. I might very well be drafted.

Chapter Twenty-Six

December 1945

Dear Mammy and Daddy:

I've put my name down for the school camp next summer but they may already have enough applicants for it. What I'd really like to do would be to (don't laugh at this) would be to hitch hike with Phil or Phip or someone out to Cleveland. There we could get defense jobs for about a month and then try to get a job on one of the boats which goes around the Great Lakes and that goes up the St. Lawrence River to Quebec. From Quebec we could hitch hike back down to Maine. The reason I want to do something along this line anyway before I have to go in the Army is because I want not only the kind of education you get at a school but the, I think, even more valuable kind of education that you can get from mixing and working with common people and I should think that by this means I could learn how the other half live.

Lots of love,
Clint

Phil and I both got into Princeton. So did Johnny Gray and Phip and three other guys. We were ecstatic. Phil and Johnny and I were going to room together. We would go to New York every other day, hang out at The Three Deuces, Café Society Downtown, and wherever else there was good jazz; and to save money we'd eat at the automat or Hamburger Heaven. We would go to classes only when we felt like it. "It's not going to be that easy," said Phil. "Art says he works all the time."

"Art's a brain," I said. "Brains have to work. We don't have to get 'A's."

"Bill told me it's not too hard to get a '3'," said Johnny. "That's a 'C'," he added, for our benefit. " '1' is for brains, '2' is for grinds. '3' is for gentlemen—they even call it the gentleman's '3'. '4' is for dummies. And '5' is for failing. You have to maintain a '3' average to stay in."

"So you have to grind away at something," said Phil.

"Music Appreciation," I said, and we all laughed.

Phil would have no trouble getting good grades. He'd been getting nothing but 'A's and 'B's since the beginning of fifth form year, and he could probably get straight 'A's if he wanted to. I'd gotten on the honor roll myself that past spring—once. And it felt good, no denying that. But for me that meant a monumental effort. Phil could goof off most of the semester and then stay up all night and pull an 'A' on the exam. Johnny got by mostly on his athletic ability.

Half the class was going to Harvard: John Train, of course, and Charlie Gardiner, and Cooper. About ten were going to Yale, including Jock and Harry Welsh. Monster Bob and Brewer and a few others were headed to offbeat places: MIT, the University of New Mexico, Penn. Chas would join the Marines. Two others weren't going any place at all. Most of us were going where our fathers had gone, and in many cases their fathers and grandfathers. Phil's family had gone to Harvard for generations. He was going to Princeton because I had talked him into it; and, anyway, Harvard was too stuffy. At Princeton you could study and have fun at the same time. Yet it wasn't Joe College, like Yale. That was why I was going to Princeton. That there was a bust of my grandfather sitting in the alcove of the dining room in the graduate school—for ten years he had been the dean—and that both my father and Uncle Corny had gone to Princeton; these were purely coincidences.

Sixth form year had turned into pretty much of a breeze. One of the benefits of getting on the honor roll that past spring was that I could skip study halls. That privilege was worth the effort all by itself. But sixth formers were automatically exempt from study hall. The pressure was off. From Christmas on, even though college was still not in the bag, you could relax. When the news finally came, and it was good, life was nothing but smiles.

"Tlo-bitch! Shtop now!" Three heads in front of me turned, lips smirking. Loewenburg was ringing the final bells before noon dismissal, and I'd been saying something to Phil when the blast came. Me? I looked at Loewenburg in what I hoped was a way that would allow him to acknowledge his mistake. I was a sixth former after all. "Tlo-bitch!" he shouted again. "Come here!" I heard Phil stifle a laugh, and naturally there were others. I started to make my way down the aisle. I'd been standing in the very back with the others. We weren't even required to be there. We were just being polite—observing the scene. I felt myself redden as I walked through the forms, right down to where the first formers sat. Then I turned right, and marched over to the big desk.

"Yes, Sir," I said in my coolest voice. "You wanted me?"

"You vas talking, vispering," he spluttered, in a loud voice. "Vot about doesn't concern. You should know better. Go now."

"Yes, Sir," I said, and started back along the side of the room this time, feeling the eyes of the whole school upon me. My embarrassment had turned to fury. What did that stupid Loewenburg think he was dong? He'd been here long enough to know the rules. You weren't supposed to chew out a sixth former even in private unless he'd done something practically criminal. And to bawl me out in front of the whole school, and for something as insignificant as whispering, was inexcusable. No one else would have done it; not Freiday, not Gallien, not Niehaus, not anyone. I would go directly to Crocker and complain.

"Tlo-bitch! Shtop now!" It was a perfect imitation, beautifully muted. I glared at Phil. Loewenburg, of course, was looking the other way.

"Tlo-bitch! Shtop now!" My second formers greeted me in a chorus when I came into the dormitory to see if they were getting ready for lunch. I jumped at Hunter and pinned him up against the wall, my hands on his neck.

"You vant de S.S. men mit zee firing squad, you little shtruddle?" I spat at him, in my best Nazi accent.

"Come on," he said, his face turning a pleasantly tomatoish red. "I wasn't the only one."

"Dot goes for all ov you," I said. "Any more ov dat, unt ve line you up unt bang, bang, bang, you ist all dead." They were getting hysterical. Fat little Sargeantson was laughing so hard he was bent over double; and Pawling,

198

who had tears in his eyes was batting him unmercifully on the back.

"Five minutes to the first bell," said Charlie in a loud voice from the hall. By the time he'd walked in, the boys had scattered to their cubicles and the scene was over.

"Tlo-bitch! Shtop now!" the words followed me everywhere during my final months at Groton. But I learned how to turn them to my advantage. I found I enjoyed making people laugh.

"Bulllllbssssss!" Ever since he was about eight I could make my brother Gus literally wet his pants laughing just by saying that. And there were other examples. Who knows? It might even turn into a career.

Careers were very much on everyone's minds. Phip was gong to be a minister, though some of the masters tried to talk him into government instead. Chas was going to be a drummer, after he got out of the Marine Corps. Jock was undecided. Half of him wanted to go with the piano; but the other half, the stronger one, I suspected, urged him into the woolen business, where there was a place waiting for him. David Krumbhaar was planning to be an architect. There had never been any question about that. Johnny Gray was dying to get into professional baseball, and Cushing thought he had a chance. Phil didn't know yet, and neither did Charlie. Something interesting, that was the main thing. After all, there was still college. I seemed to change my mind every couple of weeks; or, rather, half the time I still wanted to be a minister and the other half I alternated between forestry, playing in a jazz band, acting, and just living in the country on a small farm—raising a family. In her letters, Kate told me not to worry about it. College would change everything anyhow. She added that she didn't see me in any of those things.

I talked it over with Paul Abry, and he seemed to agree with Kate. Time would tell. I hadn't even fully matured yet. He was non-committal about the ministry. You had to receive a call, he said.

"Just wait for it, you mean?"

"I can't explain it. All I can say is you'll know if it's right."

The Army was taken care of, in any case. We had to register for the draft, but if we were going to college, we were automatically deferred. Everything was settled, in fact; yet nothing was sure. In a few months we would graduate. What about the summer? What were my plans? Kate already had a job lined up on a farm. What was our future? Did we even have one? What about the ministry? I couldn't sit around waiting for a call forever. I had to do something.

"If you really want to be a jazz trombonist," Grampa Whiting had said to me that past Christmas, "why waste your father's money going to college?" The statement jolted me. I wanted to play the trombone *and* I wanted to go to college. Anyway, if I didn't go to college, I wasn't protected from the draft. So there really wasn't any choice. Grampa Whiting had not gone to college and he claimed he was the smarter for it. He'd started life as a boot black and worked up to being head of his own coffee company, as he'd often told me. He was sharp. That was for sure. Maybe college would have dulled him.

That past Christmas I'd taken him out for lunch on his birthday to Sweets, the fish restaurant we always went to on Fulton Street. When the meal was over, he pushed back his chair, the way he always did, and took out a cigar. "Tell me something, Clint," he said, "How's he going to bring the change?" The check had come to $3.73, and I'd handed the waiter a five-dollar bill.

"Either a one dollar bill and change, or all change," I said.

"A dollar says he brings you five quarters and two pennies."

"You're on."

Five quarters and two pennies it was.

"Why?" my grandfather said.

"I don't know."

"Because he wants a good tip; not a quarter, not 35 cents, not 40 cents, not 48 cents. So he brings all quarters and counts on 50 cents."

"Okay," I said, handing over a dollar. It was worth it. He'd taught me something. Obvious, now that he'd explained it.

"Another thing," he said. "You didn't check the bill. Another dollar says it's wrong."

I looked at Grampa Whiting to see if he was kidding. Was he trying to give me back my dollar?

"Okay," I said. Your Finnan Haddie was $1.85. My fried shrimp was $1.65. Tax, .03." I was beginning to redden.

"Total of $3.53. Hand over the dollar."

"You added it up," I said.

"Of course. But to make certain, I told him to get it wrong." I looked at him in astonishment and saw the

201

twinkle in his eye. I gave him another dollar. And he smiled.

Grampa Whiting wouldn't sit around like this, wondering what to do. He'd make up his mind and do it. College was set. I'd either get a ministry call or I wouldn't. What I had to do now was find myself a summer job.

Chapter Twenty-Seven

19 December 1932

My Dear...:

There has been a good deal written about Franklin Roosevelt when he was a boy at Groton, more than I should have thought justified by the impression he left at the school. He was a quiet, satisfactory boy of more than ordinary intelligence, taking a good position in his Form but not brilliant. Athletically he was rather too slight for success. We all liked him...
I voted for Hoover...

Affectionately yours,
Endicott Peabody

Ashburn, *Peabody of Groton*, p.341.

Phip, as predicted, would give the graduation speech. He would also take away most of the prizes and go down in the history of the school as one of its outstanding athletes as well as scholars. He was the senior prefect, too. What was surprising was that he wasn't a bad guy. Success had not utterly destroyed him. It had left him a little tight around the mouth; his laugh was a bit too hearty; and though he'd probably had the prettiest girl to the school dance, he couldn't compete with Chas, or a half dozen others, as a ladies' man.

The school dance on the Washington's birthday weekend had been the biggest flop imaginable. At the last minute, a fourth former had come down with scarlet fever and only those dates who had already been exposed were allowed to come. There were eight of them in all, for eighty-six boys, my own Kate substitute, a girl I barely knew from Philadelphia, not among them. The only fun we had was with a girl I'd gotten up as a blind date for Cooper. Her name was Delores Fields, and I'd gone out with her a few times in New York. She was the fastest girl I knew, just how fast I'd had no idea.

Cooper took a dislike to her the minute he saw her and she to him, and from that moment on she played the field. She would undoubtedly have played the field in any case, but now she did so with a vengeance. As one of the eight girls on campus, and certainly the sexiest looking, she enjoyed the dance weekend as if it had been created just for her. Wherever she went she was surrounded by a crowd, a crowd that included Sloan, one of the younger masters.

"Her perfume!" said Cooper, his aristocratic nose twitching. It was not the most subtle kind, admittedly, but it drew the bees to the honey. It fell to me, as the person who'd arranged it all, to play the surrogate. Sloan, a thirty-year-old bachelor, who also happened to be my advisor, was the most difficult to control.

"Who can help me find the ping pong ball?" Delores would say, having dropped it down the front of her dress in full sight of everyone; and ten boys would immediately offer their services. She accommodated them, one by one, in the darkened corner of the hall, only the thickness of a few doors between herself and the Crockers, until Sloan dragged her off late that night and had, we presumed, his way with her.

The graduation class, by tradition, had to prepare a song recital for the whole school. Our renditions included "Tea for two," "Deep Purple," "Smoke Gets in Your Eyes," and "The Animals Are Coming,"

"The animals are coming, two by two
The old fat pig cries, 'Who dat shovin'?'"

Tlo-bitch, the pig, shouting out the 'Bulllbsssss' routine to the who-hahing of the multitude. The Three Shots of Rhythm gave its last concert—"Take the 'A' Train." Take any train. This was not Fort Devens and we could do no wrong.

What dominates my mind about the graduation ceremony itself was the expression of intense pride on the face of Aunt Mary Zabriskie each time Phip walked up to the podium to accept yet another prize. The Zabriskies, all six of them, were seated in the front row next to my parents and Katherine and Gus, but Aunt Mary's face stood out from the others for the way it shone. This was it, the moment she'd been waiting for for eighteen years.

Kate had wanted to come to graduation, but I'd told her not to. I wouldn't have been able to spend any time with her, I'd said. There was too much going on. I would hardly have a chance to talk to my parents or show Gus or Katherine around the school. Now I wished I'd let her come. It would have been enough just to see her out there in the audience.

Gus was crazy about our log cabin. He was supposed to look around the school and talk to the masters, in case he ended up going to Groton himself; but what really interested him was the cabin. He'd have spent the night in it if he'd been allowed. The cabin held me, too. It was part of me after all, and would be there long after I was gone. I visited the hut as well. One of its roof boards had collapsed. It would cave in before long, become the home of badgers or skunks or woodchucks. The log cabin would not last forever, either, I knew. Nothing lasts, I thought, feeling suddenly sad.

In two days I would be gone and all of this would be over, forever. I had been looking forward to this for six years. Relief, gratitude, joy, a sense of accomplishment, perhaps; these were the emotions I had expected and I felt none of them—only sadness, inexpressible melancholy. It was the last thing I had expected. Without being conscious of doing it deliberately, I walked around the grounds, taking leave of places, saying goodbye. I opened the door to the fives courts and sniffed for a final time the pungent odor that always lingered there; stopped at the baseball cage and rubbed between my fingers the fine, dry dirt: then let it fall. I visited the schoolroom in the Schoolhouse when no one else was there and walked slowly around the room studying the plaques. All the graduates of the school were there, right back to the class of 1886: George Rublee, the first graduate. Form by form, the plaques went round the room, the name of each student chiseled into the wood, immortalized there. Our plaque would join the others in the fall—1946.

I looked up at the windows we had spent all those days cleaning, at the desks, five of which had been my own. I had hated this room in particular. This was where I had sat in detention all those afternoons, copying pages from the dictionary, pained to the point of misery by the sounds of laughter floating in from outside, the crack of baseball bats, even by the distant whirring of the mowing machines. Yet I would miss this room, too; maybe more than the others.

Saying goodbye to the masters was surprisingly painful too. Fat Freiday's face was a comforting one, I realized; Mommsen's thin line of a mouth with its ever-present cigarette was somehow heroic. Abry, Cushing, Moss, DeVoe, even Gallien; these were people I had come to know. The Crockers. Mr. Nash. Mr.Niehaus. It was awful.

"Come back and see us," said Miss Winterbottom, and the emotion I felt was as unexpected as it was strong. Niehaus favored me with a rabbit punch, for which I thanked him in kind, grateful for the opportunity.

Even the rituals of packing held emotions that I had not foreseen. When Phil and I cleaned out our study, we couldn't believe how much we'd accumulated: tobacco, pipes, dozens of them. A well-secreted, very stale, pack of Luckies. Books, pictures, clothes, cartons of papers, cocoa packets.

"Look at this," he said. It was the old whoopee cushion. "You want it?"

I thought for a minute. "Naw," I said. "Leave it here." We left that and a good deal more, finding it hard to throw out anything.

Saying goodbye to your friends, that was the worst, of course. Some of them you'd never see again. Phil and Phip and Johnny and I were going on to college together, but what about Chas and Jock and Charlie and David Krumbhaar and John Train? "Skin, man," said Chas as we clasped hands for the last time, pretending how happy we were to be out of there.

"See you at the Deuces," I said, maintaining my cool. I would probably see Chas again, but I doubted if I would see much of Jock.

"So long, then," he said, looking up from the suitcase he was packing. We shook hands.

"So long," I said. Neither of us gave a sign of anything.

It was over, finally; but I thought, even at the time, that in another sense it would never be. When our cars were packed, we drove away, shouted a last goodbye to whoever happened to be there, and tried very hard not to look back.

Changes at Groton
1946-1975

1946 First Upper School dance with a girls' school: Concord Academy..

1947 First cafeteria meals served at Groton: Sunday breakfasts.

1948 Thanksgiving weekend extended to four days for Upper School. ˙

Committee formed for the study of the curriculum

First off-campus overnight student trip: sixth formers go to Newport, R.I. for two days at sea on aircraft carrier *USS Philippine Sea*

1951 Four day Thanksgiving weekend extended to lower school.

Other weekends become established. .

1952 First Negro admitted.

1958 Recommendations of study committee *not* to enlarge the student body from two hundred to four hundred and *not* to form a companion girls' school accepted by the board of Trustees.

1963   Parents' Weekend established.

       First Lower School dance with girls' school
       Concord Academy.

       Two-day visit to the campus by Martin
       Luther King, Jr.

1965   Headmaster leads eighty-five boys and several
       faculty members in Boston civil rights march.
       Speaker: Martin Luther King, Jr.

1968   Elimination of First Form.

1970   Introduction of restricted smoking privileges
       for fifth and sixth formers.

       Relaxation of the dress code.

1971   Abandonment of the dress code.

       Introduction of pass-fail grades for sixth
       formers in the winter and spring terms,
       as well as electives, independent study and off-
       campus projects.

       Trustees approve recommendations that (1)
       cubicles be replaced by sleeping-studies;

(2) girls be admitted; (3) student body be increased to three hundred.

1972 Prize Day exercises held outdoors for the first time.

1975 Groton School becomes coeducational.

Printed in the United States
4413

OFF THE BEATEN TRACK
Rethinking Gender Justice for Indian Women

OFF THE BEATEN TRACK
Rethinking Gender Justice for Indian Women

Madhu Kishwar

OXFORD
UNIVERSITY PRESS

OXFORD
UNIVERSITY PRESS

YMCA Library Building, Jai Singh Road, New Delhi 110 001

Oxford University Press is a department of the University of Oxford. It furthers the
University's objective of excellence in research, scholarship, and education
by publishing worldwide in

Oxford   New York

Athens   Auckland   Bangkok   Bogota   Buenos Aires   Calcutta
Cape Town   Chennai   Dar es Salaam   Delhi   Florence   Hong Kong   Istanbul
Karachi   Kuala Lumpur   Madrid   Melbourne   Mexico City   Mumbai
Nairobi   Paris   Sao Paulo   Singapore   Taipei   Tokyo   Toronto   Warsaw
with associated companies in   Berlin   Ibadan

Oxford is a registered trade mark of Oxford University Press
in the UK and in certain other countries

Published in India
By Oxford University Press, New Delhi

© Madhu Kishwar 1999
c/o Manushi, C 174 Lajpat Nagar 1, New Delhi 110 024

The moral rights of the author have been asserted
Database right Oxford University Press (maker)
First published 1999

ISBN 019 564 8161

Typeset in Garamond Light
by S.J.I. Services, New Delhi 110 024
Printed by Saurabh Print-O-Pack, Noida
Published by Manzar Khan, Oxford University Press
YMCA Library Building, Jai Singh Road, New Delhi 110 001

For Babul
A loved and cherished friend

Acknowledgements

My ability to make my work with *Manushi* the highest priority of my life for over twenty years owes much to the supportive attitude of all my family, but especially my parents. Their unconditional and undemanding love and care, no matter how outrageous my actions, or how much trouble I gave them, or how much I neglected them, has been my most important source of strength. I thank them for raising me so that I could take living in freedom as my birthright. It is their upbringing that nurtured in me the desire to see a similar freedom become a universal condition in our country rather than the privilege of a mere handful.

I would never have contemplated preparing this book or written so regularly, if numerous *Manushi* readers and friends had not responded with such warmth and enthusiasm to my writings. It is their deep involvement in our common work that goaded me to share my thoughts and ideas with them so frequently.

My former colleague at *Manushi*, Ruth Vanita, played a crucial role in the magazine's survival during the initial, most difficult years. Her vital contributions are reflected in some of these essays, though she and I have developed different perspectives and emphases over the years. I still wonder at my incredible good fortune in having had her as a companion, and in the endless store of love, nurturance, generosity and companionship she lavished on me during those thirteen years of our working together when we were so overworked and I suffered frequent bouts of ill health.

I am also thankful to Rukun Advani and Anuradha Roy at OUP for being so decisive and enthusiastic about publishing this and the earlier collection of my essays. It has been a pleasure to work with Anita Roy and Shalini Sinha, my editors. They have been painstaking in discussing the selections with me and in helping prepare the essays for publication. They were also extremely understanding, patient and helpful—even when I often delayed meeting my deadlines due to numerous other preoccupations.

Contents

Introduction

The essays I selected for this volume cover a whole range of issues concerning women. They were originally published in *Manushi* during the period 1980–97. Most remain pretty much as they were originally published, though I've made a few minor editorial corrections, and in a few cases condensed or cut short an essay to squeeze it into this volume. I made major revisions in only one of the essays, 'A Horror of Isms' (originally published under the title 'Why I do Not Call Myself a Feminist').

After long consideration, in preparing the rest of the essays, I concluded that it would be more useful to readers to have before them the originals rather than for me to revise them for this volume, with the aid of hindsight, to reflect further developments in my thinking. I have separated them by theme. The dates of publication are highlighted for every essay so that the reader may view each in the light of the debates underway at that time and to get a sense of where my notions arose from and what direction they took. Indeed, if it were feasible, I would, alongside these essays and for each theme, publish related articles by others which triggered off my reactions, or those which were written in reaction to some of my writings.

Many of these essays were written in the heat of the moment, and reflect the debates, my analyses and the extent of my comprehension of the issues at that particular point in time. They illustrate a fairly consistent action-oriented social mobilization approach to reform that allows women more options and choices rather than presenting them with *one* supposedly correct way of doing things. Another common thread in most of my writings is my preference for appealing to the moral conscience of our people rather than advocating authoritarian, coercive methods of political reform that render people powerless and destroys their sense of confidence and self-esteem.

In several of these essays I also share with the readers the reasons for and the process through which I came to review and revise my own assumptions and opinions on a whole range of specific issues and strategies over the years. Both my original orientation and this process of revision led to basic and sharp differences with mainstream opinion on these issues as well as the common consensus on women's issues among most of those who view themselves as social reformers, feminists and progressive. Hence the title of this volume: *Off the Beaten Track.*

My work and writing on women's issues is inspired by the belief that women will receive their due rights and place in society only if they go beyond petitioning the government to make symbolic gestures and concessions on narrowly defined women's issues. I would like to see women play a leading role in restructuring our politics and economy to safeguard the rights of all. The focus of most of my writing is how to make our society more humane and compassionate while we seek to make it more just; how to ensure that the means we use are in conformity with the ends we seek. This is another reason for my uneasiness with exclusive reliance on the *sarkari danda* for social reform.

India is a vast, complex and heterogeneous society and civilization. Unfortunately, the post-colonial educated elites in India are systematically alienated and estranged from the lives and concerns of the people. Most of the elite emerge from universities with advanced degrees but very little information or knowledge about our own people's lives, values and aspirations—especially those of other less advantaged castes and classes and those living in rural areas. In the absence of sufficient and accurate information, urban educated people tend to assume that the problems of Indian people are as we imagine them rather than as they actually are.

Unfortunately, due to the deference offered to us because of our privileged education and social status, advocates of social reforms carry a disproportionate influence in our society—at least in the realm of ideological formulae. Our dim and inaccurate perceptions come to dominate social and political thinking as well as policy-making. This has often produced disastrous results by obscuring women's actual options and real concerns.

One of the most important things I have learnt is that even the most well-meaning efforts to help improve people's lives can end up in disaster if you do not take people's actual lives, dilemmas and perceptions sufficiently seriously, or if you fail to understand the effects of any particular effort at change on other parts of a complex social situation. Contributing to social change involves deliberate attempts at mobilizing opinion in a particular direction—but if the interventions are guided primarily by the activist's own predilections and ideas, without taking into account the situation, perceptions, wishes and aspirations of those on whose behalf we seek to help bring about change, we can easily end up either as irrelevant pompous impostors or ineffectual authoritarian manipulators.

During the freedom struggle and in the first years of independence, India experienced substantial progress on women's issues, especially among those groups which took the initiative for social reform. For example, women acquired the right to vote without having to struggle for it; we were allowed entrance into higher education and some enclaves in public life with less harassment and hostility than women in most countries of the industrialized West had to face. Those parts of family law that are state administered underwent important changes and the Constitution included directives banning discrimination on the basis of gender. However, by the mid-1970s, we awoke to find that the gains we made went only a limited way and opened up opportunities for only a small section of women. They did not bring security against violence and brutality and the right to equitable non-discriminatory participation in the family, the society, the economy and the polity for the vast majority of women.

These essays are primarily an attempt to grapple with and find answers to one of the most serious challenges facing women in India today: why is it that despite all the attention focused on contemporary women's issues and the numerous high profile interventions by women's organizations, we as social reformers have a very poor record of resolving women's basic problems? While new examples of the oppression and suffering of women are regularly added to our agenda, almost none of our work has yet resulted in more than a symbolic resolution of some problems, such as passing some righteous sounding but inappropriate law that has no beneficial effect on the lives of oppressed women. Even worse, the few laws that have the slightest chance of improving ordinary women's lives are not implemented, nor does it seem were they ever intended as anything more than a rhetorical and symbolic expression of pious sentiment. In most cases, laws are simply misused—often to make women's lives even more vulnerable.

The main connecting theme in these essays is to uncover the reasons why social reform efforts to alleviate women's dire situation in contemporary India have, in general, stopped making genuine progress? Indeed, in many areas, women's suffering has increased. Most of the essays in the book attempt to review and re-evaluate interventions made by *Manushi* or those of other leading women's organizations in India on specific issues. This kind of self-audit, I believe is essential and needs to be attempted on a much wider scale within the movement.

For example, the practice of dowry has come under consistent and vigorous attack during the last two decades. Yet, despite all the protests, *dharnas*, and attempts at making anti-dowry laws more and more stringent, the peculiarly extortionist versions of dowry have grown and thrived in India and brought many new regions and communities under its influence. Nowhere has the practice of dowry been halted or contained. The first three essays—'Beginning with Our Own Lives: A Call for Dowry Boycott', 'Rethinking Dowry Boycott' and 'Dowry Calculations'—delineate how, starting with a simplistic but determined abolitionist approach, I was compelled to revise and reform our mode of intervention when we found that our initial efforts were altogether fruitless. The abolition efforts followed a characteristic pattern: misplaced reforming zeal based on poorly reasoned theoretical premises without an adequate understanding of complex social forces which bolstered the practice and institution of dowry. Our failure to make a dent on this charged issue convinced me that the practices concerning dowry, as they exist in India today, are a consequence, not the primary cause, of the devaluation of women's lives. The main reason for the continuation and growth of dowry was not 'growing greed', as many believed, but the culturally determined disinheritance of women most fully revealed within their natal families.

Major changes in women's position in their natal family and in the society and economy at large must precede and provide support for women's security against oppression and exploitation before dowry will be abolished or its practice transformed into a more gender-neutral transaction, the way that it functions in some other societies. The essays reproduced here, and related articles I wrote sharing my rethinking on dowry and property rights, created a major furore within mainstream thinking. In particular, many feminist(s) responded with great hostility to my changing perceptions and suggestions for reform. That entire debate, carried out both through the pages of *Manushi* as well as in newspapers and academic journals, cannot be reproduced here in full for reasons of space.

The essay 'Knocking at the Portals of Justice: The Struggle for Women's Land Rights' (originally published under the title 'Public Interest Litigation: One Step Forward, Two Steps Backward') illustrates a miserable failure we experienced trying to combat the culture of disinheritance for women relying primarily on law courts and legislation. The legal aid work we undertook—both in individual cases as well as on behalf of large communities of women—forced us to conclude that a dysfunctional, corrupt and insensitive legal system within a culture not sincerely committed to providing justice for women could not be expected to provide a remedy for women's culturally sanctioned disinheritance. These legal interventions have, very often, on balance, unfortunately resulted in further jeopardizing the already fragile existence of women.

The next group of articles—'The Burning of Roop Kanwar', 'Co-ownership Right for Wives' and 'When Daughters are Unwanted'—analyses the actual negative consequences of well-meaning but misplaced efforts by political groups, including women's organizations, to get poorly constructed and unimplementable new laws enacted, ostensibly to protect women from abuse and exploitation. As subsequent events show, none of these new laws have succeeded in achieving the purposes for which they were meant. The essay 'A Code for Self-Monitoring' offers an over-all critique of the statist approach to social reform, that is, the tendency of the educated elite to attempt to play God and issue commandments in the form of ever newer versions of ineffectual legislation for the rest of society that pretend to offer remedies for the oppression of women. The article analyses why this approach has been so harmful.

The three essays on electoral politics—'Violence and the 1989 Election', 'Out of the Zenana Dabba' and 'Women's Marginal Role in Politics'—analyse the reasons for the low rate of participation and the ineffective leverage of women in the political institutions of our country. They try to figure out what would be the essential preconditions to bring about an enhanced and meaningful participation of women in representative institutions.

'Love and Marriage', 'Women, Sex and Marriage', and 'Yes to Sita, No to Ram!' have been as controversial as the essays on dowry and inheritance rights—and for similar reasons. They essentially argue against the common tendency among many feminists to dismiss with disdain the choice(s) that ordinary women make among the limited alternatives available to them. These articles attempt to understand why most women in our society struggle so hard to keep even bad marriages intact; how ordinary women in our culture explain the rationale for their choices on issues that affect them most deeply; how they try to negotiate their intimate relationship with men; why Sita—a symbol of women's slavery for most feminists—continues to be such an important role model for women in India; why so many women prefer family-arranged marriages to self-arranged ones; whether it is appropriate to call all self-arranged marriages 'love marriages'; the absurdities in our definitions of sexual liberation; and why most married women seem less interested in their own sexual liberation and more concerned about keeping their husbands within some restraints.

The conclusions I arrived at on these issues proved extremely unpopular with some political groups and with most feminists. As with the dowry articles, I was accused of having turned into an apologist for the oppression of women, after having started off as a radical proponent of women's rights. I confess I have never been able to deal with women's rights issues in terms of labels such as 'radical' versus 'traditional', 'feminist' versus 'non-feminist', or 'progressive' versus 'conservative'. I am more concerned about being sensible, trying to understand what different groups of women want, and to find concrete and pragmatic ways to actually strengthen their abilities to live without fear or oppression, rather than to make women's lives an experimental lab for our supposedly radical ideas. I have tried to respect other women's choices and aspirations even when they have gone against many of my cherished beliefs concerning what is a fulfilling life.

The essay on sex harassment explores the social and psychological reasons why many women fall prey to sexual harassment, including those who are from well-off and supposedly privileged families. It also explores some of the implications of restrictions on women's status and opportunities and offers some strategies women may find useful in resisting sexual exploitation.

'When India "Missed" the Universe' critically evaluates my own past activism with regard to opposing beauty contests. The fallouts from that experience inhibit me today from adopting a one-dimensional oppositional role, even while I recognize and wish to continue to combat the harmful impact of the culture of beauty contests and its obsession with purveying of women's bodies as decorative objects for display and consumption. Once again I find myself facing the same old moral dilemmas: these contests may be seen as strategies to make women more self-hating while they are diverted into chasing manufactured dreams. Nevertheless, if this display is something women *choose* of their own free will, do we, the self-appointed guardians of social, morality, have the right to call for a ban?

'Who Am I?: Living Identities vs Acquired Ones' explores the many harmful effects of pushing people towards unidimensional identities—a strong trait among followers of various 'isms', including feminism. It also explores the question why and under what circumstances certain aspects of a person's identity come to overwhelm all other concerns and layers, and why we have to build safeguards against such a tendency.

Finally, the article 'Why I do not Call Myself a Feminist' deals with my own reservations about being labelled a feminist. It is at one level a personal statement tracing the process of and reasons for my estrangement from the version of feminist ideology implemented in many of the dominant groupings in India. However, I have tried to go beyond the personal dimensions of that strife to raise certain basic theoretical and practical questions about 'ism-driven' politics not just in India, but throughout the world.

Some of these essays don't go beyond raising questions, but in most there is some attempt to provide tentative directions for future action. I emphasize the world 'tentative' because I am only too aware that I still have limited knowledge and experience of the social and political dynamics of women's lives among a wide spectrum of communities and regions in India. I am also acutely conscious of the fact that I have had to face very few of the disabilities imposed upon most women in most societies. I have been fortunate to live a life of my own choice without facing the usual social constraints. Therefore, my experience of handling the social and familial pressures that hamper most women's lives is rather limited. I have tried to offset this predicament by making a special effort to sympathetically understand the choices women make, the values they hold dear and how they go about trying to negotiate a better deal for themselves and their children. I have tried to understand what they see as the hurdles in the way of their well-being, the forces that weigh them down and the types of interventions that they think might make life better for them.

I would like my work to meet their requirements as far as possible, to make new options available and known to them rather than insist on imposing my own ideological agendas. I leave it to each reader to decide whether these essays are anywhere close to the goals I set for myself.

Madhu Kishwar
July, 1998
New Delhi

I

Beginning With Our Own Lives*
A Call for Dowry Boycott

Though we feel very encouraged by the fact that over the past year, many more individual women, women's groups and organizations have become activized around the issue of dowry and dowry murders, we have noticed with concern a rather disappointing trend. Many of us see our role as that of women 'activists' mobilizing 'other' women in protest action against atrocities like dowry murders. Many, who take upon ourselves the task of changing society's attitudes, continue to live our own lives almost untouched by the ideas with which we seek to influence others.

We, at *Manushi*, feel that initiating any kind of social and political action is meaningless unless it begins with our own lives, that those of us who assume the role of mobilizers, lead protest marches and speak or write against dowry, owe it to ourselves and to all those whom we try to draw into collective action not to in any way be party to such crimes as the giving and taking of dowry. We have no moral right to shout slogans like '*Dahej mat do, dahej mat lo*' ('Do not give dowry, do not take dowry') if we privately continue to participate in marriages where dowry is given or taken. If we do not dare to boycott the marriage ceremony of even our own brothers or sisters where lavish dowry is given, if we do not start the campaign in our own homes, what moral right have we to preach to others? We are not for a moment suggesting that every woman who participates in a protest action or starts getting involved in the campaign should be called upon to make such a commitment. We are referring only to those who take upon themselves the task of mobilization or consciousness-raising with other women, those who see themselves as leading the anti-dowry movement.

It is unfortunate that the viciousness of the dowry custom comes to be noticed only when a woman is murdered for it. We feel that all

*First published in *Manushi*, No. 5, May–June 1980. A statement for dowry boycott issued by Madhu Kishwar and five others.

those who give and take dowry or participate in this ritual are also responsible for making such murders possible. Are they not helping perpetuate a vicious custom which reduces women to articles of sale and barter? Why cannot a protest or public meeting begin or end with the organizers making a commitment that they will not be a party to dowry giving or taking in any form, that they will boycott all dowry marriages?

We, therefore, appeal to all women's groups and organizations to ensure that the movement begins with our own lives, that all of us be prepared to pay the price of our convictions. At least the women actively involved in taking up any issue should seriously discuss how it touches their lives and make commitments to personally and collectively battle against it.

Some of us have been practising this form of boycott for a while. But now we publicly affirm that:

1. We will not attend or in any way participate in a marriage where dowry is either given or taken in however veiled a form (as gifts, trousseau, or as money deposited in a bank in the girl's name at the time of marriage), even if the marriage be that of a close relative or a dear friend. We will openly make known our reasons for boycotting such marriages, rather than just quietly staying away from the ceremony. We will also boycott all rituals wherein dowry continues to be given after marriage such as customary gifts to the son-in-law's relatives at festivals and childbirth.

2. We will henceforth not confine protest actions to dowry murders but will also protest when dowry is given at extravagant marriage ceremonies.

3. We will not attend marriages in which the woman has no active choice in deciding whether she wants to get married at all or in choosing the person to whom she is to be married.

By protesting only when murders take place, we are keeping our own homes untouched, because dowry murders, for all their frequency, are still rare as compared to the high frequency of dowry giving and taking. Almost all of us participate in or connive with the giving and taking of dowry—not just in the form of cash, jewellery, household goods, and gifts to the husband's family on every conceivable occasion—but the various bribes that the woman's family is forced to continue offering so that she may not be taunted and maltreated.

Only when dowry itself is attacked in all its forms and manifestations does the battleground shift to our own homes and personal lives. It is there that the real struggle begins.

II

Rethinking Dowry Boycott*

For years now, we have participated in the common refrain that dowry is a social evil. Slogans have been raised against it; politicians have condemned it from public platforms; Parliament has legislated against it. Some of us at *Manushi* were also caught up in the euphoria and took a pledge in 1980 not to attend any dowry weddings.

This pledge was prompted by the fact that almost everyone, including those who are at the forefront of anti-dowry campaigns, continues to give and take dowry. We hoped that the refusal, even by a few people, to attend dowry weddings, would build pressure within their families and commumities against the practice, and that the boycott would spread.

However, the pledge did not have the desired effect, nor has it borne fruit even when taken on a larger scale, in the course of campaigns by other organizations. Very few, even from amongst *Manushi* readers, responded when we gave a call for more signatories. Amongst my family, friends, and neighbours, my stand was viewed with respect, even appreciation. But it did not lead anyone (except my two brothers) to refrain from taking (or giving) dowry, even though some were apologetic about their compulsions.

All these years, I have adhered to the pledge, even at the cost of annoying many friends and relatives. Simultaneously, however, I have also been forced to re-examine the question, given that most young women, for whose benefit we wish to 'abolish' dowry, are not willing to give it up. This raises a political and ethical question—do we, as self-appointed social reformers, have the right to promulgate measures for the supposed welfare of any group when that group itself does not perceive the reform as being in its interest?

*First published in *Manushi*, No. 48, Sept–Oct 1988.

Instead of dismissing the refusal of young women to say 'no' to dowry, as being a sign of their 'low consciousness' or lack of awareness, we would do better to examine why they are not willing to give it up. The answer is simple. Under the existing family structure, giving up dowry does not entail any alternative advantage for a woman. She loses the little she would get, and gains literally nothing. And yet, we the social reformers have shied away from this simple answer, and have continued to demand that women, as proof of their 'liberated' thinking, should refuse to take dowry.

Most women see their dowry as the only share they will get in their parental property. In a situation where women do not have effective inheritance rights, dowry is the only wealth to which they can lay claim. To suggest that women refuse dowry and go empty-handed to their marital homes is to suggest that they make even greater martyrs of themselves than society makes of them. Until we can ensure inheritance rights for daughters, we have no right to ask them to sacrifice the inadequate compensation they get by way of dowry.

The few women who, motivated by idealism, do not claim what society recognizes to be their due—a dowry—are rarely able to enforce their claim to inheritance rights since society does not recognize this as their due (regardless of what the law may say). Take the example of a colleague of mine, who is the only woman in her family to have built a career and stayed unmarried. She abstained from taking her share of her mother's jewels when it was offered to her because she does not like wearing jewels. Nor did she get a dowry or its equivalent. The result is that while her brother's son inherited the ancestral house and business, and her brother's daughters got huge dowries in cash and kind (much of it of their own selection), she had to start from scratch to build her own assets, and is not sure of where she will live after retirement. Needless to say, no one in the family expects her to demand her share in the family house. If she were to do so, it is likely to lead to a complete rupture with the family. So she ends up staying briefly in what should be equally her house, but is viewed as a semi-dependent of her nephew.

While in some cases the woman is not allowed to enjoy her dowry, in many other cases she is able to exercise control, partial or total, over it. To go dowryless is to be deprived of even this chance. Hence, women's commonsense desire for a dowry.

Her wedding is the one occasion when a daughter is specially indulged and made much of. She has, to some extent, the chance to select clothes and jewels, to demand and to get. This is a valuable experience for most girls, given that, in general, a daughter's desires are much less indulged by parents than a son's. Further, a woman never knows whether, after marriage, she will be given any money to spend on her own needs or will be provided with clothes or jewels. We have heard many women complain that for years after marriage, they were not given money by their in-laws to buy a new blouse or pair of slippers, and continued wearing what they had received in dowry or what their parents continued to give them from time to time—part of an extended dowry. In many cases, therefore, dowry is a woman's lifeline. To ask her to do without it is like asking workers to protest against wage-slavery by working for free and abstaining from taking their wages.

What is dowry? The transfer of wealth at the time of marriage. In itself, this is neither good nor evil. In many societies, marriage payments have been made in different forms. The practice of giving the daughter wealth of some kind—in the form of a settlement or a trousseau or family jewels passed from mother to daughter—has been prevalent in many societies, including throughout Europe until very recently. While this system prompted men to look for women with bigger fortunes, there is no evidence that this always in all societies led to the woman's maltreatment. It may even have enhanced her status under certain circumstances.

The harassment of wives is related to the utterly dependent and powerless position of women in our present family structure which concentrates economic and decision-making power in the hands of men. What we need to fight is not a phoney symbol such as dowry but the power relations within the family. Not giving dowry will not by itself alter the fact that property control is in the hands of men and that women are deprived of it.

Social and political activists have tended to single out dowry as the prime cause of maltreatment of wives, and have attributed increase in dowry demands and payments to growing greed and materialism in our society. In an earlier article, 'Dowry: To Ensure Her Happiness or to Disinherit Her?' (*Manushi*, No. 34, 1986), I tried to demonstrate how this analysis is extremely misleading, if not useless, in combatting dowry. Yet this analysis continues to be popular because it is relatively easier to give sermons to people to be less greedy than to work out ways to actually restructure relations, even within our own families, in such a way that power and property control is redistributed.

There is also a widespread tendency amongst activists to confuse the issues by condemning lavish and ostentatious weddings and gift-giving as somehow evil and harmful to women. A critique of waste and ostentation should not be confused with a critique of what goes specifically against women's interests. The pressure to make a lavish display is not confined to daughters' weddings, or even to weddings alone. To take just one example, there is great pressure amongst the middle-and upper-classes in urban areas to make increasingly lavish displays—more recurrent than weddings—on children's birthdays. Parents do complain even while they comply, but the pressure certainly does not lead them to harass or kill their children. Nor does it act as a deterrent to having children. Therefore, we should take with a pinch of salt the argument that it is only the fear of having to give dowry and arrange ostentatious weddings which makes people prefer sons to daughters, or makes them neglect their daughters.

When, in the late 1970s, it was discovered that many of the deaths of married women which used to pass off as accidents were in fact suicides or wife-murders, women's organizations and the press too quickly assumed that the main cause of these deaths was the greed for dowry. One possible reason why this happened is that when the woman's parents narrated the story, they always projected dowry demands as the most torturous part of the harassment inflicted by her husband and in-laws.

To the woman's parents, dowry demands loom largest because this is the one form of harassment which has to be borne by them. All the other forms of torture have to be borne by the woman alone. If she is taunted for her looks, culinary or housekeeping skills, mannerisms, inability to bear a son or inability to 'please' her husband, as almost every woman in such a situation is, the near invariable response of her parents is to tell her to try to improve herself, to 'adjust' and 'mould' herself to her marital family's requirements. But when the taunt relates to dowry the woman's natal family, especially the men, find themselves in the dock. No adjustment on the woman's part will do—it is her father who has to adjust to the demands for more wealth. That is why this particular aspect of the harassment pinches the woman's family most, and eclipses all else in their minds.

If the woman is killed or thrown out by her husband, her parents have yet another reason to project dowry demands as the primary or only cause of harassment—they hope to get the dowry back. Even if the woman is alive, it is relatively easier to get part of the dowry back than to ensure that the woman can live with dignity in her in-laws' home.

When the woman is dead, it is always her parents or brothers who bring the case to public attention; even when she is alive, she is almost invariably accompanied to the police station or the social organization by her father or brother because she badly needs their support. In most cases, the father or brother is the one to draft the complaint and narrate it to the authorities.

In this narrative to the police and the social workers, the parents, or even the woman herself is usually compelled to highlight dowry demands and to downplay other problems because today, dowry demands are perhaps the only form of harassment which will be unequivocally condemned, even by the police. Other forms of harassment, including even wife-beating, are much more likely to be condoned. When told that the husband berates or beats his wife, the police tend to ask why he does so, implying that she must be provoking him. That under no circumstances should a man beat his wife is not yet universally accepted in the way that it is accepted that dowry demands are wrong. So, highlighting dowry demands is one of the simplest ways to get a complaint to be taken seriously and registered as a criminal case. In the process, it comes to be projected as the main cause of harassment. The downplaying of other forms of harassment tends to draw public attention away from the inherent powerlessness of women in the existing family structure.

If one listens closely to the narratives of women, a number of elements recur as regularly as do dowry demands. One such recurrent element is the flinging of insulting remarks about her family, ancestry and upbringing. Another is the strict control over her movements, contacts, associations and expenditure. After years of listening to the detailed narratives of harassed wives, and working to provide legal advice to such women, I have realized that it is a fallacy to see dowry as the root cause of the harassment of wives. I have not come across a single case amongst the hundreds I have heard, read about or dealt with, where the husband and in-laws harassed the woman because of dowry alone, and were, in all other respects, satisfied with her. Dissatisfaction is expressed, not only with the quality and quantity of the dowry but equally with the woman herself. She is told that the husband could have got not just a better dowry but also a better wife. Criticizing the dowry, like criticizing her family, is a way of criticizing her, and the package deal that she represents. This is one reason why meeting dowry demands almost never induces husband or in-laws to view with greater favour a woman whom they otherwise view with contempt.

It is highly significant that it is not only when the dowry is considered inadequate that a woman will be harassed; this can happen equally if the dowry is considered large and ostentatious. She may be accused of arrogance, of trying to show her in-laws up and dazzle them with her parental affluence. In the same way, great beauty is made a pretext for humiliation just as much as its lack; high educational qualifications or a good job become a pretext for taunting just as much as lack of education or her unemployability. If a woman's parents are loving towards her, this can become an occasion for insult; so can their being neglectful.

There is almost no attribute—negative or positive—which a woman may possess, which cannot be used against her if her husband and in-laws so wish. Clearly, what requires rectification are not her attributes or possessions but her position of dependence and helplessness which forces her to put up with harassment and violence. To expect that harassment will stop if she is dowryless, is like advising a wife to give up her job because her violent husband resents her having a better job than he does.

Dowry is only one among many pretexts used by in-laws to legitimize abuse. A certain degree of ill-treatment is built into the subservient and dependent status of a wife in the existing family structure. This ill-treatment only comes to public notice when it crosses certain limits. In those cases where a woman is not maltreated, this is because her in-laws refrain from using their power. But the fact of their having the power still remains.

Dowry in itself does not always and under all circumstances lead to blackmail. In several cases, harassment and violence occur without any relation to dowry. In the few cases where the woman is in a strong position because of her independent earnings, profession and status in society, and has managed to acquire self-confidence, gifts given by her parents, whether or not they are termed 'dowry', do not make an appreciable difference either way.

The real problem lies not in the wealth itself—the furniture or gadgets or vehicles or clothes or jewels, however abundant or expensive—but in who controls them. In our society today, women are not expected to control wealth but to surrender it—in favour of brothers or husband. A wife is treated not as an individual who controls her own life and assets but as herself an asset who must perform several functions. One function is to bring wealth just as another function is to provide services of various kinds, and yet another to provide a male heir.

She is usually unable to resist this role because her parents have not treated her differently. Even as unmarried daughters, most girls are made to live a narrowly confined and dependent life. Most parents do not allow daughters to have money or other assets in their own name or to learn to manage family property. In rural areas, where the overwhelming majority of Indian women live, they may toil on the family farm but are seldom given the right to inherit it as sons are. Even among non-agricultural families and in urban areas, daughters' education is not taken as seriously as that of sons. Frequently, daughters are actively deterred from taking up paid employment. A life of economic independence tends to be seen as almost a stigma for a woman.

A girl who has been crippled on the pretext of being 'sheltered' is not likely to be less helpless just because no dowry is given at her wedding. The well-being of such a girl is at the mercy of chance— whether her husband and in-laws are good enough to refrain from exercising the arbitrary power they have over her life. If they decide to be nasty, no amount of dowry or lack of it can help her. Most women realize this. That is why they are not convinced by the argument that to refuse dowry would be to ensure their own welfare. They are aware that as their lives are structured today, the chance of getting a kindly disposed husband will play a more important role in their welfare than anything they can do.

If, on the other hand, a woman is equipped to take care of herself and of what belongs to her, her having a dowry will be no disadvantage. If ill-treated, she will know how to resist, how to guard her interests, and how, if necessary, to walk out taking her dowry with her. It is in this context that the recent Supreme Court judgement defining dowry as *stridhan* is important. Changing a name does not make a social evil a social good. What the judgement stresses is that shifting control of the assets would render them advantageous to women, whereas today they can be used to her disadvantage.

Today, I find it irrelevant to talk of abolishing dowry. Instead, we should single-mindedly work to ensure effective inheritance rights for women—but not on paper alone. We should forget the slogan '*Dahej mat do, dahej mat lo'* ('Do not give dowry; do not take dowry') and raise the slogan *'Betiyon ko virasat do, Betiyan, apni virasat lo'* ('Daughters must be given property rights; daughters must claim inheritance rights').

A number of steps need to be taken to facilitate this:

1. Any will which disinherits daughters should be considered invalid.
2. All land, property and succession related laws, including land ceiling laws, should be amended to ensure equal rights to women, particularly over immovable property such as housing and land.
3. Any document whereby a woman surrenders her right in favour of her brothers, husband or in-laws, should be considered invalid.
4. A woman should not be able to pass on to her husband or in-laws property inherited from her parents. If she dies childless or under suspicious circumstances, the property should revert to her natal family. This would ensure that her inheritance does not become an incentive for her husband and in-laws to kill her. Her inherited property should be inherited by her adult children or, if she is childless and dies a natural death many years after marriage, it may be inherited by her husband, as his would be inherited by her under the same circumstances.

If women's inheritance rights were to become real, dowry in its present form would almost certainly disappear. Gifts at a son's or daughter's wedding could not then be at all objectionable, even if termed 'dowry'. Equal inheritance rights would also ensure that a woman who does not marry does not end up empty-handed.

We should work to equip women with the resources and abilities to define, control and guard their own interests and their own lives. Whether or not they are given dowry will then become irrelevant to their essential well-being.

Is Dowry the Real Killer?

We made a count of all marital violence cases mentioned in *Manushi* from No. 1, 1979, to No. 50, 1989, in order to see what pattern of causality, if any, emerged. We included here only cases where physical violence was used against the woman by her husband or in-laws. The cases are described in varying degrees of detail, from a paragraph to several pages, in the form of reports by activists, victims or their families, letters from readers, interviews, and interview- or survey-based articles.

A pattern we noticed in the reporting was that when the woman spoke or wrote about the violence she suffered, dowry was almost never mentioned as the sole cause and, further, that most of the reasons were merely pretexts, the violence being actually irrational and causeless, a straightforward expression of power. When a third person who was not a continuous witness to the violence, such as the woman's parent, sibling, other relative, or an activist, reported the case, the description tended to be briefer and more unidimensional, and more frequently focused on dowry as the only or primary cause of violence.

This pattern is evident from the fact that in cases where the woman had died, and had left no account of her suffering, about half the cases (reported by others) were ascribed simply to dowry (36 out of 79). But in cases of torture or attempted murder where the woman either reported herself or would have spoken to the person reporting, only 14.7 per cent of the cases cited dowry as the sole cause; 13.2 per cent cited other causes as primary while mentioning dowry, and 72 per cent cited other causes (or none) and did not even mention dowry. It is noteworthy that the violence in these cases was not of a negligible kind, ranging from being attacked with an axe, or having her nose chopped off, to repeated rape by father-in-law, severe battering and sadistic torture.

III

Dowry Calculations*
Daughter's Rights in her Parental Family

The practice of dowry has drawn a great deal of criticism in the last century or so among the socially influential urban-educated middle-classes in India, and has come to be identified as one of the key aspects of Indian women's oppression. The opponents of dowry base their critique on the fact that the pressure of providing dowry for daughters makes daughters appear burdensome, and therefore unwanted. Dowry is condemned for being an economic burden on parents. Yet dowry opponents seldom base their criticism on sensible economic calculations. This article focuses on just such calculations. It ignores the no less important cultural and social dimensions of dowry, some of which have been covered in other pieces of my writing in the issue.[+]

This is not intended as a comprehensive analysis of the role of dowry in Indian marriages. I have deliberately limited my analysis of dowry payments to those of urban middle- and upper-class families, who are also among the most articulate critics of the institution of dowry. They continue to decry it as a social evil even though they have emerged as the trend-setters in escalating the scale of dowry.

Carrying wealth from parents to in-laws should enhance a woman's position in her marital home rather than being a source of grief for her. In many societies, dowry-giving does not worsen women's lives, but in India, tussles over dowry payments have become a major source of conflict between families. Dowry requirements are used as another excuse for viewing daughters as a burden. All forms of violence against daughters, including female infanticide and the growing practice of aborting female foetuses after amniocen-

---

*First published in *Manushi*, No. 78, Sept–Oct 1993.

[+]See *Manushi*, No. 34, 1986; No. 53, 1989; and also my documentary film on dowry available from *Manushi*.

tesis, have been attributed to the economic burden that a daughter is said to represent.

However, dowry payments are not the cause of women's devaluation and oppression. These payments do not by themselves transform girls into burdens to their parents. For instance, all those parents who happily pay lakhs of rupees as capitation fee to get their sons admitted to medical or engineering colleges, or provide money for their sons' business investments, do not think of sons as 'burdensome'. Dowry makes daughters 'burdensome' only because daughters are unwanted to begin with.

The particular form dowry payments take in our country, and the ugly tussles between the groom's and bride's family undoubtedly often add to women's vulnerability. However, they are not the cause of her vulnerability, but only a symptom of her fragile rights, especially in her natal family. In recent decades, as dowries have become more and more extravagant, the belief that daughters are an unwelcome burden has grown increasingly dominant. The anti-dowry movement, by limiting itself to the constant repetition of 'abolish dowry' as a mantra, has only helped further legitimize the conventional belief that daughters are an economic liability.

Dowry vs *Stridhan*

Some of the defenders of dowry payments justify the custom by depicting it as a form of pre-mortem inheritance. According to this interpretation, daughters, unlike sons, don't have to wait until their father's death to get their share of inherited property. Instead, they get their share at the time of marriage. They view dowry payments as the equivalent of *stridhan*[1] in traditional Hindu law.

However, there is a world of difference between dowry payments as they are made currently and *stridhan*. Traditionally, *stridhan* was considered a woman's own inalienable property over which she had full and absolute right. *Stridhan* was supposed to pass from mother to daughter and not travel via the male line, as does most other property. Dowry payments as currently made, however, are rarely considered female-owned or inherited property. Instead, they increasingly take the form of offerings over which the daughter retains uncertain rights. They are made to the groom's family as a token of gratitude for accepting the girl into their family, and for allowing her natal family to get rid of her. Some vestiges of the ideology that once surrounded *stridhan* do remain. There is usually a tacit understanding, for instance, that a bride can retain some rights in the disposition of some of the jewellery, clothing, and other items meant for her personal use which she brought as part of her dowry.

But that is only one part of dowry payment. Another part is offered to the groom and his family. Cash, as well as major items such as automobiles, however, are almost always given directly to the groom's father or to the groom himself. These gifts are expected to be commensurate with the status of the groom's family and with that of the groom himself. The groom and his family consider a poor or shabby dowry an insult. Such dowries can, and often do, become the cause of enormous conflicts between the families.

The Dowry Prohibition Act, which outlaws dowry payments, also provides that in cases where the marriage breaks down, dowry payments must be returned, arguing that dowry payments should be considered as *stridhan*. However, return of dowry payments have become highly problematic in a world where they are seen as unconditional gifts to the groom and his family.

Burdensome Daughters

Hardly any historical research has been done to show how *stridhan* was transformed into dowry payment. All we know is that there is little mention of exorbitant dowries causing the ruin of families in the literature of pre-British India. Ruin due to exorbitant dowry payments became a major theme only in late nineteenth century literature. This period seems to have witnessed the large-scale erosion of women's economic importance and inheritance rights due to the manner in which the colonial rulers carried out land settlement operations in India.

In conformity with the Victorian norms they were familiar with, the British legislated that land entitlements be given to 'male heads of the family', bypassing the customary laws which allowed various categories of entitlements to women. This concentrated property in the hands of men in an unprecedented way and paved the way for the disinheritance of women. In addition, the rapacious land revenue demands drained large amounts of the economic surplus from the rural economy. It made the peasants extremely cash poor. The destruction of traditional crafts pushed large sections of impoverished artisan groups back to a total reliance on their small landholdings, and the consequent increasing pressure on land bestowed a special power and status on those who owned land.

However, with rural society and artisan groups becoming extremely cash poor, the tradition of *stridhan* seems to have become burdensome. The traditional view of daughters as *paraya dhan* (someone else's wealth) achieved a new and deadlier meaning. The term *paraya dhan* had the connotation of viewing women as wealth. This is an apt description in a society in which women carried their *stridhan* with them—property that was theirs by right. Traditionally, the entry of a bride into her new family would be referred to as the coming of Lakshmi—the Goddess of wealth. Even today vestiges of that tradition remain in most communities. *Yeh hamare ghar ki Lakshmi hai*, is still a commonly used expression. A young bride enters her marital home with *haldi* (turmeric) soaked feet, leaving auspicious marks on the floor, which are associated with Lakshmi.

As women were increasingly disinherited, however, daughters began to appear as liabilities. *Kanyadan*, the gift of a daughter, became not so much a matter of earning *dharmic* merit (the merit of performing one's social obligation) so much as getting rid of an unwanted burden. It is in this context of the devaluation of women's lives and the marginalization of their economic rights, that dowry payments began to assume the form of offerings to a groom's family so that they would take a burden from the bride's family.

Women's Work Devalued

But why should women begin to be considered economic liabilities? Even in a peasant household, a woman's labour is of crucial importance for the family's economy. Labour power, however, is valued most in those societies with surplus land and scarce labour. Hence, in many traditional rural communities of Asia and Africa, paying bride-price was the norm, as is still the case in some tribal pockets of India. Bride-price is a way of compensating the woman's natal family for the loss of an adult woman's labour power, which in most agricultural societies is considered a valuable asset. However, as land becomes scarce and population pressure increases, as happened with the colonization of India, possession of land becomes the all-important asset. If, in such a situation, ownership of land is vested exclusively in the hands of men, women begin to be treated like mere dependents and considered liabilities, rather than assets, as are sons. Hence, bringing a bride into the house is seen as adding to the economic burden of the family, except in those peasant households where women's labour is the mainstay of agricultural operations.

New Power Centres

The increase in dowry payments is also related to certain other trends which marginalized women's lives in an unprecedented manner. Following the establishment of a new administrative machinery in the nineteenth century, women's economic worth was downgraded with the creation of new power centres outside of the traditional peasant economy. The new jobs and opportunities created by the colonial machinery provided avenues for rapid economic advancement and political power, in a way that working or owning small or average holdings of land never did. The job of a *patwari* (village accounts keeper), a police constable or even a clerk in a government department provided a person with enormous clout, and the accompanying ability to harass people and extract bribes. The system has accumulated even more powers in post-Independence India. Since this countrywide government machinery was first opened only to men, their power was enhanced dramatically in the last century-and-a-half. In recent years, women in small numbers have begun to enter government service, but mostly in relatively powerless jobs, such as nurses or school teachers.

In a rural household where both husband and wife work on land for their family's sustenance, there is less scope for a power imbalance between the two, because a woman's labour is more, not less, valuable. But when the husband becomes a police or a bank officer, or even a municipal clerk, his status changes dramatically. By virtue of the regular cash income, in addition to his income from the land, his family becomes more prosperous than a landholding peasant family which does not have this other source of income, power and influence, and acquires a dominance they could never have attained solely as peasants. This influence and income is exclusively his own, unlike the income from land, in which the wife's labour plays a visible role. Since most women continue to work in the peasant economy, while an increasing number of men are gaining access to new jobs and business opportunities, there has been a dramatic increase in the economic and political clout of men.

Dowry Variations

The contemporary marriage economy reflects this power equation fairly accurately. For instance, the amount of dowry required to get a police officer groom for one's daughter is far more than for making a match with an engineer in a private firm. All those government job holders whose power invites hefty bribes, such as income tax, excise and customs, or IAS (Indian Administrative Service) officers, are offered the biggest dowries. The going rate for an IAS groom is about Rs 80 lakh in states like Andhra Pradesh. (Now increased to about 10 crore). This is viewed more as an investment than as a dowry, because having an IAS officer as a son-in-law means making an alliance with a powerful family, thus gaining access to vast economic opportunities and political influence not available by any other route. The 'licence-permit-raj' in India, for instance, puts enormous power in the hands of bureaucrats to bestow licences for such money-making ventures as sanctioning trade quotas of scarce commodities and getting prime land allotted at dirt cheap prices to their favourites. The amount of dowry in such cases reflects the amount of power the groom commands. An officer in the postal department will never fetch as high a dowry as an officer in charge of giving licences in the Ministry of Industries, no matter how well-educated or good-looking the former may be. A university teacher, despite all his fancy degrees, will fetch far less dowry than even a low level officer in the public works or excise department.

What about women who themselves earn handsome salaries in urban professions? Why does dowry persist even in such marriages? To begin with, very few women are employed in professions which are citadels of power and corruption. Those few are not sought after as brides to the same degree as grooms who have attained such a position. Corruption requires wheeling-and-dealing with a network of other corrupt people. The prospect of a daughter or a daughter-in-law involved in shady deals would frighten most families. An IAS officer would rather marry the daughter of a rich businessman who brings in lakhs as dowry than a woman colleague from his own service, because the former assures a far more stable marriage. It is a common joke in India that the marriages of male IAS officers are the most stable because the deal is clear. Men marry money and women marry the three letters: IAS.

Income Gap

Even women professionals are seen as salary earners and no more. Their salaries alone do not bring them at a par with their husbands, because this small flow of money gets pooled in along with the husband's earnings for current consumption. The husband's position is far more solid due to his expected inheritance. He is likely to get, in one stroke, much more than she is likely to save or earn in a lifetime. In addition, in today's world, most men among the professional or business groups earn far more than women.

Let us take a concrete example. Pratibha (a pseudonym) is a college lecturer. At the time of her marriage to Vivek she was earning Rs 3,000 a month. Vivek was in business and earned around Rs 12,000 a month at that time. His business grew fast and within seven years of his marriage he was earning no less than Rs 30,000 to 50,000 per month. In the same period, Pratibha's income increased by no more than Rs 2,500 a month. The fact that the couple stayed at Vivek's family home added to the imbalance. Since theirs was a dowryless wedding, she could call nothing in that house her own, except for her clothes and a few personal items of daily use. Vivek, along with his brother, is going to inherit property worth Rs 60 lakh at current prices. Pratibha is well aware that she will not inherit anything from her father. If her marriage were to break down, her standard of living would fall dramatically because she would have to move out of this house. She has a right to live in it as Vivek's wife, but certainly cannot claim any share in her father-in-law's property in her own right, especially since she did not add anything to it. Legally she is entitled to inherit her husband's share of the property as a widow, if the property has already devolved upon her husband. But most important of all, she is not legally entitled to a share in his lifetime, whether the marriage stays intact or it breaks down, unless Vivek or his father decide to make her a co-sharer, out of generosity or some compulsion such as saving taxes or bypassing property ceiling laws.

Disinherited Daughters

Disinheritance of daughters by their natal family is the crux of the problem. The share women acquire in their marital family's property is not allotted to them in their own right, but comes to them through their husbands. Hence, women inherit more often as widows than as daughters or wives. This is the main reason why the dowry given at the time of a daughter's wedding comes to be seen as an offering to her in-laws, rather than her exclusive personal property. Through this dowry her parents are buying a share for their daughter in her husband's family property. At the time of her marriage, a woman ceases to be a full member of her natal family without simultaneously gaining full membership in her husband's family with immediate effect. That often accrues to her with time as she proves her loyalty to the interests of her new family. The roots of her insecurity lie in her fragile rights in her natal family.

In most traditional societies, including India, the concept of inheritance differed enormously from the modern, western concept which allows a person to will away property to whomever he or she chooses. Traditional societies recognize the rights of each and every member, including the handicapped or crippled, to be at least maintained by, if not exercise control over, the family property which is primarily seen as a form of kinship wealth, not individual wealth. Several communities in India allowed women the right to inherit parental as well as marital property. Many others, which followed the *Mitakshara* system, had a provision for *stridhan*. But even in communities where the right to control and administer family property rested with men, all women members had clear-cut rights of life-long maintenance as wives, as daughters, widows, sisters, and certain other kin.

The Hindu Succession Act, however, under the guise of giving women equal rights, has in fact lost them some of those traditional guarantees. The mischief centres around two points:

1. The deliberate inclusion of the provision allowing a person to will away property in whosoever's favour they prefer. This is alien to traditional Hindu customary laws. This provision has been used to enable fathers to altogether disinherit their daughters by writing their will in favour of sons only.
2. Giving sons a right by birth in Hindu joint family property, while daughters are allowed a nominal and uncertain share in joint family property held by males as coparceners.

Women in the Modern Economy

In the coparcenary property, daughters are supposed to get a small and very unequal share, but the law allows even this to be willed away to whoever a person chooses to sign away his property. This provision has been used to force daughters to surrender their rights in favour of brothers. Thus, while sons cannot be disinherited even by the father in the Hindu joint family coparcenary property, there is no similar guarantee for daughter's rights. Thus, our modern inheritance laws have increasingly moved in favour of men and against the interests of women. The few communities which practised matrilineal inheritance, such as the Nairs and Moplahs of Kerala, have been steadily moving towards patrilineal inheritance. Systems which provided reasonable or adequate protection of women's economic rights have all been rail-roaded out of existence. With the modernization of the Indian economy, property is today much more heavily concentrated in the hands of men.

The present day dowry system in India is a result of the disinheritance of women and the desperation of parents to push their daughters out of their homes after marrying them off, no matter how, because failure to do so is considered a severe stigma. Since the woman is being sent as a disinherited dependent, the receiving family must, therefore, be compensated.

Changing Marriage Patterns

Before the enactment of the anti-dowry laws, dowry payments were regulated by community norms. The gifts would be put on public display to ensure that the amount of wealth given conformed to the personal standing of the family as well as to the standards and limits set by the community.

A poor family would often be given a helping hand by better-off members of their community to make the payments appropriate to the norms set by the *biradari*.[2] One major purpose of the custom of publicly displaying all that was given to a daughter at the time of marriage was to make sure the community witnessed the transaction. This ensured that the amount given to a daughter was proportionate to her parents' means. Moreover, in case of marriage breakdown, the groom's family could not deny having received all those gifts. Thus, if that portion designated as *stridhan* had to be returned, the community elders who negotiated the terms of separation knew the exact amount that was due to the bride's family. While the Dowry Prohibition Act certainly did not succeed in curbing the practice of dowry payments, it enabled the transaction to be hidden more easily. Currently, dowry payments are more surreptitious due to the illegality of making them, as well as to the pressure to hide one's wealth from tax authorities. Therefore, it becomes harder for the woman's family to establish what they gave in the face of conflicting claims. Many of the conflicts also result from the bride's family trying to back out of commitments they made at the time of marriage negotiations.

Traditionally, when marriages were performed within pre-determined *jati*[3] and *gotra*[4]-boundaries far fewer economic differences existed between members of the same *jati* in a particular region. Even if certain families possessed more wealth, their standard of living did not vary dramatically in external manifestations. Flaunting one's wealth and trying to be one up within one's *jati* was looked down upon. However, with the emergence of class differentiations within the same *jati*, vast differences have emerged between the day-to-day standard of living of families within the same *biradari*. Consequently, we witness an increasing breakdown of community-set norms for dowry payments. Traditionally, the culture of dowry went hand-in-hand with hypergamy—that is, the practice of marrying one's daughter into families with higher social status and of a higher *gotra* within one's own *jati* and *biradari*. Thus, marrying off daughters provided an opportunity to forge alliances with influential families. However, the transformation of *jatis* into castes and the emergence of enormous class differentiations within the same caste have changed the priorities that go into determining a suitable match. The real or potential earning capacity of the groom has come to occupy a far more important place in deciding marriage alliances than the traditional notions of social status or higher *gotra* status. Thus, *gotra* and *jati* boundaries have been replaced, especially among the urban-based communities, by the modern and far broader category of caste. Higher dowries now go to grooms with a higher earning capacity even if they are of lower social or *gotra* status. Thus, a doctor will command a far higher dowry even though he may be from a poor family of relatively lower ritual status, than someone who is a mere school teacher, no matter how high his *gotra* status.

With the spread of geographic mobility in urban areas, marriages are increasingly being arranged through matrimonial ads and other modern institutions of match-making where families largely unknown to each other enter into marriage alliances. This anonymity has contributed a great deal to downgrading the importance of non-economic factors such as *'sharafat'* (goodness and honesty), the personal qualities of the groom, and the social respect commanded by the family. All those factors tend to be overshadowed by the economic criteria, provided the match is broadly speaking within the same caste. In the terminology of marriage advertisements, a 'respectable' family is one which is well-placed and economically well-off, just as a family promising a 'decent' marriage is dropping a hint that they will pay a handsome dowry.

Dowry payments are increasingly being viewed as:
1. Gratitude payment to get rid of the unwanted burden of a daughter;

2. An offering made to the groom's family commensurate with their *izzat,* that is, their social and economic standing;

3. A lingering notion from the tradition of *stridhan* whereby a family feels their daughter should be given her due share in parental property; however, the payments are given not to her but to the groom's family and considered as an investment to secure a share for her in her husband's household property.

The association of dowry payments with *izzat* (respect, honour) acts in two ways. An extravagant dowry acts as a confirmation of the family's social standing, and enhances their *izzat*. A small dowry is viewed as a social insult both for the receiving and the giving family. That considerations of *izzat* are far more important than mere economic considerations is borne out by the fact that much of the conflict between the groom's and the bride's family centres around whether the groom's party was treated with due respect or not. An indication of the importance of *izzat* is that the bride's family often spends as much money on decorations, *shamiana,* and other paraphernalia around the marriage feast, as it does on their daughter's dowry and gifts to her husband and in-laws.

Dowry as *Izzat*

Conversely, one often witnesses cases where some of the few families that defy the custom and go for a dowryless wedding are treated shabbily and insultingly by the bride's family, who often assume that a groom without a price tag is worthless. The dowry payment negotiations reflect this perception in financial terms fairly accurately. A widower or a man with some disability is unlikely to fetch a high dowry, no matter what his family or job status. I've often heard brides' families say that when they read a matrimonial advertisement in the newspaper from a groom's family saying they would go for a dowryless wedding, the message they read between the lines is that the fellow must have some physical or other defect. The fear of being considered 'defective' and being treated shabbily is one important reason that keeps some grooms' families from seeking a dowryless wedding. Any family daring to defy the custom is at once advised not to say they don't want dowry, since they will not be treated with respect (*izzat nahin milegi*). Unfortunately, too many families which have had dowryless weddings for their sons have mostly negative experiences to narrate.

The increase in dowry payments is not primarily due to an increase in greed in society as a whole; after all, those who have to give are balanced out by those who receive, and are often the same families. It has more to do with the sudden and swift increases in cash incomes of a small but significant proportion of the population. Since one of the key determinants of the dowry payment amount is the perceived economic status of the groom's family, families which seek upward mobility through marriage alliances are usually the ones who pay more exorbitant dowries. However, despite the uproar concerning the growing exorbitancy of dowry payments, the amount that is spent on dowry is usually far less than the sons' inheritance.

Exorbitant Dowries?

Let me illustrate this point with a couple of concrete examples. A lower middle class Punjabi family lives in our neighbourhood; let's call them the Kapoors. They have two daughters and one son. All three are married. Mr Kapoor worked in a low-level government job. Throughout those years, the family lived modestly. After retirement, Mr Kapoor, along with his son, set up a small shop in the front portion of his house, selling daily provisions. Both the daughters got very modest dowries. The net expenditure on the second daughter's wedding, which was fairly recent, was no more than Rs 1 lakh. This included the daughter's trousseau, jewellery, the gifts to in-laws, and the money spent on the reception. Being a lower middle class family, the Kapoors no doubt felt the pinch when they had to put together that much cash to marry off their two daughters. They might, there-fore, be held up as an example of pressured parents who had to pay supposedly exorbitant dowries to their daughters.

However, their one son will inherit at least thirty times what the daughters got by way of dowry. The tiny plot of land on which their house stands is worth Rs 36 lakh at current market prices. They recently entered into a collaboration with a builder and built four-and-a-half apartments on that small plot, two of which went to the builder. Apart from the two apartments, they retain the basement floor, which has been converted into a shop. One of the apartments has been rented and the other is retained for the use of the family. The son lives with his parents so that he lives virtually free of rent payments and other household costs.

The entire property, household goods, and savings of his parents will pass to him with no share for the daughters. No doubt he will have the responsibility for taking care of his parents in their old age and for making occasional gifts to his two married sisters and their families. At the moment, however, his father, though in his 70s, is still working and earning, and not yet a liability to the son. Neither is the mother. She provides child care and other support to her daughter-in-law, who works as a school teacher. If anything, the son has many advantages staying with his parents since, if he moved out, he would have to start his own household from scratch. The dowry payments and the small flow of post-marital gifts to his sisters are thus a small price to pay for the sum he has gained when his sisters do not claim what should legally be their share of the property, at current prices about Rs 9–10 lakh each.

Let me take another case of a wealthier family. My friend Anu was married in 1970. Her father was a rich businessman and spent about Rs 5 lakh on her wedding, which was considered an excessive amount in those days. She has also continually received expensive gifts from her parents over the years. It is understood that Anu does not get any share of the property which will go to her two younger brothers. This consists of a prospering business worth a few crores plus a palatial house in New Delhi worth at least Rs 2.5 crores. The two sons have been business-partners with their father since they grew up and have drawn princely incomes from this family business. They also live in the family house.

The mere Rs 5 lakh that the Khanna family spent in marrying off Anu is considered an undesirable expense; anti-dowry campaigners want such payments abolished. But they do not seem to be as concerned that Anu gets her due inheritance. In neither Anu's case nor in that of the Kapoor family did the daughters get anything near that given to the sons, despite their supposedly exorbitant dowries.

Complaints about exorbitant dowries gain legitimacy when families are cash poor, as is the case for most peasant families. Even among the peasantry, the land and other assets which sons inherit are worth much more than daughters' dowries. However, since most agricultural land usually does not yield an amount of cash surplus that matches the sale value of the land, the pressure on parents at the time of a daughter's wedding is enormous. This may also be true for certain salaried employees in urban areas. But even a modestly paid salaried employee will leave his sons much more than his daughters. Even if he leaves nothing more than a moderate house, the value of that property would far exceed that given to daughters as dowry.

Daughters vs Wives

Beginning in the nineteenth century, social reformers in India placed much more emphasis on the maltreatment of women as wives and sought to strengthen their position in their marital homes without strengthening their rights as daughters. We have failed to pay sufficient attention to the fact that women's parents leave them at the mercy of other families and do not think of equipping them financially for their future lives as they do for their sons. The disinheritance of women is caused and supported by a culture which does not treat daughters as full members of their natal families. A daughter continuing to stay with her parents after her marriage is considered a social disgrace. An even greater disgrace comes upon a family which fails to marry off their daughter. Even when she is in dire need, her continuing to live in her natal household is dependent on her brothers' goodwill.

The Hindu Succession Act provided very little security for the inheritance rights of daughters. However, the rights of wives, especially as widows, are relatively better protected. The husband's property automatically comes to the widow, unless he has willed it otherwise. Fathers disinheriting daughters is a very common occurrence. But far fewer husbands disinherit their wives, because that is not as socially accepted as the disinheritance of daughters. This has created a peculiar anomaly. The moment a bride enters her marital home, she legally acquires the right to be her husband's heir, even if she has no children. A wife's right has a stronger social sanction than the right of daughters. For instance, if a man dies prematurely, his insurance policy and provident fund would go in favour of his wife unless he has nominated someone else. A government pension will also automatically go to his widow. His mother may have been a dependent too, but she would not be legally entitled to any part of that money.

Thus, a newly-wedded bride affects the interests of all members of her marital family by acquiring the legal right to inherit her husband's share of the family property. Hence, the dowry she brings is not just her individual property but is meant to be added to the family kitty in order that her future right to that family's property, apart from her current maintenance, is assured. However, since she brings in far less than what she will be entitled to as an inheritor, her legal rights are dreaded. That is why in the early years of her married life a woman is expected to prove her loyalty to her new family in order to be accepted as a full member with rights of inheritance. In such a situation, the rights of young widows, especially if childless, are very vulnerable because they are not likely to have had the chance to be fully absorbed into their marital family, and consequently feel pressured to return to their natal home. There, too, their rights are not secure. Once they have been married off, they are perceived as someone else's responsibility.

Take the case of Reena who got married to Ashok after a love affair. Theirs was a dowryless wedding. Reena was employed in a multinational company and earned a handsome salary. However, her husband came from a very wealthy family, whereas she was from an ordinary middle class family. Far from being a burdensome daughter, she helped her parents financially, especially when her father fell ill and required expensive medical treatment. However, when he died, the little property he had, including the family house, went to his two sons. This came as a big jolt to Reena because she had insisted on a dowryless wedding, believing she was as good as a son and, therefore, did not want to burden her parents with a dowry. In a few years, her husband died in a road accident and a couple of years later her father-in-law also died. As his property was being divided between his children, she expected to be given the share that would have been her husband's had he been alive. Her in-laws found her demand preposterous because a) they felt she had not added to the family wealth by bringing a dowry; b) as a young widow she might remarry and carry away their property into another family; and c) if her own father did not care to provide for her, why should she expect her in-laws to do so? They were only willing to earmark a portion for their two grandchildren and leave it in a trust for when they became adults. Reena was not able to get any part of that property for herself. In this case, Reena was not left destitute because she was earning a good salary. But her father's negation of her inheritance rights, his refusal to treat her as a full member of the family, made her demand for a share in her father-in-law's property appear unreasonable.

In the Parent's Own Interest

Secure inheritance rights for daughters are desirable not just from the woman's point of view. Old parents benefit no less from it. In cultures where daughters are routinely disinherited, families are more stringently patrilocal and the responsibility of taking care of old parents falls to the sons, who have to rely on their wives to provide much of the day-to-day care. This leaves old parents at the mercy of someone who is a new entrant to the family and, therefore, does not have the same emotional attachment to her husband's parents. Too often, daughters-in-law consider this an unwanted liability. As a result, most parents who are financially well-off and keep their property under their own control—with the subtle threat of disinheritance if they are treated shabbily—are looked after with respect.

Parents who are poor or have made the mistake of handing everything over to their sons in their own lifetime are often treated very shabbily. Apart from the fact that a young bride feels no great inner urge to nurture her husband's parents, there is another reason that makes her resentful of having to serve her husband's parents. She has no right to take care of her own parents in case of need. Her relationship to her natal family is restricted. Her own brothers would discourage her close association with her parents, lest she begin to harbour the expectation of being given a share of the inheritance.

In my own neighbourhood I witnessed such a case closely. Mrs A's mother lives with her two married sons, with whom she doesn't have a very smooth relationship because their wives resent this old, widowed mother who was naive enough to pass on her meagre assets to her sons, thinking they were going to take care of her. Once they had the house transferred to their name, their widowed mother began to appear totally dispensable. Every time she has a tiff with her daughter-in-law, she approaches her daughter, Mrs A, for help and requests that she be allowed to come and live with her. But Mrs A feels terribly resentful that her mother remembers her only in times of trouble but forgot her at the time she passed on the family property. The old woman is consequently unwanted everywhere.

In cultures where daughters inherit equally or better than sons, where keeping daughters close to the parental family is not looked down upon as it is in many parts of India, and in cultures where daughters are free to take responsibility for their old parents, the latter are much better looked after than when they have to depend on daughters-in-law.

Similarly, conflicts between sisters-in-law are more ferocious in patrilocal families which disinherit daughters. A wife will look upon a husband's sister as a rival, an unwelcome burden, only when she comes as a disinherited daughter herself and her well-being is consequently dependent on her husband's share of the property. The wife is only too eager to cut down on her sister-in-law's fragile rights. Likewise, the mother, sisters and brothers of the groom view a young bride as someone who is going to adversely affect their respective shares in family property. One of the key criticisms of the dowry system has been that the money goes to the in-laws or husband, and that they come to acquire greater control over the money than the bride herself. This often occurs because dowry payments serve the purpose of buying a right for the woman in the husband's family property. If daughters inherited in the same manner as sons, they would enter their marital homes not as dependents but as equal partners. Such a woman could well insist on keeping property in her own name.

There can be no equality in marriage if women enter their marital homes as dependents or as disinherited daughters. Women cannot be strengthened as wives if their parents treat them as burdens and do not equip them to fend for themselves as they do sons. It is absurd to think that a husband can be persuaded to part with half his property in case of a breakdown of the marriage, or that the in-laws would be willing to hand over to a young widowed daughter-in-law the inheritance due to their deceased son, when a woman's own father does not treat her on par with her brothers and does not consider her worthy of being an equal inheritor.

Our struggle ought to focus on equal and inalienable inheritance rights for daughters in parental property, especially the right to live in the parental home as well as the right to take care of her parents in old age. It is only when parents begin to see daughters as worthy of providing them security in their old age, as much as sons, and are in turn willing to provide them with the economic security they try to provide for sons, that the culture of women's devaluation can be combatted. Merely outlawing dowry without ensuring inheritance rights for women only makes women still more vulnerable.

NOTES

1. *Stridhan* has many complex meanings. At its simplest, it means property gifted to a woman, either by her parents or in-laws, which is considered her own.
2. *Biradari.* Locally-based kinship group.
3. *Jati.* An endogamous group now used interchangeably with caste.
4. *Gotra.* An exogamous sub-division within *jati* whose members ascribe their lineage to a *rishi* (seer) either by pupilhood or biology.

IV

Knocking at the Portals of Justice
The Struggle for Women's Land Rights

With the introduction of the concept of Public Interest Litigation (PIL) in the late 1970s, direct access for citizens was provided to the High Courts as well as the Supreme Court. Progressive judges such as Justice P.N. Bhagwati began to actively encourage social and political activists to bring instances of injustice to exploited groups and vulnerable individuals directly to the notice of the Supreme Court. The Supreme Court had even ruled that letters to it could be treated as petitions. Poor prisoners, inmates of Nariniketans, marginalized tribals, bonded labourers and similar groups whose voices had never reached the citadels of power began to get a hearing in the highest court in the land through social workers and political activists who brought their cases from remote regions to the country's apex court. For a brief period it appeared that one didn't need to hire expensive lawyers or follow long cumbersome procedures to get the voice of the poor heard in the Supreme Court. A few sympathetic judges even made allowances for the activists who tried to plead the cases directly without the mediation of lawyers. What was most encouraging was that there was no difficulty in getting some of the best lawyers to take on these cases *gratis* or for only a nominal fee.

However, if one were to review the various high profile Public Interest Litigation cases of the last decade and-a-half, one would find that, despite all the fanfare of media coverage, Public Interest Litigation has very rarely actually benefitted those victims whose cases were brought to the Supreme Court. This is my impression not only from talking to various people and organizations who filed PIL cases, but also from *Manushi's* own experience with Public Interest Litigation.

*First Published in *Manushi*, No. 81, March–April 1994.

Maki Bui's Ordeal

I would like to share the story of one of our experiments with PIL to illustrate its actual workings. This case is not unusual. In 1981, *Manushi* filed a petition in the Supreme Court on behalf of Maki Bui and her daughter, Sonamuni, Ho tribal women of Lonjo Village in Singhbhum district, Bihar. The petition sought to overturn the denial of equal inheritance rights to women of the Ho tribe. Maki Bui died last year, but the Supreme Court has not yet delivered a judgement on the case, which has remained pending for the last 13 years.

I met Maki Bui in 1980 while I was travelling through Singhbhum gathering information on police atrocities against tribal women. During the course of police raids carried out on a number of villages, the police had arrested and intimidated tribal women who were taking part in a movement to reclaim forest lands from the government. I went to Lonjo village to meet Pilar, a social worker based there at the time. Many village women would come to her with their family or health problems. Among the women Pilar told me about and introduced me to was Maki Bui.

When I first met her, Maki Bui was in her early fifties. She had recently been widowed. Her husband had been a retired police constable who had served for many years in other parts of Bihar, often getting transferred from one local post to another over his long career. Only after his retirement did he live in Lonjo village with his wife and daughter for a sustained period of time. Like most rural women with a husband who worked outside the village, Maki Bui stayed in the village, working on the land through most of the period he was employed elsewhere. The couple had no sons, just one daughter. Their daughter, Sonamuni, had been married off while her father was still alive. Many of Maki Bui's husband's relatives living in Lonjo village were among the most influential families in the village. This included his elder brother and the brothers' sons.

After her husband's death, Maki Bui continued working on the land inherited by him, using her usufructuary rights according to the customary law of her tribe. According to this customary practice, Maki Bui was entitled to occupy her husband's share of the family land during her lifetime. After her death, the land would revert to one of her husband's agnates (relatives in the male line) rather than her already married daughter, Sonamuni. If the contemporary Ho custom were followed, Sonamuni would have been allowed limited usufructuary rights in her natal family land only if she had remained unmarried.

As soon as she gets married, a Ho woman loses all rights to her natal family's land, even her limited usufructuary foothold. This loss of usufructuary rights is permanent; she never gets those rights back, even if her husband abandons her immediately after her wedding. An implicit assumption of the customary law is that the daughter's right has been transformed into a right to sustenance in her marital family. Since tribal marriages are not always stable and men often take a second or even a third wife, women's usufructuary rights in their marital household are frequently violated both legally and customarily. In such situations they end up not being able to claim a maintenance right in either their parental or marital home. This is an important reason why a large number of Ho women stay unmarried. Census reports since the early decades of this century have consistently recorded that about 11 per cent of adult Ho women remain unmarried. This is a high figure for any society; for India, it is astonishingly different from the almost universal rate of marriage in other communities.

A Ho woman's position as a wife is particularly vulnerable if she has no sons. A woman with an adult son is more likely to have her rights honoured since a son cannot legally be disinherited from coparcenary property by his father. In addition, a man is not likely to be able to beat his wife out of the house if she has the moral and physical support of her able-bodied sons. However, a woman who is childless or only has daughters is hard put to enforce her rights if her marriage breaks down or her husband dies.

Maki Bui found herself in precisely such a situation. After her husband's death, his male relatives became impatient and began to put pressure on her to give them all rights to her land, threatening to take away even her limited usufructuary rights. Maki Bui faced a particularly difficult situation because she wanted to pass on the land to her daughter, Sonamuni, who had been married into a poor family. At first she tried to get her daughter and son-in-law to come and live in Lonjo so that they would have some customary claim to her land after her death. Customary law does have provisions for adopting a son-in-law for inheritance purposes. The strategy was resented by Maki Bui's husband's family, who began to threaten her with violence.

Worried that her attempts to pass the land on to her daughter and her son-in-law were being thwarted, she tried surreptitiously to mortgage her land so that she could give the money thus raised to her daughter in lieu of the land itself. This strategy evoked great hostility amongst her husband's male relatives. One of her husband's brothers was the village *mukhia* (headman). Their sense of their own dominance in the village made them feel they could get away with murdering Maki Bui if she seemed likely to succeed in passing the land on to her daughter.

The first time I met Maki Bui she was living in constant fear for her life. An examination of cases before the Chaibasa Court revealed that the labelling of single or widowed women as witches (*daiyan*) in order to deprive them of their property, and even life, was a common pratice used by tribal men. Maki Bui first approached Pilar for help, and through Pilar, me. In my naive, enthusiastic way, typical of many of our English-educated elite who think of rights in terms of modern jurisprudence, something to be enforced by the state machinery, I suggested we challenge the constitutional validity of the discriminatory tribal law. The constitutional case seemed straightforward and clearly in Maki Bui's favour. Non-discrimination on the basis of gender is a fundamental principle of the Constitution; it appeared that it would be simple to get the Supreme Court to rule that those aspects of tribal customary law that discriminate against a woman's inheritance rights were unconstitutional. I promised Maki Bui that I would return to Delhi, explore the possibility of obtaining legal help for her, and come back to Lonjo with some solution to recommend.

That was during the heyday of enthusiasm for Public Interest Litigation in India. I consulted a number of lawyers and people in the judiciary. They all encouraged me to proceed with my petition, indicating that the Court was likely to look on it favourably.

Petition Admitted

I then went back to Lonjo and told Maki Bui that we had found a solution to her difficulties. The Supreme Court itself would listen to her case. If her petition succeeded, and we were confident it would, then not only her rights but the rights of millions of other tribal women would be secured. She seemed enthusiastic. A short while later, *Manushi* filed a public interest case in the Supreme Court on behalf of Maki Bui and her daughter. This case was admitted to Justice Bhagwati's court. We felt particularly elated since he was reputed to be sympathetic to the plight of the poor and vulnerable, especially women.

Public Interest Litigation cases attracted a lot of media attention in those days. The Maki Bui petition, received some coverage in the national press, but it received far more publicity in Bihar. Following Maki Bui's petition, which was published in *Manushi* No. 13, of 1982 many other people showed an interest in joining this battle. People from different regions wrote to us saying that the situation was similar among several other communities and therefore, they wished to join us in challenging this discriminatory law. One of *Manushi's* subscribers, Mary Roy, who belongs to the Syrian Christian community, wrote to say, inspired by the *Manushi* petition, she had filed a petition along the same lines challenging similar discrimination against Syrian Christian women. From Maharashtra's Dhulia district, Sharad Patil, a prominent political activist working among the tribals, also filed an intervention petition because many tribal communities in that area practised similar denial of land rights to women. From within Bihar some activists working with the Jharkhand movement brought more intervention petitions involving other tribal communities. Maki Bui's case seemed to have a large ripple effect. Within a short time, we had succeeded in getting the issue of women's land rights debated and discussed among a whole range of social and political organizations. In Bombay, some activists of Nivara Hakk Samiti, who were fighting for the housing rights of pavement dwellers, wrote to say that they had decided to demand house *pattas* in the name of women.

Framing the petition was not simple, given the sensitive nature of the issues involved. Thus far we only knew the situation from the point of view described to us in discussions with Maki Bui and a few other village women. I knew next to nothing about inheritance procedures and land settlement patterns and precedents of that region. The petition for relief had to give an accurate idea of what the customary law was at the operational level. Several lawyers who offered to fight the case for us knew even less than we did about these customary laws.

The solutions they suggested were, therefore, mostly simplistic and inappropriate. Most of them suggested we should ask the Supreme Court to apply the Hindu Succession Act (HSA) to resolve this problem in tribal law. We explained that doing this would be politically suicidal. The tribals had learned from a long history of exploitation at the hands of *dikus* (outsiders) to be hostile to attempts at Hinduization. *Dikus* have snatched away most of the tribal lands by force or fraud with the active connivance of the colonial British government as well as of its successor regime, the Government of India. Many tribal difficulties stemmed from the period when the British government opened this area for outsiders to start business and mining ventures on land traditionally owned by tribals.

Officials Flout Court Orders

Getting the case admitted to the Supreme Court was no problem. Getting the case heard was a far more difficult matter. The years that followed were full of unending petty harassment, slipshod court procedures and interminable delays. After the case was admitted on August 20, 1981, the Supreme Court served notice to the Bihar government to send its response. They also ordered the Bihar government to ensure that during the period that the case remained before the court and until final orders were passed, they were to see to it that Maki Bui continued to enjoy her customary rights as a widow without fear or hindrance. We had expected that Maki Bui's relatives would behave in a more restrained fashion when they got to know that she had gained access to the Supreme Court and that if they tried any mischief, we could pressure the local administration to provide her protection through the orders of the Supreme Court. But this proved to be a naive hope.

The Bihar government took an exceptionally long time to file its reply. Finally, when it did reply, the Bihar counsel submitted that the 'custom' we had challenged was in accordance with 'natural justice, equity and good conscience.' The Bihar counsel also denied that Maki Bui had been harassed by her husband's male agnates. Their basis for this denial was an affidavit submitted by the Block Development Officer (BDO) of Sonua, who claimed to have visited the village and found that Maki Bui was 'living in the same house where she used to live during the time of her husband and appropriating all the lands inherited by her late husband, and enjoying the produces [sic] according to her own sweet will....' The BDO asserted that 'through cross examinations among the 16 *annas raiyats* [sic] of the village, I came to the conclusion that the allegations against the respondents ... is totally bosiless [sic] and false.'

We pointed out to the court that the BDO never visited the village to talk to Maki Bui or to any other woman in Lonjo. In fact, on a date prior to the date the BDO claimed that he visited the village, Maki Bui had left Lonjo out of fear for her life and was staying in her son-in-law's village. The very officer who was assigned the task of providing security to Maki Bui seemed to be lying in writing to the Supreme Court. He had probably summoned Maki Bui's male relatives, and enacted a drama of threatening them with a view to extracting a bribe in return for lying in their favour to the Supreme Court. The judges seemed also to suspect he was lying but seemed helpless to take any action.

The Bihar government further added that the said custom is based on reasonable and sound principles of natural justice and economic stability of the tribes and as such it does not offend Articles 14 and 15 of the Constitution. This assertion clearly showed that the Bihar government identified the interests of the tribe with that of the men of the tribe. We argued that since women constituted half the tribe and were the primary workers on land, any custom which was detrimental to their interests and to their economic stability could not be said to be beneficial to the economic stability of the tribe as a whole. The misery caused to the women by the denial of their inheritance rights in land resulted in destabilization of the tribal family and damaged the community as a whole.

Inappropriate Solutions

At the end of their various and mutually contradictory submissions, the state of Bihar recommended the extension of the Hindu Succession Act (HSA) to the Ho tribals.

The judges also seemed in favour of this measure. But we argued against extending the Hindu Succession Act on the ground that it would be detrimental to the integrity and well-being of the tribal community as a whole.

Applying the HSA would be problematic because not all tribals are Hindus. A large proportion are animists and many have converted to Christianity. Yet, in matters of succession, the customary law is the same for all, no matter what their religion. The tribal identity is not defined by religion alone. Any extension of the HSA to tribal Hindus would mean that the Christian Succession Law would have to be extended to Christian tribals; tribal animists would need a separate set of laws. This would have the undesirable effect of splitting up the tribe on religious lines and contribute to destroying their distinctive cultural identity.

We knew from our experience providing legal aid for Hindu women that the HSA offered inadequate protection to Hindu women. Daughters could be equal inheritors in self-acquired property, but the provision allowing father to disinherit whomever they pleased invariably tended to be used against daughters. The distinction in the law between self-acquired and coparcenary property added further loopholes in the Hindu Succession laws. Sons had rights by birth equal to that of fathers, whereas daughters had a minuscule share in coparcenary property. Even this tiny share they could be made to sign away in favour of their brothers or other male members of the family. In this respect, the Hindu Succession Act was similar to the discriminatory aspects of tribal law which gave full rights by birth only to sons, and excluded daughters. Nevertheless, the exaggerated rhetoric about gender equality, supposedly incorporated in that Act according to its advocates, had mesmerised the educated elite, including most lawyers, into believing that the reformed Hindu law could be used as a model to show the way to other communities to shed gender discrimination. In actual fact, few Hindu women have benefitted from its provisions.

Extending the Indian Succession Act (ISA) to these tribals would be viewed by Hos and other tribals as a conspiracy against them by the outsiders. The ISA has a provision allowing people to will away or sell their properties to whomsoever they please, including people outside their family. This would harm the overall interests of the tribals by facilitating the alienation of whatever land they had left. The little foothold that these tribals have retained over parts of their traditional landholdings is only possible because of the restrictions incorporated in the Chhota Nagpur Tenancy Act, which does not allow tribal men to sell or will away their land to anyone they please. The land has to pass on to a predetermined set of heirs. It can only be alienated under special conditions with the permission of the Deputy Commissioner, ostensibly for 'development' purposes. This provision has been frequently misused in the takeover of tribal lands by large industrial interests, as well as for exclusion of tribals from their own lands, and in the appropriation of the region's mineral and forest wealth by the government. There are many instances where industrial or other interest groups have used these provisions to defraud tribals of their lands, for example, getting them drunk and making them sign away their ancestral rights with the active connivance of the government officials. Bringing in the provision for willing away or freely selling landed property along with the Indian Succession Act would altogether nullify the pitifully small amount of protection the tribals had under the existing law. On the pretext of helping tribal women, if our petition facilitated and furthered land alienation, women would be as much the losers as men. Therefore, we asked for minimal changes in the Chhota Nagpur Tenancy Act and went no further than saying that the expression 'he' whenever it occurs should include 'she' so that women are entitled to inheritance rights equal to men. This interpretation would ensure that there was no vacuum in the legislation if the provision challenged were held *ultra vires*. We demanded that 'in pursuance of the spirit of the Chhota Nagpur Tenancy Act which sought to prevent the alienation of tribal land to non-tribals, and to ensure that the rights granted to women were not rendered nugatory, the court direct that in the event of a marriage between a tribal and a non-tribal, the land of the tribal must not, on the death of the tribal, pass to the non-tribal but must revert to the natal family of the tribal.'

Under customary law, if a tribal man marries a non-tribal woman, the children of the marriage do not inherit their father's land which reverts to his male agnates. We asked for the same principle to be extended to women.

Findings From Lonjo

In order to learn for myself whether allowing full inheritance rights to daughters were likely to produce any negative repercussions, I decided to study Lonjo village with the help of Pilar and find out from detailed family histories whether Maki Bui's case was an exception. I also hoped to learn about women's relationship to land under the existing system.* The results were a surprise, even to me. They showed that:

- Maki Bui was far from atypical. A large proportion of women faced similar problems and were living precarious lives. A large number had been deserted by their husbands, who had remarried.
- Women do not marry far off. In most cases marriages come to be settled within walking distance of the woman's natal village. Therefore the argument that after marriage women could not exercise rights over the family land does not hold good.
- Men migrate away to far off places much more often than women; the primary responsibility for both agricultural and household work rests with women. At least 80 per cent of agricultural tasks are performed by women. Men's participation is confined to occasional tasks such as ploughing.

*For a detailed report and analysis see, Madhu Kishwar's article, 'Toiling Without Rights: Ho Women of Singhbhum', *Economic and Political Weekly*, Vol. XXII, Nos. 3, 4, 5, 1987.

At this point the case was due for a preliminary hearing. For about a year, it kept appearing in the list for admissions rather than where it should have appeared: on the list for arguments. Every time our lawyers would draw the attention of the Supreme Court to this error, the judges would order that it be listed in the proper slot; but despite the order, somehow, the next time the lists were issued, the case would be back in the wrong list. Our lawyers attributed the error to a typist's mistake. However, if a typist can go on making the same error so many times in the face of repeated directions from the court to correct it, and not be called to account for causing such an immense amount of precious time to be lost in such cases, then there is something seriously wrong with the functioning of the simplest aspects of the court. It took about two years for the preliminary hearing and notices to be sent to the Bihar government.

Unofficially, we were told by the court registrar's office that they had lost all five copies of the case we had prepared and submitted to the court. We were advised to replace the files quietly without comment if we wanted the case to be heard. There was no point in kicking up a fuss. We did as we were told.

Getting a Hearing

There were many more problems to come. Between 1983 and 1985, the case was listed for a final hearing numerous times but was not heard because it was placed too low down on the list. Therefore, its turn would not come before the court adjourned for the day. During this period, the Bihar government kept on seeking adjournment after adjournment on the flimsiest grounds. The court continued granting those adjournments even though it was clear that they were resorting to blatant dilatory tactics.

However, on each of the days when the case was listed, even if it was on the wrong list or in a spot too low on the list to get heard, some of us from *Manushi* would be present all day. Several times when the court listed the case, I was out of Delhi and would cut my trip short before my work was finished and rush back to Delhi only to find that our turn never came.

In the meantime, Maki Bui was getting desperate. After the BDO's enquiry, her in-laws' family began to harass and intimidate her even more for having dared to take them to court. On one occasion, when it seemed that the case might actually be heard, we arranged for Maki Bui to come to Delhi for the court hearing in the hope that: a) she would see for herself that the case was being argued and would feel reassured that we were not lax; b) we might somehow get the judges to notice her in court. If the lawyers told the court that this poor village woman had come all the way from a little village in south Bihar to seek justice, perhaps they might feel moved enough to expedite the case; and c) that we might be able to arrange some newspaper publicity regarding the case by requesting some sympathetic journalists to interview her and demand the case be heard and decided upon without further delay.

Maki Bui was indeed very impressed with the physical grandeur of the Supreme Court, and told me, 'I am sure such a big court will give me big justice.' However, her case never came up for hearing on that day. Seeing her sitting in a sort of daze in the court, I realized that even if the case had come up for a hearing, this woman could not possibly have understood what was being argued on her behalf. For the judges, she was not a human being but a case number. Maki Bui's fate depended on people who neither knew her language nor considered her worth their notice.

Our attempts to organize newspaper publicity on her behalf was also a flop. She was neither glamorous nor colourful enough for any newspaper reporter or editor to pay attention to her. While several newspapers would willingly publish interviews with me on this case, no one found her worth a conversation. She, however, went back to Bihar under the illusion that we would soon have a solution for her.

We renewed our efforts to get her case expedited. The Bihar government kept requesting postponement after postponement on one pretext or the other. In the meantime, we heard from Pilar in Bihar that Maki Bui had been even more aggressively threatened by her relatives and consequently had to leave Lonjo and go far away to her daughter's village. Maki Bui had started off by asking our help to enable her to pass on her piece of land to her daughter. Instead of assisting her to get more than the discriminatory customary law allowed, her coming to the Supreme Court had actually endangered her life even further.

Who Cares for Court Orders?

We filed a petition alleging contempt of court against the Bihar government for violation of the court's interim orders that Maki Bui be offered protection. They had submitted an affidavit assuring the court that Maki Bui's traditional rights were not being tampered with in her village. We informed the court that she had in fact been forced to flee Lonjo and the Bihar government had done nothing to protect her and her rights in the land. I felt responsible for having suggested the legal route to her and thus helping bring her troubles to this awful point. The then Chief Justice, Ranganath Mishra, himself heard our contempt application. I joined with our lawyers in pleading that there was danger to her life, that the Court should take action against the Bihar government for having flouted the Supreme Court's interim order. Even though by now our expectations of the Supreme Court had been scaled down considerably, we were still not prepared for what happened. Justice Mishra said openly in a packed court: 'We can pass a contempt order if you insist. But what good will it do for the petitioner? The Bihar government or its police are not going to heed it any more than they did our original order. Better that you advise that old woman to continue staying with her daughter so at least she is more safe than in her own village. Or else bring her to Delhi and keep her with you so she is safe.' (Justice Mishra's comments quoted above are from my notes. They were not included in the written record of the Court). Justice Mishra prevailed upon us not to press the contempt petition but reiterated the court's order that the superintendent of police, state of Bihar, should provide adequate protection to Maki Bui and her daughter and ensure their personal safety.

What was the point of fighting this case for so many years if the highest court of the land was admitting that its orders carried no weight whatsoever with the government of Bihar, that even a BDO does not have to pay any heed to it? What good would any final judgement be in such a situation? Even if the Supreme Court actually gave a judgement in Maki Bui's favour, there would be no machinery to implement that judgement, even in such a simple case of one poor old woman in a tribal village in Bihar. We had approached the Supreme Court in the hope that its judgement would help millions of women, not just Ho women but other tribals as well. Now the Supreme Court was itself admitting that it could not even provide this one woman with any protection.

In the course of the hearing, the judges also suggested to the Bihar government that it should consider amending the provisions in Sections 6 and 7 of the Chhota Nagpur Tenancy Act on the lines we had suggested with a view to conferring inheritance on the female heirs. The Bihar counsel agreed in February 1987 to consult the appropriate authority and come back with a proposal. Several adjournments later, in August 1987, the state of Bihar submitted an affidavit through a section officer, Revenue and Land Reforms Department of Bihar, saying that some of the deputy commissioners and divisional commissioners had not yet sent their comments on the matter. But the Regional Development Commissioner of Ranchi had given his view against the proposed amendment: 'Since this amendment may have very far reaching consequences, affecting the age-old customs of the tribal population, the matter has been referred to the Bihar State Tribal Advisory Council... which is likely to meet and consider the proposal in near future. Only on receipt of their recommendations state government would be able to finalise its views on the subject.'

Years passed. The Bihar government showed no inclination to propose a solution and the Supreme Court insisted on forever waiting for the Bihar government's proposal. Even so, we had not yet given up. Over the years, I met several bureaucrats connected with Bihar in order to find out if they could suggest ways that we could get the judgement from the Supreme Court to take effect if and when it was delivered. None of them could make any workable suggestions, even though they were among the most senior and skilled of our civil servants.

Maki Bui is Dead

Last year we got the news that both Maki Bui and her daughter, Sonamuni, were dead. We were unable to maintain touch with Maki Bui after Pilar moved out of Lonjo district to another district in Bihar. It is likely that Maki Bui gave up hope and did not think it worthwhile to maintain contact with us.

In September 1993 Pilar and I visited Lonjo to find out the causes of Maki Bui and Sonamuni's death. It was easy to get information about Maki Bui from Lonjo village residents because Pilar knew several families very closely. But no one in Lonjo knew how Sonamuni died. We found that Maki Bui had left her daughter's village some years ago and had come to stay in a village within walking distance from Lonjo—probably fearing that if she stayed in a far away village then the chances of her claiming her land would become altogether dismal. While living in that village she fell ill and became very weak.

At this point, when it was clear she was going to die soon, her brother-in-law's family insisted on bringing her to their house in Lonjo. She was extremely unhappy staying with them because it was they who had initially driven her out of her home. She kept requesting some of her women friends in the village to take her to their home. But no one dared interfere for fear of annoying the *mukhia*'s family. He was probably keen to have her die in his house to strengthen his claim to her land. Her daughter, who had been no more than 30 to 35 years old, was already dead. No one in Lonjo knew how she died.

The case is still dragging on, even though the final hearing and arguments were completed in 1990. The Supreme Court continues to insist that the Bihar government must come up with proposals listing what they intend to do regarding the discriminatory provisions. And the Bihar government keeps on procrastinating on one ground or another, seeking adjournment after adjournment. Even though it was obvious that the Bihar government was deliberately dragging the case, not once did the Supreme Court refuse to grant adjournment at the request of the Bihar counsel.

Who Benefits from Courts?

Over the years, only in rare cases have we been able to provide a modicum of help to a few individual women through the law courts. By and large, our experiences in the courts have been frustrating and demoralizing, especially when the litigants are poor and vulnerable and come into the legal system via the Public Interest Litigation route.

We were not the only group to be misled by the rhetoric of the proponents of Public Interest Litigation. Scores of activists all over the country enthusiastically participated in the rush to enter Public Interest Litigation cases in the Supreme Court. It gave us all an exaggerated sense of our importance and potential influence in making changes on basic issues. Judges were going out of their way to encourage activists to bring such cases to them. Lawyers were more than willing to fight these cases free of charge. Activists like us only had to take the pleasant role of heroic interveners. My impression is that the outcome in the overwhelming majority of these Public Interest Litigation cases was not substantially different from that of the Maki Bui case.

The only 'beneficiaries' of this wave of cases have been the progressive judges, lawyers and social activists. Many of us made a name for ourselves as defenders of the rights of the poor and the powerless without going to too much trouble or expense. We read out reports of these cases at international conferences on human rights. We received a great deal of positive media publicity both within India and abroad. Despite all the praise the social activists received for initiating Public Interest Litigation, the actual victims on whose behalf we raised these issues have not often found their situation improved. Indeed, many of them found themselves in ever-worsening circumstances as a result of agreeing to participate as complainants in these celebrated cases. The press publicity made them more vulnerable at the local level for they came to be big threats to the local vested interests. This has caused a great deal of resentment at the local level against high-profile interventionists coming from Delhi and other big cities and state capitals.

For instance, there is no way I could have provided day-to-day protection to Maki Bui. By encouraging her to enter into a heightened confrontation with her own community and giving her the illusion that my privileged status as part of the urban elite with connections in Delhi could offer her a measure of protection, I was in effect endangering her life even more. For her, the goodwill of as many parts of her community as possible was her main source of protection in a dangerous situation. By going to court and seeking redress outside the community and hoping to use the government apparatus with its hypocritical rhetoric of equality and social justice in her favour she came to be perceived as a threat by her own community. Her relatives probably found it relatively easy to neutralize, through bribes, the government functionaries expected to ensure Maki Bui's safety. All our high-powered petitions in the Supreme Court could not combat the local forces of one influential family and a corrupt and inefficient local administration.

Am I suggesting that we leave the poor and vulnerable to their fate, that we make no effort from the outside to strengthen their rights? Far from it. In fact, I think we should redouble our efforts to provide whatever assistance we can to those subject to these injustices. But we must seek more appropriate methods, those that are more likely to be helpful and do not claim to accomplish more that they are capable of achieving. Outside intervention often heightens the con-frontation level without ensuring adequate protection for the con-cerned individuals or groups especially if we are relying on the government to do the job. No matter what the official rhetoric, in actual practice the government functionaries invariably tend to pro-tect the wrongdoers because that brings bribes. Yet we, the urban activists, continue to rely on the same government machinery simply because we ourselves are beneficiaries of this *sifarish raj* (getting our work done through influence at the top). But what may work for well-connected people like us does not work for the poor and vulnerable. Thus while high-profile well-connected activists themselves do not face much personal risk, those that we lead into a high pitched battle end up becoming even more vulnerable. We think we can neutralize local pressure by newspaper publicity. However, while this may help make us more known and famous, it rarely succeeds in making officials behave better. It is often counter-productive—the more the newspaper publicity, the higher the bribes extracted by local officials to protect wrongdoers.

Why Courts Fail in Justice

The existing legal machinery exists mostly to tyrannize and harass rather than to enforce laws or deliver justice. Some of its outstanding flaws result from the origins of the system; this legal machinery was originally created to facilitate colonial rulers in imposing their will on the people. It was often used to snatch away their property and other rights. The legal system is alien to our land and insensitive to the needs of our people. It remained essentially the same even after Independence and was allowed to spread its tentacles much more widely than during the British days. To make any real headway we need to change some of its basic flaws:

- The laws are framed and administered by individuals who do not understand basic facts about the diverse life situations and customs of our people. The English educated administrators, parliamentarians, judges, lawyers, police officials and others who are part of this legal apparatus are often as ignorant about the actual ways of life of the people as were the English rulers after whom the present rulers modelled themselves. There seems very little relationship between this country's formal statutes and the actual social arrangements that govern economic and social relationships within various communities and occupations. The statutes are based on principles of British jurisprudence that have very little in common with the traditional dispute settlement methods that still maintain some of their legitimacy among many communities in India. Unless our laws reflect a measure of social consensus, they will continue to be breached.
- Our laws are written in archaic English and are thus beyond the comprehension of even most of the English-educated Indians, leave alone the hundreds of millions who do not know English. Our courts need to switch over to careful use of local languages and dialects.

- The procedures and legal provisions are so cumbersome that dependence on lawyers becomes inevitable. Once the case is handed over to lawyers, a petitioner becomes a helpless spectator in the whole legal proceeding that may decide the person's fate. It also makes the system too expensive and thus beyond the reach of the majority of the people. Clearly written and logically presented laws should enable us to discourage and minimize the use of lawyers.

- The courts are physically distant from the people. The long delays and erratic functioning of the courts act as another source of harassment against those least able to bear the burdens of frequent attendance at these locations. Travelling the long distances to court involves needless expenditure leading to economic ruin of those few among the poor who seek relief from the courts.

- The judgements are delivered on the basis of what is 'proven' to have happened rather than the actual facts. The convoluted rules and procedures that dominate court proceedings actually thwart justice rather than facilitate it. The system is run by poorly trained and meagerly endowed court officers and judges. The true account of what actually happened has little effect on the court. The burden of proof falls most often on the victim. In cases where the victim is helpless and poor and cannot hire smart, expensive lawyers, the person can lose the case even while being in the right. Crooks can often get away with fraud and even murder if they have lawyers smart enough to know how to find the multitude of technical loopholes in the law. The facts of the case come to matter far less than the minute procedural errors that astute lawyers know how to avoid. If people are made to argue their case personally they are less likely to be able to argue only on the basis of technicalities rather than substance. If cases are decided locally it will be more difficult for the litigants to lie openly and blatantly.

- Even in those rare cases where the courts decide a case correctly in favour of a poor and powerless victim, that person seldom gets the relief provided for in the judgement. The corrupt and lawless behaviour of the police makes them totally unfit as an instrument for enforcing these judgements. We need to focus our attention on evolving a functioning enforcement machinery for court judgements.

- There are no effective laws to ensure that the government apparatus, the judges, the police and the bureaucrats behave lawfully. There are no enforceable provisions for an aggrieved person to get a judge punished in those instances where he gives a blatantly false judgement for a bribe. There are few instances where a police officer is punished for lawless, corrupt behaviour, or for sabotaging the court's verdict. There is no deterrence against those who cause criminal delays in the law courts. Unless we overhaul our administrative machinery and enshrine principles of accountability in it, we will not be able to alter the existing situation whereby judges keep getting their salaries and perks, lawyers keep making lots of money, and innumerable government functionaries—from court peons and clerks to magistrates—keep drawing secure salaries and extracting large bribes while the citizens end up getting more fleeced with every passing decade.

Addendum

A three-judge bench of the Supreme Court finally delivered its judgement in this case on April 17, 1996. One of the judges, K. Ramaswamy, strongly dissented from the combined judgement of Justices M.M. Punchhi and Kuldip Singh, who were of the opinion that, even at the risk of appearing 'conservative for adopting a cautious approach', the court should avoid 'entering the thicket... [since] there would follow a beeline for similar claims in diverse situations' from other communities.

They issued directions to the State of Bihar 'to comprehensively examine the question of the premise of our constitutional ethos and the need voiced to amend the law. ... to examine the question of recommending to the Central government whether the latter would consider it just and necessary to withdraw the exemptions given under the Hindu Succession Act and the Indian Succession Act at this point of time insofar as the applicability of these provisions to the Scheduled Tribes in the State of Bihar is concerned'. Thus placing the onus for change squarely with the Bihar government.

As a signatory to CEDAW and the UN declaration on 'the Right to Development', Justice Ramaswamy held that it was 'imperative for the State to eliminate obstacles, prohibit all gender-based discriminations as mandated by the Articles 14 and 15 of the Constitution of India. By operation of Article 2(f) and other related articles of CEDAW, the State should, by appropriate measures including legislation, modify the law and abolish gender-based discrimination in the existing laws, regulations, customs and practices which constitute discrimination against women'. Accordingly, he held that Scheduled Tribe women should succeed to the estate of their parent, brother, husband, as heirs by intestate succession and enjoy equal rights with men in this and other respects. Following this judgement, male tribal leaders held demonstration protesting against the court's interference in their customary laws. The judgement has, therefore, not made any difference to the situation either legally or at ground level.

V

The Burning of Roop Kanwar

On 4 September 1987, eighteen-year-old Roop Kanwar was burnt to death on her husband's pyre in village Deorala, Sikar district, Rajasthan. In one sense, there is not much difference between the death of Roop Kanwar and the deaths of thousands of women burnt alive in their own homes in may parts of the country. But her death was significantly different in its social and cultural resonance.

Wife-burning, like many other acts of violence, occurs with the tacit consent of society, but it incurs public disapproval. Therefore, it is perpetrated secretively, behind locked doors. The woman's husband and in-laws invariably claim that her death was a regrettable suicide or accident, and that they made every attempt to save her.

Modern day sati, on the other hand, though rare, is a public spectacle, conducted with the approval and applause of the local community. It is this aspect that is particularly alarming. If the widespread implicit acceptance of wife-murder in our society today expresses the low value set on women's lives, the public burning to death of a woman is an open endorsement of that devaluation.

When parents advise their daughters to endure maltreatment by a husband and in-laws, and to 'adjust' at all costs in the marital home, they too are endorsing the norm that a woman's life is worthless except as an object of use or abuse by her husband. In this context, the reaction of Roop Kanwar's natal family to her death is not very surprising. When we met her brother in Jaipur, he said that though their family was mourning her death, they had no complaints regarding the manner of her death. Although Roop Kanwar was burnt in the presence of thousands of people from around Deorala, her family, who live in Jaipur, a mere two-hours drive away, were not informed

*First published in *Manushi*, No. 42–43, Sept–Dec 1987, co-authored with Ruth Vanita.

that she was about to become a sati. Yet, they condoned her being burnt alive and say she has brought honour to them.

In most ordinary wife-murder cases, the husband and in-laws of the woman try to defame her after her death, as an unstable woman with suicidal tendencies or a bad character. But Roop Kanwar's past is being recreated to mythologize her as an embodiment of the best womanly and wifely virtues. In a culture where a woman is considered a burden, easily dispensable and replaceable, it is a rare woman who is honoured in her death. No wonder, then, that so many women are awe-inspired by the new sati cult. Roop Kanwar's glorification may even appear some sort of acknowledgement, however bizarre, of the many unrewarded sacrifices women make in everyday life for the husband and family.

The Roop Kanwar case has sharply polarized public opinion. Those who are glorifying her death are trying to project it as part of a 'glorious tradition' of Rajput and Hindu culture. Unfortunately, those opposed to it have inadvertently strengthened this myth by their inaccurate descriptions of the phenomenon and the forces behind it.

Most reformers have attributed the Deorala episode to the 'ignorance and illiteracy' of the rural masses that they describe as prone to 'blind superstitiousness and excessive religiosity'. The phenomenon is seen as an indication of 'how backwardness and primitiveness has been preserved in India's villages.'

This kind of characterization of the Deorala episode assumes that it is a tradition of the masses to which the modern and the educated, supposedly stand opposed. But the fact of the matter is that Deorala is not a neglected village, nor are its inhabitants, illiterate rustics. Nor are leaders of the pro-sati campaign mainly rural-based people. They are in large part urban-based politicians, who are not excessively religious but excessively greedy for power of a very 'modern' kind.

Thus, what was essentially a women's rights issue has been distorted into an issue of 'tradition' versus 'modernity', a struggle of the religious majority against an irreligious minority.

The People of Deorala

In failing to recognize that the Roop Kanwar's sati is a thoroughly 'modern' phenomenon in its political, economic and social moorings, the reformers have played into the hands of the pro-sati camp. The Roop Kanwar case has as little to do with tradition, as Ramanand Sagar's Sita has to do with Valmiki's Sita.

In an attempt to understand the context of Roop Kanwar's death and the forces behind its subsequent glorification, we visited Deorala and Jaipur in the last week of October, 1987.

Deorala is about two hours drive from Jaipur, the capital of Rajasthan, and about five hours drive from Delhi, by another route. It is an advanced prosperous village by Rajasthani and even by all-India standards. Its initial prosperity may have been based on agriculture because this part of the state is well-irrigated by private tubewells.

But, today, its prosperity is entrenched in its intimate connections with employment in the urban sector. Almost every family in Deorala has one or more male members who has a job in nearby towns. Most of these men are in government employment. A large majority of them are in the police or the army.

Deorala has many schools, a very high literacy rate (about 70 per cent) and has produced many matriculates and graduates. Roop Kanwar was a city-educated girl, her husband a science graduate, her father-in-law a school teacher and her brothers well-educated men, running a prosperous transport business in Jaipur.

The village has a population of about 10,000; the dominant castes being Rajputs and Brahmins. Almost all the houses are brick and cement structures. There is a market where a wide variety of consumer goods are available; the village has electricity and tap water. Many people own TV sets, cycles and motorcycles.

We saw hardly any visibly poverty-stricken people. The villagers looked well-fed. Most of the young people were dressed in fashionably tailored outfits of mill-made cloth. The men all wore western dress—trousers and shirts. The young women wore Punjabi or Rajasthani dress, tailored in an urban style, clearly influenced by Hindi films.

The Sati Sthal

The Sati Sthal (the sati site) is situated at one end of the village, in an open ground. It is a temporary structure, a platform topped by a pavilion. When we reached there, four schoolboys, who appeared as aged between seven and fifteen years old, were walking round and round it, with sticks in their hands, chanting slogans. They wore shirts and shorts with outsize turbans perched incongruously on their heads.

Nearby, a group of young men were selling coconuts and other offerings, and distributing *prasad*. At a little distance, another group of young men were selling reprints of the now famous photo-collage showing a beatific Roop Kanwar on the pyre with her husband's head in her lap.

Clusters of women sat around talking, among them a number of schoolgirls. They were very different from the filmy stereotype of the village woman, as a shy secluded belle. They assumed that we were journalists and kept staring at us with overt hostility for about 45 minutes. Since we refrained from asking any journalistic questions or taking photos, they finally called us and began cross-examining us with great confidence. Their hostility melted into the warmth and hospitality characteristic of an Indian village only after they were somewhat assured that we were not seeking to extract any statements from them. None of the women were veiled and they talked, joked, teased and laughed unabashedly in the presence of men.

Religion or Politics?

Most of the slogans being shouted at the Sati Sthal were clearly modelled on electoral slogans and had not the remotest connection to any kind of religious chant. One boy would shout the first line and the others would then shout the second line, in the manner that slogans are raised at political rallies:

> Sati ho to kaisi ho?
> Roop Kanwar ke jaisi ho.
> Model: Desh ka neta kaisa ho
> Rajiv Gandhi (X, Y, Z) jaisa ho.

> Jab tak suraj chand rahega
> Roop Kanwar tera naam rahega.
> Model: Jab tak suraj chand rahega
> Indira tera naam rahega.

Others were victory chants of an inappropriate, even meaningless kind:

> Ek do teen char
> Sati Mata ki jai jaikar
> Sati Mata ki jai
> Deorala Gaon ki jai
> Sati ke pati ki jai.

A couple of slogans had a pretence of religiosity but were linked to a generalized term denoting god, not to any specific cult associated with sati:

Hari Om nam karega par
Sati Mata ki jai jaikar.

The most interesting slogan, clearly an offshoot of cow protection slogans popularized by political organizations like the Vishwa Hindu Parishad, was:

Desh dharam ka nata hai
Sati hamari mata hai.

The entire exercise had the flavour of a political rally, a show of strength *vis-à-vis* a political adversary rather than devotion to a deity.

We also attended the daily evening worship. The ground was floodlit. The schoolboys were replaced by young men with naked swords in hand. The *arti* sung was *Om Jai Jagdish Hare*, an *arti* of recent origin in modern Hindi which has been popularized by Bombay cinema to the extent that it has now assumed the status of a sort of national *arti*, sung indiscriminately on all occasions. It has nothing at all to do with sati, and certainly is not of Rajput or Rajasthani origin.

A majority of those gathered at the worship were young men and women, most of them educated. That the *arti* was a recent imposition on village culture was evident from the fact that most of those who sang it had no notion of the tune and only a few of them knew the words, with the result that the rendering was ragged and unintelligible. The *arti* was performed by educated youths whose idea of religious ritual seemed more influenced by Hindi films than by any local religious tradition.

The fascination with the sati cult has been attributed to the superstitious ignorance of illiterate village women, but it is noteworthy that the entire cult being created at Deorala is in the hands of educated men. Women participate by standing at a respectable distance, and joining in the singing.

Urban-based Campaign

The pro-sati campaign is not an indigenous product of Deorala. It is based in Jaipur. Its leaders are urban, educated men in their twenties and thirties. These men have landed property and family connections in rural areas so their influence extends over both urban and rural areas. Some of them have government jobs, others have political power. The two networks are closely connected through kinship ties and with contacts in New Delhi also.

Thus, they constitute a powerful regional elite. They project themselves as representatives of rural India. In fact, they have no more claim to such a position than most urban dwellers, including many anti-sati campaigners, who have an ancestral village that they visit from time to time.

The secretary of the newly-founded Dharm Raksha Samiti (original name Sati Dharm Raksha Samiti, changed after the ordinance was passed forbidding glorification of sati), Mr Narendra Singh Rajawat, is an educated man in his thirties, running a prosperous leather export business. His wife seemed in most ways to go along with the politics of the Samiti, although she has no official post in it. She is in her late twenties, a product of Lady Shri Ram College, one of Delhi's leading elite colleges for women. Even though she admitted being habituated to wearing modern western clothes as also the fashionable salwar kameez, the day she met us she was wearing traditional Rajasthani *ghagra choli*, as though ready to go to a fancy dress party or a ceremonial occasion like a wedding. By contrast, none of the village women we met wore anything as exotic as that.

We met a well-educated, young Rajput man in Deorala, who said he had rushed there from Delhi as soon as he had heard of the sati, and had been camping in Deorala ever since, helping organize the pro-sati campaign. He admitted to having played a prominent part in organizing the pro-sati rally in Jaipur. It was this man and his ilk who kept claiming that miraculous cures had been effected by the Sati Mata's powers.

The lifestyle of this urban-based elite is far removed from any traditional rustic lifestyle. It has little understanding of tradition. This was evident from the phoney ritualism that surrounds the Sati Sthal in Deorala. Several Rajputs from traditional families told us that satis in the past were never worshipped in the fashion that is being institutionalized at Deorala today. There was no tradition of offering *prasad* and singing *artis* to worship a sati. People would silently fold their hands before a Sati Sthal. Families, who had a sati in their ancestry would invoke her blessings but there was no big ceremonial cult around the satis.

Chunri Mahotsav—A Victory Celebration

Another example of how a newfangled cult is being created today is the *chunri mahotsav* held after Roop Kanwar's death, which we saw notified in handbills on the walls at Deorala. The leaders of the Sati

Dharm Raksha Samiti and Roop Kanwar's brother pointed out that the *chunri rasam* is a ceremony performed for any deceased woman and is the counterpart of the *pagri rasam* for men. It is a solemn ritual, held in the days of mourning. They were trying to say that ordinary ceremonies like this one should not have been objected to even by opponents of sati. But they could not explain why the ceremony had been termed a *chunri mahotsav* when no one would traditionally hold a *mahotsav* (festival) after a death, or why the ceremony became a militant celebration, a show of strength.

The pro-sati rally in Jaipur was another example of departure from tradition. It totally lacked the solemnity that would befit a procession connected with a death. The bulk of the demonstrators were young, educated men. Contingents of Rajput young men had come from many cities all over India. They shouted slogans in a militant fashion, posturing and dancing as if part of a victory celebration. In contrast, the anti-sati rally by women in Jaipur was an absolutely silent procession.

The sati cult in its present day form is primarily the product of a phoney religiosity that is the accompaniment of newfound prosperity, harnessed by political leaders for their own vested interests. This religio-political combine is being imported into villages from cities. It is not really a traditional residue from the rural backwaters of the country.

It is commonly found in many parts of the world, that as groups become more prosperous, they become more institutionally and ostentatiously religious and begin to spend money on building temples and promoting rituals. It is no coincidence that the largest number of new temples are springing up in cities, built by big businessmen. The dozen or so big sati temples in urban and semi-urban areas that have become centres of a cult have been built in the last decade by the rich Marwari businessmen and not the Rajput community.

Hindu Custom?

Proponents and opponents of sati have embarked on an examination of ancient texts to establish whether or not these texts 'sanction' sati. This search for a sanction or prohibition of various practices is an empty exercise that nineteenth century British administrators began and that Indian social reformers picked up.

The British assumed that every religion like Christianity, would have one book which all believers would accept as the 'gospel truth', and began a search for such a book for Hinduism. The search is a futile one because Hinduism is not a closed body of doctrines nor does it treat any text or set of texts as the final truth.

In different times and places, different Hindu communities follow widely different social and religious practices. Many of these practices are not mentioned in any text, but are nonetheless rigorously followed. Many practices sanctioned in texts are never practised and would be viewed with horrow if proposed—for example, the practice of *niyoga* whereby unmarried persons may, at prescribed times, cohabit for the purpose of bearing children and satisfying their desires.

No society has one, single-track tradition. A whole range of ideas and beliefs, many of them contradictory, coexist and are handed down by each generation. In the process, they are continually transformed. Particular sections of community leadership pick up and glorify different traditions at different times. Therefore, we must enquire what forces are at work at a particular time and place to create an aura of legitimacy around an event, and why they choose to do so?

In Rajasthan, women who became satis were not the only ones traditionally glorified and revered by Rajputs or by Rajasthanis in general. Mirabai too was a Rajput woman (born *circa* AD 1512) who has been deeply revered over the centuries and whose songs continue to be sung today with love and devotion by Rajput and other Rajasthani women and men. She did not spend her life serving her husband, let alone giving up her life for him. Her songs openly proclaim her determination to undertake a spiritual quest, resisting the opposition of her husband and in-laws. In one song, she addresses her husband thus:

> Ranaji, you cannot stop me now
> I love to be among the wise
> I throw off the veil of modesty...
> Take your necklaces and jewels
> I tear and fling your finery...
> Mira wanders, a mad woman,
> Her hair flies free.
> (*Ranaji, Ab no rahoongi tori hatki*)

She lived a highly unconventional life, breaking out of seclusion, travelling widely with a following of women, and singing and dancing in temples. In many songs, she stressed her defiance of social opinion:

Mira dances with bells on her feet...
'Mira is mad' people say
'Destroyer of family' kindred call me
Mira dances with bells on her feet...
(*Pag ghungroo bandh...*)

In one song she even states:

I will sing of Girdhar
I will not be a Sati
(*Girdhar gasya, Sati na hosya*)

Mira continues to have a powerful grip over people's imagination in Rajasthan. One evidence of this is that over the centuries, more and more songs have been added to the body of her work, and scholars have difficulty sifting them. Women add to and change the songs as they sing them. Her songs are in Rajasthani, the people's own language, unlike the songs being sung in worship of Roop Kanwar today.

The urge towards self-definition and freedom that Mira represents is more integrally a part of Rajasthani traditions relating to women than is the cult being created around Roop Kanwar today. That the new self-proclaimed leaders should choose a Roop Kanwar rather than a Mira as a symbol of Rajasthani womanhood indicates what they believe of woman's place, but it is not evidence that a major section of Rajasthani women have chosen that ideal for themselves.

Many politicians used the Deorala episode as a pretext to attempt to unite the internally divided Rajput community and capture it as a vote-bank. Many other leaders of Hindu revivalist organizations are trying to use the issue as a symbol of Hindu unity.

The call to boycott Diwali celebrations if government did not release those arrested at Deorala was first issued to Rajputs, but later extended to 'all Hindus'. At the rally organized by the Dharm Raksha Samiti in Jaipur, the call to save religion was issued in nasty, communal terms. What this portends can be gauged from the fact that burning a woman to death has become the symbol of this unity.

A number of saffron robed religious figures were collected, and sat on the platform at the pro-sati rally. However, they were not the organizers of the campaign. The campaign was not led by religious leaders, but by politicians under the facade of newly floated organizations like the Dharm Raksha Samiti.

These politicians pretend to be ordinary non-political religious Rajputs. For instance, we met Rajendra Singh Rathore, an ex-Yuva Janata student leader. Asked about his affiliations, he said, 'Here, I am just a member of the Dharm Raksha Samiti. I am not a political person.' But, a little later, he gloatingly remarked that V.P. Singh had lost Rajput hearts and votes by issuing a statement against the Deorala sati. It was clear that he was enjoying his new found power as a Rajput leader able to mobilize the votes of sections of his community.

Fortunately, the diversity of Hindu society still lends it strength and sanity. The sati symbol is not likely to carry much weight beyond certain parts of the Hindi belt. In fact, the symbol has further divided Hindu opinion. For example, the Shankaracharya of Puri's pro-sati pronouncements have not convinced even Hindus in south India, let alone in Bengal or Gujarat, the North-East or the Arya Samaji, Radhaswami and other Hindu sects in the north.

It is important to remember that many Rajputs are also totally opposed to sati. Several Rajput women and men were active in the protests against Roop Kanwar's death. A Rajput man was one of the advocates involved in filing petitions against the proponents of sati. Those who took a public stand had to face considerable hostility. Rani Chuhrawat, a well-known public figure, expressed her opposition to sati on public platforms. She was *gheraoed* and abused and is being defamed by many pro-sati elements in an attempt to silence her.

She pointed out that sati cannot be equated with the right to suicide because even where the right to suicide exists in law, suicide is not a socially encouraged act. One's family members would try their best to dissuade one from committing suicide and would certainly not help in any way. If one still wanted to commit suicide, one would do it privately, in solitude, not as a public spectacle. Even technically, sati is not suicide since someone else lights the pyre, not the woman herself.

Second, and most important, she asked how many women have the right to decide anything voluntarily?

If a woman does not have the right to decide whether she wants to marry, and when, and whom, how far she wants to take a particular job or not—how is it that she suddenly gets the right to take such a major decision as to whether she wants to die? Why is it that her family meekly acquiesces in her decision, when in the normal course, they would not scruple to overrule decisions she made of which they did not approve? Given women's general powerlessness, lack of control over their own lives, and definition of their status by their relationship to men (as daughters, wives, widows, mothers), can any decision of theirs, particularly such a momentous decision, really be called voluntary and self-chosen?

Women's groups in Rajasthan made an effort to work as a concerted lobby. They conducted a public debate on the issue, and mobilized women from different strata of society to protest the Deorala incident. A large rally was held in Jaipur. Many organizations from outside Rajasthan supported these efforts in various ways. These were positive developments.

State Action

However, it is unfortunate that opposition to sati took mainly the form of seeking government intervention. Our government, by its skilful use of progressive rhetoric, has convinced reformers that even though it has a consistent track record of being both dishonest and ineffective, it is ultimately on the side of progress. Reformers seem to accept the government's own evaluation of itself rather than going by its abysmally poor record.

In fact, our government machinery, far from being progressive, is not even neutral. It is controlled by politicians, for whom considerations of power and profit are far more important than human rights. The machinery is not only corrupt but often outright murderous. Witness the Indian police record of atrocities, ranging from the Arwal massacre, to innumerable rapes in custody, to the recent PAC killings in cold blood of arrested Muslims in Meerut.

In Deorala, too, the police is living up to its own traditions. The village has become a police camp. The police is actively obstructing journalists and anti-sati campaigners from investigating the case.

It is likely that the actual facts of the case—whether it was murder or suicide—would have come out, were it not for the heavy police presence in the village. Under the Ordinance, any one who admits to having witnessed the sati is liable to prosecution. Most villagers are afraid to say anything for fear of being implicated by the police. Those who are determinedly pro-sati are camping at the Sati Sthal under police protection.

Any attempts to challenge the cult are prevented by the police. The march by anti-sati Hindu religious leaders, led by Swami Agnivesh, from Delhi to Deorala, was prevented from entering Deorala, and the marchers arrested. Women activists of Jaipur also say they are not allowed to enter the village in groups. The facts of the case are being suppressed and the cult built up under police protection.

About two kilometers from the village, a police picket stopped us, saying no journalist was allowed further. In Deorala, most of the policemen were in plainclothes. They mingled with the local people in a very friendly manner. It was hard to know who was a villager and who a policeman. When we tried to take photos, some men aggressively forbade us. We thought they were villagers but they turned out to be plainclothes policemen. We were told there were 'orders' forbidding photography at the site but no one could explain why.

The ostensible reason for the police being there was to implement the Ordinance forbidding glorification of sati. But they were making no attempt at all to do so. They were quite as involved in the worship as other villagers. One policemen reminded us to take off our shoes when approaching the Sati Sthal, and another cheerfully advised us to attend the *arti* at 7 p.m. We saw many jeeps and matadors (vans) full of worshippers from other areas coming to the village. Not one was stopped by the police.

Yet, the villagers claim the police victimized them. They claim that press publicity has led to police repression and that indiscriminate arrests have been made. Scores of persons had been arrested from Deorala, most of whom have been released in subsequent months. The villagers we met claimed most of those arrested were innocent bystanders.

The people of Deorala, whom we met, young and old alike, were highly suspicious and hostile towards the press and anyone who looked like a journalist. The police seemed to share this hostility. Whenever we began talking to any one villager, many others would immediately gather around and suspiciously demand: 'What are they asking? What are you telling them?' So effective was this mutual policing of each other by the villagers that we ended up answering more questions than they did.

This mutual policing within the community, hostility to outsiders, particularly journalists, and the mingling of the police with the people they are accused of repressing, was highly reminiscent of the situation we encountered in those parts of Meerut, which had witnessed mass burnings and the death of Muslims during the recent riots.

Role of Government

The government and the police failed to prevent Roop Kanwar's death in an area that is teeming with government servants and police personnel. There was no way local government and police personnel could have been unaware of what was about to occur. There was a two-hour gap between the announcement that Roop was to become a sati and the actual immolation. People gathered from surrounding areas to witness it, and it took place in broad daylight.

No special anti-sati law was needed to prevent Roop Kanwar's death. The existing law was perfectly adequate. Both murder and suicide are illegal, punishable offences under the Indian Penal Code. The police is duty-bound to prevent their commission. A policeman who knows that a murder or suicide is about to occur, and neglects to intervene, also commits a serious offence.

Where a whole community chose to collude in a woman's being murdered or pressured to submit to immolation, the local government and police, which are not after all a separate species but a part of the same society, also colluded in the crime. The upper levels of government, at the State and Central levels, reacted with delaying and evasive tactics, succumbing to different pressure groups, and did not investigate the crucial question of why the local police had not intervened. Instead, that same local police was posted in the village to create an intimidating atmosphere to prevent proper investigation. It remains to be seen whether Roop Kanwar's in-laws' prosecution actually proceeds effectively.

It was the lack of will on the government's part, not the lack of a law, that resulted in its failure to intervene. Yet, the anti-sati campaigners assumed that a stringent law was all that was needed to solve the problem. If sati is just a cover used to get away with hounding a woman to death why is a special law needed to deal with such incidents? Does this not amount to conceding to the view that sati constitutes a special category distinct from murder or suicide?

Our government has perfected the art of passing draconian laws which it then uses not to solve problems but to acquire additional arbitrary powers and then uses these powers to intimidate the citizenry even further. For example, the Anti Terrorist Act has not resulted in an end to terrorism but is used as a new weapon by policemen to threaten ordinary people and petty offenders and extract even larger bribes.

The anti-sati Ordinance passed by the Rajasthan government, with its vague definition of 'abetment of sati' as including presence at the site as a participant, has ample scope for misuse. The police can easily pick up any person from the area whom they wish to harass. It is alleged that they have already arrested several innocent people from Deorala. A person has to prove that he or she was not present at the site since the Ordinance, in violation of the principle that a person is innocent until proven guilty, lays the burden of proof on the accused.

The Ordinance also prescribes the death sentence for abetment of sati. At a time when most countries are considering abolition of the death sentence, as it has proven futile as a way of reducing the murder rate, that we should be introducing it for more offences is a singular irony. The Ordinance also has a ridiculous provision for punishing the victim. A woman who attempts sati is to be imprisoned for one to five years and fined Rs 5,000 to Rs 20,000. Central legislation along the same lines is now being drafted.

What Went Wrong?

Somewhere along the way, the anti-sati campaign became somewhat counter-productive. The campaigners became characterized as a handful of anti-Hindu, anti-Rajput, anti-religion, pro-government, anti-masses, urban, educated, westernized people, and the pro-sati lobby as those sensitive to the sentiments of the rural, traditional poor. This completely false polarization occurred because:

1. The reformers wrongly characterized the Deorala episode as the product of illiteracy and backwardness among the rural poor, whereas it was the product of a modernized, developed, prosperous combine of local people.
2. The reformers saw the Deorala episode as the product of an old tradition, whereas in its present form it is a newly-created cult, organized primarily by political, not by religious leaders.
3. The reformers entered into a debate on the religiosity or otherwise of the Deorala Sati. It is important that we demystify it and see it as a case of a woman being hounded to death under a specious religious cover, and of her death being made a symbol by certain power-groups to demonstrate their clout.
4. The main thrust of the anti-sati campaign took the form of petitions to government authorities asking for more stringent laws. This gave government the opportunity to pose as progressive by introducing a repressive law, and let the government off the hook for its complicity in Roop Kanwar's death.
5. The reformers asked that the police be used as an agent of social reform, forgetting that the police is incapable of performing this role. The police acquired more powers which it used to aid and abet pro-sati forces and to prevent the reformers and the press

from purveying information about the case. In addition, it made a lot of money on the side.

What Might Help

We have to consider what course of action could create a state of affairs wherein people could not be able to justify and escape retribution for burning a woman to death in public. To prevent any more such incidents from occurring must be our main concern. Any course of action that has the negative, unintended consequence of heightening the aura around the Deorala episode and of arming with more arbitrary powers those who colluded in Roop Kanwar's death— namely, the local government and police—should be avoided.

When we consider the question of what is to be done, we have to bear in mind that not everyone in every part of the country can be equally effective in acting on every issue. Where we are placed inevitably affects our sphere of influence and effective activity.

Alternative courses of action that are being pursued, but unfortunately, with much less vigour than the course of demanding more legislation and more police, are:

1. Indicting the local police for not having intervened to save Roop Kanwar. All the local police officers who failed to stop the burning should be treated as abettors of Roop Kanwar's murder, immediately suspended, and tried under the Indian Penal Code. This is one way to ensure that other policemen know what the consequences will be of condoning any other such deaths.

2. Monitoring the case against Roop Kanwar's in-laws to see that all the facts are uncovered, that it is not quietly dropped for 'lack of evidence' as too many wife-murder cases routinely are; following it up consistently to see that the accused are exposed, prosecuted and convicted.

3. Instead of relying on ordinances, stay orders and the police to prevent glorification of the Deorala episode and the construction of a temple, it would be better if local human rights and women's organizations mobilized all concerned persons to offer indefinite *satyagraha* at Deorala to facilitate dialogue and debate with those involved in the sati cult. Outside activists might be permitted to join in on a relay basis. This could have been done better if Deorala had not been converted into a police camp. But it should still be possible, though it will now involve fighting the government for

the citizens' right to protest the murder and its subsequent glorification.

4. Some laudable attempts have been made to engage the wider public in a debate that goes beyond the newspaper pages. One such attempt was a *yatra* from Delhi to Deorala, led by Arya Samaj *sanyasis*. This is an important symbolic statement that anti-women forces do not have a monopoly on defining Hindu traditions and do not represent all Hindus.

The Women's Development Programme and other social work organizations in Ajmer district, Rajasthan, have organized a *padyatra* through villages, with plays and songs that raise questions of concern to people including the drought, women's issues, and sati.

More such efforts could mobilize a broader social consensus in Rajasthan against maltreatment of women, and provide an atmosphere conducive to expression of dissent from amongst local communities themselves.

That a woman could be burnt to death in public is a stark indication of women's vulnerability in our social system. Roop Kanwar's death was only one expression of the general devaluation of women's lives. Unless the consensus within our society changes in favour of a more dignified and self-sustaining life for women, any number of repressive laws and policemen are not likely to preserve women's lives.

Update on Roop Kanwar, 1998

After a great deal of pressure and agitation by women's organizations and human rights groups all over the country, the government of Rajasthan filed a case in the court of Additional District Judge, Neem Ka Thana. The case dragged on for years at the level of the lower court. In the meantime, all the witnesses had turned hostile, further weakening the case. Finally on 11 October 1996, a judgement was delivered acquitting all the accused.

There were a number of protest demonstrations in Rajasthan against this judgement, including a siege of the secretariat. All this to pressure the Rajasthan government to file an appeal in the High Court—something it should have done on its own initiative. The case has not even been listed for hearing since then.

It is noteworthy that the anti-sati Ordinance passed in response to Roop Kanwar's sati, cannot be appealed to in this case (except for preventing glorification of sati) since the law came into effect after her death.

VI

Co-ownership Rights for Wives
A Solution Worse than the Problem

An important reason for the limited appeal of the women's movement in India among women themselves is its narrow focus on the rights of women as wives, with little appreciation of their rights as daughters, or as sisters, mothers or grandmothers. This is partly due to the fact that most women's organizations are flooded with complaints of harassed wives and have thus come to focus on women's problems in their role as daughters-in-law or wives.

A new offshoot of this narrow concern is the demand that the existing property laws of all communities be amended to create joint matrimonial property. In deference to pressure from women's rights activists, the Maharashtra government has declared a New Policy for Women which provides that as soon as a marriage is solemnized, the wife becomes a joint owner of the properties and assets earned by the husband. Efforts are being made to pass all-India legislation along the same lines. The assumption is that a wife should be treated as a co-owner in her husband's property from the time of marriage and be able to claim half of the joint matrimonial property in case of divorce.

Inappropriate for India

This proposal is beset with several difficulties. To begin with, the proponents of women's rights tend to forget that at least 70 per cent of our population lives in villages and a large majority of these people belong to peasant families. Very few of these families are nuclear. In the vast majority of instances, land and other property are jointly owned and get partitioned among the sons, usually after the death of the father. How do we make the wife a co-owner in her husband's property and earnings when the husband in most cases does not have

*First published in *Manushi*, No. 84, Sept–Oct 1994.

a separate property or income at the time of his marriage, and often for years afterwards?

In most peasant families, income is jointly shared. Even if one or more sons are earning a wage through urban employment, they contribute much of their earnings to the common family kitty. In most cases, elder brothers take responsibility for the education and even marriages of the younger brothers and sisters—often even of their nephews and nieces. Thus, there are many more claimants to a man's earnings in the Indian family set-up than in the West. Are we giving the wife the right to negate the claims of other members of the family, claims that include old parents and younger siblings?

The move to make wives co-owners in the husband's property is out of tune with social reality in many other important respects as well, especially when combined with, another important plank of the women's movement, that is abolition of dowry. Women's organizations continue harping on the need to put an end to the dowry system without ensuring that in lieu of dowry, daughters get equal inheritance rights with sons. Dowry has been seen only in terms of a financial burden on the bride's parents, overlooking the fact that dowry exists only among those communities where families are not willing to treat daughters as co-inheritors with sons.

One Way Sharing?

The absurdity of trying to abolish dowry without ensuring inalienable inheritance rights for women is sought to be further extended by proposing new laws which make it possible for a woman to be an equal share-holder is her husband's property from the moment she gets married—with the implicit right to demand partition in case of divorce. Are we willing to allow husbands to be co-owners in the wife's inheritance? If the idea is joint matrimonial property, this follows logically. Or is it to be only a one-way sharing?

The idea of joint matrimonial property would make sense only if women brought their share of inheritance from their parental home at the time of marriage, merging their own property into that of their husbands'. The couple could then become co-owners of their genuinely 'joint' property. Though there is mention in the Maharashtra Policy that the Hindu Succession Act be amended to give women coparcenary rights in their natal property, there is no mention whether a woman's husband will also acquire a joint right in her property. Most important of all, merely amending the Act will not ensure that the daughters actually claim and get their share.

Andhra Pradesh has already given coparcenary rights to women but reports show that daughters continue to be deprived of their due share through the instrument of the will. It is a common practice in India to make a daughter sign away her rights in favour of her brothers even before she gets married. Thus to combat the culture of disinheritance we would need a law which prevents women from signing away their rights in their parental property in favour of their brothers.

It is absurd to expect that a woman's husband will willingly make her an equal co-sharer from the day they get married, while her own father and brothers are allowed to disinherit her. The culture of keeping women economically dependent can be fought only if we start at the root of it all—namely, the woman's natal family. If a woman enters her husband's house, as an economic dependent, she is bound to be more vulnerable, as well as desperate to push other claimants out of her way.

The concept of joint matrimonial property being currently proposed by feminists in India has been unthinkingly borrowed from some western countries without taking into consideration the radically different economic and social organization of Indian families. Even in the US, a wife can usually claim a share only from that portion of property or income which is earned after her marriage to that particular man. Moreover, men can also claim maintenance, as well as inheritance from wives. Our social reform advocates are making no such distinction between self-earned and inherited property—the assumption being that a wife has a right to even what was earned and inherited before the two got married.

As it is, women are viewed as economic liabilities to be passed on from parents to husbands. With this change in the law they will also be viewed as grabbers out to snatch a man's wealth from him. This will only strengthen the image of women as an economic drain and the entry of a daughter-in-law would be even more dreaded than the birth of a daughter.

Wives Versus Others

An important reason for the ferocity of battles waged by women with their sisters-in-law and mothers-in-law is that they usually come into their marital homes after being disinherited from their parental inheritance, and are taught to believe that they are to find economic security through a stake in their husband's property. Consequently, the desire to push the other dependents—husband's younger brothers and sisters and aged parents, out of the way.

The flip side of the coin is that many women continue to prefer maltreatment in their husband's homes rather than return to their parental home, because of the hostility and humiliation they face at the hands of their brothers' wives, who want their husband's sisters out of the way. Most women would rather be dead than come and live with their natal family, even when in need, because they fear the taunts and maltreatment at the hands of *bhabhis* (brothers' wives).

This ugly tussle between women is primarily due to their fragile rights in their natal homes. For a daughter, a *bhabhi* represents a threat, for she affects her already fragile rights in her own parents' house. Similarly, mothers-in-law fear a daughter-in-law's entry into the house lest they be either pushed out or left uncared for. Attempts to strengthen the rights of women as wives at the cost of their rights as daughters, sisters, and mothers-in-law is bound to be counterproductive and lead to still more murderous power tussles between women in the family.

It is a mistake to think that women face maltreatment only as wives and daughters-in-law. Maltreatment of women as mothers-in-law is no less frequent. In cases, where a wife manages to get the upper hand, one often finds old mothers made to live a life of humiliation and callous neglect. But it has not yet become acceptable to consider the full significance of such instances.

The maltreatment tends to be more severe in cases where the old parents have handed over their property to their sons in their own life-time or are too poor to leave an inheritance, and therefore, get treated as liabilities. One comes across numerous cases where a widowed mother-in-law was left uncared for when grievously ill, or not allowed even a small amount of pocket money and treated as an unpaid domestic servant and *ayah* rolled into one.

Even in cases where the family property has not been formally passed on to sons, given our cultural conditioning, sons are usually secure in the knowledge that they will not be disinherited no matter how badly they behave. Thus, it is not uncommon for even propertied parents to be neglected or maltreated by their daughters-in-law when the latter are able to win over their husbands on their side.

The problems of widowed mothers are also due to the absence of secure formal and legal property rights for them. In cases where the sons take over control of the father's property, widowed mothers become as vulnerable to abuse as a powerless daughter-in-law. An important reason why such instances do not get to be highlighted is that in most cases mothers cannot bring themselves to lodge police complaints or seek newspaper publicity against their daughters-in-law because of their attachment and loyalty to their sons. Wives do not have a similar sense of loyalty, especially as new brides. For all the stereotyping of Indian women as silent-suffering Sitas, maltreated wives today, are more likely to seek outside help than mothers or even sisters. Our law courts testify to this. Hardly any mothers or sisters take their sons or brothers to court for maltreating them or denying them their share of property. But wives have relatively fewer inhibitions fighting court cases against their estranged husbands. Even among those of my friends who are very assertive of their rights as women, I find that hardly any of them have fought with their fathers or brothers when they were disinherited from parental property. But virtually none of them would be similarly willing to surrender their rights in their husband's property.

Misuse of Section 498A

One is beginning to hear complaints that Section 498A, which pro-vides for a jail term for 'cruelty' to a wife or daughter-in-law is being misused by wives and their parents. This should not come as a surprise. Our police has perfected the art of using legal provisions for personal enrichment. The stricter the law, the higher the bribe rate of the police, who do not hesitate to use any and every law in favour of anyone willing to bribe them adequately. While misuse of stringent laws like TADA (Terrorist and Disruptive Activities Act) is being acknowledged, women's organizations are reluctant to acknowledge a similar misuse of Section 498A of the IPC.

I quote from a letter I recently received, from Anil Agarwal of Bombay. This is just one of the several cases I have come across in recent years of misuse of this legal provision. He writes:

… Section 498A has given a ready-made tool in the hands of unscrupulous daughters-in-law to drive out an in-law and usurp their property. The police is too willing to go along with such complaints [provided they are adequately bribed] and lock up anybody named in the complaint to languish in jail, since Section 498A allows for no bail. I know a case where the daughter-in-law and her husband succeeded, with the help of an unscrupulous lawyer and the police, in driving out the mother-in-law (the owner of the house) and her two mentally retarded daughters from the house by lodging a complaint of harassment against them under Section 498A. This lady is now at the mercy of others. When they approached an all-India women's organization, the response they got added insult to injury: 'Kindly ask the old lady to refer her daughters to an institution where the mentally handicapped are looked after. As for the elderly lady, she can also go to a Home for the Aged.'...

Such cruelties are not confined to cases of mentally retarded sisters-in-law. One reason why most parents prefer to marry off daughters before bringing a daughter-in-law into the house is because of their fear of their son disowning all responsibility for his sisters under the influence of his wife.

However, all this is not to deny that under the present system wives deserve a better deal and that only too frequently men abandon their wives without providing for them even while their parents are unwilling to take them back. Our inheritance laws are heavily weighted against daughters and our maintenance laws are hopelessly inadequate to help women thrown out of their home by unscrupulous husbands.

The idea of joint matrimonial property is in fact a product of women's dissatisfaction with the existing maintenance laws. But the idea as it stands is a knee-jerk reaction. Far from solving the problem, it will make for even more conflicts between men and women and within families. It will open a floodgate of litigation because the provision has ample scope for misuse by wives and their families and will make the groom's family as vulnerable as wives are today.

Not at Other's Cost

If we want our family life to be less acrimonious, we have to ensure that the rights of one member do not encroach upon those of the others. The current battles between *saas-bahu* (mothers-in-law and daughters-in-law, as well as between sisters-in-law), *nanad-bhabhi* can be minimized only if every woman has inalienable rights in her parental home and property and therefore she is not treated as *paraya dhan*, a burden to be passed on to another family. It would be far more practical to propose that instead of spending money on dowry which mostly consists of consumer goods, parents give income-generating forms of property to their daughters such as cash deposits, house, land, shop or factory—all in the daughter's own name—and that she retains these as her own even after marriage so that she does not enter her husband's home as a dependent and an economic liability but rather as an economically self sufficient unit. The property may be made joint only if and when the husband and wife both want to pool their economic resources and become a single economic unit.

Practice Before You Preach

Our social reformers have perfected the art of proposing laws which are so impractical that they can only be observed in the breach. To ensure that social reformers do not propose absurd laws, we must make it mandatory that those who propose such far reaching changes in our family laws demonstrate their viability by first implementing the proposed changes in their own family and social circle.

Thus the persons responsible for recommending that women become equal co-owners in the husband's property from the day of marriage should provide undertakings from at least ten of their relatives and an equal number of friends or neighbours that they have already implemented it in their family's inheritance papers. Such a process will ensure that even social reformers become accountable for their acts and that they test out their ideas, on however small a scale, before they are unleashed on the hapless millions of this country by way of new legislation. Only through such a process they will understand the weaknesses and limitations of the reforms they propose.

VII

When Daughters are Unwanted
Sex Determination Tests in India

Technologies like amniocentesis and ultrasound, used in most parts of the world largely for detecting foetal abnormalities, are used in large parts of the Indian subcontinent for determining the sex of the foetus so that the mother can have an abortion if the foetus in the womb happens to be a female. The rapid spread of these tests has resulted in sex-selective abortions of hundreds of thousands of female foetuses.

The magnitude of the problem can be gauged by noting that Dr Sunil Kothari, who runs a major ultrasound and abortion clinic in Delhi, admitted to having performed 60,000 such tests during an interview on the BBC. He declared with total conviction: 'This is the best way of population control for India.' There are thousands of doctors all over the country who are engaged in the same type of medical practice as Kothari—some operating openly and some in a clandestine manner.

India has had a lower proportion of females than of males in the overall population for at least a century. The 1901 census recorded 972 females per 1,000 males in the country's population. By 1991, the sex ratio had come down to 927 females per 1,000 males, indicating a deficit of nearly 30 million females in the total population. Selective abortions of female foetuses following sex determination tests are likely to further accelerate the deficit of females. The full demographic impact of the spread of this technology is likely to show up dramatically in the all-India census in the year 2001.

There are important regional differences in son preferences and devaluation of daughters. As the census figures testify, sex ratios are much lower in the north-western areas of the subcontinent. Traditionally, the south and the extreme North-East have recorded either evenly-balanced sex ratios or sex ratios in favour of females, as in

*First published in *Manushi*, No. 86, Jan–Feb 1995.

states like Kerala and Manipur. In the North-West, sex ratios have been imbalanced against females far more among specific landowning communities (such as Rajputs, Jats, Gujjars) and relatively more balanced among the landless poor, or among the artisanal groups. In Bihar, there is a sharp north-south divide. Among the landowning Hindu peasant communities of north Bihar, the sex ratio is in favour of males. However, in south Bihar, among the predominantly tribal population, the sex ratio is in favour of females.

An alarming aspect of the deficit of females is that, over the last few decades, the prevalence of low sex ratios has spread both horizontally and vertically. The South and the North-East (which earlier recorded sex ratios slightly in favour of females) have now almost entirely shifted to a deficit of females and are slowly moving towards the all-India pattern. Lower status groups, which not too long ago had favourable sex ratios, are beginning to emulate higher status groups in rural areas, and are recording a decline in the proportion of their respective female populations. Thus, the culture of overvaluing male lives at the cost of female lives is not a mere hangover of traditional norms, as is often believed, but is also a widespread contemporary phenomenon.

Sex Selective Abortion

Many women's organizations and other concerned citizen groups have responded to the epidemic of abortions of female foetuses by demanding a ban on Sex Determination Tests (SDTs). The state of Maharashtra was the first to outlaw these tests. It passed the Prenatal Diagnostic (PND) Techniques (Regulation and Prevention of Misuse) Act of 1988 after a government-sponsored study found that in most cases gynaecologists were performing amniocentesis solely to determine the sex of the foetus; only a tiny proportion of all tests were for detection of genetic disorders. Nearly all of the 15,914 abortions, during 1984–5, at a well-known abortion clinic in Bombay, were undertaken after sex determination tests indicated the foetus was female. Such clinics are not confined to big cities. They have sprung up in small towns and villages as well.

Three other states—Punjab, Haryana and Gujarat—also banned these tests because these clinics were indulging in aggressive campaigns to encourage people to abort female foetuses. Hoardings such as 'Pay Rs 500 now and save Rs five lakh later', playing on the anxieties of parents about having daughters, had become a common sight in these states.

The Ineffective Ban

However, the law remained a dead letter and the clinics continued to mushroom and thrive in all these states. The only difference the new law made was that huge hoardings that had earlier read, *Ladka ya ladki jaanch karaiye* (Find out if it's a boy or a girl), were replaced by barely veiled messages such as *Swasth ladka ya ladki?* (Healthy boy or girl?) or *Garbh mein bacchhe ki har prakar ki jankari* (Everything you want to know about the child in your womb).

Doctor-client complicity ensured that the clinics flourished despite the ban. A magazine reported that in a small town like Sirsa in Haryana at least a hundred tests were being performed every day. Doctors in the town declared openly: 'Earlier, we used to give our findings in writing. Now we will simply tell them the sex of their child verbally. Who can stop us from doing that?' Dr M.R. Bansal of Sirsa, who had earlier hit the headlines with his display jars containing female foetuses preserved in formalin, declared that the ban would only result in doctors 'hiking their fees' and as a result 'the poor will suffer'. (*Sunday* 24–30 July 1994, by Minu Jain and Harry Singh).

Before the ban, an amniocentesis test cost anything between Rs 70 to Rs 600. After the new law, amniocentesis could still be had for Rs 1,500 to Rs 2,000 at ordinary clinics, though prestigious clinics charge higher amounts. Another less invasive and safer sex determination test, ultrasound, is now easily available for Rs 800 to Rs 1,500.

Despite this dismal failure of new state laws to curb female foeticide, some women's organizations continued to demand comprehensive all-India legislation and even more stringent provisions to deal with the problem. In August 1994, Parliament enacted another law, also called the Prenatal Diagnostic Techniques (Regulation and Prevention of Misuse) Act, in response to their pressure. This law prohibits any genetic counselling centre, laboratory or clinic from performing any of the PND techniques unless they register under this Act. They must also satisfy one or more of the criteria which the law establishes for determining whether the test is permissible:

— the age of the pregnant woman is above 35 years;
— the pregnant woman has undergone two or more spontaneous abortions or foetal losses;

— during her pregnancy, the pregnant woman had been exposed to substances potentially harmful to the foetus such as certain drugs, radiation, infections, or exposure to certain dangerous chemicals;   ·

— the pregnant woman has a family history of mental retardation or physical deformities.

The doctor who conducts the tests is required to not only explain the possible side effects and risks involved, but also to obtain the pregnant woman's consent in writing.

Attempting to ensure that the results of these tests are not used in deciding to abort a female foetus, the law states that, 'no person conducting PND procedures shall communicate to the pregnant woman concerned or her relatives the sex of the foetus by words, signs or in any other manner'. Likewise, the law bans advertising in any manner whatsoever, the availability of PND procedures as a means of determining the sex of the foetus. Any person violating this law can be sentenced to imprisonment for a term which may stretch to three years, and with fines which may extend to Rs 10,000. A medical practitioner convicted by the court for flouting the law may lose his membership in the State Medical Council for a period of two years for the first offence, and permanently for any subsequent offence.

The Act does not limit penalties to the medical fraternity. It considers the woman's family even more culpable. The normal practice is that a person is believed innocent unless proven guilty. But not by this law. 'The court shall presume unless the contrary is proved that the pregnant woman has been compelled by her husband or the relative to undergo the PND test and such persons shall be liable for abetment of offence' and held punishable. As an indication that the law considers use of the PND test as a grave crime, it stipulates that 'every offence under this Act shall be non-cognizable, non-bailable and non-compoundable'.

The Maharashtra Act had exempted from punishment any pregnant woman who underwent this test. However, the central legislation states that any person who seeks the aid of a genetic lab or clinic for conducting PND tests on any pregnant woman is punishable with imprisonment up to three years, and a fine up to Rs 10,000. Unless the pregnant woman herself can prove that she was compelled to undergo the test, she is no longer exempt from punishment. In case of a second offence, the term of imprisonment can go up to five years and the fine up to Rs 50,000.

With such a draconian law, one would imagine that people would be too frightened to conduct or undergo such tests. This is far from the case. Delhi, the seat of the Central government, has thousands of clinics with facilities for carrying out prenatal sex determination tests. They are no more confined to towns and cities: SDT clinics have mushroomed in many of our villages as well with some doctors moving from village to village in their private cars and matadors.

Several women's organizations have demanded that the law be made even more stringent. They want genetic tests to be permitted only in government hospitals. They have also demanded that all ultrasonography equipment be registered with the government to prevent its misuse.

It is time that we face the fact that the laws that have been enacted to prohibit prenatal sex determination will not work given the dismal political and administrative functioning in our country. The more stringent a law attempting to prohibit consensual behaviour, the greater the likelihood that it will be used primarily for making money by officials. The police know the location and activities of sex determination clinics; they collect regular bribes from the doctors as protection money, just as they do from brothel owners in states where prostitution is banned. Similar issues arise in the selective enforcement of the laws against drug smuggling, or brewing illicit liquor. In fact, the moment any activity is declared illegal, the police develop a vested interest in encouraging people to undertake it—for that brings them enormous amounts of extra income.

In banning sex determination tests (SDTs) we run the risk of further criminalization of the medical profession. The popular demand for these tests will ensure that many doctors will be willing to do the tests in return for higher payments. Part of that money will be used to buy police protection. In addition, if clinics go underground, it will become impossible to monitor clinic functioning and safety, thus exposing women who go for these tests to even greater risks. The emergence of a police-doctor nexus has dangerous implications for the well-being of any society. As it is, large numbers of Indian doctors indulge in unethical practices. This law which can easily and profitably be flouted will further strengthen the hold of such people on the profession.

Moreover, the technology needed for performing these tests is easily available and relatively inexpensive; just about anyone can set up such a lab if he or she so desires. There is no way to police these mushrooming clinics, especially since many doctors have begun to use portable ultrasound machines which they carry in their cars, performing the tests in people's homes. Since ultrasound is a valuable technique for a whole range of other diagnoses of the internal organs, there is no way the use of ultrasound can be banned altogether.

New innovations in this field will make it even easier to choose the sex of children. Recent research indicates that it may soon be possible to prevent the very conception of female children by manipulating male sperm to ensure that a mother desirous of having a son will conceive only a male child. Things are likely to move in this direction in the near future, making any attempt to ban prenatal sex selection even more absurd.

Pro-SDT Arguments

Sadly enough many people feel that sex selective foeticide can serve as an important solution to India's over-population. Most families in India keep producing children until they feel they have the desired number of sons. In the process, often several daughters are born before the desired number of sons arrive. Therefore, it is argued that if families could ensure the birth of a son or two without risking the birth of too many unwanted daughters, it is likely that they would have more of an interest in smaller-sized families.

Many people even argue that as women become scarcer their lives will be more valued. One reason why bodies like the medical associations have failed to take a stand against these tests is that most doctors involved in this business are convinced that they are providing an important social service, that they are doing 'noble work'. Dr Pai, a pioneer in providing cheap and safe SDTs and sex selective abortions in Bombay, speaks on behalf of many in his profession when he says: 'Happy and wanted children is what we desire.... Unwanted babies must be aborted.' A woman doctor, Sudha Limaye, Head of the Obstetric and Gynaecology Department of Bokaro General Hospital in Bihar, is reported to have said, 'Our priority is population control by any means. Amniocentesis should be used as a method of family planning and be made available to everyone at a minimum cost or even free.'

Some studies have revealed that most parents obtain sex determination tests only after the birth of one or two children. For instance, the data so far collected by Ritu Juneja of Delhi University in her doctoral research on pre-natal gender selection shows that the majority of parents come for SDTs only if they already have one or two daughters. In her sample, she found that 40 per cent women came for SDT after the birth of one daughter, 29 per cent after two daughters and the rest after three or more daughters. In her sample, she did not find a single case of a woman using a SDT for her first pregnancy. Her respondents saw SDTs not just as a family planning (keeping families small) measure but also as a way of 'balancing' (having children of both sex) their families. However, the anxiety to 'balance' the family through SDTs is far more pronounced in families who only have girls than in those who only have sons. Juneja came across only one woman who had undergone two sex-selective abortions with a view to having a daughter after two sons. However, Sunil Khanna's study indicates that among a certain community a SDT is resorted to even in the case of a first pregnancy. This is unlikely to be a general pattern (see *Manushi*, No. 86, Jan–Feb. 1995, pp. 23–9).

Many argue: what is wrong with helping people achieve their desired family size? Most of those who are pro-choice and want women to have autonomy tend to support a woman's rights to abort. Why then do some of these very same people object to sex selective abortion, especially if the woman herself is averse to producing more than one or at the most two daughters? If we do not want the government to prevent women from aborting unwanted children, how can we remain consistent and support it when it tries to prevent women from aborting unwanted daughters?

Perpetrators or Victims?

Most of those supporting the laws against SDTs respond by saying that women are being socially coerced into getting rid of daughters; they are not viewed as free agents. Therefore, banning sex selective abortions does not amount to encroaching on a woman's right to decide how many children she should have. However, several studies have revealed that in large parts of the country and in many communities, a mother's aversion to having more than one daughter is no less strong than that of male family members. Investigations have revealed that many women go for these tests on their own initiative; they are not mere victims of coercion, though other forms of constriction of choice may be salient considerations.

A recent MSc thesis by Meenu Sondhi entitled 'The Silent Deaths: A Study of Female Foeticide in Delhi' found that most of the women clients coming to SDT clinics that were included in her study were highly educated and from well-off families. Several of the interviewed women suggested that SDTs must be legalized since this technology is an advance in science and optimum use should be made of it. Some talked about the social pressure to produce a son. Others pointed out the need to 'balance' their families since they already had a daughter. Though the doctors performing the tests and subsequent abortions claimed that they provided this service only to those women who already had two daughters, the researcher found that several of the women who opted for the test already had a son. (Reported in the *Indian Express*, 28 October 1990, by Sharmila Chandra).

All these socio-economic factors, therefore, make it virtually impossible to enforce such a ban in our country where the police is unable to enforce the law impartially and effectively even for those activities that people agree are harmful, such as manufacture of spurious medicines. Few of the parties involved in SDTs and subsequent abortions or their families and neighbours view themselves as doing anything wrong. Abortion is legal in India and is frequently advocated as a family planning measure. Aborting female foetuses to limit family size has a widespread legitimacy. It is socially sanctioned among several communities. A law can work only when at least some people have an interest in enforcing it and see in it some benefit for themselves.

When Women Are Scarce

This brings us to vital questions. Is there any truth in the argument that the killing of unwanted girls will ultimately help make the lives of those daughters that are allowed to live any better? Is greater scarcity of women likely to lead to the surviving women becoming more valued?

From what we know of the existing low sex ratio regions, it appears that the market law assigning a higher value to items scarce in supply does not appear to operate in this realm. Communities with low sex ratios tend to be more misogynistic and those with high sex ratios tend to allow for greater female autonomy and dignity. Compare the lives of Jat and Rajput women with Nair women of Kerala or Meitis of Manipur and the point becomes obvious. Seclusion and purdah, disinheritance of women from property, low female literacy rates, poor health, and low employment rates are all characteristic of low sex ratio regions, as is a greater incidence of domestic violence against women. In contrast, among the high sex ratio regions and communities, women do not live under as many crippling restrictions, have more secure inheritance rights, are rarely forbidden the right to earn independent incomes, and tend to have higher literacy levels and relatively better health. They also tend to have better opportunities for political participation at the local level.

Dread of Daughters

If women's own lives are so negatively affected by discrimination against their daughters, why then are women so wrapped up in the culture of son preference? Aversion to having daughters is a culturally conditioned choice rooted in certain economic and political power relations within the family and community. For instance, a study done in a Punjab village (*Family Life: The Unequal Deal* by Berny Horowitz, and Madhu Kishwar, *In Search of Answers: Indian Women's Voices from Manushi*, eds Kishwar and Vanita, 3rd edn. Manohar, Delhi 1996, pp. 50–79) found that both peasant women and landless agricultural labourers displayed an overwhelming preference for boys and a serious dread of having daughters. Some women wanted no daughters at all. Even those who mentioned that daughters provide valuable support to their mothers, share their problems and give a helping hand in domestic work, still did not want any daughters. Two of the fifteen peasant women interviewed got sterilized after they gave birth to two sons because neither they themselves nor their families wanted a daughter. One of these women said that because she had eight sisters and had suffered so much as a result, she herself never wanted to give birth to a girl. Almost all the women said that girls are unwanted because they are a burden. One of them reported that her own mother had died within days after the birth of her fifth daughter because her husband had become very unhappy at the birth of yet another girl.

Even among the agricultural labourers, nine out of the fourteen interviewed stated a clear preference for male children. Not one of them said that she preferred a girl, but their reaction to the birth of daughters was not as adverse as it was among peasant women. However, most of these women did clearly admit, that from their own point of view, daughters would be good for them, be more emotionally supportive and help them in household work more than the sons.

Why is it that women dread having daughters? Some reasons could be that:

- Their own lives as women and what they saw of their mothers' lives give them an aversion to producing another sufferer like themselves.
- Their own status in the family is downgraded and they become vulnerable to more abuse every time an unwanted daughter is born to them or if they fail to produce a son. A woman often even seems to become incapable of breast-feeding her girl child when she herself has an insecure place in the family. If the birth of a girl child makes her life more miserable, there is reason for her to hate that child, and even to want it dead.
- Most women do not see their daughters having a better life than they themselves have experienced.
- As distinct from the mother's own interest, the family as an economic unit sees these daughters as burdensome on account of dowry and the limited employment opportunities for women.

Thus, we find that women's responses to their children are not just a matter of unconditional nurturing and caring but are also determined in part by their own perceived interests. Motherhood gets expressed in a variety of ways, depending on the woman's own situation in the family.

Since in our culture, men and women are expected to subordinate their individual interests to that of the family, it is to be expected that ultimately women themselves see their own interests as indistinguishable from the family's interests, and consequently become actively involved in favouring male children at the cost of daughters, just as they ignore their own health and nutritional needs but seldom those of their husbands'.

Why Are Women Devalued

However, the culture of self-neglect and self-depreciation is more prevalent among women of certain communities and regions. One can identify some of them by their low sex ratios. Misogynist attitudes are much stronger in the north-western plains of India, for example, because this region has been a frontier area for centuries. It witnessed constant warfare, facing outside invaders, as well as fighting among the diverse groups inhabiting this area. The people of this area came to pride themselves on their martial traditions. They adopted more stringent forms of female seclusion and *purdah* that went far beyond those practised in other parts of India.

In this region, ownership of land was the hallmark of higher status and there was a constant drive toward acquiring more and more land. Since maintaining possession of land was so precarious, the importance of males was enhanced considerably in comparison to areas which did not experience so much turbulence. The landowning communities in the north-west came to value physical strength, skills in wielding weapons, and equated 'manly' qualities with aggressiveness and virility far more than is healthy for any society.

In such a situation, women came to be valued primarily as the bearers of sons and were seen as liabilities in most other contexts. The fiercely patrilineal family and kinship structure that evolved made it mandatory for daughters to be sent away to their husband's family after marriage. Not only were daughters, a constant source of anxiety because of their assumed need for greater protection against an outside world full of enemies, they were also seen as an economic drain because they take away wealth rather than add to it.

The establishment of British rule brought an end to internecine warfare, as well as to external invasions but exacerbated land hunger even more. The most important and far reaching of the changes introduced by the British, involved imposing changes in land ownership patterns. Cultivators now ended up as tenants of a much more interventionist and rapacious state. While creating these new tenancy rights, women's rights in the land were disregarded and bypassed. Even among communities where women were the primary workers on the land, in the process of converting communal property rights of the clan into individual property rights, women were almost completely excluded.

Labour power is more valued in societies with surplus land and scarce labour. As land becomes scarce and population pressure increases, a woman's labour power loses its value and possession of land becomes the all-important asset. If ownership of land is vested mostly or exclusively in the hands of men, women begin to be treated like mere dependents and are considered as liabilities rather than assets.

Take the case of tribal communities of South Bihar, which until the nineteenth century practised shifting cultivation combined with hunting. In these tribal groups, families value their daughters highly because women's labour is the mainstay of agricultural operations. Men's labour plays a very peripheral role in their rural economy. Consequently, most tribal girls fetch a bride-price instead of taking a dowry. They are not perceived as a burden on the family and their birth is far from dreaded as is evident from their sex ratio figures. According to the 1971 census, there were 1,041 females for every 1,000 males amongst the Hos in Bihar. The comparable figures from the 1971 census for other northern states were: Punjab and Haryana (874), UP (883), and Rajasthan (919).

However, these communities were forced to become settled agriculturists by the British, and their communally-owned land parcelled out to individual families, the title being vested with the male head. The tribal's switch to sedentary agriculture, forced upon them by the British is documented at length in my study of the impact of this on the women of the Ho tribe in Singhbhum district, Bihar (*Economic and Political Weekly*, vol. 22 nos. 3, 4 and 5: January, 1987). It shows how the society was forced by outside forces to fall in line with the culture of son preference even though these communities did not traditionally devalue daughters, as is evident from their sex ratios.

The new ownership patterns introduced by the British were crystalized in the Chhotanagpur Tenancy Act of 1908 which conferred exclusive rights on men as the owners of cultivable land; widows and unmarried daughters were only allowed limited usufructory rights. For instance, as soon as a daughter marries, she loses even the right to be maintained from her father's land. She does not inherit land as a son does. Even if an unmarried daughter is raped or has a brief sexual affair with a man, she loses her right to live off the family land, in the same way as she would if she were to get married.

A tribal woman cannot claim a share in her husband's land in her own right even if she is the one cultivating it while he may have migrated elsewhere for employment. She is only allowed to claim a right through her son, if she has one. If a man has no sons, the land he cultivates will revert to his brothers and their sons after his death. A man is assured of his right over the land in his lifetime, but his wife's position is not so secure.

A woman's ability to hold on to the land is also determined by the age of her sons at the time of her husband's death. Women who have only daughters or baby sons tend to be relatively powerless in the violence-charged atmosphere of the village. The land of such widows is often snatched away from them through force or fraud. Thus, women are forced into a situation of son preference for their own protection.

Another reason for son preference is that the outside world of education and employment is extremely male-oriented and male-dominated. Therefore, if tribals have to seek a foothold in the mainstream economy, they can do so only through sons.

Most of the 37 women interviewed in the course of my study of a Ho village stated that they personally preferred daughters. One of the women, Jasmati Sundi, explained this preference in response to my question as to whether she wanted a son or a daughter:

I want a daughter even though having a son will improve my position *vis à vis* my husband's land. Even if I have a son, my husband may throw me out before the son is grown up enough to defend me. If he does allow me to stay on, what do I need a son for? If our land goes to his uncles or cousins after we die, what do I care? If we don't have a daughter who will give us some affection and care when I am old? A son and a daughter-in-law will never do that. When my mother was sick I cared for her, none of my brothers looked after her.

That the culture of son preference has largely been imposed on the Hos by patriarchal land relations dictated from above becomes evident when one considers the attitude of the Hos to children born out of wedlock. Daughters born out of wedlock are not as unwelcome as sons, even in cases where the father refuses to acknowledge responsibility for the child. A baby boy whose father does not accept him runs a higher risk of being killed or allowed to die through neglect than does a girl. A boy's life is not seen as worth much if he is not going to inherit land, since that is seen as his most important function in life. Also, if an unmarried woman is saddled with a son, she will find it more difficult to get married because a prospective husband would not like another man's son in the house as a possible claimant of the land, whereas a stepdaughter is welcome because she is seen as an additional worker on their land and can earn a bride-price for the family.

Increasing Land Hunger

At the heart of these battles is the growing land hunger among the peasantry—both tribal and non-tribal. Land hunger is leading to constant conflicts in villages. The relatively more powerful families are constantly on the lookout for opportunities to usurp the land of less powerful families. Often, the influential families get widows' land surreptitiously transferred in their own names by bribing local officials. They push out those women who have no adult male family members to protect their land. Given the corruption and lawlessness of the government machinery in India, those who cannot resist aggression and physical force tend to lose their land. There is a popular saying in the north: *Jitney ladke utne lath, jitney lath utna kabza* (the more the sons, the more your capacity to wield *lathis* [inflict violence]—and the number of *lathis* decides how much land a family controls).

As the scale of violence increases in society, its importance in controlling and gaining access to new resources is enhanced; daughters then appear more and more frequently, as liabilities.

The increase in insecurity bolsters the ideology of keeping women in the house. In many parts of India, working outside the home is seen as a sign of a family's low social and economic status. Refusing to let women work outside the home does not save women from drudgery, but rather ensures that they stay confined to all the unpaid jobs on their family farm—field labour, harvesting, weeding, caring for family livestock, basic home processing of their farm produce, housework of all kinds, and care of children.

While they may play an important role in producing food, women are usually not allowed to engage in other economic activities that might give them access to cash, such as the marketing of produce, which involves exposure to and contact with the world of commerce and men. Since cash is highly prized in rural areas, and women have few opportunities to earn cash, this is another way that women are kept dependent and are usually considered an economic liability rather than an asset no matter how much labour they put into the running of the household.

Summing Up

Thus, if we want to stop the female foeticide or neglect of women, it is not enough to simply pass a law and hope that it will succeed in countering all those social and economic forces which make women's lives appear expendable.

However, when I argue that a legal ban on female foeticide won't work, I do not mean to imply that we should leave things as they are nor that the resultant scarcity of females will inevitably raise the value of female lives. What I am suggesting is that we stop looking for quick fixes and instead face the problem squarely. There is no way to ensure the healthy survival of baby girls unless families find them worth nurturing. That is indeed a complex task which allows for no easy short-term solutions. Activist intervention has not led to curbing SDTs. If anything the practice has grown and spread.

The real challenge before us is to figure out ways in which a realization of the value of daughters can be enhanced in the eyes of their own families.

VIII

A Code for Self-Monitoring
Some Thoughts on Activism

Today, there is widespread dissatisfaction with the way things are run in our country. Among other things, we are dissatisfied with our government, our economy, our educational institutions, our public health system, the bureaucracy, the police, and the judiciary, as well as the way we have ordered our family structures and social relations. Because of this disgruntlement there has emerged a whole range of social and political activists who have taken it upon themselves to change things for the better. I too belong to this growing tribe of 'self-appointed reformers'. .

It is not as if people have demanded that we intervene in their lives. Nor have they elected us to represent their political or economic interests. We are essentially 'self-appointed' guardians of social and public morality.

It took me many years to realize that good intentions are by themselves no guarantee that my work will inevitably produce good results. It is much easier to do harm than to do good. Therefore, I must constantly attempt to evolve meaningful criteria for judging and evaluating my interventions and actions, especially, since most of us unfortunately are not accountable to the people whose interests we claim to serve.

An MLA or MP who does not represent people's interests can at least be voted out by his constituency. There is no such check on a self-appointed reformer, except that people might choose to ignore him or her. And that is precisely the kind of external check we must make space for in our work. We must make sure that people have the option to ignore us if we don't make sense to them; they must not be coerced to take notice of us or do our bidding. It is for this reason that I have avoided, as far as possible, taking *sarkari* or statist approach to social reform. This approach relies heavily and at times exclusively

*First published in *Manushi*, No. 85, Nov–Dec 1994.

on the state machinery for carrying out the agenda of social reform and justice.

The Statist Approach

Unfortunately, the *sarkari* route has become all too popular among the educated elite of India. They have inherited this tendency from their erstwhile colonial rulers who, after looting various parts of India to build an empire, subsequently became enamoured with the idea that they had been engaged in a 'civilizing' mission all along. With this as justification, they began to imagine they could banish those activities and people they considered undesirable, immoral, and uncivilized by simply declaring them unlawful. Their norm was an idealized notion of how their own society functioned—its imperial beliefs, laws and customs.

Due to our western education we have come to deeply imbibe the colonial view of Indian society and to relate to our people in the same way as the British did, especially if those people happen to be poor and uneducated. Every time we confront social practices that we do not like, we demand that they be outlawed and that people be forced to act as we think right. For instance, when confronted with any aspect of social oppression or violence against women, the characteristic response of progressive organizations has been two-fold:

• To ask for a stringent application of existing laws;
• To ask for new, even more strict legislation, with a view to controlling the wrongdoers by strong punitive measures such as long prison terms.

Most activists tend to see such legislation as a precursor to changing social norms, without ensuring that the laws are enacted judiciously and implemented with care. Consequently, new laws have rarely achieved the desired results. If anything they have added to our problems. Most of our legal interventions only succeed in estranging us further from the people we wish to reform through law.

For example, in 1987, when the Roop Kanwar sati case came to light, progressive-minded people all over the country joined with women's organizations to demand that sati be outlawed and that strict action be taken against Roop Kanwar's in-laws for either forcing or allowing her to commit sati. The outcry was so strong that, after a lot of initial confused dilly-dallying, the Rajasthan government sent a heavy police contingent to Deorala for the ostensible purpose of preventing the Sati-Sthal (the site of sati) being made into another religious shrine and to stop the deification of Roop Kanwar for having committed sati.

In addition, under pressure from women's organizations, the government passed an anti-sati Ordinance which is both foolish and draconian as a piece of legislation. Among other things, anyone who admits to having witnessed a sati is liable to prosecution under this law. The law became more of a hindrance than a help to people interested in investigating what actually happened, because under the new law many were afraid that they would be prosecuted as abettors to the crime if they admitted they had been present when it took place. That did not, on the other hand, prevent the police from making a number of arrests of ordinary villagers, mostly with a view to harassing them and extorting money from them. Thus, what really took place could never be established. Did Roop Kanwar voluntarily climb onto her husband's funeral pyre or was she dragged there, as some journalists alleged?

When we visited Deorala nearly a month after the incident we found it was like a police camp. But that did not prevent the villagers from performing regular *arti* at the Sati-Sthal with the very policemen, posted there to prevent such activities, themselves joining in the *arti*. The arrests and the harassment caused by the heavy police presence had made the villagers both angry and hostile to all those outsiders who, they felt, had no right to interfere in their internal community affairs. Social activists were often prevented from even entering the village. Even if they got inside the village, no one was willing to talk to them (see the article 'The Burning of Roop Kanwar', Chapter V for a detailed description).

It was not just the men of Deorala who reacted with such hostility to outside intervention. The Rajput women, for whose supposed benefit the campaign had been launched, were no less hostile to outside intervention. They joined their men in vociferously defending the cult of sati.

The backlash was largely due to the fact that the anti-sati campaign had been carried out mainly through the press and not in direct communication with the people concerned. This led to a complete breakdown of communication between the reformers and the supposed beneficiaries of the reform. Consequently, the activists were unable to carry out a proper investigation to establish whether the sati was voluntary or a product of coercion.

If it turned out to be the latter, as many suspected, there was no need to invoke anti-sati legislation or pass a new draconian law. It could simply be dealt with as plain murder without the reformers needing to enter into a debate on the sanctity of the Roop Kanwar sati. If it could be proved that Roop Kanwar was forced onto the pyre, even the pro-sati enthusiasts would not dare call it sati. That would destroy the myth of sacredness which they presently bestow upon it by insisting that it was Roop Kanwar's divine *sat* which prompted her to commit self-immolation.

Crime vs Culture

If Roop Kanwar had indeed been murdered, we have strong provisions in the Indian Penal Code for dealing with murderers. They can be sentenced to life imprisonment, or even given the death penalty. We did not need another law to deal with Roop Kanwar's murder. By using the anti-sati Ordinance against her in-laws rather than the Indian Penal Code provision for murder, the government gave their alleged crime a measure of respectability.

The unfortunate truth is that the state and the police were not really interested in stopping sati. To expect a government, which doesn't implement even the existing laws for people's protection to enforce even more stringent laws is laughable. For instance, Deorala has a very large proportion of families in which the men are employed in the police. A good number of these policemen were in the village on the day Roop Kanwar allegedly committed sati. These policemen were duty-bound to prevent the sati; they did not do so. Our demand could well have been that they be punished for dereliction of duty so that those in charge of law enforcement understand that they are being closely monitored.

If Roop Kanwar had been forced to immolate herself, then the act falls in the realm of criminality. But if it was voluntary, it comes in the realm of cultural traditions. If it turned out that Roop Kanwar had indeed decided to immolate herself and, therefore, commanded genuine reverence from her community, then the problem needed to be dealt with altogether differently. In such a situation, mere condemnation and punishment would not do. It would require a genuine dialogue on why women among certain communities like the Rajputs are culturally conditioned to consider their own lives worthless after the death of their husbands. Instead of a dialogue, there was only a confrontation between the villagers and the activists, leading to a hardening of positions on both the sides, thus defeating the very purpose for which the campaign was launched. While the progressive outsiders continued to condemn sati, Rajput women joined their men in sati's defence.

We need to learn to distinguish carefully between crime and culture. No self-respecting society can promote crime in the name of tradition, though it may support repressive norms. In an orderly society, dealing with crime should be left to agencies of the state such as the police and the judiciary. Crime might also be controlled by judiciously worked out social sanctions and punitive measures. But dearly held and deeply cherished cultural norms cannot be changed simply by applying the instruments of state repression through legal punishments. Social reform is too complex and important a matter to be left simply to the police and law courts. The best of laws cannot substitute for approaching the people directly to build a new social consensus, rather than talking *at* them through the newspapers, as many of us are prone to do.

Encouraging Criminalization

In fact, our obsession with outlawing the social practices we find harmful is encouraging the widespread criminalization of our society. For instance, the zealots who fight to get prostitution banned have not succeeded at all in stopping, or curbing it. The anti-prostitution law has meant simply that the police have been armed with too much power to harass prostitutes. Consequently, brothels function under police protection and the flesh trade provides a lucrative source of income for policemen. They not only collect regular *haftas* (weekly or monthly money bribes) but also extort sex bribes from prostitutes. In addition, the police stage occasional dramas of carrying out raids during which arrests are made to instil greater fear among prostitutes, their pimps and the brothel owners. This helps the police to raise their bribe rates even higher. The criminalization of prostitution and the police-pimp nexus makes it much harder for women to escape from prostitution if they so desire.

Yet, all these unfortunate results of our activities have not dampened our enthusiasm for continuing to use laws in ways that are counter-productive. For instance, ever since it became clear that pre-natal tests for genetic defects were being used almost exclusively for detecting and aborting female foetuses, women's organizations have been demanding that such tests be banned. As a result, a series of state laws were enacted, followed by central legislation along the same lines, which provide for jail terms of up to five years and heavy fines for any doctor performing these tests. The recent Central government law states that the woman who undertakes these tests, and even her family will be punished with imprisonment.

However, the law has not curbed the practice. Far from it. Sex Determination Test clinics continue to flourish. The only change in the situation is that the ban has made the tests more remunerative for doctors. Earlier the test cost between Rs 100 to Rs 600. After the ban, doctors have begun charging anything ranging from Rs 500 to Rs 8,000, depending on the status of the doctor and the paying capacity of the family. One can be certain that a part of this money is going to buy police protection. Now that the test has gone underground there are no ways to monitor malpractice. All we have succeeded in doing is to criminalize large sections of the medical profession and to increase corruption in police.

Those who asked for the ban also failed to realize that technological advances are moving along at such a fast pace that it is impossible to control the spread of these tests through mere legislation unless the doctors could be made to act with social responsibility. For instance, it took successive governments within India, nearly a decade and a half to respond to an earlier SDT technique called amniocentesis by passing an ineffective law against it. In the meantime, ultrasound techniques came into vogue. There is no way this new technology can be controlled because it is used for a range of diagnoses, from detecting kidney stones to checking inflammations of intestines or various other organs. One would have to police hundreds of thousands of ultrasound examinations in the country round the clock in order to ensure that the machines are not used for SDTs. Even if one managed this impossible feat, where is the guarantee that the police won't stand there merrily collecting bribes for each test they let pass? In all likelihood, they themselves will be keen to bring their own wives or sisters in for the test.

We had better face up to the fact that SDTs cannot be controlled, as long as those who perform them and those who take them are convinced they serve an important need. As things stand, most doctors feel they are doing an important social service, a noble job, by providing this facility. They see it as a valuable device for population control that prevents the birth of unwanted daughters. Most families are also convinced that they should have not more than one daughter while ensuring the birth of at least one or two sons. This creates a real demand for the test. Unlike prostitution, there is no shame associated with wanting sons and being averse to too many daughters.

When proposing a social reform measure, it is important to remember that the people for whose benefit it is meant must envision their lives as improving due to the change, if they are to adopt it willingly. In the case of SDTs, most women who go for the tests believe that producing more daughters will adversely affect their lives and make them more vulnerable to abuse. Unless we are able to change those pressures which make people averse to having daughters and devalue female lives, our campaign will not be heeded. By using punitive measures we will only become more estranged from the society we wish to reform.

Campaigns cannot work if they stay confined to the ideological level. We activists need to work for those changes in our economy and polity which will contribute toward making daughters far more desired than they are at present. To accomplish this preference-change we will have to do many things, including changing our inheritance patterns and family structures, which allow sons to act as the main supports of the family. At present, families concentrate property in the hands of sons and wilfully disinherit daughters. This culture of disinheritance of women has in turn led to harmful institutions such as the modern-day forms of dowry, which only strengthen the popular prejudice that daughters are an undesirable financial burden.

Thus foeticide cannot be controlled unless this equation changes and families begin to value their daughters more than they do at present. It doesn't take much to kill an infant daughter even without the aid of technology, if she is unwanted. Simple neglect of infant girls does the job as efficiently. Trying to solve the problem of our low sex ratio through a law about foeticide or even one about infanticide is like trying to stop someone from sneezing by forcibly holding and blocking the person's nose rather than by attempting to find out what is wrong with his or her health, and providing treatment.

Reform Government First

I am willing to concede that a legal ban would have a salutary effect if we had an honest law enforcing machinery. For instance, if the government could honestly enact and implement a law that any doctor who provided an SDT test would lose his or her licence to practice medicine, I would be perfectly willing to support such a law. But as things stand, those doctors who pay off the police or other enforcement agencies would be allowed to continue with the tests and the police would simply harass those doctors with whom they have some personal scores to settle.

Thus, for anyone seriously interested in using law as an instrument of social reform, the task of reforming the legal machinery ought to be taken up as a high priority. We cannot set lawless tyrants upon people in the name of reform. This is not to suggest, that in the meantime we sit quietly and let things continue as they are. Nor am I proposing that we activists and reformers should meekly accept the cultural values and social norms of every group across the country simply because they are widely cherished by most of the people. I am only trying to emphasize that we need to work harder at changing those cultural norms through a process in which people become voluntary participants in adopting more humane values. Otherwise, the effects of our campaigns opposing harmful practices will not be enduring.

Given the present state of our law enforcement machinery, it would be better if we let our opposition be known through protests demonstrations and even *dharnas* and picketing outside SDT clinics. We should try to prevail upon the various medical associations in the country to condemn such practices and debar membership for such doctors. In short, through our rigorous publicity campaigns we should ensure that we do not let people rest in peace until they recognize the harm that comes from virulent son preference.

Avoiding the overuse of the statist route to social reform ensures that you get a proper feedback from those whose lives you seek to improve. If you are not using coercive methods like the threat of imprisonment, arrest, and so on, then you are more likely to find out if your ideas are indeed workable. The process of persuading people to a different mode of thinking necessitates dialogue with them. If they are not frightened by punitive measures, they would have no hesitation in pointing out the limitations or weaknesses of what is proposed for their benefit. This ensures that the many complexities of the situation are taken into account, and that potentially harmful approaches are eliminated from the social reform agenda.

Practise Before Preaching

Too often activists themselves cannot implement what they preach. Take, for example, the anti-dowry campaigns in which activists demanded stricter anti-dowry laws to abolish the practice altogether in all its forms because they saw it as very harmful to women. We at *Manushi* started on the same note in the late 70s. I found it very distressing, however, that many of the activists would participate in anti-dowry demonstrations condemning those who give or take dowry one day, but would not themselves hesitate to participate in a dowry wedding the very next day. When I argued with them, they offered excuses such as that they couldn't annoy or displease their family or friends. I was terribly distressed by this gap between what we preached and what we were practising, and thought this might be the real reason why the anti-dowry movement had no impact.

Some of us at *Manushi* decided to try to implement our anti-dowry campaign in our own lives before we condemned others for taking dowry. We took a public vow that we would not attend any wedding where dowry was given or taken, even if it involved our close relations or friends. We hoped that others would also take this oath and help in curbing the dowry menace. In addition, we called for a boycott of such weddings by other activists, arguing that we ought to begin with implementing the reforms we advocated in our own lives. No more than a dozen women responded. This list did not include any of the prominent women activists. However, I personally carried out my boycott vow meticulously for more than thirteen years, even at the cost of hurting dear friends and close relatives. The only totally dowryless wedding I was witness to during this period was that of my own brother. In most other cases, the women to be married would come and argue with me heatedly, pointing out the foolishness of my stand given that they themselves wanted to take dowry. Why should they be forced to give up a dowry, they argued, when they knew their parents would not give them a share in the family estate? If I did not have a means of ensuring that daughters got their due share in parental property, what business did I have to prevent them from getting dowries? In their view, it would only serve their brothers' interests, as they would get an even larger share of the inheritance.

It was this process of feedback which compelled me to reconsider my stand and shift its focus to fighting for an equal inheritance right for daughters. I am convinced that if I had not practised what I advocated, and simply asked for a more ferocious anti-dowry law than already exists, I would not have understood the weakness of my position. I believe activists should attempt to put their ideas into practice at least among their own relatives and friends before they propose important changes in law. We should not make a mockery of legislation, by enacting unimplementable laws.

Start with Existing Laws

For instance, though we already have a Dowry Prohibition Act, it has no effect. If anything, the practice of giving dowry has grown and spread. Before asking for a new law we need to find out why the existing plethora of laws are not functioning. The anti-dowry law does not work not only because it is stupidly devised, but also because even the dowry-givers are by and large convinced that dowry must be given. Most of all, the women concerned don't see the anti-dowry campaign as a help. Since in most cases, they are going to be denied property rights anyway, most women feel that dowry is their rightful due, and that entering their marital homes 'empty-handed' would only reinforce their dependence on their husbands and in-laws. The early years of a marriage, before the woman has had time to develop a relationship with her husband and his family, can be particularly uncertain, and entering the house without a dowry could make her position seem even more insecure.

We also need to understand that most people are not anti-dowry per se, but against 'dowry demands'. It is the harassment of brides to extract more money from their parents which is disapproved of, not the voluntary giving of dowry, which is indeed seen as both necessary and desirable. We would have done better had we made this existing social consensus our starting point for combating some of the negative aspects of dowry-giving. Our attempts to outlaw dowry outright are inherently absurd. How can parents be prevented from bestowing gifts or property on their own daughters? Why outlaw *stridhan*, especially if the daughters themselves are keen to receive it?

We could easily have focused our efforts on preventing extortion, and received greater social support. For those efforts, we need no new laws. The Indian Penal Code defines extortion (putting someone in fear of injury or death with a view to extracting money or property from him or her) as a criminal offence for which a person can be sentenced to up to ten years of imprisonment. With this as a starting point, we can launch rigorous campaigns to persuade parents to change the forms of dowry from consumer items such as television and furniture, which depreciate in value, to income generating forms of property such as land, fixed deposits, or shares in business, which appreciate in value. This would be a pre-mortem inheritance and ensure that a daughter would not need to enter her marital home as an economic dependent, but rather would possess some independent assets of her own. If we could offer a genuine choice to a woman between a dowry and an inheritance share, we would find that most would probably prefer the latter, because it is likely to be more substantial and enduring, and our reforms would be effective. Instead, we are saddled with an anti-dowry law which is universally flouted, including by the law-makers themselves, and a mockery has been made of our reform campaign.

In short, whenever we see people bypass or ignore a social law which has been enacted for their supposed benefit, we must ask what is wrong with this law that its alleged beneficiaries ignore it, rather than assume that there is something wrong with the people who disobey its dictates.

I am not suggesting that laws have no use in our society, or that our society is uniquely lawless and therefore does not heed legislation. I am however arguing that:

- We should take laws more seriously and try to ensure that the gap between what the law says and what people practise is not so large as to make a mockery of these laws. In other words, we need to ensure that the laws are implemented fairly and honestly.
- Before asking for new legislation we should find out whether or not there are existing laws that can do the job but are not being implemented. If this is the case, there is no way of ensuring that a new, more stringent law will do the job any better.

The Colonial Legacy

Unfortunately, such a basic exercise is seldom undertaken. We also tend to forget that we are saddled with a largely lawless government which does not follow its own laws and dictates. If anything, the laws are mainly used by the enforcing agencies—the police, the judiciary, the bureaucracy—to harass and tyrannize people so that they are compelled to pay bribes. This is not only the case in India, but in most of those societies which have had the misfortune of being colonized by a western power. The state machinery that the British built for colonial rule was devised as an instrument of economic and political subjugation. It was in no way accountable to the people over whom it ruled. Since those who inherited power from the British failed to overhaul the government to make it both sensitive and accountable to people's needs, it therefore fostered unbridled corruption and lawlessness in our society, emanating mostly from the rulers themselves.

Since our bureaucracy gives open protection to criminals, we have to be careful in asking for more and more stringent laws. Also, because our law-makers and bureaucrats have never tried to honestly implement even the existing laws, and are mostly interested in finding ways in which laws can be used for extracting bribes, they are extremely inept when it comes to making meaningful new laws. They tend to think that legislating frightening provisions, allowing for more arbitrary powers in the hands of the state, will convince the public of their bona fides and demonstrate their moral outrage at the crime being committed. However, the actual effect of the law is simply to add to corruption and criminalization.

The use of law as an instrument of social reform has worked reasonably well in many western societies because while they built lawless states in the colonies, the western powers ensured that within their own societies governments are not quite so tyrannical nor viewed with as much hostility. Even there, however, law does not act as a magic wand. Much effort goes into making people change their value systems in accordance with the law. However, in India we tend to use law enactment as a substitute for all else. Often people are neither aware what laws are passed for their ostensible benefit, nor how to get the laws they are aware of enforced. It is time we understood that at the heart of our own efforts to make social change, there has to be a reform of the government machinery itself.

Even if we had a government sincere about implementing good laws we should not overlook some special characteristics of our society. This society has no history of external law-makers. The diverse communities of India have for centuries been governed by internally evolved customs rather than by textual commandments.

The Hindu faith has no equivalent of the Bible with its commandments or the Quran with its list of dos and don'ts. In fact, all of our supposed law-makers, including the much maligned Manu, repeatedly emphasized that custom must override textual authorities to remain a living force, and must adapt to the changing times and needs of society. Even today the most common justification people offer for following a certain custom is not 'because that is what the law of a sacred text says', but rather 'that is how we do things in our *biradari* (kinship group)'. Therefore, attempts at centralized law-making by small elite groups without seeking the endorsement of those for whom they are meant tends to be counter-productive, especially since laws are written in an alieu language which most people in India do not understand.

Embodying Your Message

People in India may not heed laws but they are willing to be challenged in their cherished beliefs by those whose words and life they respect. In our culture people who succeed in changing the hearts of other people are usually those whose life is their message. Through their compassion, generosity, wisdom and love, they often manage to make people adopt new, more humane values, or bring about far-reaching behavioural changes. A famous fable, told in virtually every Indian language, describes what kind of messages people are most sensitive to in India. The story goes as follows:

A mother once took her son to a Mahatma complaining that the child ate too much *gur* (jaggery), and was consequently ruining his health. The Mahatma asked the mother to return with the child a week later so that he could think of how to get his message across to the child. When she came back a week later, the Mahatma simply told the child, '*Bete, gur* eating is bad for your health. You should control this habit.' The mother found this very annoying and asked the Mahatma irritably, 'If this is all you had to say why couldn't you do it last week? Why did you make me take this extra trip? As if I don't keep saying the same words to him all the time!'

This Mahatma calmly answered, 'Till last week I was myself fond of eating *gur.* How could I forbid him from doing what I did myself? It took me one whole week to give up the habit. Now I can advise him in good conscience.'

Needless to say the child never ate *gur* again.

Mahatma Gandhi understood this secret of reaching the hearts of his people. He began all his campaigns for reform with his own life—whether it was the removal of untouchability or cultivating the spirit of *swadeshi*. That was why he touched such a deep chord in people and succeeded in mobilizing them for far-reaching changes in their personal and political behaviour. Unfortunately, most contemporary reformers think mere preaching is enough and do very little to embed the changes they advocate in their own lives. Nor do they live sufficiently respectworthy lives which alone can inspire confidence in people.

Need For Accountability

In all previous ages those who wished to mobilize society towards certain goals communicated directly with the people whose lives they sought to influence, and therefore understood what worked and what did not. In our modern age of technological communication, however, we activists are increasingly resorting to the use of mass media for getting our messages across—barring those few who are working in small communities where the directly spoken word of mouth still matters most.

This makes us far less accountable to the people on whose behalf we speak. They have no way of ensuring that we take up issues that are most important to their lives and require urgent attention. Since most of us are well-connected to the media world, we can manage to get good coverage even if what we say does not have much relevance to the everyday privations people are undergoing. Moreover, the press prefers sensational issues to everyday mundane ones. That too, often influences the priorities of activists.

For instance, the lack of access to clean and adequate sources of water in our country is killing hundreds of thousands of children every year with diseases that are easily preventable such as cholera, diarrhoea and jaundice. Yet, we choose to tune in to the alarmist sensational concerns of the West because our media is heavily influenced by the western media and its concerns. In recent years, there has been much more talk of the hole in the ozone layer and the need to fix our refrigeration technology, while scarcely any attention has been paid to the scarcity of basic survival requirements such as clean water for the bulk of our population.

The year 1980 witnessed one of the most severe droughts in the country, leading to great distress for the rural population, particularly the women. But the most influential group of our activists spent their entire energy focusing on changes in the rape law. It is no doubt important to improve our rape laws, but we need to have a better sense of priorities. The concerns and troubles of the most disadvantaged sections of our society ought to get greater attention from us if we wish our work to be meaningful. We need to be vigilant to prevent being swayed by issues that the media finds fashionable in a way that makes us lose sight of our initial goals. The media is constantly looking for either sensational issues or those that are made respectable by powerful lobbies.

The moment, for example, that the UN declares a particular year to be the Year of the Girl Child you find a spate of articles on the subject. Activists begin to organize workshops and seminars on the theme, some hoping to encash on the current political fashion and get media publicity. The next year they will move on to whatever new subject is at the top of the media list. Much of this is related to the flow of funds from various national and international agencies which is increasingly determining the priorities of activists who depend upon such grants. The priorities of fund donors often end up determining the agendas of activists in the same way that much social science or science research is determined by the allocation of funds and research grants.

It is crucially important that we learn to make our work self-supporting, instead of relying on grants from government or private funding agencies. This will help our attempts to stay close to priorities we set for ourselves. The challenges of creating an independent economic base for our work requires people's active participation, and thus builds a viable support base for the movement.

Another equally important rule we activists need to be forever vigilant about is that when we are dealing with poor, disadvantaged groups who are being exploited by others—say a group of landless poor being made to work for low wages by rich peasants—we need to be cautious that we do not escalate the conflict to levels which cannot be sustained by the group concerned. One of the prime reasons for the collapse of radical left politics in most parts of the country is that it did not recognize people's own fighting capacity, and indulged in acts of violence which brought about such high-pitched confrontations that there was fierce retaliation aimed not just at the activists but more ferociously at the group being mobilized. This tends to make people frightened and forever wary of political activity and usually sets the clock back rather than taking things forward.

This is true whether we are intervening in the lives of vulnerable groups, such as the landless poor struggling for better wages, or particular individuals who might come to our organizations for help. For instance, in the early years of *Manushi,* we would often encourage a woman to break out of an abusive or oppressive marriage when she sought our intervention, and sounded desperately unhappy with her situation. Due to our inexperience we were often unable to tell how much of it was posturing and whether the woman herself was prepared to take decisive steps to effect change. Over the years, we realized that many of those who were influenced by our advice and encouragement could not sustain the break for long, and would quietly return to their husbands, often on even less favourable terms than before. They would then hesitate to tell us about it, due to their feelings that we expected a certain behaviour pattern from them which they could not sustain.

Need To Be Open

Equally important, we should avoid hidden agendas in our politics. For instance, if we find that the group we are mobilizing is interested in improving its economic situation and fighting for a wage increase, but we ourselves have other political goals, we should not try to impose our agenda on others through the back door. There should be as little gap possible between what we say and what we do. Politicians, and social workers, have come to be so mistrusted because people have come to realize that they do not mean what they say. Pious platitudes cannot be a substitute for honest words and honest actions. We should try to be as transparent as possible in our politics so that we are assisting people in achieving *their* ends rather than using them as a means to achieve our *own* ends.

Our politics and social reform strategies must attempt to be inclusivist rather than exclusivist, aiming towards the ultimate end of minimizing social conflict rather than resulting in greater disharmony, which is unfortunately often promoted as a virtue in itself by those who consider themselves radicals. Sectional politics are inherently limited, especially if we are constantly pitching the interests of one group against those of others. We can move towards a just society only if the widely varied segments of that society are conscious to observe more humane norms in their mutual relations.

For instance, if a woman approaches an organization to complain of marital abuse, it is not enough that she be encouraged to be more assertive of her rights. It is equally important that her husband and in-laws be brought to respect her rights. Merely heightening the level of confrontation in the family will not achieve that end. Raising the level of mutual understanding on both sides of the conflict should be our goal, and we can only do that if we remain genuinely non-partisan.

Naturally, there will be cases where it is neither expedient nor effective for activists to spend considerable energy on the reformation of individual criminal behaviour. In these instances, the immediate concern may be to rescue the victims and obtain just punishment for the offenders. Nonetheless, even in these instances, we must observe a stringent code of non-partisanship, where the fight is not motivated or influenced by malice or hatred. We must remember that for change to occur and to last on a broad social level, beyond the rectification of individual cases, there must be tremendous effort made not simply to punish those who oppress others, but to change the social attitudes and institutions which permit such oppression.

Another problem activists face is that many of us begin our work with the naive assumption that the poor and vulnerable are more virtuous than the powerful and wealthy. When our actual political experiences do not bear this out we tend to become demoralized and cynical. Consequently, it becomes increasingly difficult for activists to sustain their faith in working for the disadvantaged. A woman who seeks aid because she is suffering marital abuse may be abusive to others herself, or there may be mitigating factors for the husband's violence. Personal virtue must be kept distinct from individual rights, and activists must keep themselves from expecting consistently moral behaviour in those whose cause they are espousing. If our commitment to women's equality and dignity begins to falter when we find that many women do not fit the stereotype of the 'virtuous oppressed', it shows that we are more attracted to abstract causes rather than to fighting for the rights of real human beings regardless of their personal failings. At the same time, we must remain impartial enough to be able to openly acknowledge and distance ourselves from any harmful aspects in those whose causes we espouse. Our interventions can be effective only if our words are believed—if people credit us with the ability to be fair and truthful even if the truth weakens our own position temporarily.

Our Self-View

At the heart of it all is the question—how does an activist see her or his role? Is an activist a person whose purpose is to raise other people's awareness level, someone who assumes people do not know their own interests and need to be guided into choosing the path the activist thinks best? Are people to be told what is good and bad for them, educated into being more aware in the way the activist sees awareness? Or is the job of an activist to try and learn how people define their problems? Find out what hurts them? Learn what improvements they want to make in their own lives?

There are certainly problems in attempting to follow this route. What if the group you are working with wants to destroy another group? Or what if parents see it in their family's interest to marry off a daughter when she is no more than a little girl? In such cases, it would be irresponsible not to try to intervene to stop such a practice, especially if it involves violence and coercion. Two things, however, must be remembered:

- We must minimize the use of instruments such as police and instead resort to moral persuasion as much as possible.
- We must learn to distinguish between situations where a person or a family is choosing a harmful practice or a self-demeaning way of life due to cultural conditioning, or lack of options and those choices which are made with evil motives.

People will not heed us if they do not have viable options to behave differently. For instance, if one sees someone drinking filthy gutter water which is potentially lethal, it would be foolish to merely stop at giving that person a sermon on hygiene or forcibly preventing the person from swallowing the water. You would need to find out if clean drinking water or other safe drinks are actually available at a price the person can afford. If they are not, you would first have to assure the easy accessibility of clean water before expecting that your advice will be heeded. That is to say, whenever someone is behaving in what seem to be self-destructive ways, start by exploring the availability of real options. Then your job need go no further than merely acquainting the person with the available options and information about their consequences.

Finally, it is important to avoid making social causes out of our own personal grievances. Feminists in the West came up with a powerful slogan: 'The personal is political'. They encouraged women to speak out about their own experiences of oppression, and fight against the discrimination they personally encounter. However, those of us who wish to play a catalytic and organizational role in mobilizing *others* to fight against injustice, would do well to avoid turning our personal problems or injustices into social causes. We should have the capacity to resolve our personal problems without using our activist organizations as vehicles for our personal empowerment, or for settling scores with those who may have wronged us.

We are living in an age wherein we who speak on behalf of the poor and oppressed can build political careers out of it—become heroes and heroines in the eyes of the rest of the world—fight and win elections, occupy positions of power on the strength of our activism, get a lot of media coverage, become celebrities and so on. In such a situation, activists often tend to mistake their personal celebrity status with the success of the cause. We need to remember that the two are not synonymous. Instead, we need to develop self-evaluating procedures to help us stay finely tuned to the needs of those we set out to serve.

I am also old-fashioned enough to believe that one should not make one's social and political work a source of personal livelihood, but that this should be undertaken in the spirit of unconditional giving, in the same way that people do *seva* in a gurudwara. The modern tendency to put a price tag on everything and to reduce social work to the status of merely another job spells the doom of social altruism, and is a symptom of an unhealthy society which only promotes greed and self-centredness. These days one frequently sees that those who talk on behalf of the poor have the potential to earn five-figure salaries while the poor remain pretty much where they were. Even if one were to take a salary for this work, we need to ensure that what the activists pay themselves is modest enough so that the poor do not feel that the activists are making rich careers out of poverty mongering. We should try and serve the cause rather than make the cause serve us.

IX

Violence and the 1989 Election
Implications for Women

India is not only the world's largest democracy, but it has also, one of the most politically aware electorates in the world. The Indian people may indeed be said to live and breathe politics. Conversations, whether between friends or strangers, whether in elite drawing rooms, village *chaupals* or buses and trains, almost invariably veer around to politics sooner or later. India is one of the few countries where most people would, if forced to choose, perhaps prefer to hear a V.P. Singh or Atal Bihari Vajpayee speak, than to watch a pornographic film or a football match. This intense involvement in monitoring the doings of those in power and those vying for power makes the average Indian voter a formidable customer for the politician. Even the most authoritarian of our rulers dare not tamper with democratic institutions beyond a point. For instance, although two and a half years of Emergency had not aroused much open rebellion, yet Indira Gandhi felt compelled to hold elections in 1977. The Indian people have not allowed their rulers to hijack democracy as has happened in most other Third World countries.

The 1989 national election was in some ways the most heartening of all the elections we have had so far. In the face of the most blatant attempts by criminalized elements in all major parties to use violence as an instrument to manipulate the elections, the people's quiet determination to use their independent judgement in exercising their voting right proved stronger. Both at the centre and at the state levels, most ruling parties—the Congress(I), the Janata Dal in Karnataka, the Telugu Desam in Andhra Pradesh, the Left Front in Kerala—were humbled. More important, we, for the first time, had at the centre a multi-party coalition government—the National Front, supported by the Bharatiya Janata Party (BJP) and the Left Front, with the Congress(I) as a large opposition. It is to be hoped that the various groups

*First published in *Manushi*, No. 54–55, Sept-Oct-Nov-Dec 1989.

represented in parliament will act as checks and balances on one another so that no one group or coterie is in a position to run amok. The situation is still fluid, as the coming assembly elections are likely to render it yet more complex.

Many of the implications and consequences of the election have been analysed and debated in the media. We shall here focus on two issues which particularly affect women—the use of violence and the nonfunctioning of political institutions.

The Congress(I) government had systematically undermined the normal functioning of government and other public institutions. Almost nothing works without a bribe or stringpulling. While this was detrimental for all citizens, it is especially so for disadvantaged groups like women. Women have relatively less ability to use money or muscle power and other forms of influence in the public sphere. Hence, when the apparatus of public affairs and of welfare services become intransigent, women's powerlessness and dependence on male members of the families to get things done is increased. Women's presence in public affairs also declines.

The peripheralization of women in the 1989 elections was apparent. Here, we refer not primarily to the decline in the number of women members of parliament (though this too occurred—from 44 to 27) but rather to the complete absence of any women's issue from the electoral scene. Even high priority women's issues did not become voting issues. Women were not organized outside of political parties in a way that they could choose and support those candidates who committed themselves to women's interests. During the election it became amply clear that, despite all the rhetoric of 'integration of women into development', despite the crumbs thrown to women like the Indira Mahila Yojana announced by Rajiv Gandhi on election eve, politicians do not have to reckon with women as a constituency.

The new visibility of women's issues in the media should not mislead us into thinking that women are organized on any significant scale to press for concrete demands. Almost every other deprived section has a list of demands (however relevant or irrelevant to their situation) which have to be taken into account when politicians make electoral calculations, but apart from dangling the carrot of 30 per cent reservations for women—a commitment they have no intention of fulfilling, all political parties totally bypass women.

Violence was an equally important factor in marginalizing women. The election took place in a turbulent atmosphere rife with different varieties of violence. Violence always has the effect of further confining and restricting the lives, movements and activities of women.

An important reason why women cannot make it on their own in electoral politics without a male protector is that our political milieu as it is constructed today actively pushes out independent women. This it does by various kinds of violence, overt and covert. Electoral politics in India today increasingly relies on violence and intimidation. A candidate is considered a 'winning' candidate if he commands money power and hoodlum power—to capture booths, rig votes, and terrorize weaker sections and opponents. No party can claim to be free of such gangsterism or even claim that none of its candidates are criminalized. According to one estimate, 100 people died in the course of the 1989 election, not of course counting the hundreds killed in pre-election communal violence engineered with an eye on the election. It is a truism that women will not participate in large numbers in activities that generate violence as Indian politics does today.

The only women who can venture to campaign or contest in such a violent atmosphere are wives and daughters of powerful male politicians. These women are protected by gun-toting brigades. The few women politicians like Jayalalitha who are bold enough to venture into the field on their own are surrounded by coteries of criminalized male politicians and consequently fail to draw out women as active supporters or workers.

The offices of political parties today are no more secure for women than are our police stations. A lone woman would hesitate to enter for fear of risking her very life in the process. Witness the unruly behaviour of Youth Congressmen at national and international conferences, or of Devi Lal's green brigades at party rallies. As important as actual violence in repelling women from the political arena is the ever present threat of violence.

Even if some intrepid women do venture into party networks on their own, they would not get far. In order to climb in the party hierarchy they would have to attach themselves as a wife or girlfriend to some party high-up. This is true of all parties, right or left. And even veterans among women politicians are unlikely to have much say in party decision-making. An important reason for their exclusion is that in our political culture today, real decisions are taken not at open deliberations which tend to be staged shows, but at late night drink sessions where women would not be invited, even if they were hardy enough to wish to be present. It is at these booze sessions in hotel rooms and private residences that male politicians get together to form and break alliances. It is here that the real horse-trading is done and the deals worked out that decide which stated policy will be acted upon and which quietly dropped, which candidate supported and which stabbed in the back. Of all the kinds of violence used during the 1989 election—intimidation of certain sections of voters, booth capturing, rigging, attacks on candidates, shoot-outs between hoodlum gangs attached to rival parties, the most fearful was the violence and threat of violence against Muslims in northern and western India. This was also the form of violence that most directly and intimately affected women, invading their homes and families, violating their domestic relationships, and victimizing them individually and collectively.

If women were ignored by contending politicians, Muslims were in the less enviable position of being manipulated and bullied. In contrast to the prevalent stereotype of Muslims as a pampered minority who blackmail government into granting them concessions, this election clearly demonstrated that Muslims are the victims of political blackmail. While the election eve massacre in Bhagalpur was by no means the first of its kind, it was remarkable because of the cynical way violence was engineered as an electoral weapon.

It suits the Congress(I) now to claim that its defeat in the North was because it was 'secular' while the opposition appealed to the electorate on a communal basis. However, the fact is that the Congress(I) spared no effort not only to make its electoral appeal on a communal basis but also to terrorize people into voting on that basis. That the vast majority of massacres of Muslims with the connivance and active participation of government machinery, police and paramilitary forces have occurred in Congress(I) ruled states over the last five years was not a coincidence. Further, the Congress(I) deliberately fanned the flames of communal hatred in 1989 by dragging its feet on the Ram Janambhoomi-Babri Masjid issue, preventing any settlement from being arrived at, and simultaneously throwing a sop to the Muslims by conferring second language status in Uttar Pradesh on Urdu, in the full knowledge that this would be used as a stick to beat Muslims.

Faced with this reality, Muslims in the North could no longer buy the claim of the Congress(I) that it was secular, and swung away from it. Where faced, as in Delhi or Maharashtra, by the Hobson's choice of the Congress(I) versus the BJP or the Shiv Sena, many Muslims refrained from voting, or chose a losing candidate. Others, with fear in their hearts, chose whichever of the two main contenders seemed to them the lesser evil. Wherever a real choice existed, as in Uttar Pradesh, they took it—the Janata Dal, the CPI or CPI(M), the Bahujan Samaj Party (BSP). More significant, however, is that Hindus did not vote as a monolith any more than Muslims did.

It would be simplistic to interpret the vote for BJP or the Shiv Sena as a vote for more anti-Muslim violence. If the Hindu voters wanted more Muslims killed they could not have done better than return the Congress(I) to power in Uttar Pradesh and Bihar. Yet, in this supposedly Hindi-Hindu heartland, neither the Congress(I) nor the BJP met with any substantial success. It was the Janata Dal, whose most visible leader in this area, V.P. Singh, had openly opposed the Congress(I) and had also refused to share a platform with the BJP, which got a clear majority, while a number of smaller parties with an avowedly non-communal position (CPI, CPI-M, BSP) did surprisingly well. Very significant, for instance, was the victory of a CPI candidate in the Faizabad constituency, where the disputed Babri Masjid is situated, and where the CPI and CPI(M) had just held a rally opposing the Congress(I)'s, BJP's and Vishwa Hindu Parishad's communalization of the issue.

In rejecting the Congress(I) the electorate in north India rejected a party with a proven track record of anti-minority violence, in favour of other parties which, even if they are not decidedly better intentioned, have, at least at the moment, less blood on their hands. Disgust with the Congress(I) misrule of violence and corruption was reflected in a vote for whichever alternative existed.

If the BJP and Shiv Sena interpret this as a vote for more anti-Muslim violence and fail to act responsibly, they will make the same mistake that Rajiv Gandhi made in 1985. His government interpreted the anti-terrorist vote that they got as a mandate for more violence of the kind they had perpetrated on the Sikhs in November 1984. Consequently, they pursued a bloody, strong-arm policy in Punjab, continuing to heap violence and humiliation on the Sikhs. But this backfired in 1989 when they lost both the Sikh and the Hindu vote. If the Congress(I) has not benefited electorally from the massacres it has perpetrated, there is no reason to believe that the BJP or the Shiv Sena will benefit from a similar strategy. Their leaders would do well to realize the long-term implications for their parties and to change their tendencies to violence and authoritarianism.

The issue of violence in the polity is directly linked to that of women's participation in politics. Women, in any case, have to negotiate many forms of violence both in the home and outside. When, in addition, violent conflict erupts in society, women get pushed back into the domestic sphere, made further invisible and silenced. For example, when a minority community is under siege, it is not just the women of that community who are terrorized but also the women of the majority community. Hindu-Muslim conflict is bred on prejudice, fear and lies. Thus, even when it is Muslims who are being killed, many Hindus genuinely believe that they are under attack. Hindu women are scarcely less afraid to step out of the house at such times than are Muslim women. If one cannot even move out freely, how can one participate in any kind of political activity?

Further, in an atmosphere where communal issues are mischievously made into top priority issues, women tend to submerge their own interests in what they imagine are the interests of the community. Thus, many women in Maharashtra, identifying the Shiv Sena as a supposed protector of 'Hindu interests', would support it despite its blatant use of hoodlum power which can never be conducive to women's greater freedom or security.

How women's issues are subordinated and sacrificed to pressures from communal forces was demonstrated by the fate of Pramila Dandavate. She is perhaps the only national level woman politician who has consistently worked on women's issues and attempted to make them her main political plank. She was allotted a ticket by the Janata Dal as part of the National Front, but in the negotiations with the Shiv Sena, her ticket was bargained away in exchange for a seat adjustment. Her candidature was withdrawn in favour of a Shiv Sena candidate and in return the Shiv Sena did not put up a candidate against her husband Madhu Dandavate, also of the Janata Dal. This deal has an almost symbolic significance, involving as it does the sacrifice of a woman politician standing for women's issues to a Shiv Sena candidate standing on a blatantly communal platform.

If Indian women today are not organized as a political pressure group, it is not because they are indifferent to public affairs or are delightedly submerged in domestic matters, as some newspaper

comments insultingly make out. One proof of women's interest in
changing society for the better is the substantial number of women
who are active in non-party organizations ranging from civil liberties
and women's groups and mahila mandals to social, charitable associations, even in rural areas and small towns.

It is also a fact that Indian women are enthusiastic about exercising
their franchise. Over the years, the gap between the proportions of
men and of women who cast their vote has been steadily narrowing.
Under normal circumstances, that is, when there is no violence or
blatant intimidation, women come in large numbers and wait in long
queues to vote. The familiar newspaper photos of women in *ghung-
hat* or *burqa* casting their vote express not just a cliche but a significant aspect of our political reality—that even women who lead
confined lives are not indifferent to their right to vote. Several studies
have also eroded the notion that women always vote as their families
decide. While not enough is known about women's voting pattern,
there is reason to believe that many use the secrecy of the ballot to
vote autonomously despite the preferences or dictates of dominant
male family members.

In the last five years, an increasing ferment and unrest has also
been evident amongst women, witness their large-scale participation
in many movements, especially the new peasant movements.
Women's potential for participation in political life and for bringing
about change can be encouraged, however, only if violence is somewhat curbed. Violence is being used by all major parties today.
However, more frightening than the use of hoodlum brigades is the
attempt by some parties to legitimize and give respectability to special
kinds of violence.

The appeal of the Shiv Sena, for example, is twofold. First, it claims
to 'get things done', by cutting through, violently if necessary, the net
of corruption and inefficiency that envelops government functioning.
Fed up with the inefficiency, corruption and nepotism that the Con-
gress(I) rulers had developed into a fine art, people are lured into
believing that a strong hand is required—that government functionaries will work only when terrorized from above. It is in this hope that
they turn to a Bal Thackeray, even while they are afraid of him. The
logic of this choice is evident in the Amitabh Bachchan films of the
eighties—when nothing works, only a ruthless strong man, a Shahen-
shah or a Toofan, can bludgeon the rusted government machinery

into yielding results and can check the criminals who are ruling the
roost in all spheres of public life.

The second part of the appeal to violence is based on the stereotyping of a minority community as 'fundamentalists', 'backward',
'violent', 'treacherous', and of the majority community as 'secular' and
discriminated against even though it is a majority. This strategy is
pursued with a view to unifying the majority community through
hatred and fear.

Perhaps the most fortunate feature of our political and social life,
demonstrated in this election too, is that we, as Indians, have many
allegiances, and our vote is not normally determined by any single
allegiance that overrides all others. Thus, for example, a Hindu or a
Muslim also has an allegiance to a particular regional group, local
devotional community, linguistic group, caste, clan, village or town,
and these loyalties are often as strong as, or stronger than, the
so-called 'Hindu' or 'Muslim' identity. It is fashionable to decry these
cross-cutting allegiances as divisive and backward looking. In fact, it
is precisely these loyalties which act as obstacles in the way of unreal
loyalties and artificial, abstract, pan Indian 'Hindu' or 'Muslim' identities which would steam roller other, frequently more salient, identities. For example, a Hindu and a Muslim from Kerala who meet in
Bombay will probably have more experiences and goals in common
than either would have with a co-religionist from Haryana. This
communality may help prevent them from being willing to legitimize
murder in the name of religious oneness. Real unity is unity with
people among whom one lives, the commitment to stand against the
murder of one's neighbour, not unity with killers on an all-India level
who claim to share one's religion.

Parties like the BJP and the Shiv Sena, by appealing to our worst
prejudices and by systematically promoting mistrust and hatred
among different groups, try to make anti-Muslim violence legitimate
and respectable in a way that other forms of violence have not
achieved. They can do this only because of our lack of knowledge of
the real situation, especially of other communities than our own, from
whom we are often socially cut off.

Fear breeds on misinformation. For example, each time a massacre
takes place it is called a 'riot'. This misleading word suggests that two
equally matched groups clashed and both suffered equally. Newspapers, because of poorly thought out, foolish laws, are not allowed to
report how many of those killed belonged to each community. Taking

advantage of the gap in information, parties like the BJP and the Shiv Sena spread the lie that as many or more Hindus lost life and property as did Muslims. In fact, wherever studies have been conducted in the eighties, the pattern of violence has clearly emerged not as a clash between communities but rather a systematic attack on the minority by police in collusion with hoodlum brigades. A *Manushi* team that investigated the 1987 violence in Meerut, for example, found that the vast majority of those killed were Muslims (most of them murdered in cold blood by the police and The Provincial Armed Constabulary (PAC)), the majority of those arrested as 'rioters' were also Muslims, and the majority of commercial establishments, houses and vehicles destroyed belonged to Muslims. Yet almost all Hindus we met in Meerut were convinced that Hindus had been the primary victims of violence and would have been wiped out if the PAC had not come to their defence.

To explode such myths by presenting the facts is important, because these myths are built and used to legitimize the continuing use of violence in political life. Such lies can be exposed only by actually going to the sites of violence and observing the reality (for example, in Meerut we did a colony by colony count of burnt shops and houses and a house to house count of the dead and injured in affected areas). The reality cannot be understood merely by talking to authorities or to members of both communities because these are too often blinded by fear and propaganda; some deliberately make use of it.

Women's groups are among those in a position to expose the anatomy of violence in our society. They have already contributed to this task in significant ways. For example, in the aftermath of the November 1984 massacre of the Sikhs in Delhi, women formed a large component of the Nagrik Ekta Manch, which did relief work, and also of the groups which produced investigative reports on the way the violence was engineered by the Congress(I). These reports played a crucial role in preventing the legitimization of the massacre. The Congress(I) was put on the defensive, nationally and internationally, and compelled to realize that their strategy of pogroms against the Sikhs outside Punjab would not yield dividends. Women's groups continue to work with the 1984 riot victims, and to keep the issue alive in public memory.

A similar role on a smaller scale has been played by women activists in Bombay, Ahmedabad and Hyderabad in exposing the role of government and police in massacres of Muslims. Our efforts in this direction need to be far more systematic as a necessity for making life safe for all of us.

Some of the steps we could take immediately:

1. As soon as a so-called 'riot' occurs, an active group could organize to go to the spot and investigate the situation, observe and examine the actual losses, and record the facts, not just what is reported. For example, we must try to establish how many of each community actually got killed, injured, arrested, tortured, and lost how much property. Also, what part police, paramilitary forces, government machinery and political parties played in the violence.

   We should then make this information available to the media as widely as is possible, to combat the mischievous and lying propaganda spread by communal forces.

2. We can play a similar role during elections. We should select those constituencies where there is the greatest likelihood of violence and intimidation, and should be present there to observe and record events. Very small efforts made in this direction during the national election indicated that even the presence of an alert team of two put the officials on their best behaviour and may have acted as some sort of check on blatant rigging.

By repeatedly exposing the mechanics of violence we can build pressure on the forces, governmental and other, that perpetrate it. Only when there is a public or political backlash against such moves that instigate murder, will they think twice about continuing to spark riots. And only in a polity where violence is not the norm can women begin to participate in significant numbers and to press for their own priority issues.

X

Out of the Zenana Dabba
Strategies for Enhancing Women's Political Representation

The Prime Minister himself could not make it that day. At a conference organized by the National Commission for Women in the last week of July, a few of us had been asked by the Commission to pose questions to the Prime Minister on his views regarding 33 per cent reservation for women in Parliament and state assemblies. At the last minute, we were informed that the Prime Minister could not keep his commitment and had sent his Minister for Social Welfare, Mr Ramoowalia, as a substitute.

I asked Mr Ramoowalia:

The United Front (UF) government has been rather quick to announce that they will introduce 33 per cent reservation for women in Parliament and in the state assemblies, along with a 33 per cent reservation in government jobs, through an amendment of the Constitution. Why is it that the politicians who committed themselves to these measures have done nothing to enhance the participation of women within their respective parties? How can 33 per cent reservation for women in Parliament and state assemblies work if there aren't enough women active in parties, if the parties don't have enough viable candidates to field? What measures of internal reform were these parties contemplating in order to include women in party decision-making and leadership roles?'

Mr Ramoowalia graced me with an answer, which I must present in brief or I will have no space for anything else. He started off by saying, 'I agree wholeheartedly with my sister, Madhu Kishwar, that social reform is the most important matter before us' then quickly launched into a sermon on what he thought were important issues for social reform. He advised the august gathering of women leaders and activists come from all over the country that women needed to be saved from three social evils—first and foremost from the dowry

First published in *Manushi*, No. 96, Sept–Oct 1996.

system. The second important evil women need to be saved from are 'evil mothers-in-law'. And then he went on to describe how during his trip to England he had read a moving novel about the viciousness of an evil-hearted mother-in-law, who made her daughter-in-law's life miserable. Thereafter, he launched into a vituperative but hilarious attack at a 'new social evil'—the corrupt non-government organizations (NGOs). He warned women that in the name of helping them and other vulnerable sections of society, these greedy NGO leaders were actually exploiting women just like evil mothers-in-law do and lectured us on how our women needed to be saved from the evil designs of NGO leaders whose funds and grants his ministry was beginning to cut down. It is obvious that his answer had as little to do with my question as chalk with cheese.

His skirting of my question shows how little thinking has been done by our political leaders about this vital measure to provide 33 per cent reservation for women through a constitutional amendment.

If those in ministerial positions like Ramoowalia haven't given a minute's thought to this issue, one can imagine the paltry extent of discussion and debate that must have taken place among the top leaders, as well as among ordinary party workers on the subject. Unfortunately, even women lobbyists and MPs who have campaigned in favour of reservations do not seem to have done the required homework before putting forward their demand. The proposed bill mindlessly follows the reservation scheme for women already in operation at the zilla parishad and panchayat level, which has by now demonstrated many inherent flaws and weaknesses. The new reservation bill fails to avoid those same mistakes.

The Magic Number

The provisions of the reservation bill as presented before the Parliament in the monsoon session that year can be summed up as follows:

- One-third of seats will be reserved for women in the Lok Sabha and state legislatures through a constitutional amendment.
- These reservations are meant for an indefinite period, unlike reservations for SCs and STs which lapse unless extended after every ten years.
- The reserved constituencies are to be determined through a lottery system. For SCs and STs, constituencies are reserved on the basis

of population proportion. Constituencies with a high SC/ST population are selected for a period of time and are supposed to be delimited after some years. But since the population of women is evenly spread throughout the country, this formula cannot be applied for them. The lottery system will mean that before every election a different set of constituencies will be declared as reserved for women.

• There is also a provision for parallel reservations for SCs and STs, which is to say women belonging to SCs and STs will be getting one-third of seats reserved for people of that category—in other words there will be reservations within reservations.

There are several problems inherent in this particular scheme. To begin with, why a 33 per cent quota? What is the significance of this number? Why not 13 or 43 or even 73 per cent? The reservation quota for all other groups such as the Scheduled Castes and Tribes has been determined on the basis of their numerical strength in the overall population. Not so for women. In India, the proportion of women as compared to men is a little less than 50 per cent. So why not 49 per cent reservation for women? Does the magical figure of 33 per cent represent some projection into the near future of our declining sex ratio? Are our policy-makers anticipating the advent of all kinds of new technologies to bring down the already low sex ratio so that women will soon only be one-third of the population?

This is not at all to suggest that 33 per cent reservation is a small amount. Even in Sweden, a country considered the most advanced democracy with the highest percentage of women in positions of political power anywhere in the world, women occupied 40 per cent of elected parliamentary seats in 1994. This, after nearly a century of effort and struggle. The figures for other 'leading' democracies are pretty dismal. According to a survey done in 1994, women occupied 9 per cent of parliamentary seats in the UK; 11 per cent in the USA's House of Representatives; 7 per cent in India (which has dropped to 6 per cent in 1996); 6 per cent in France; 8 per cent in Australia; 4 per cent in Thailand; 3 per cent in Japan; and 2 per cent in Egypt and Turkey. Thus by reserving one-third of the seats in legislatures, India will be ensuring a quantum leap. The very presence of 181 women in the Lok Sabha will make them much more visible, a drastic difference from their minuscule presence today.

However, accepting the present scheme of 33 per cent permanent reservation for women is like demanding that some seats be reserved in every bus for women or the equivalent of a *zenana dabba* (ladies compartment) in every train. Men then come to expect women to remain confined to the 'ladies section' and assume that all the rest of the seats are reserved for them.

Even though there will be no legal bar on women standing from general constituencies, it is highly unlikely that women will be given tickets from outside the reserved constituencies. This same pattern is evident with SCs and STs, who have been permanently confined to reserved constituencies. At the panchàyat and zilla parishad level, in most states party bosses are not giving tickets to women to contest from general constituencies—which are assumed to be reserved for men. Only in Karnataka and West Bengal have women managed to go beyond 33 per cent. For our state legislatures, it will be much harder for women to secure tickets beyond the stipulated quota because of intense competition at this level.

The present scheme of reservation will ensure that women will enter the electoral battle only against other women and never get an opportunity to contest against men, a sure way to perpetually ghettoize women's politics. As it is, women in India have deeply imbibed the notion that 'women are women's worst enemies' because of the way they are pitched against each other in the family structure. Their dependence on men estranges them from other women because men mediate women's relations with the outside world. Therefore, political solidarity among women is hard to build. If even in the political realm, women are constantly pitched only against other women, there will be far less possibility of their working together as a concerted lobby cutting across party lines, at least on some crucial women-related issues. It will strengthen the tendency to view other women as permanent rivals rather than possible allies.

The lottery system of gender-based reservations will lead to a fresh set of constituencies being earmarked for women at every election. There would be no way to predict which constituencies will be reserved in the next election. In most functioning democracies politicians are expected to develop and nurse a constituency. However, an unpredictable and rotating reservation policy, already implemented at the zilla parishad level, has resulted in killing women's incentive to build their own constituencies because politicians have no way of knowing which ones will be declared as reserved constituencies next election. A similar set-up for legislatures will result in women candidates becoming even more dependent on their male party bosses, rather than working within their own constituencies to win elections. Even after being elected in a particular area, there will be no pressure to responsibly serve that constituency because if in the next draw of lots that constituency is dereserved, these women will have to shift elsewhere for the next election. This will lead to even more irresponsible politics in general, as well as among women. A man may have worked hard in his constituency after being elected. But he will not be sure of being able to stand from the same one if the lottery system decides that that constituency is to be earmarked for women. This will inevitably produce a backlash from men and damage the legitimacy of women's participation in politics.

Women from the Backward Castes are not covered by the reservation quota announced by the government, while women belonging to SCs and STs will be getting one-third of the seats reserved for people of that category.

Within the Backward Caste-based parties, the few upper-caste women that are members, will be the automatic beneficiaries of reservation. But chances are that we will be saddled with more *biwi-beti* brigades because Backward Caste leaders are likely to resort to fielding their mothers or sisters or wives to ensure that the women's quota stays within their caste control and women legislators do not pose any challenge to their power. The current scheme of reservations makes this easy and may further encourage formation of caste-blocs in a party. The men from the OBC communities representing a range of peasant castes and communities including Yadavs, Gujjars, and Vokaliggas have come to dominate politics in almost all the states of India. They have come to acquire power even at the national level, after the formation of, first, the Janata Dal government at the Centre in 1989 and, a coalition of various OBC parties in the United Front government. However, women of these communities continue to be among the most oppressed in India and politically insignificant. An obvious proof of this is the near total absence of notable OBC women leaders within the OBC parties. For instance, the few prominent women leaders in the Janata Dal like Pramila Dandavate and Mrinal Gore are from Brahmin families.

The UF government had only one woman minister, Kanti Singh, a total non-entity. Her only claim to fame was her sycophantic relationship to the Bihar Chief Minister, Laloo Prasad Yadav. The women from various OBC castes in rural areas live under the most crippling restrictions, especially in north India. While certain upper-caste groups like Brahmins and Kayasthas have initiated widespread internal social reform movements ever since the nineteenth century in order to improve the status and rights of women within their communities, very little internal reform work has been undertaken by OBC groups or by the SC and ST communities in relation to women's rights. As a result, their social and political culture remains far more hostile to women's participation in public affairs within their villages and communities. That is why these caste leaders are more likely to capture the women's quota through their wives and daughters, who can then be used as puppets and rubber stamps.

Biwi-Beti Brigades

At the panchayat level *biwi* brigades can still serve the useful purpose of getting men used to including women in village debate and decision-making, even if the women are totally lacking in political experience and are used as puppets. The tasks expected of a panchayat or corporation member are relatively simple, often concerned with organizing civic amenities in the locality with which most villagers have close familiarity. Therefore, a woman who may initially enter village politics as someone's wife does not necessarily require much time to become a fully functioning panchayat leader, provided some of her family restrictions are removed. But the presence of such proxy figures in Parliament and state assemblies is not only counterproductive, but actually harmful. Political socialization of such women legislators into the parties, required for being effective members of state assemblies and Parliament, cannot take place smoothly when women members remain filially attached to and politically dependent on the male party leaders. Reproduction of kinship-groups within existing caste-groups in the parties in Parliament and state legislatures is likely to further contribute to the breakdown of our party system and of representative democracy.

Many argue that if sons and nephews can enter politics on the strength of family connections, if such useless men, who are members of mafia and criminal groups, can be selected to represent us in Parliament and state assemblies, why do we have such exceptionally high expectations from women?

There is nothing inherently wrong in anyone using family connections in politics to gain an advantage, as happens in other professions. The problem arises only when women are used as proxies—a position which even untalented male kin do not allow themselves to be forced upon them. Those women who grow to have an independent existence do not get to be treated derisively even if to begin with they have entered through family connections.

In Chandrika Kumaratunge of Sri Lanka and Aung San Suu Kyi, we have two very outstanding examples of women, who got a tremendous initial advantage from their political parentage but then emerged out of the family shadow and outshone their respective fathers in politics both in terms of political vision, as well as quality of political leadership.

It is time we began taking our legislatures seriously or they will never function effectively. Parliament ought to be a forum for the most seasoned, thoughtful, and well-informed individuals. It is supposed to perform the awesome responsibility of legislating and policy-making at the macro level for nearly a billion people. It is no place for political novices to learn their first lessons in Parliamentary democracy. Our Parliament and state assemblies are being treated like a joke, contributing seriously to misgovernance in our country. Most of those who get elected are simply ill-equipped for the required political task of devising and improving upon existing legislation, and for facilitating new equations among various social perspectives and political interests. Our entire population is saddled with idiotic laws because many of our legislators don't have the elementary skills or interest in hammering out sensible, implementable legislation. Whenever serious laws are being debated and passed, both the treasury and opposition benches tend to get emptied out. Our legislators are more adept at coming to blows and staging walkouts than actually debating issues of importance. We should try to bring about a qualitative change with women's participation in these fora, rather than bring down the level of functioning further with women simply joining as puppets in this disgraceful enterprise.

What Works Better

Fixed quotas in legislatures exist only in a few countries like Nepal, the Philippines, and the erstwhile Soviet Union. None of these are great success stories for women's political participation. Unfortunately, we insist on following that same route.

The Scandinavian and other European countries which arrived at a relatively high level of female representation did so without reserving seats in Parliament. Rather than freezing women's representation at a quota ceiling, these countries have moved in the direction of equal (and sometimes more than equal) participation in a steady and enduring fashion. Women in these countries are especially active in local institutions of governance. In Sweden, 48 per cent of those elected to county councils in 1994 were women and 41 per cent of municipal council members were women. This broad-based participation at the lower levels provides a rich training ground for intervention at the very top levels as well, as evident by the rising proportion of women in the European Parliament where international affairs are sorted out.

However, in all of these countries these gains have not been made without special efforts. Widespread pressure was created by women's movements which succeeded in organizing female voters around pro-women programmes and policies. Secondly, most of the political parties committed themselves to a quota system within their parties in which a certain percentage of candidates for all elections have to be women. Even within the party decision-making fora, a certain percentage of posts are reserved for women by voluntary commitment, rather than legislative coercion. In Sweden, the Social Democratic Party, the Left Party, and the Green Party have committed themselves to a 50 per cent quota for women while the Liberal Party has a 40 per cent quota.

In Germany, according to the statutes of the Green Party, at least one-half of the party's posts must be held by women and on electoral lists, women must be represented with a minimum share of 50 per cent. In the Social Democratic Party of Germany, the quota for appointed candidates is 40 per cent for both men and women. All the parties in Norway have adopted a 40 per cent minimum quota for women for each level of the party's governing bodies, as well as for elections to the legislature. The New Labour Party of New Zealand, as well as the Green Party have 50 per cent quotas for women. In the Netherlands, it varies from 26 per cent in the Christian Democratic Party, 33 per cent in the Socialist Party to 40 per cent in the Green Party. In all these countries, internal party quotas have yielded a higher representation of women in legislatures without needing to reserve seats because these parties themselves function democratically with a fair degree of financial and political accountability.

In our country, even the best of our women parliamentarians feel sidelined and powerless within their respective parties. The few women leaders who exist in various parties have not been able to facilitate the entry of greater numbers of women in electoral and party politics, and therefore are an ineffective minority within their own respective parties. The very same male party leaders who compete with each other in announcing special quotas for women have shown little willingness to include women in party decision-making or even to create a conducive atmosphere for women's participation in politics. The representation of women within the decision-making fora of various political parties is even lower than their representation in Parliament. Unless change occurs within each of these parties, women's participation cannot be enhanced because under the present system, parties are the only platform for political socialization for electoral purposes. If women are not allowed to play an active role in the day-to-day functioning of the parties, it becomes far easier for powerful male politicians to corner the women's quota by presenting their own wives and daughters for ticket allocation at election time.

Therefore, my initial response was to suggest that instead of quotas in legislature, we should ensure quotas within parties through an amendment of the People's Representation Act. Any party which failed to include a certain per cent of women in their decision-making bodies and give a certain fixed quota of party tickets to women would merit disqualification. (See my article, 'Why Feminise Corruption?' in *Indian Express*, 4 Oct 1996) However, on second thought this does not seem to be an efficient and workable proposal. Our political parties don't function according to well-defined democratic norms, nor is there much financial transparency. Consequently, thugs and crooks have come to dominate them. Even important posts are often reduced to rubber-stamp status. For instance, ever since Indira Gandhi's time, Congress Working Committee has not been allowed to play the role of a collective power centre. Most decisions came to be taken in the Prime Minister's Office. Even in the recent past despite a crisis in the Congress, all the heavyweight dissidents put together could not prevail upon the former Prime Minister P.V. Narasimha Rao to call a meeting of the Congress Working Committee at the time they wanted to elect an alternative president. Rao gave up power only when court cases and press exposure made it impossible for him to continue. At the district and state levels, organizational elections have not been held for so long that Congressmen have lost the memory of how to function as a party and instead act like gangsters. Ticket distribution of all parties is controlled by powerful coteries sitting in Delhi rather than being decided locally on the basis of a person's merit and commitment.

As a result, seeking patronage through sycophancy and pay-offs has become the hallmark of our political culture. Most parties maintain no accounts. Money collected in the name of parties is simply siphoned off into personal accounts, not just by petty local leaders but right up to the Prime Minister's level. Here again, Indira Gandhi played a pioneering role in legitimizing this kind of corruption. A large part of the money she collected in the name of the Congress Party through kickbacks, pay-offs, and plain extortion is known to have been siphoned off into sundry foreign and Indian accounts which she and her sons controlled personally. This is how she became independent of (and above) the party and began to use the money for horse-trading of MPs and MLAs to ensure that only her sycophants stayed in power. The recent scandal involving the 'purchase' of Jharkhand Mukti Morcha MPs by Rao to defeat a no-confidence motion against his minority government is not an isolated incident—it has been a routine happening since Mrs Gandhi's time. Likewise, the recent *hawala* scam demonstrates that other parties have enthusiastically emulated the Congress Party as a role model, despite all the noises they make against its misrule and corruption. The pay-off list mentioned in the Jain diary includes BJP, Janata Dal and Congress leaders of all political shades. Even the left parties tend to adopt this political culture wherever they get into power. Party tickets are increasingly being purchased with pay-offs to top leaders. In such an atmosphere, whether women's representation in party forums is 20 or 50 per cent hardly makes a difference.

Moreover, to compel a party, by law, to include a fixed quota of women, militates against the very principle of democracy. Every political party ought to be free to define and act on its own ideology and principles, including those parties that do not believe in women's political participation. Internal quotas can be meaningful only when parties commit to them voluntarily, as happened in some of the European democracies.

At the same time, it is urgently required that we take special measures to enhance women's political participation in ways that help them influence decision-making. Our democracy will remain seriously flawed if it fails to yield space to women.

An Alternative Proposal

A proposal put forward by Shetkari Sangathana of Maharashtra in its Aurangabad Conference of 1993 on seat reservation for women, seems to be more promising than the mechanical, rotating, quota system being currently proposed. This proposal was formulated after the Sangathana carried out a review of the results of the one-third reservation quota for women at the panchayat and zilla parishad level.

The proposal advocates the creation of multi-seat constituencies, with one-third of the seats reserved for women. For instance, three constituencies could be clubbed together to make one and these clubbed constituencies can be represented by three people, one of whom must be a woman. The first two seats would go to the two candidates who poll the highest number of votes—whether the candidate is a man or a woman. The third seat would go to the woman who polls the highest number of votes among the women candidates. This same principle of guaranteed representation for women of at least one-third of all seats could also be extended to a 50 per cent reservation for women which is what I would personally favour and fight for. In that case, each constituency would be represented by two members in Parliament—one man and one woman. This could be done while maintaining our current 'first-past-the-post' system, or even if we adopted a proportional representation system.

There are several advantages this system:

- Representation of women would not be frozen at a 33 per cent limit. Every constituency will be represented by at least one woman but it would not be limited to one if women candidates manage to win general seats as well.
- All the voters in every constituency would get a chance to vote for a woman candidate, if they so desire, as opposed to the presently proposed quota system, in which voters of only one-third of all constituencies will get an opportunity to elect women candidates.
- The tendency to ignore one's constituency (due to the uncertainty that comes with rotating reserved constituencies) would be reduced. Women would be able to opt for the constituency where they have built support, rather than be shunted around from one constituency to the other.
- Men would not feel forced out of their nursed constituencies, but simply be asked to share space with women. All candidates,

regardless of sex, would have an opportunity to win one of the first two seats if they are able to garner enough votes. If a party does not wish to field women candidates, it could choose to put up only one or two male candidates. It would not have to draw a total blank in a constituency simply because it did not have eligible women or simply did not want to put up women candidates.

• Women will not be fighting only against other women, but would compete with men as well. They would also get an opportunity to team up with male colleagues to cover their joint constituency on behalf of their party, so they would not be confined to the *zenana dabba*.

In multi-seat constituencies, voters will have the choice to elect leaders from more than one party. If the three (or one of the two) winning candidates are from different parties, they are likely to act as a check on their colleagues and compete with each other in serving the constituency.

It may well be argued that clubbing two or three constituencies together will make them unduly large and unwieldy. But then three candidates of the same party are required to campaign and serve it jointly. This may promote a measure of team spirit among our legislators. Moreover, a big constituency is a disadvantage only for those who step into the electoral fray at the last minute and have no real roots in that area. They have to 'cover' the entire constituency in the few weeks given for the election campaign. Those who have nurtured their constituencies by prior hard work would not be so handicapped.

Another alternative would be to double the number of seats in parliament. We have an exceptionally low votes to representative ratio as compared to other countries. Doubling the size of our legislatures will help to redress this imbalance and allow for fifty per cent assured seats for women.

However, this system of dual member or multi-seat constituencies is likely to throw up its own problems which will need careful handling. For instance, what if the woman candidate who is to get elected on the reserved quota for women gets an insignificant or minuscule percentage of votes? To ensure that such non-viable candidates don't sneak in merely because they are women, it could be stipulated that whoever is to be elected under the quota has to secure a respectable percentage of the total votes cast. She may have still gotten far fewer votes than the male candidate who comes in third, to which extent it is 'unfair' to the man. But that is the logic of reservations. They cannot be accomplished without a measure of positive discrimination. The chief advantage of this system over the currently proposed system is that it does not disqualify men altogether from one-third of the country's constituencies. The two seat constituency with 50 per cent quota for women cuts down on many of these complexities.

If, in addition, we could put an end to the control over party tickets by the 'High Commands', better quality people might emerge within the various parties. To do this, we would have to ensure by law that the political parties follow democratic procedures, including party elections held regularly in each and every party, and that there is financial accountability of the parties through strict laws concerning campaign contributions and regular yearly audits of party finances. Parties which fail to fulfil these two criteria could be disqualified from contesting elections. Public funding of elections would also go a long way in reducing the role of money power, provided strict checks are kept on election expenditure. Candidates for the legislature as well as at the panchayat and zilla parishad level should be selected through primary elections at the appropriate levels by party members and not nominated by state or national level bosses. Parties which are sincerely interested in seeing women participate actively in politics ought to begin by activizing their women's fronts at all levels and by including women in their decision-making bodies through a voluntarily committed quota system.

These changes ought to be simultaneously accompanied by other electoral reforms with well-defined rules that allow for public monitoring. However, the real cleansing of our politics will take place only when being in a position of power in the government (whether as a politician or a bureaucrat) no longer provides a license to loot the public exchequer. The license-permit-kickback raj has to be thoroughly dismantled before democracy can work in this country and we can begin to live as free citizens and participate effectively in the governance of our country.

XI

Women's Marginal Role in Politics

The law to reserve one-third of the total number of seats for women was implemented at the panchayat and zilla parishad level in most of the states of India without any opposition from any political quarter whatsoever. Ramakrishna Hegde's government in Karnataka started this process in 1983 before the Central legislation mandating representation for women was passed. It provided for 25 per cent reservation for women at village panchayat levels. This was before any powerful women's lobby emerged in Karnataka to press for this move and before there was any popular groundswell of opinion in favour of women's reservation. In the mid 1980s, the Shetkari Sangathana of Maharashtra, led by Sharad Joshi, pioneered the move to field all-women panels for panchayat elections in that state and subsequently, focused on getting women elected to zilla parishads in as many constituencies as possible, with men of the Sangathana playing a supportive role. However, the Bill introduced in the Parliament in September 1996 to reserve one-third of the seats in Parliament and state legislatures has evoked a good deal of resistance and opposition. This despite the fact that all our major national parties—the Congress, the BJP, the Janata Dal, and even the two Communist parties have committed themselves to reserving 33 per cent of the seats in legislatures for women by including this promise in their respective election manifestos.

The Common Minimum Programme (CMP) agreed upon by the various parties constituting the UF government started its section entitled 'Social Justice' with the declaration that

one-third of the elected membership in Parliament and state legislatures will be reserved for women. Legislation, including an amendment to the Constitution, if necessary, will be introduced to reserve one-third of all posts in government for women.... All laws will be reviewed to remove provisions which discriminate against women.

*First published in *Manushi*, No. 97, Nov–Dec 1996.

News reports indicated that the greatest opposition to this Bill was coming from the United Front MPs. Some of them openly declared their intention to even defy the party whip (if one is issued) and vote against the Bill.

Compare the present day controversy over the issue of women's representation in legislatures to the atmosphere that prevailed in the 1920s. In response to the Indian agitation for representative government, the British government set up a committee headed by Montague and Chelmsford in 1919 to work out a proposal for constitutional reforms aiming at the inclusion of some Indians in government. Many groups presented their case for representation before the committee. Among the many delegations that met this committee, Sarojini Naidu and Margaret Cousins led a small delegation of women to demand that women be granted the same rights of representation in legislatures as men. The British government predictably thought this demand was quite preposterous because women in most western countries had still not been given the right to vote, despite a protracted struggle. The Southborough Committee stated that 'the extension of the vote to women would be premature in a society which continued to enforce purdah and prohibitions against female education.'[1] However, instead of taking on themselves the onus of rejecting the demand outright, the British government simply skirted the issue by leaving it up to each of the individual provincial legislatures that they had just set up in India to grant or to refuse the franchise to women. Their assumption was that since Indians were so 'backward', they would never accept the idea of equal political rights for women. But despite the fact that at this time there was no mass-based women's suffrage movement in India, each of the Indian provincial legislatures voted to make it possible, within a short span of time, for women to be represented at par with men without much fuss.

The testimony of Margaret Cousins, an Irish feminist who played a major role in women's organizations in India, as well as in Britain, brings out the contrast between the western and Indian response to women's political rights very clearly.

Perhaps only women like myself who had suffered from the cruelties, the injustices of men politicians, the man-controlled press, the man in the street, in England and Ireland while we waged our militant campaign for eight years there after all peaceful and constitutional means had been tried for fifty previous years, could fully appreciate the wisdom, nobility and the passing of fundamental tests in self-government of these Indian legislators....

Between the Madras Legislative Council in 1921 and Bihar Council in 1929 all the legislative areas of India had conferred the symbol and instrument of equal citizenship with men on women who possessed equal qualifications— a certain amount of literacy, property, age, payment of taxes, length of residence.[2]

These limitations were included solely because the British were only prepared for limited suffrage for those who possessed a certain amount of property and education. They were not willing to consider universal adult suffrage. When a meeting of representative women's organizations in 1930, drafted a memorandum demanding immediate acceptance of adult franchise without gender discrimination, it was turned down by the British government. The same demand received a totally different response from the Indian leaders. The very next year, in 1931, the Karachi session of the Indian National Congress took the historic decision committing itself to the political equality of women, regardless of their status and qualifications. This proposal met with virtually no opposition.

Laws claiming to protect women's rights have seldom evoked the same amount of hostility or opposition in India that they provoke in many other countries of the world and get to be easily endorsed by the entire political spectrum. In fact, in India there is very little difference between parties of the right or left on women's issues. For instance, the BJP's current manifesto sounds even more progressive than the left parties on women's issues.

It took women in Europe a century-long struggle to win the right to vote. By contrast, the right to vote and other legal rights came without a fuss or fight in India. The right to abortion, right to equal employment and educational opportunities, equal remuneration for equal work, protection against domestic violence—all came to be passed as laws in India without any hostility or resistance. However, since our government neither has the political will nor the appropriate machinery to implement any of its laws (not just those relating to women but even traffic laws) little of our progressive legislation makes an impact on citizens' lives.

People's Response

Our country has had a well-entrenched tradition, whereby a party, politician or public figure bad-mouthing women in public or opposing moves for women's empowerment are strongly disapproved of and usually rejected. As far as I can remember, among our male politicians, only Bal Thackeray of the Shiv Sena some years ago and more recently Sharad Yadav of Janata Dal have made some brazenly anti-women statements. In the assembly elections that followed, Shiv Sena, Thackeray's party suffered a major setback in Maharashtra, which was attributed to Thackeray's indiscreet anti-women remarks, among other things. Sharad Yadav too was given such a drubbing for bad-mouthing women politicians that no one from his party dared defend him. He himself was forced to rein his tongue by the force of reaction against him. Because of this, very few politicians dare attack women from public platforms except when they are in direct electoral competition with a woman.

This is not just due to the pressure on our politicians to be 'politically correct' on women's issues. Indira Gandhi as the first woman prime minister of India was rarely attacked on account of her gender. If anything, she was able to use her gender to her advantage projecting herself as Mother India and Durga incarnate rolled into one. There was no fuss made over her assuming the highest political office in the land. By contrast, many of the supposed advanced democracies of the West are still not ready for women in such high offices. The first woman prime minister of France was constantly derided and attacked for being a woman till she simply resigned from the job.

There is indeed a widespread social opinion in favour of women's active political participation. The recent countrywide post-election opinion survey conducted by the Centre for the Study of Developing Societies for *India Today* provides the most encouraging and definitive endorsement that there is no real divide between men and women in India on this issue. 75 per cent of men and 79 per cent of women favour active participation of women in politics and 75 per cent of men and an equal number of women favour the principle of reservations for women in legislatures. Though this does not mean that they will necessarily favour women candidates simply on account of their gender.

On the eve of assembly elections in Uttar Pradesh, I interviewed scores of men and women in Meerut constituency to gauge people's responses on a range of political issues, including reservations for women. Barring one Sikh couple, everyone I interviewed expressed strong feelings in favour of reservations for women. This included men and women from supposedly conservative Muslim families, illiterate working-class Hindus and Muslims, and representatives of

the Balmiki and Jatav (sweeper) communities, apart from the middle-
and upper-classes. Men and women alike said that the inclusion of
women was both necessary and desirable and would be beneficial
not just for women but for politics as a whole.

Despite all this, women have been politically marginalized in our
country and most of them live extremely restricted lives. They are not
allowed to have much of a voice even within their own community's
decision-making processes, leave alone having a meaningful say in
national politics. In addition, today we are witnessing a serious
backlash. Not just politicians but even many intellectuals are angrily
rejecting the idea of reservations for women and calling it a retrogres-
sive move.

Peripheral Role of Women

Most countries in the world have failed to give due space and
representation to women in political institutions. Even in societies
where women exercise relatively more freedom in day-do-day living,
they remain politically marginalized.

Women have done extremely well in the Scandinavian countries—Sweden, Norway, Denmark and Finland, where they are moving in the direction of near equal participation. In these societies
women have begun to seriously alter the very nature of politics and
have made enduring and substantial gains for themselves in every
field. In India, the problem is more serious because while in many
other countries women are inching forward bit by bit, in India the
participation of women in politics is actually declining. There were
many more outstanding women leaders and workers in the Congress
Party at all levels during the freedom movement than in today's all
parties put together. Thus, women's declining representation in the
legislatures of a few states and the stagnant representation of women
in the Lok Sabha since Independence is apparent today.

One of the most puzzling features of low political representation
of women in our legislative bodies is that it seems to have no direct
correlation with literacy and other seemingly logical indicators. A
comparison between the states of Kerala and Rajasthan, whose literacy rates are at opposite ends of the spectrum, demonstrates this
clearly. In Kerala, the overall literacy rate is reportedly 90 per cent
with 86 per cent female literacy. By contrast, in Rajasthan, female

literacy is a mere 20 per cent and only 12 per cent of the females are literate in rural areas.[3]

Kerala has a matrilineal tradition in which women have a much larger measure of autonomy and freedom of movement. Kerala's women also tend to marry at a much later age compared to women in other states. Most women in Rajasthan live far more restricted lives in aggressively patriarchal communities, many of whom still practise purdah very early or even child marriages. However, all these cultural and educational advantages that women acquired in Kerala have not translated into higher political participation. The percentage of women in the Kerala legislative assembly rose from less than 1 per cent in 1967 to 6 per cent in 1991. In Rajasthan, the representation of women was 4 per cent in 1967 and reached 8 per cent in 1985–90. Since then it has been going down. Similarly, the state of Manipur, which has a tradition of women playing a dominant role in family and community, again due to a matrilineal heritage, never elected a single woman legislator up to 1990—when it elected its first. A similar low level of women's representation is true for Nagaland and other north-eastern states, which are known for a less repressive culture for women. By contrast, UP, Bihar, and Madhya Pradesh, which are known for their low education levels and repressive cultural norms for women, have not only sent a relatively larger proportion of women to the Lok Sabha but have also elected relatively more women MLAs.

Post-Independence Politics

In independent India, politics has proved to be very inhospitable for women. One important reason is the pervasive gender discrimination which results in making even veteran women politicians feel by-passed and ignored. For new entrants, discrimination makes it very difficult for them to establish a foothold without patronage from powerful men in the party.

However, it is important to recognize that the sidelining of women in our polity goes beyond gender discrimination. It is part of a larger process in which most honest, decent people have become politically marginalized as our politics and government have become the hotbed of crooks, thugs and even outright criminals. Very few honest men or women have survived in electoral politics and kept their honesty intact.

Today, the political scene has come to be dominated by anti-social elements because we have reduced our democracy to the sole ritual of the electorate casting its vote whenever called upon to do so. After they vote, the people have virtually no role in the functioning of civic and other institutions. After Independence, the brown *sahibs* led by Nehru, who inherited power from the *gora sahibs*, allowed the colonial bureaucracy to strengthen its stranglehold over our civic, administrative, and political institutions from the village to the national level. Even today, a young collector in his twenties rules supreme like a colonial master over the district he governs. He can dismiss panchayats and zilla parishads at will and people have to appear before *sarkari babus* as hapless supplicants for every little thing. In such an atmosphere, local leaders, including elected representatives, tend to establish a nexus with bureaucrats so that both can join in unrestrained loot and plunder of public resources. No effective monitoring mechanisms exist to restrain our *netas* and *babus* or call them to account when they systematically abuse their authority. Politics has become the quickest and shortest route to getting rich without doing any work other than brokerage. If the rules of the game remain as corrupt as they are now, only those women politicians who are good at emulating the worst of male politicians in the art of power-grabbing and plundering will be able to survive.

The career graphs of Indira Gandhi, Jayalalitha, Mayawati, Rithambara, Sheila Kaul, and a host of other prominent women in power politics is a testimony that women can become as vicious, corrupt, and authoritarian as the worst of men when they occupy positions of power, which demand little or no accountability. Such specimens of the female gender serve neither the cause of women nor that of society. They are as harmful for our deomocracy as are the Bal Thackerays, Chandraswamis, H.K.L. Bhagats and Advanis. The presence of this type of woman is neither worth fighting for nor celebrating.

This is not to suggest that I am in favour of leaving the political arena to the male crooks who dominate our Parliament and state legislatures today. Far from it. But I would like to see women enter politics with a vision for restoring the health of our dysfunctional political system, to make our politics truly representative and overhaul our institutions of governance—the local corporations, police stations, courts, and various government offices—in such a way that they become actually accountable to ordinary citizens in their every-day functioning.

Extra Load of Morality

Many argue that to expect women to carry an extra load of morality is to make unreasonable demands of them, which only strengthens the stereotype of women as self-sacrificing creatures, who can be easily sidelined. I confess that I am still stuck to the perhaps somewhat outdated, naive, and romantic vision of Mahatma Gandhi regarding women entering politics, not to compete with men in loot and plunder but with a view to cleansing politics. While it is legitimate for women to demand a share of the pie, it is equally important to ensure the pie is worth eating and that there is enough there for everyone to share. Women's entry into politics will not change anything for the better if the overall character of politics does not improve. If women join politics in greater numbers through the present scheme of reservation this change alone is not going to create a new political culture by itself. While the inadequate representation of women in governance is a serious flaw of our democracy, which needs correction, to stop at merely that would be suicidal as it will only lead to making a sizable space for women in the world of organized corruption and crime.

Politics at What Cost?

As things stand today, even those women who have made a mark in electoral politics find it hard to sustain their involvement unless they too become money-making racketeers. For the honest, the heavy investment of time and money that is required proves too burden-some to be sustained for more than a short time. A good example from among the many accounts I have heard of the special hurdles women face in politics, is that of Sarojatai Kashikar, who was a member of the Maharashtra assembly between 1991 and 1995. Sarojati was initially drawn into politics through her husband's close associa-tion with the Shetkari Sangathana. Before her exposure to the San-gathana, she was an ordinary housewife, whose only connection with political life for years was cooking and serving her husband's col-leagues in the movement. Though she was well-educated, she had no interest in or knowledge of the political world.

However, as the Sangathana leader Sharad Joshi insisted that women must participate actively in the movement, she slowly came to be one of the leading cadres of the Sangathana. In 1991, the Sangathana fielded her as a candidate for the Maharashtra state assembly elections as part of their campaign to get as many women elected as possible. Though new to electoral politics, she won by a convincing margin and within a short span of time came to be one of the most respected legislators in the state assembly. She took her work seriously, studied the required documents, kept in good contact with her constituency and was respected even by district officials for her honesty and integrity. However, her job as an MLA required that long periods had to be spent away from home attending assembly sessions in Bombay. Since she did not feel safe living alone in the MLA's hostel in Bombay, a young brother-in-law was deputed to accompany and stay with her in Bombay. She told me that even for a middle-aged married woman like herself, to be seen chatting and freely socializing with male political colleagues was likely to be misunderstood and become the cause for character assassination. To avoid this, her brother-in-law remained by her side to act as a protective shield.

In addition, in Sarojatai's case she could also count on four other male colleagues from the Sangathana, who also became MLAs at the same time as her. Having been trained in the political culture of the Sangathana, her colleagues were not only exceptionally honest and decent but also used to dealing respectfully with women. These men acted as buffers against the ugly aspects of politics, yet provided her the necessary communication channel with the world of politicians without her having to directly hobnob with all kinds of unsavoury characters. Since they were all close and trusted friends of her husband, interaction with them provided much less scope for misunderstanding, Yet, she did find herself handicapped in many respects and had to watch her every step. Hence the dependence on her young and relatively inexperienced brother-in-law.

Sarojatai's accomplishments would have been nearly impossible without her supportive husband and even more supportive sister-in-law who cheerfully took over the entire load of her domestic responsibility, as well as caring for her two growing sons. Fortunately, her two sons were already responsible teenagers and were cooperative, but they missed her during her long absences from home. If her kids had been small, political work would have been even more stressful.

Apart from the substantial sum of money that had to be spent on her election campaign, her husband had to spend a lot of additional money to support her politics because, unlike most other MLAs, she did not make any 'extra' money. The amount of money and resources officially provided to each MLA for their salary and political work simply does not cover the actual expenses of nursing a constituency.

Due to all this, Sarojatai simply refused to stand for the recent parliamentary election though she continues to be active in Sangathana work. They say behind every great man there is usually a great woman. However, behind each politically effective woman, not just a cooperative husband is required, but an extremely supportive and resourceful extended family and in addition a strong movement-based organization ready to encourage women into public life.

The Inhibiting Factors

A key component of politics is the art of building alliances. In a culture, where even formal interaction with men unconnected to one's own family is frowned upon, women are severaly handicapped in politics because they cannot cultivate close association with men without jeopardizing their position in the family. A woman operating on her own strength in a party filled with corrupt politicians, who think nothing of slandering their own women colleagues would find the going very tough, even if she can somehow mobilize other compensatory resources by her own special efforts.

Not too long ago, Uma Bharati of the BJP was driven to a suicide attempt because of the slander campaign unleashed by her own colleagues who saw her independent mass popularity as a threat to their power. They used her supposed personal closeness to one of the BJP's important male leaders to spread all kinds of vicious rumours about her, both within the party and in the media. The fact that politics is dominated by the most unsavoury kind of men makes most women themselves reluctant to break taboos regarding free intermixing with men. A woman risks her reputation by even being seen with many of them, whereas a man does not have to prove his credentials by such fierce avoidance.

Thus women are handicapped from getting crucial information which men pick up easily from casual gossip with all kinds of people. So much of our politics is carried out in late night sessions, often over booze, where deals are made and strategies planned. Most women politicians, including the corrupt ones, don't dare to be seen participating in such sessions.

The breakdown of institutional politics in favour of gangster politics has made things much tougher for women, especially given the strict regime of restrictions that most women are made to live under. Even though most men in India favour women's political participation, this does not easily translate into relaxing restrictions on the women of their own families. Behavioural change at the family level will require consistent hard work to change cultural norms and reduce women's domestic responsibilities.

Even in educated, middle-class neighbourhoods of Delhi, *mohalla* associations are usually run by men. While a few families are willing to relax some restrictions on women and are supportive of their activism, the workload of women and the nature of their domestic responsibilities makes it extremely hard for them to spare the kind of time required for making even a small difference in politics.

When I was studying the functioning of an all-women panchayat in a Maharashtra village, one of the leading members described the difficulties of keeping women active and involved, except intermittently:

For every little thing, we have to go and petition the district level officials—whether you want a road repaired or a bus service extended to your village, a water tank built or a phone connection sanctioned—each of these tasks require numerous trips to district headquarters with each trip involving loss of one full workday for a woman. Often meeting officials won't get the work done. You have to organize protests, sit on *dharnas* and what not. Women simply can't spare that kind of time even if their husbands are not objecting to their participation. Men enjoy meeting officials, having *chai-pani* with them, because that is how they build contacts which can be encashed for personal benefit in various ways. But women are always in a hurry to get back. They don't want to hang around gossiping in tea shops, chatting with officials and *netas*—all of which seem to be a necessary part of men's political world.

As long as working in the political realm involves endless petition-mongering to uncaring, unaccountable authorities, as long as decision-making remains remote and in the hands of bureaucrats, as long as politics cannot be easily integrated into the everyday life of people without causing severe disturbances in domestic life, men are likely to control and dominate it. There should be no requirement that a person become a full-time politician and make it a profession (as well as a means of livelihood) if we want meaningful participation by large numbers of women in this country's political life on a consistent, long-term basis, rather than fitful, sporadic involvement in *morchas* and *dharnas*, as happens at present. The more centralized and authoritarian a polity, the lower will be the involvement of women in it.

Additional Disadvantages

By keeping more than three-quarters of India's women illiterate and providing shamelessly poor quality education to the few who manage to reach *sarkari* schools, the bureaucracy plays a crucial role in discouraging and obstructing women's participation in public affairs. Even for participation at the panchayat level, it is no longer possible for an illiterate person to function effectively because the *sarkari* panchayats have been integrated into the vast bureaucratic network, with its reams of forms to fill out and its dust-covered volumes of rules and procedures.

Moreover, the rules are rendered either in Victorian English or in such opaque Hindi or regional languages that even the literate members of panchayats find it difficult to make any sense of them. Wherever the panchayat members are incapable of or diffident about handling rules and accounts, the government-appointed *gram sevak* simply takes control of the panchayats. Most women, especially those who are uneducated, feel helpless and lost when they are required to deal with the impenetrable maze of the bureaucratic world which defines the parameters of the panchayat's role. What appears to be a woman panchayat member's incapacity is actually proof of our system's ridiculous procedures and insensitivity to people's requirements.

What goes by the name of politics in our country is an overly time-consuming and debased activity. Even for those who are honest and sincere in their work, the nature of our political institutions makes it very difficult to make a real difference. Nothing comes to our citizens without *sifarish* and influence because the government encroaches on too many aspects of our lives in negative ways.

Our MPs and MLAs are constantly mobbed by favour-seekers and petition-mongers. They waste a good part of their time doling out favours to their supporters and people who seek their intervention in getting a water or electricity connection, a telephone or gas cylinder sanctioned, jobs or school admission, out-of-turn railway reservations from the MP quota, and generally mediating with various *sarkari* offices for 'getting work done' (*kaam karwana*) since our *babus* don't believe in doing anything unless kicked from above or bribed from below. This includes intervening in cases of harassment by the police, corporation or other government agencies.

In addition, an MP or an MLA is expected to lobby to get funds sanctioned for repair of roads or to get *sarkari* approval for the opening of an engineering or medical college. Even to get a primary health centre opened or a public sector enterprise started in their constituency requires lobbying. In other words, all those things that ought to happen in the normal course of events require constant string-pulling in India.

The kind of politicians who can thrive in such an atmosphere are not likely to have the time or the skills required of a legislator such as initiating meaningful changes in government policy and making appropriate laws to translate that policy into action. This cultivation of a network of favour-seekers is essentially the only political activity commonly recognized as 'political work' and 'constituency building'. Within this system how can a legislator do any meaningful work in her/his constituency? No matter how hard an MLA may try, she/he is not likely to succeed in getting a primary health centre or primary school of that constituency to function properly. However, very little effort is required for an MLA to become a part of the corruption network and make money by keeping the malfunctioning system intact. The constant pressure from favour-seekers means that an MP/MLA has no time for a normal family life. Women find this part of politics especially hard to cope with. That is why most of our women legislators tend to be from political families which are conditioned to withstand such a stressful lifestyle. No ordinary person can put up with so much strain and stay sane.

Staying Power of Women

The staying power of women in politics is also limited due to the fact that while they may get support and even get to be treated as heroines if they win an election, very few women are allowed to remain politically active once they lose an election. According to Sharad Joshi, whose Shetkari Sangathana worked hard to bring a large number of women into the electoral arena, it is extremely difficult to keep women politically active after they have lost an election because a woman who continues to devote time to politics even after an electoral setback gets to be looked down on, as a hopeless addict, like a wayward man hooked on drugs or liquor. Therefore, unlike men, women cannot take defeat in their stride and tend to fade out soon thereafter.

Considering all this, it is perhaps not a coincidence that the few women who have developed an independent political base and are able to compete with men in electoral politics are mostly single or widowed—as for example, Uma Bharti of the BJP, Mamta Banerjee of the Congress Party, and Maneka Gandhi of the Janata Dal. These women are able to give their undivided attention to politics because there is no man to hold them back, and therefore, they are not easily cowed down by scandal or character assassination. These three women have had to wage relentless battles within their respective parties for due recognition because their popularity, mass appeal and their organizational skills are resented by their male colleagues. Yet, these women have mostly emerged triumphant because they are celebrities to their supporters.

While Indian society may not be very kind to ordinary women, it loves to celebrate women who appear and prove themselves to be stronger than men.

In Maneka Gandhi's case, the aura around the Gandhi family name has played an important role in adding to her charisma, while both Uma Bharati and Mamta Banerjee come from very ordinary families and were not groomed by any powerful patriarchs. Women who show extraordinary resilience, courage and the capacity to withstand character assassination get to be treated with special awe and reverence in our country. Despite all the muck-raking regarding Uma Bharati's alleged affairs, her opponents in the party have not been able to eclipse her. She is a popular cult figure among the BJP followers, far more influential in electoral campaigns of the party than even Rajmata Scindia with all her royal antecedents. However, none of these women have the clout their popularity should have earned them within their respective parties.

At the same time, it is ironic that none of these three women make a special point of mobilizing other women. They would see that as a downgrading of their status if they were projected primarily as leaders of women. The more successful among women politicians do not like to be seen as representing women's interests. It is unfortunate, that by and large only those who find it hard to maintain a secure foothold for themselves in elective politics tend to gravitate towards women's issues.

Politics for Ordinary Women

Our democracy will become more meaningful when ordinary women can take part in political deliberations without having to make heroic sacrifices and prove themselves stronger than men, over and over again.

In the existing circumstances, even talented women cannot stay in politics on their own steam, especially if they are married and have families. Women need the following conducive conditions in order to participate effectively in the public realm:

- a supportive family, preferably one with a political background;
- someone from within the extended family willing to take over a large part of the family responsibility, especially the care of children;
- a good amount of surplus money in the family.

Not only in India, but even in the West, very few women can count on all these factors combining together in their favour. The nuclear family and the high divorce rate in the West make it that much harder for women to give much time to sustained political activity, especially since most western women are simultaneously engaged in employment outside the house. If a woman's day revolves around dropping off and picking up kids from creches after an eight or ten-hour job outside the house, there is not much energy or time left for political work, except sporadic participation in campaigns and demonstrations. If the nature and demands of politics are such that a woman has to choose between her children and politics, most women are likely to avoid politics.

Therefore, it is crucially important for women to have more leisure for them to want to participate in politics. They tend to prefer political work that doesn't take them too far away from home on a regular basis. Thus women can be effective only in decentralized polities where decisions affecting people's lives can be taken locally.

Where Women Succeeded

If we look around the world, we find that women have secured a strong political foothold only in those societies where institutions function according to well-defined democratic norms, where the crime, violence, and overall corruption levels are low, where decision-making is not concentrated in the hands of a few, and where citizens actively participate in local governance without needing to become full-time politicians.

It is no coincidence that the representation of women is highest in the parliaments of the Scandinavian countries. By contrast, in the more macho and aggressive political climate of the USA, women's representation in the Senate is barely 9 per cent. This is despite the long history of a militant women's movement in the United States. Apart from the above mentioned factors, family life in the Scandina-vian countries has changed dramatically due to changes from above and below, allowing women relatively greater leisure and freedom. According to 1994 statistics, 66 per cent of Swedish women in the age group 25–29 were never married or remained single. In the 40–49 age group this figure drops to 16 per cent—still high by Indian standards, where marriage is nearly universal. This doesn't count the people who are divorced and separated, but only those who remain single.

In Sweden, according to 1994 data, the average number of children a woman has in her entire lifetime is 1.9, and according to 1992–93 figures, 28 per cent of Swedish couples were cohabiting without children. In 1990–91, Swedish women spent an average of 17 hours per week on household work excluding childcare, with men contributing 6 hours. In 1990–91, women had 33 hours per week for leisure activities with men having only a slight advantage with 35 hours of leisure per week.

The state provides high-quality childcare through municipal institutions and in 1993, 58 per cent of kids aged one to six attended state-supported daycare centres. The state also provides 'cash benefits' up to 450 days after a baby is born for both fathers and mothers of young children. There are many other special benefits provided for children who have special needs.

The functional and streamlined democracies typical of Scandinavia have opened up a substantial amount of time for both women and men who are interested in political work or any other work outside the domestic sphere.

However, the support system that is enjoyed by people living in Scandinavian countries is only possible because these countries have:

- very high income levels;
- not a very dramatic gap between the rich and the poor;
- small and culturally homogeneous populations;
- well-developed traditions of the state playing a social welfare role;
- a substantial number of women living independently;

- very high education levels for both men and women and high participation of women in the income-earning labour force. For instance, in 1994, only 5 per cent of women were unemployed in Sweden while the figure for unemployed men was a little higher at 7 per cent;
- a situation in which families are spending less and less time on housework and care of children. They have minimal interaction with 'other family members', such as elderly parents, and other relatives.

It is no wonder that having freed themselves from the domestic sphere, Scandinavian women lead the women of the world in political participation. However, this has been achieved at a very heavy cost which most of us in India may not be willing to pay. Care of others outside the family takes up about 30 minutes a week for both women and men in Sweden. By contrast, Swedish women spend 32.6 and men spend 35.2 hours a week on leisure activities.[4]

All of this paints a picture of an increasing atomization of human life and rapid erosion of family ties. If one compares the time involvement of Swedish parents with their children or relatives to the amount of importance given to family life in India, including time with children, old parents, relatives, neighbours, and friends, it becomes obvious why most people in India, not just women, are averse to sustained political work.

However, the gains Scandinavian women have made in the public realm are indeed substantial.

In this respect, Japan provides an interesting contrast where politics at the top is highly male-dominated but at the bottom is becoming rather woman-centric. In Japan, a majority of women do not work outside the house, while men are expected to work extremely hard to support their families. Employers control not only men's long working hours, but also their leisure time when they are expected to socialize with male colleagues going in groups to bars or *geisha* houses. Consequently, men have hardly any time for family life. They come home too late, too tired, and leave too early to be able to take an active interest in family or neighbourhood affairs. Consequently, the whole domestic terrain and neighbourhood is left to women, who have lots of free time on their hands once their husbands and kids leave the house. In addition, men are expected to hand over their earnings to women—family finances are controlled and managed mostly by women.

The male-centric traditional culture of Japan does expect women to remain servile to men and nurture them obediently. But since men are home so little, the time women spend serving and pleasing men is very small. During such time they tend to wear a Kabuki-mask-like expression and do the required rituals, only to shed that mask of servility, as soon as men leave home. Unlike women in India, they socialize with other women freely, especially in their neighbourhoods and they do not live under a regime of restrictions over their movements and interactions with the outside world, provided they are not spending too much time with other men or having extramarital affairs. Consequently, women as a group have the time and the resources to take an active interest in local neighbourhood affairs—including civic matters. The politics at this level is heavily female-centred.

The famous Socialist Party woman leader, Takako Doi, came into prominence by quietly building a vast political base by mobilizing such female networks and energy into the political mainstream.

Thus, women in Japan have carved out a special space for themselves in politics at the base level, without the confrontational militancy of the western feminists. In this case, the fact that most Japanese women are relatively leisured housewives proved to be a positive asset. It would have been much harder had they been running from high-pressured jobs, to household shopping, to creches, and to the kitchens, as most western women do.

All this only goes to underscore the fact that the problem is far more complex than simply that Indian women are lagging behind due to discrimination. We have to make politics worthy of women, tune it sensitively to their requirements or else even with reserved seats, only those who become like saree-wearing men will be able to survive in politics.

NOTES

1. *Report on the Committee for the Status of Women*, pp. 284–5.
2. Margaret Cousins, *Indian Womanhood Today*, Kitabistan Series, Allahabad, 1937, pp. 32–3.
3. *A Status Report on Participation of Women in Panchayat Raj*, Institute of Social Sciences, New Delhi, 1995.
4. *Women and Men in Sweden: Facts and Figures, 1995.* Gender Statistics Unit, Sweden, 1995.

XII

Sex Harassment and Slander as Weapons of Subjugation

The problem of sexual harassment is part of a whole syndrome of discrimination and exploitation that women are subjected to in most societies. It is important not just because this form of oppression is more gender specific than most others, but also because women become even more vulnerable as they protest about it. The veil of silence cast over this particular form of exploitation makes it much harder to fight against or seek redressal for.

The problem of sexual harassment affects women of all classes, strata and communities. Very few women, even among the supposedly privileged sections of society, are likely to have altogether escaped various forms of sexual harassment, especially if they do not stay within the extremely narrow and debilitating boundaries and norms set by their community and family.

Sexual abuse for women comes first and foremost at the hands of those supposed to be their near and dear ones—the very people meant to protect them from aggression from the outside world. But in this article I will not be dealing with this aspect of the problem. I will also not be talking about the vast majority of the poor, urban or rural women who bear the worst forms of sexual violence and coercion nor will I be dealing with blatant forms of sexual violence such as rape.

I have confined my attention to the experiences of a tiny segment of our population—university students and teachers who come from middle and upper-middle class homes. The reason for narrowing down the focus to this group is simply that as someone who has taught in Delhi University for several years, I have been a close witness to the problems of these women. However, I am well aware that women

*First published in *Manushi*, No. 68, Jan–Feb 1992.

in universities, coming, as many of them do, from relatively elite backgrounds, are the least vulnerable among the various categories of women who venture out of the home to seek employment. Yet, they are not free from sexual exploitation and are more likely to take their humiliation silently for fear of seriously jeopardizing their status and survival within their own family and kinship group.

If most well-educated women from well-off families are unable to effectively resist sexual harassment and abuse, how much more difficult is it likely to be for women from vulnerable and poorer sections of society to resist such abuse? The accounts I have put together point to a general pattern. Sexual harassment is not so much rooted in individual inclinations or class characteristics. Rather, women become more or less vulnerable depending on how much control men have over their ability to earn a livelihood or to thwart their chances of acquiring a degree or skills which will equip them for entering the job market.

I extend the theme to include another related dimension of the problem: the use of sexual slander as a weapon to keep women in a perpetual state of fear, the fear of losing *izzat* (honour) in a way that can affect a woman's very chances of survival, and result in loss of family support, loss of a job, and the risk of becoming a social outcast.

Sadly, women may be subjected to sexual slander not only in situations where they are suspected of having violated some norm of sexual behaviour. Equally often, they may become targets of slander when, as victims, they dare to openly protest against sexual harassment or abuse. It is fairly common for a man accused of sexual harassment to start a counter-campaign against the woman, alleging sexual misconduct on her part. In fact, threatening to make such allegations is one of the most frequently deployed weapons used by men to frighten women, and to keep them subjugated.

How do we define sexual harassment? Sexual harassment occurs when a woman, despite having clearly indicated her disinterest, is pressured into tolerating or accepting undesirable sexual advances by someone who is in a position of power over her and is able to harm her interests if she declines these advances or to have sexual relations with him. For example, a boss who threatens, overtly or covertly, to withhold the promotion of a junior colleague or get her fired from the job if she snubs his sexual overtures; or a professor who uses his power as a member of a selection committee to coax or coerce a woman student into a sexual affair—can be accused of sexual harassment.

Even if a woman takes the initiative in making sexual advances to a man in a position of power in order to escape a difficult predicament or extract a favour, the man in a position of power who accepts a sexual favour, would still be guilty of sexual harassment. As someone in a position of power, he has a special responsibility to ensure that women working under him do not have to debase themselves simply to get their due or offer their bodies as a bribe to extract extra favours.

If a boss repeatedly makes sexual propositions to a woman employee, with or without any physical overtures, despite her repeatedly indicating that she finds his advances offensive, he can be rightly accused of sexual harassment. As someone working under him, the woman has little choice but to suffer such treatment. In most jobs, she has no way of escaping these unwanted sexual advances except by quitting. If she quits, she may not be able to get another job at all, or one that pays enough. Repeatedly making advances, even if they do not go beyond the verbal, toward someone who has no option but to suffer them, makes a boss guilty of sexual harassment.

I may well be accused of applying too wide a definition of sexual harassment that is unfair to many men. However, we need to acknowledge that we live in a world where men have a near total monopoly of power—economic, political, and social. There is, at best, a microscopic sprinkling of women, mostly token figures, at the top decision-making levels of our society. Therefore, women have to enter the job market or the political world on men's terms, which are more often than not, highly disadvantageous to women.

A Weapon for Dominance

Aggressive sexual encounters are used by men as one of the means of maintaining dominance and control, and frequently as a weapon for humiliating women. When men use their power to seduce or compel women into sexual relations, it often has little to do with mutually sought after physical pleasure. Sex is used as a weapon to try to debase the woman, to train her to accept a demeaning self-view, to see herself as a thing rather than a person in her own right, a person who can demand and get her due. If, in any society, men feel safe in demanding sexual bribes or inflicting sexual harassment with impunity and getting away with it, this is a good indication of a gross power imbalance between men and women. This is well-illustrated by a recent case at one of the prestigious IITs, (Institutes of Technology).

Whereby *Manushi's* help and intervention was sought by a group of concerned students. I give below an abridged version of their letter:

... A joined the Department in early 1991 under Dr S, who is also the Head of the Department. From her first day on the job, Dr S tried to cajole and coax her into having sexual relations with him, initially by way of suggestive hints and then overtly indicating that it will be in her 'best interest' for a bright future and career that she subject herself to his wishes.... Dr S resorted to daily pestering of A, giving examples of the girls whom he had similarly 'helped' in reaching excellent career tracks. When the advances became too overt and also since she did not receive any support from other lab mates A gave her resignation letter indicating that she was not able to continue due to continuous harassment by the project leader. However, her resignation letter was not accepted and instead she was served with a termination letter by Dr S citing that he had been 'observing her progress since she joined and it has not been up to his expectation and satisfaction'. What his 'expectations' were and how she could have 'satisfied' it is disgusting but obvious....

Since the Dean, Research & Development is the competent authority in charge of project staff, Dr K submitted the resignation letter. However, instead of promising her that an enquiry would be initiated and strict action would be taken against Dr S if found guilty, the senior professors and the custodians of the Institute, using pseudo affection as a facade, suggested that it would be better for her reputation and future that she withdraw the present resignation letter and substitute it with one giving some other excuse....

A however did not accept the proposal. One evening a jeep full of goons went to her house, showered her with abuses and threatened her with dire consequences if she ever dared to enter IIT. She was totally upset at this turn of events; the dramatic coincidence of this and her meeting with Institute authorities clearly speaks of criminal collaboration....

The group who wrote us this letter ended by requesting that an outside enquiry be instituted because they had failed in their efforts to get a fair hearing from the IIT authorities.

When we tried following up on the letter, we were informed by a professor working at the same IIT that after having stood up to intense pressure for a while, A 'took a complete U-turn'. She had given a written statement to the Acting Director saying that she had a lot of respect for Dr S, who was a 'great man' and 'an internationally reputed scientist' with whom she wished to continue working in the lab. But since her resignation had already been accepted earlier, her project post had fallen vacant. It was, therefore, re-advertised. She was the only candidate who appeared and the selection committee recommended her for the job. One suspects that she made a deal under pressure, not just in order to retain her position but more for fear of not being ever able to get her doctoral degree. She had already submitted her thesis but had to go through the interview to defend it. Since Dr S was likely to be on the committee to approve her Phd. thesis, years of her labour would have gone waste if he went against her. But her backtracking in this fashion left the students very confused and scared. They had openly supported A when she took a stand. There was a signature campaign and an open protest encounter with the Director. But after she wrote this letter to the Director, the students became so demoralized they refused to even talk about the incident. The position of the concerned professor seems fairly secure and he has continued to occupy the same position of power, though he is alleged to have a long track record of similarly exploiting many of the women who have worked under him.

This particular case is fairly typical of the atmosphere of exploitation in many science establishments and labs. By all accounts it seems that women working as researchers or project officers in such institutions are far more vulnerable to sexual harassment than those in other disciplines. The reasons are obvious.

The power that a research supervisor holds in a science institution is vast because he can effectively block all avenues of research including lab facilities. A woman who has spent several years working on her thesis or research project is totally dependent upon the whims of this one person for completing her research and getting her degree. Being denied access to lab facilities or certain equipment can completely mar a researcher's career. Leaving one institution and joining another is not an option as easily available to science researchers as it is to those in social sciences because in scientific establishments, control over funds and grants affords to professors almost total power over their subordinates. Most important of all, perhaps, is the fact that the system obliges the student to depend on the supervisor's recommendation for further studies and academic positions. This too, appears to be more strongly institutionalized in the natural sciences. Falling out with one's supervisor means putting one's entire career in jeopardy. In the event of a rift between a researcher and her supervisor, the entire faculty closes ranks. In most cases, the unfortunate student will not find another supervisor since he or she has violated the unwritten code of servility. Mild exploitation of the guide-student relation is fairly common with students of both sexes. 'Where are you going?' 'To buy vegetables for my guide' is a standard joke among

Phd. students in the sciences. But exploitation can take far more humiliating and deadly forms for women researchers.

In the last few years, there have been several cases of suicide by women who were unable to cope with the debasing forms of sexual harassment in some of Delhi's science departments and research institutions. On the few occasions when the aggrieved students decided to make a public issue of it, the outcome was not very different from that of the case mentioned above. Some years ago, the Department of Physics in Delhi University was rocked by a serious protest movement by students against the gross forms of sexual abuse and harassment by one of the professors. Despite long drawn-out efforts to get an enquiry instituted, nothing much came of it except that the professor accused of financial corruption and sexual harassment left and got himself an even better job, of a higher status, as the head of a prestigious research institution on account of his political connections.

However, the problem is not confined to science establishments alone. It occurs wherever women have to work in a situation of job insecurity combined with the lack of accountability of those in positions of power.

Some years ago, *Manushi* had to intervene in an incredibly sad story of degradation related by women employees of the Department of Adult Continuing Education and Extension of Delhi University (DACEE) which demonstrated clearly that even women from relatively better-off families are extremely prone to be exploited if they are working in a situation where their job is totally dependent on the whims of one man or a small coterie who have tremendous powers placed at their disposal. We were surprised to find how diffident most of them were in fighting back sexual exploitation even though the Department Head, S.C. Bhatia, had indulged in extremely gross forms of sexual exploitation of his numerous female colleagues. He hired twenty-two women employees in the period from the founding of the Department in 1978 to his suspension. Most of them were young and attractive, and few were married. He sexually harassed virtually every one of them. Those who resisted, he physically assaulted. He pawed these female colleagues, made lewd comments and sometimes even tried to force sex on them. He enacted many violent sexual assaults on these women in his office. From whatever information we could gather, it appears that some of these young women succumbed to Bhatia's advances. Such women would be given special monetary allowances, taken out to conferences and introduced to influential and powerful people. Some had open affairs with him, some did it surreptitiously. One of these women even went to the extent of nearly marrying him though he had a wife and she knew of his behaviour with other women. Some resisted him. As long as he was pawing them and forcing kisses on them many didn't resist but when he began demanding sex and intercourse, some became frightened. Only one woman, Dr Sushma Merh, gave him a tough fight; she continually protested and refused to succumb either to his sexual advances or to his physical violence. She fought it out alone for years at the cost of her health and career. When she found that the University authorities continued protecting Bhatia despite her best efforts to institute an enquiry, she approached *Manushi* for help. After *Manushi* took up the case and campaigned for an independent probe, an enquiry committee was instituted into Bhatia's conduct. The enquiry committee was seriously hampered by the fact that twenty of the twenty-two women he had hired had left the department quietly. The two remaining in the department, agreed to give evidence. Some simply could not take his continued demands beyond a point. I doubt whether Bhatia would have dared to go as far as he did, had he found his women colleagues offering him tough resistance rather than leaving quietly when they found that they could tolerate it no more.

Why did so many women—young, educated and none of them from poor families—not protest more effectively when forced to undergo such humiliation? Many of their colleagues think it was the lure of career promotion. Others think that they simply enjoyed the attention. We will never know for sure what complex sets of motivations or compulsions led each of them to act as they did. But we do know that a crucial factor in all this was that Bhatia ensured everybody else in the academic department was employed on a temporary or *ad hoc* basis. He was thus not just a colleague, not just a man, but a power figure who controlled everyone's livelihood.

Unfortunately, we do not have the versions of many others because they had left by the time we took up the case. But from the accounts I have heard from various employees of the department it seems many of the women found it hard to openly resist him because he was a figure of authority. The tendency to obey men in power is in part due to the fact that women are too often trained to think that their business is to please men, especially if the man is in a superior position. The same woman who would react violently to a poor man—say a rickshaw *wallah* who makes a pass at her—is much less likely to offer firm resistance if a powerful man, say a vice-chancellor or a minister, makes sexual advances towards her.

Not surprisingly, even though the women employees of DACEE confess that they were for years subjected to highly offensive and sexually exploitative behaviour by the head of the department, the matter came to a head only when a majority of the employees, including men, were faced with the near certain fate of being fired from their jobs. And it is quite likely that most of them would lose interest in pursuing the allegations of sexual harassment if they won their case concerning job regularization.

The fact that some of the women of DACEE fell for the crumbs and 'perks' that were offered them in return for sexual favours created an atmosphere of mistrust and hostility among them, pre-empting the possibility of their being able to make common cause with each other. The fact that too many of the women kept quiet for years or, at best, chose to leave their jobs without as much as a formal protest, and that the male employees who are making a big issue of it were likewise silent all these years, makes people suspect their motives today, even if their grievances are legitimate. For the natural question asked is: Why are they taking up the issue now? Could it not be motivated? It is no coincidence that women employees have raised the issue in such strong terms only when their male colleagues decided to make common cause with them at a time when most of them had been threatened with likely dismissal. Thus by becoming embroiled with the battle of the employees to retain and regularize their jobs, it becomes much harder for the issue of sex harassment to retain its integrity. On the other hand, one cannot ignore that the primary reason why the women employees were so vulnerable to exploitation and abuse was that not one member of the staff, except the head of the institution, had a regular and permanent position.[1]

Why do Men Gang Up?

However, even when women do raise timely protests, the outcome is not necessarily very encouraging. In the vast majority of cases where such instances of sexual abuse come to light, the authorities protect the culprit and further punish the victim—in those few instances where they have not succeeded in silencing her in the first place. Let me illustrate this by another example from Delhi University.

J had opted for a newly introduced course during her final semester studies for an MA. Most of the books required for the course were not available in the library or in the market. The professor teaching the course offered to lend her the books before the exams. When she went over to his house to collect the books, he tried molesting her. His wife and children were present in the house not far from the room in which they were sitting. J tried resisting, but he refused to stop. She slapped him and ran out of the house. A few days later, when the exam results were announced, she found that while she had done fairly well in all her other papers she had been given a failing mark in that one paper which was corrected by that professor. Convinced that this was an act of vindictiveness on his part, she went to lodge a complaint with the head of the department, demanding a re-evaluation of her paper. The head simply refused to accept her written complaint, asserting he was doing so in her best interest, because if she made it a public issue, 'mud would only stick to her name'. J, who was only 20 years old, was thus left with no choice except to drop that particular course and take an additional one in the next semester. She later happened to learn that the head of her department was himself regularly subjecting his own niece, who was a student at the same university, to even worse kinds of sexual harassment.

Among the many reasons men spontaneously tend to protect each other when they learn of other men's misdemeanours against women, is that many of those who have attained such power have themselves committed such abuses. Thus in protecting each other they are essentially protecting themselves from present or future potential exposure. Any woman who dares make a public issue of sexual harassment must run the risk of being put down and humiliated so that she becomes an object lesson for others and few will dare follow her example.

This happens not only when women are in clearly vulnerable and dependent positions, but also in those rare cases where women occupy relatively higher positions of power and prestige. A senior IAS officer of the Punjab cadre, was treated no better by the higher bureaucrats when she dared complain against sexual misbehaviour by a senior IPS officer. This occurred despite the fact that the sexual misbehaviour took place at a public party in full view of dozens of people, and he was known to have acted similarly with other women. Yet the police chief was not only avidly protected by the bureaucratic and political establishment, but the man was actually decorated with the Padma Bhushan while this case was pending in the courts. To add further insult to injury, she was slandered and demeaned in several ways. She was accused of helping terrorists when she accused this IPS officer of misconduct because he was supposedly spearheading the anti-terrorist campaign in Punjab. A number of other irrelevant charges were brought against her. She has been fighting this lone battle for years in the courts and in the public realm. Very few of her women colleagues in the IAS dare support her openly for fear of damaging their own careers. Even fewer now dare come out and complain against personal harassment or abuse after seeing how her case has been handled. She has been able to press her case simply because she has the support of a fairly wealthy and influential family. Even so, it is an extremely unequal battle in which she is more likely to be the loser than the man who misbehaved with her.

Impossible to 'Stay Away'

Many are likely to respond to this tale of woe by saying: 'Why make such a fuss over some bit of unwanted sexual attention? How do you know women don't enjoy it? And if they don't, why don't they simply stay away from such undesirable situations?'

The unfortunate truth is that, as things stand, it is virtually impossible for women to 'stay away' from sexual harassment. All those millions of women who decide to stay at home and not to venture outside the house for a living, are not really 'staying away' from trouble. We know, from world-wide experience, that women and girls suffer the worst forms of sexual harassment and abuse at the hands of various male relatives, including brothers, uncles, cousins, brothers-in-law, and fathers. Yet the physical and ideological power of the male-dominated family is such that the possibility of sexual harassment at the work-place is used as one of the important reasons for not allowing women to seek employment outside the house. Instead they are often urged to accept a life of crippling dependence on the men of the family. Sexual abuse is one of the few crimes which are seen by most people as primarily the fault of the victim rather than the aggressor. The victimized women are the ones who are imprisoned within four walls, not the aggressive men. Such crimes set into motion a vicious cycle, entrapping women so that they end up seeming voluntarily to choose a life confined within the house.

It is proof of the low opinion men have of themselves and of each other that jobs outside the home which bring a higher degree of exposure to men are considered more disreputable for women, as though mere interaction with men will pollute women. For example, the job of a nurse is considered much less respectable than that of a primary school teacher because, in the former case she is expected to deal with a large number of men, but in the latter, this contact is minimal, especially if her colleagues are women. Unfortunately, men's mutual mistrust of each other's intentions towards women does not affect men as adversely as it does women. It virtually imprisons and severely restricts women's existence. Since those jobs that bring women social exposure are usually the ones where sexual harassment is most frequent and dangerous, women are expected to either stay homebound or take up only those kinds of jobs where their interaction with the male world is minimal. Barring a microscopic section among the educated elite in metropolitan cities, the social status of the working woman is, in many ways, much lower than that of a homebound woman.

It Ghettoizes Women

This is one of the reasons middle-class women constitute such a small percentage of the professional or organized labour force in India. This is also how middle-class women are ghettoized into certain low-paying jobs with negligible upward mobility such as school teaching. Even when they open businesses they must choose businesses in which they deal primarily with other women—such as running beauty parlours, or clothing boutiques. Otherwise, they must choose to be home-based workers—to give private tuition to children, to knit and sew for other women. Thus, the few women who do manage to seek work outside their homes have their choices and access to skills and work severely restricted. In addition, they must be willing to give up jobs as soon as their husband or other family members find their working inconvenient or objectionable.

An important reason why few girls are allowed to be educated in India is the fear parents have that their daughters will be sexually harassed if the school is situated far away from their village. Even those who are allowed education can do so only within narrow confines. If higher education means letting a daughter study in a co-educational institution, live away from home, or even travel long distances, many parents would rather discontinue her studies.

Normally, it is assumed that women coming to study in co-educational institutions are likely to enjoy a freer atmosphere and be more 'liberated'. In actual fact, it often works to the detriment of women students. As someone who studied in an all-women college, I found that we could be more relaxed and free within our college. We did not feel inhibited about how we dressed or looked. Women students freely sat and lounged around on the lawns, talked and laughed without a feeling of being constantly 'watched' and observed by leering men. Similarly, in the classroom, we were far less inhibited in discussing or asking questions. In contrast, my experience of teaching in a co-educational college tells me that women students tend to lead a ghettoized existence. They behave as though they are being forever 'observed' and most of them are afraid to draw any attention to themselves. Very few dare to intermix freely with male students for fear of inviting rowdy behaviour or even flirtatious attention. Very often, male students bully them into accepting dates and will not hesitate to blackmail them with threats of violence if they turn down their advances. Sometimes, this can take fatal forms, as for instance it did for a young girl from Bombay who was doused with acid and set on fire by a young man who felt snubbed because she refused to have an affair with him. On the other hand, being seen openly dating with this or that boy could equally well invite the wrath of her family and ruin her marriage prospects because she would be then suspected of being a 'loose' woman.

While the college compound may offer some degree of security, the streets on the campus are truly menacing for women. A woman walking down a campus street is in perpetual fear of being hit, pawed or molested and subjected to obscene or vulgar comments. No wonder then, that a large number of parents prefer sending their daughters to off-campus all-women's colleges even though that does not take care of the sexual harassment suffered by women in public buses. Many parents try to get around that by insisting that their daughter study through a correspondence course.

Very few any women students will stay back to participate in any activity on the campus, however important, if it requires their missing the 'University Special bus' and having to take a regular bus. The harassment in the latter case is far more severe than in the University Specials, even though they often face problems even in those specials. During exams, very few women students, even those living in campus hostels, will be found using the library in the evening because it would involve a 'risky' walk back to the hostel or bus stop. Thus women students lead a very marginalized existence in the social, cultural and political life of our universities. The threat of sexual harassment and violence acts as a major hurdle for women acquiring the education and skills required to equip them for an independent life.

Politically Peripheralized

Prejudice against middle- and upper-class women seeking employment outside the home, especially in secure government jobs or public undertakings, has been breaking down slowly over the last few decades especially in big cities. However, the prejudice against women engaging in politics on their own is still very strong. It seems that a much larger number of women participated in political movements during the Mahatma Gandhi-led freedom struggle, than do so today. The fear of sexual abuse, harassment and slander has only increased with time as politics seems to have been taken over more and more by *goondas* and hoodlums. An unprotected woman feels unsafe in virtually any and every political party today. That partially explains why the few women who are active in politics today, or have been elected to state assemblies and parliament, are mostly wives, daughters or sisters of powerful politicians, and thus have some protection when they need to deal directly with men.

Unlike in jobs, where sexual harassment occurs because a woman has to work as a subordinate to men, in the realm of politics the mere entry of women excites hostility from men who will unleash slander campaigns against the woman who dares enter unaccompanied by a husband or father. A woman in politics is the easiest target because politics necessitates a great deal of public contact. A woman entering politics, therefore, cannot escape slander at no matter what level—from the gram panchayat and zilla parishad to state assemblies or parliament—or, for that matter, in student unions or trade unions.

My own experience as a student of Delhi University is a fairly typical one and helps demonstrate the process through which men manage to keep women politically peripheral and, therefore, powerless in society.

In the early 1970s, Miranda House Student's Union was the first women's union to become affiliated to Delhi University Student's Union (DUSU). The reason some of us initiated this move was to try and loosen the hold of hoodlum male politicians over the affairs of the University. They could not formally oppose the move but they tried various methods to intimidate women representatives from attending the crucial meetings where important decisions would be taken. Their style of operation ensured that it was virtually impossible for young women to participate in campus politics without seriously jeopardizing their safety and reputation. For example, most important meetings would be held during late night sessions, with liquor flowing freely and the threat of inter-gang violence ever-present. If we women representatives kept away from these meetings, the very purpose of our joining DUSU was nullified. On the other hand, if we dared attend those meetings then all manner of scandalous rumours would be let loose about us. Very often the male leaders would themselves warn us that it would be better for us to stay away from certain meetings especially the late night ones to ensure our own safety. The reputation of the DUSU office was such that a woman seen entering that building at night or even in the evening, would be automatically viewed as a prostitute or a call-girl. And these were precisely the kind of rumours they would spread about us if we dared to be present at the really important meetings. The reason for keeping women out was obvious: they could not make their shady deals—which included wining, bribing and womanizing—in our presence. We inhibited those transactions by our mere presence and hence we were not allowed to have more than a token presence. Most of my fellow women students refrained from attending those meetings because of the risks it involved. I was one of the few women who persisted, but this did not make much of a dent in their political culture because there weren't enough of us to make a difference. I could afford to take the risks involved, because I was confident of my family's support no matter what slander I was subject to. But most women are frightened of their family disapproval. Even a whiff of slander associated with their name could ruin their lives.

That this problem persists even at the higher echelons of political life came out clearly in a recent interview with Sarojatai Kashikar—the Shetkari Sangathana MLA from Maharashtra. Explaining why women cannot act effectively in politics she described how she herself never dares to sit down in the Mantralaya canteen even for a cup of tea with male politicians (except the three or four who are close to her husband and family on account of their Sangathana connection) because it could easily lend itself to scandalous talk. Thus women politicians are unable to keep themselves well-informed because of the restrictions on their social interaction. Sexual slander is such a powerful weapon that anyone can end up seriously harming even a powerful woman. Mahasati Sita was after all discarded by Ram at the instigation of a *dhobi* casting aspersions on her sexual fidelity!

This is one aspect of our culture which has a very pernicious anti-woman bias. The revelations in the Anita Hill hearing in the US show how a woman could end up living a traumatized and scarred existence even in a culture where remarriage, multiple affairs, even certain types of extra-marital sex are socially tolerated to a large extent. Imagine the consequences for a woman in our culture, where even divorcees and widows are treated as 'soiled' goods, where the remarriage of even a young, divorced woman is a difficult proposition in many communities because she is stigmatized as a used and discarded woman. In such a situation, most women cannot afford to carry the stigma of being (even wrongly) suspected of sexual affairs outside marriage because the punishment can go far beyond mere social disapproval. It can take such deadly forms as murder, or can end up with the woman being discarded by her husband and family, being socially shunned and put into the category of the 'disreputable' woman—the ostracized prostitute.

The categorization of women into two mutually exclusive categories—the *izzatdar bahu beti samaj* and the so-called *patita samaj*—acts as one of the biggest factors for women accepting extremely circumscribed lives under crippling restrictions. The mere threat of being pushed into the second category through sexual slander, even when it is baseless, can jeopardize the very survival of a woman. The fear of punishment for even unwittingly crossing the *lakshman rekhas* that most women have to deal with, makes it virtually impossible for them to openly and boldly seek redressal for sexual wrongs committed against them. This is one of the special features of women's oppression. We have been trained to consider such abuse 'unspeakable'. The manner in which we are socially criticized for speaking against sexual abuse ensures our silence much better than any external censorship or bans on freedom of speech. To put up with indignity and act as if nothing has happened has been socially defined as the most dignified course for a woman to adopt. Any attempt at making a public issue of it is seen as proof of having invited trouble through some fault of our own.

The point when the censorship imposed by the family and society becomes the woman's internal self-censorship is the point of her final silencing. Unless women can struggle successfully against the bans imposed on their speaking against abuse that affects them most intimately, they are unlikely to have their voices heard on other important social and political matters or, for that matter, to act as full members of society. They will remain socially and politically marginalized, thus facilitating their continuing subjugation.

Why She Succumbs Easily

One of the reasons why women find it difficult to effectively resist sexual harassment and abuse is that in the existing state of male-female power relations, women do not receive very respectful kinds of sexual attention from men, even within 'normal' family and other relations. They are used to being manipulated and having men take decisions on their behalf, as well as trained to accept sexually passive roles. With such conditioning, they often mistake sexual advances as a sign of genuine interest or attraction on the part of the man and may succumb to it in part or full, especially during the early stages of what may appear as a harmless flirtation. If, in addition, the man is in a position of power and influence, the idea of being sexually wooed may even be gratifying to a woman's ego, even if it is a blatantly manipulative relationship. It may also appear attractive because of the potential enhancement in career prospects. It may be that when the attention which initially appeared to be flattering begins to assume threatening dimensions, that a woman discovers she is unable to draw the line, and becomes a hapless object (whose futile objections are ignored) rather than a consenting beneficiary. It is in situations like these, when it is hard to tell where consent ends and harassment begins, that women have the least chance of being taken seriously, and later attempts at protest often backfire to her detriment.

Steps Towards Protection

Yet the battle against sexual harassment and slander will have to be a central one if women want to affect meaningful changes in their currently powerless and vulnerable position.

If we had a functioning judicial system, I would have begun by emphasizing the need to make and enforce laws which stipulate heavy fines and damages for men who indulge in sexual abuse and harassment. But knowing full well that our judicial system is a near total disaster and is not likely to undergo major changes in the foreseeable future, we need to create other channels for redressal:

- The first step in this direction is to recognize that living confined lives at home does not offer any real protection to women. It only enhances our vulnerability. Like Sita we may spend a lifetime zealously guarding our chastity, but Ravans are lurking even within our homes and the Rams of this world have never had any compunctions about discarding their Sitas when even baseless accusations are made. In fact, the solution lies in the opposite direction. The larger the number of women entering the public realm, the safer each woman is likely to be, just as currently our presence in small, insignificant numbers renders the few who venture out far more vulnerable. If we enter the public realm in respected positions, we are less likely to be treated shabbily, than if we try to fit into the glamour-doll roles in the job market which seem to attract large numbers of women from western-educated elite families. A female personal secretary or an air-hostess, for instance, is more likely to get sexually harassed than a woman doctor or a bank officer. Yet, large numbers of women from elite families tend to gravitate towards glamorous but vulnerable jobs. This despite the fact that they have the option to qualify for and pursue less glamorous but more remunerative and respected careers.

- A woman who has an independent source of income, assets and resources is less likely to experience or need to succumb to sexual manipulation than if she lives a life of dependence.

- It is equally important to try and break out of the demeaning behaviour patterns men have taught us to adopt for seeking advancement. We would do well to recognize that flirting with those on whom you are dependent can land you in real trouble. At the risk of sounding prudish, I would say that with the present gross imbalance in male-female power relations, flirtation, especially with men in authority, is too dangerous a game for women to play. It may become harmless in a more egalitarian society but in today's context, the failure to say 'No' at the right moment only conditions women into accepting the role of playthings.

- It is important to recognize that this is one battle in which we can expect very little support from men. They have a tendency to protect each other unless, of course, they have some other score to settle, in which case the whole issue gets politicized in such a way that the wronged woman becomes a mere instrument for men's political ends.

- Women, unfortunately, make it easy for men to get away with exploiting them because, unlike men, they seldom rise to defend each other in this type of situation. In fact, in such situations women tend to remain hopelessly divided against each other, each one trying to safeguard her own interest. It is time we understood that women's safety is indivisible. None of us is truly safe till each one of us is safe. The most powerful of male protectors cannot provide us the safety that a socially safe environment can.

- We have to fight to make the workplace safe for women by stipulating a code of conduct which is enforceable even more stringently than service rules. We have to demand a permanent machinery at every level of employment to handle women's grievances and complaints of sexual harassment, one which has well-defined rules and the obligation to see every complaint through within a specified period of time. At the same time, women have to learn to take an active interest in the politics of their respective workplaces, so as to have a say in their many important decision-making processes, as well as in the functioning of the grievance machinery.

- Men will not feel as bold as they presently do in their misbehaviour if such acts are routinely made public. Even if the man cannot be punished through the legal machinery, public exposure and building social opinion against men who abuse their positions of power is bound to act as some kind of check and balance. However, such exposure can go against the interests of the victimized woman herself, unless every workplace has women's support groups who protect the woman from further harassment and slander, and raise public awareness to ensure that men who harass and abuse women are socially despised and ostracized. If men cannot feel 'manly' in sexually abusing women, they are less likely to try and do so. However, these collective efforts are likely to take a long time to materialize. In the meantime, each one of us has to learn to protect herself in the best possible ways that we can individually devise.

Playing Durga Helps

I will end by sharing with you a strategy which I find has been usefully employed by many women who have learnt to deal effectively with men. However, I do not claim universal application or a uniform success rate for this strategy.

One of the characteristic features of our culture is that men in India are habituated to fearing and respecting strong female figures. The very same man who thinks nothing of beating his wife or daughter has no psychological barrier to bowing in reverence and fear before a *chandi* or a *durga.* Our culture worships two kinds of goddesses. The benign, consort goddesses like Parvati, Sita, Lakshmi are revered but not feared. The other kind are far more numerous and culturally more powerful. Each region, often each village in India, worships its own local version of the *Chandi/Durga* type of deity. Such goddesses have some common features. Frequently, the story of their origin is derived from that of a woman who transformed herself into a ferocious being in order to defend herself from being wronged by some man or the other. The all-pervasive religious folklore has thus made available to the women of India certain powerful forms of social protest and redressal not available to women in many other cultures. This includes the socially and culturally-sanctioned right to assume the *Durga/Chandi roop* to defend herself against wrong. I have found that men in India are conditioned to accept and fear this aspect of women. This is not true for cultures with less varied patriarchal religious traditions, in which God and other authority figures are invariably male. If men are aware that a woman is capable of rising to her defence, with ferocity if necessary, they are less likely to attempt to harass or abuse her than if they see her as trapped in the female stereotype of a helpless creature and sex object. The reputation of being upright and ferocious may invite ridicule or hostility in many cultures, where women have been more successfully manipulated into playing the decorative sex object role with pride. But in India, such ferocity brings an unusual kind of respect and saves a woman from many potentially exploitative situations. However, we have to remember that becoming *Durga* can be very self-destructive if we don't regulate our anger and keep it under control. If turned inwards, it can harm us both physically and emotionally, as well as destroy our ability to receive and give affection without fear. And once that happens, then we are defeated anyway.

In short, the simplest way to render men powerless is to stop fearing them—without at the same time hating them. We are lucky that men in India have the good sense to fear women who are not afraid of them.

However, it is not enough that some women manage to keep men at bay by provoking in them a fear of a woman's wrath. Ultimately, our aim has to be to create a society in which no man can abuse or exploit a woman with impunity, to build new social norms whereby it is considered despicable rather than admirable for men, especially those in positions of authority, to use sexual aggression as an instrument of abusing and exploiting women.

NOTE

1. We did not simply publish this case in *Manushi* but initiated in Delhi University a Forum against Sexual Violence and Abuse named *Swabhiman*. Through this forum we organized protests, *dharnas*, and other forms of mobilizing opinion to press for an impartial probe. After *Manushi* took up this case, various teachers' and student bodies which till then had remained inactive on the issue, also became involved and a strong movement emerged in the campus demanding Bhatia's dismissal. The University establishment tried to protect Bhatia for years, but had to finally give in to the demand for a judicial probe.

    A committee headed by Justice Wad, a retired High Court judge was appointed to handle the case. Its report passed a strong indictment against Bhatia and recommended his dismissal, upholding virtually all the charges that had been levelled against him. The Delhi university establishment which had been going out of its way to protect Bhatia was forced to put him under suspension. However, when Bhatia went to court and obtained a stay order on his suspension, the university lawyer did not challenge or object to the stay indicating complicity in getting him reinstated through the back door. The battle is thus not yet over.

XIII

When India 'Missed' the Universe

"I have a terrible tendency to put on weight. If I have more than two chapatis at a go, I bloat. If I have one extra biscuit, I feel so guilty, I wander around the house moaning that I look fat. Of late I have become obsessed with food. If I see a two-day chapati that a dog wouldn't eat, I start drooling."

Madhu Sapre, fashion model and former Miss India

The winning of the Miss Universe crown by Sushmita Sen in 1994, and the Miss World crown by Aishwarya Rai later that year were celebrated by the Indian mass media and the urban elite as though they were momentous events in Indian history. Manpreet Brar's qualifying as first runner-up this year in the Miss Universe contest has convinced many Indians that the winning of the earlier two crowns was not a fluke—that India has indeed arrived on the international scene. Many educated Indians behaved as though they had conquered the world, whereas in Europe and America little attention was paid to our grand accomplishments.

Up until the 1970s, beauty contests used to be peripheral affairs, only covered by specialized women's magazines such as *Femina* and *Eve's Weekly*. They were hardly ever a topic of animated discussion in middle-class homes. But now they have acquired a prominence in our social life totally out of proportion to their significance. Millions sat glued to their TV sets in India to watch the crowning of Sushmita and Aishwarya. The Prime Minister and the President received them as though they were high dignitaries. Big national and international companies spent millions of dollars promoting their products and image through association with the contests and the winners.

Beauty contests now get prominent front-page coverage in leading national newspapers. It is inconceivable that a high status paper like the *New York Times* would organize a beauty contest to boost its

*First published in *Manushi*, No. 88, May–June 1995.

circulation. But in India, where earlier the Miss India contest used to be a more *Femina* event, it has now been converted into a grand *The Times of India* gala. For instance, on 14 May 1995, *The Times of India* gave the lead story of Manpreet Brar, the first runner-up in the Miss Universe 1995 contest an eight column space across the entire front-page. The burning of Charar-e-Sharif in Kashmir was relegated to a much less prominent place.

The victories of Sushmita and Aishwarya had been even more lavishly praised—their achievement was celebrated in India the way America celebrated its first astronaut's walk on the moon. Even Doordarshan telecast it live on the national hook-up at prime time.

The Indian beauties who won international crowns gave hope to the inferiority complex-ridden Indian elites that if they continued to ape the West in its mannerisms, lifestyle, consumption patterns, fashion designs and what have you, they would one day make it to world class, just as Sushmita and Aishwarya did by learning to walk, talk, dress, smile and wear make-up like Hollywood stars. On the surface, participation in these beauty contests may even give the impression of having a liberating effect on the supposedly tradition-bound Indian women by encouraging them to enhance their physical and sexual appeal. To see Indian women parading confidently in front of men and being sexually provocative could be seen as a sign of self-assertion of their womanhood and sexuality. But in actual fact, these contests are hardly a celebration of women's beauty. The participants end up reducing their bodies and their whole existence to well-packaged products and vehicle's, for displaying consumer goods. Most of these are useless products, and therefore, must rely on media hype to generate an artificial demand. It is no coincidence, for instance, that Pepsi hired Sushmita and Aishwarya to boost their sales in India soon after they won the crown. It is only by using such glamourized models that they can hope to persuade people to buy—a flavoured sugar water costing no more than a few paise, at Rs 6 and in the process harm their health bottle!

Protests against beauty contests, the use of women as sex objects, and the commodification of women's bodies have been key components of women's movements in the West. Western feminists realized that beauty contests, by their demonstration effect through various media, had the serious potential to harm women—physically, mentally and emotionally. Unfortunately, we in India are catching this western fever years after thinking women in the West have challenged and discarded those concepts of beauty. The Miss India Contest has become an important national event. Beauty contests have proliferated in thousands of women's colleges and in hundreds of local clubs and hotels.

The 'Beauties' of Miranda

The euphoria whirling around these Indian beauties brought back memories of the days in 1971 when, as president of the Miranda House Students' Union, I worked very hard to get the Miss Miranda beauty contest abolished. In those days the Miss Miranda beauty contest had pretty much the same glamour among its more restricted audience as the Miss India contest. This time, when eushmita won the Miss Universe contest for India and the country went ecstatic over it, I just could not react in a manner I did in the 1970s. This is not because I've changed my mind about the harmful effects of beauty contests, but because looking back at the fall-out of our campaign in the university, I am left with very ambivalent feelings.

When I joined Miranda House as a starry-eyed 16-year-old in the late 1960s, I got the first and the longest-lasting culture shock of my life—one that played a substantial role in shaping my life and thinking in the years to come. In those days, Miranda House was considered to be India's premier institution for women's education and attracted daughters of the bureaucratic and business elite in large numbers. The college population was divided into three distinct categories—the westernized Mirandians who came from elite schools; the science types; and the Hindi-speaking *bhenjis*. Not everyone who came from an English-speaking school qualified to be admitted into the first group. Ragging not only served the purpose of sifting the freshers into neat categories but also showed each group its place in the Miranda House scheme of things. Without any formal sanction, fairly strict and visible forms of segregation were practised routinely and viciously. The 'real' Mirandians would never condescend to even rag a fresher if she did not come from the right background. You had to be from a school such as Welhams, Loreto, Tara Hall or Convent of Jesus and Mary in order to qualify to be admitted to the charmed circle. Someone from Salwan school or Guru Harkishan Public School would be automatically ruled out, even if the school taught through the medium of English. Your father had to be a highly-placed bureaucrat, preferably from the IFS or the IAS, or a senior army officer, or a top business executive for you to qualify to be ragged by the 'hep' seniors. You had to be able to speak English with the right public school accent. If you were a day scholar, your parents would need to have a house in some prestigious south Delhi colony, unless you lived in the princely bureaucratic part of New Delhi. Often, the seniors could tell from the way someone dressed if she 'belonged'. Occasionally, a *bhenji* type dressed in ways resembling the elite would be summoned for ragging. But the first few questions would decide whether she was considered worthy of ragging or not. 'Your name, fresher? Where do you stay? What does your father do?' Only if you had 'satisfactory' answers to each of those qualifying queries did the select few condescend to rag you. If a fresher answered that she lived in Kamla Nagar or Shahdara or a trans-Yamuna colony or that her father owned a dry cleaner's shop or was a postal clerk, she would be asked to 'get lost' at once. Through this process, the seniors sifted and selected the freshers they considered worthy of notice and friendship. The ragging period ended on a celebratory note—with the famous Miss Miranda beauty contest. Though entry to it was not formally forbidden to the *bhenji* types, it was well-understood that the prestigious title could only go to the hep elite: the *bhenjis* hardly never even dared to enter the contest.

A Hallowed Tradition?

The beauty contest set the tone for the whole institution. The college seemed to function more as a finishing school for a large number of young women, where they came to acquire airs rather than academic qualifications. Undoubtedly, there was a facade of selecting as Miss Miranda House, someone who combined beauty with 'brains' and 'good grooming'. That usually amounted to asking a few questions like, 'What would you do if you found yourself on the moon?' The fresher who managed a cheeky and funny answer usually was considered brainy enough to deserve the crown. All the intelligence required of you amounted to no more than being able to come up with an instant joke or a smart alec response.

This crowning event was followed by a series of parties organized by the boys of the St. Stephens' College. The senior Mirandians would take the Miranda House freshers along in order to facilitate pairing-off with the Stephenians. The height of a Mirandian's ambition was to get a boyfriend from among the Stephenians, preferably someone with a car who could take you out to fancy discotheques and parties every weekend. In all the years that I studied in that supposedly premier institution, I heard very few of my fellow classmates discuss books or ideas except to borrow each other's notes for examination preparation. Most of their time and energy was spent on talking of boyfriends, shopping trips, dressing up, and planning for parties and outings. In that sense, the beauty contest was not an isolated event in which a few participated for fun. It set the tone and cultural milieu for the hep Mirandians all year round. The message was clear: Your body shape, waist and bust size, the way you dressed, the accent in which you spoke English and the kind of male attention you were able to attract were far more important than any other qualities you might have. For instance, while Miss Miranda was considered the celebrated heroine of the campus, very few students knew who topped the university in various subjects or won medals in debating or various sporting events. The beauty contest promoted vicious elitism and low-level competitiveness among women at the cost of talent and other human qualities.

Ironically enough, these contests and fashion parades were organized by the college Students' Union which, until then, was monopolized by the same beauty culture elite. This Union hardly ever concerned itself with academic issues or various legitimate problems faced by the students. The president and the secretary of the Union sat as judges in the beauty contest along with former beauty queens of Miranda House.

In 1969, Akhila Ramachandran took over as president of the Union. I was vice-president of the Union that year. We tried to transform the Union into the voice of organized student opinion on various issues relating to the university, as well as the general society and polity. When our elected team tried to raise the issue of abolishing the beauty contest, we met with vigorous opposition from the dominant elite of the college. Akhila worked out a compromise and tried to tone down the beauty-cutie part of the contest by asking a few 'intelligent' questions of the contestants and selecting someone who was not beautiful in the conventional sense. I, personally was not satisfied with this 'beauty-cum-brain' contest idea because it kept the basic derogatory message intact while bowdlerizing the notion of intelligence in women.

Therefore, when I got elected as president of the Union in the following year, the two issues we began the year with were—an end to nasty and often obscene ragging of freshers by the seniors and an end to the beauty contest.

We began our campaign by calling a General Body meeting to discuss the issue. At the end of it, when we called for a vote, an overwhelming majority of the college students voted against the beauty contest and in favour of a freshers' week of cultural activities. It was decided that the emphasis should be shifted from competition to exposing the first year students to various extra academic aspects of university life, and encouraging more and more students to take part.

The hep elite were clearly in a tiny minority, but they were so used to having their writ obeyed all these years, that they could not stomach the idea that the college *bhenjis*, who they considered riff-raff, could dare vote out one of their most sacred rituals—one that affirmed the superiority of their way of life in the college. Even though the function was supposed to be organized under the aegis of the Student's Union and more than ninety per cent of the student body had voted against it, the beauties and cuties were not willing to accept this verdict. This unleashed a virtual civil war in the college.

They sought and got the support of the college administration for holding the beauty contest.

In those days, the English Department, along with a sprinkling of faculty from the History and Economics Departments, used to dominate college affairs in pretty much the same way as the hep, English-speaking elite dominated the student body. The college principal, along with a group of influential teachers, declared their support for the beauty contest, defending it as one of the 'hallowed traditions' of Miranda House. On our side, we began a vigorous signature campaign in the college, going from class to class, holding long discussions with small clusters of students, and thereby, successfully mobilizing a very large body of determined opinion against the beauty contest. Since we were accused of manipulating a majority vote in the general body by rabble-rousing, we asked for a secret ballot, a sort of referendum on the desirability of holding the controversial contest. A day was fixed for it. But the beauty contest lobby felt insecure knowing that they were a small minority, and therefore, with the help of the then college principal and a few supportive teachers, they decided to hold the contest surreptitiously, a couple of days before the agreed date of the secret ballot. As soon as we got to know of it, we were able to organize, at short notice, a massive *dharna* at the proposed venue and pre-empt the holding of the contest. The beauties in all their finery trooped out of the college and held a contest in a private apartment on the outskirts of the University. They had the satisfaction of having held the contest anyway. We were satisfied it could not be called the Miss Miranda beauty contest any more. That was the last beauty contest in Miranda House.

I remember reacting with a great deal of annoyance at being labelled a feminist and being called the 'Kate Millet of India' for spearheading the campaign against the Miranda House beauty contest. My response was to reject such parallels because, until then, I had practically no knowledge of the western feminist movement, nor the issues it had raised. In those days, I saw western society mainly though the Marxist prism as a 'decadent bourgeois' society and wanted as little to do with it as possible. Indian papers in the early 1970s carried very little information about other countries. What little trickled though carried with it the stereotyping and biases of the western media on women's issues. Books by feminist authors had not yet invaded the Indian market as they came to do in later years.

Interestingly, it was not just my response which was based on sheer ignorance. The hep elite of Miranda House ended up by taking such a hostile stand against our efforts to abolish the beauty contest and indulged in a vicious hate campaign against us because these camp followers seemed unaware that the beauty contests were being similarly challenged by a newly emerging women's movement in the West. Beauty contests were on their way to becoming unfashionable, at least among the intellectual elite. In those days, there was a much larger time lag in ideas and technology from the West to Third World countries like India, unlike today, when Star TV, CNN and BBC are able to bridge the information gap almost instantaneously.

Self-inflicted Racism

One aspect of our opposition to the Miranda House beauty contest echoed some of the issues raised by western feminists in their protests against beauty contests. For instance, among other things, our campaign leaflets talked about how the beauty contest trained women to view themselves as sex objects and to remain engrossed in attempts to become sexually attractive to the male eye at the cost of developing other talents and human qualities. But that was only a small part of our objection. For me, the more important motivation behind the campaign was to fight against the vicious forms of elitism perpetuated by the super-westernized elite of our college. Their contempt for those who did not dress according to the correct fashions of the day, did not speak English with the appropriate public school accent, or did not boast of a suitable address in one of the elite colonies of Delhi was so corrosive that it destroyed the self-confidence of many who felt rejected by this group. The beauty contest was a mere symbol of this nasty elitism which enveloped all aspects of student life. In order to be part of that charmed circle you had to have a taste for western music, see western films, read only western literature. If you were seen viewing Hindi films or listening to Indian folk songs, that action stamped you as an unfashionable *bhenji* forever. Likewise, you were expected to speak in Hindi, Marathi, or whatever your 'mother tongue' may have been, only to servants and drivers. If you read Agatha Christie or even the silly *Mills and Boon* novels you were 'in'. If you were seen reading a Hindi novel by Premchand or a Tamil book, you would immediately be considered 'out'. Not that everyone who tried to be part of this 'in' group came from thoroughly westernized homes.

I recall the pathetic case of one of my classmates from English Honours who came from a wealthy, but not so westernized *bania* family. Her family still lived in the unfashionable old city. However, she never gave her correct address to anyone, including her close friends, and made out that she lived in a fashionable suburb of south Delhi. For this she had to incur a great deal of inconvenience every day. Since your social status in the college also depended on whether you took one of the college special buses to an appropriate south Delhi colony, everyday she would take a bus headed towards south Delhi along with those whose social approval she desperately desired, and then come all the way back to the Red Fort to reach her house in the Chandni Chowk area. If any one of her classmates chanced to see her near where she lived, she would refuse to recognize the person and pretend to be someone else. I myself felt a semi-outcast because though I studied in English Honours and could speak English with the appropriate Indo-British accent, I enjoyed the friendship of the pass-course *bhenjis* more than that of my own fancy classmates. I also enjoyed singing Hindi songs. As Union president, I insisted on holding all general body meetings in Hindi because the majority of students were not comfortable or fluent in English, even though they had a basic knowledge of the language. This choice provoked extreme hostility from my English language oriented contemporaries.

Copy-cat Elites

I am not against elites *per se*, but I am against those elites whose claim to superiority depends solely on their economic status and political clout rather than on any moral or intellectual worth. The Miranda House beauty lobby represented the copy-cat elite—culturally and intellectually. Miranda House was like an intellectual slum of the West. My fellow students prided themselves on knowing more about the royal family of Britain but would not have heard of a man like Chaudhary Chhotu Ram of Haryana, or have an interest in Sardar Patel. They could write a treatise on Jane Austen but would not condescend to read Mahadevi Varma. This was before the 'ethnic' became fashionable and South Asian studies departments in western universities began promoting and funding research on Indian literature and politics.

This elite prided itself on its alienation from its own people, its own culture and traditions. Its survival depended on uncritically and unimaginatively borrowing western technology, western ideas and western way of looking at the world. Therefore, it could not claim to being a genuine intellectual elite for that requires the ability to think independently, to be creative in generating ideas and providing intellectual leadership to your own society. A mentally enslaved, colonized intelligentsia cannot do that. This is why the Miranda House elite felt so threatened when a silly symbol of their hitherto assumed superiority of way of life, the beauty contest, was abolished in 1971.

Fortunately, in Miranda House, the beauty contest was never revived. However, in the last two decades, the beauty contest culture has proliferated widely and engulfed most women's institutions, including the non-elite ones. In Delhi University, you have Miss Daulat Ram, Miss Gargi, Miss Maitreyi Devi, with virtually every women's college holding its own contest. Does it represent democratization of westernization in our society? The very same *bhenjis* on whose behalf we had launched the anti-beauty contest campaign in 1970 have now taken to fashion parades and beauty contests with incredible vigour and gusto. It makes one wonder whether this is the inevitable direction in which the aspirations of the vast majority of modern women are likely to move. If this is what most women want, does one have any moral right to oppose it, since there is no evidence that women are being coerced into this culture but are happy being seduced by it?

In the meantime, many of the beauty-cutie elites of the 1960s and 1970s were admitted to western universities and got the opportunity to catch up with the latest fahions in the West. Many of them returned to India in the 1980s as enthusiastic feminists after a few years in and around western university campuses, because by then, feminism had established itself as a powerful force in western society. New academic disciplines, new departments, jobs and fellowships were created in response to the western feminist demands for equitable sharing of power in the universities and outside. These days, to declare oneself a 'Third World feminist' is to open the gates of many career opportunities which otherwise would not come your way—research grants, fellowships, teaching assignments, invitations to international conferences, project funds, and so on. You are at once admitted as a member of the intellectual elite of the world. In the last decade, with various international funding agencies promoting feminism in Third World countries, to be identified as a Third World feminist has become a very lucrative proposition indeed. So, we have the interesting phenomenon in India whereby the fashionable beauty-contest-holding elites of the 60s and 70s have taken to feminism, and have come to look down upon beauty contests as symbols of women's exploitation. The *bhenjis*, on the other hand, have now become great enthusiasts of beauty contests and fashion parades. It is a case of particular aspects of western influence reaching certain sections of our population at different paces.

Whereas earlier being pro-beauty contests was proof of one's elite status for women, today being against the 'culture of commodification of women's bodies' has become more fashionable than winning a beauty contest, for holding the latter opinion connects you to the international intellectual elite. Today, the new status symbol is the ability to use feminist jargon and be up-to-date with various fashionable ideologies emanating from the West. Witness any interaction on campus between erstwhile beauty contest enthusiasts-turned-feminists, and those who neither understand nor use the label 'feminist' and you will see how class contempt has transmuted itself into new forms and acquired a new respectibility by using feminism as a marker. It is not a coincidence that whereas the various Miss Worlds and Miss Universes used to be mostly European and American, they are now mostly from Third World countries and the contests are given undue coverage in national papers only in these countires.

There was another surprising fall-out of our campaign against the domination by the over-westernized elite in Miranda House. Earlier, the college principal invariably owed allegiance to this group and the college was unduly influenced by the English Department. While the enthusiasm to pretend that Miranda House was an extension of some British university meant that students learned very little about their country and became ridiculously Eurocentric, they also fostered some positive characteristics. The college atmosphere was relatively liberal, with far fewer restrictions on student mobility. Girls could be out every day until 8 p.m. and were allowed weekends out with no one keeping a tab on whether you went to your local guardian's home or not, as long as you brought back the leave book duly signed by the supposed guardian. Nobody bothered to check whether the signature was forged or real. Students met their boyfriends openly and went out on dates without hiding, unlike in other women's hostels which functioned mostly as prisons or *nari niketans*. The hostel was a place for fun with no restrictions on visitors into the rooms as long as they were female. Day scholars intermixed freely with hostelers and the hostel itself was the hub of activity. The westernized teachers were more likely than the other teachers to be friendly and informal with students and would invite students to their homes. Some would even offer cigarettes and drinks. All these things undoubtedly gave Miranda House girls the reputation of being 'fast', but the unusual amount of freedom available to women students allowed space to explore life—if you wanted to. For me, personally, the liberal atmosphere of Miranda House provided a space for experimenting and thinking things anew. My tenure as the vice-president and the president of the Union were really tumultuous years for the college. We turned many old conventions upside down—challenged the quality of teaching, demanded and got representation on the Governing Body, supported college workers demanding better working conditions and injected a high dose of radicalism into the student body by attempting to get it exposed to national politics—especially the radical left variety. We organized innumerable protest marches, *gheraoed* the Governing Body and the principal, frequently confronted the staff council, and got involved in Delhi University politics without being treated as pariahs. A few teachers responded with barely veiled hostility. But on the whole, in their flexible response to our activism, our westernized teachers communicated some of the positive virtues of liberalism. No matter how much we differed with them, at least some of the teachers whose decisions we were challenging remained good friends and rarely turned vindictive.

Victorianism, Indian Style

However, while I never regretted challenging the hegemony of the westernized elite in Miranda House, I did recoil in horror to see the results of a shift in power from the English Department to the non-elite departments like Hindi and Sanskrit. A few years later, when Miranda House hired its first principal from the Sanskrit Department, she brought such a repressive culture with her that the institution became unrecognizable. Innumerable ridiculous restrictions were placed on students. Iron grills and huge iron gates were introduced to bar the movement of students from one part of the college to another. For instance, day scholars were forbidden from entering the hostel and their access to the hostel was blocked off by iron grills. The college began to resemble a cage. Hearing stories of the harassment suffered by students and teachers in those days, I realized that, as was the case in the rest of the country, challenging the monopoly of the westernized elites did not necessarily bring a more benign culture. The home-bred elite can easily bring with it repressive *karwa chauth* culture and *khomeinivad* for women.

That is why I am extremely wary now of joining campaigns against beauty contests and the like. Most of those who are opposing them today have a tendency to advocate oppressive norms for women in the name of protecting Indian culture (*Bharatiya sanskriti*). While the anglicized elite tend to lag behind a few years in catching up with the latest intellectual fashions in the West, the Hindi and other regional language elites tend to absorb western notions of fifty to a hundred years ago and then, claim these as quintessential Indian values. For instance, their notion of *Bharatiya sanskriti* is, more often than not, repressive Victorianism in an Indian garb. For them, sex itself is a bad word—it is *ashlil* (vulgar)—and women's bodies something of an embarrassment.

The Barbie-doll Aesthetic

The moment one expresses a distaste for beauty contests, it is assumed that one wants every woman to look like an inmate of a Gandhi ashram, and to lead a self-repressed life.

To be opposed to beauty contests is not to be opposed to women beautifying themselves. Throughout history, women have been known to express their love of beauty by embellishing themselves and everything around them, including objects of everyday use.

Indian women in particular have been exceptionally creative in this regard. They decorate ordinary mud floors with beautiful designs, have a rich tradition of colourful clothing with intricate embroideries, create lavish mirror work and a host of rich designs. It is but natural that they would express their joy in beauty by beautifying their bodies as well. *Shringar* is an age-old tradition in India, where women put on special a variety of, and make-up and, decorate every part of the body.

However, the concept of beauty that comes to us from the West by means of these beauty contests has very little to do with aesthetics but more to do with marketing a self-view to women, whereby they all try to look and behave like standardized products—rather than normal human beings. This makes women self-hating by wanting to conform to a pre-set glamour doll image.

For years, western feminists have grappled with how men have come to define beauty in such a way, as to manipulate women into considering themselves attractive only when men find them sexually provocative. Much of this is tied in with a sick obsession with youth in western culture, which affects all strata of the society. Women have access to an extremely tenuous bit of power, as long as they are young and attractive to men. Western men, however, have a different standard for themselves. They believe that they continue to be attractive even in middle age. In fact, if they are rich and powerful, their age only adds to their charm. Streaks of silver in a man's hair are supposed to enhance his sex appeal, but not so for a woman. There is pressure for her to carefully hide them with a dye, along with other tell-tale signs of ageing.

As she starts greying, her breasts start sagging, wrinkles appear, or her waist starts bulging, she is made to feel increasingly dispensable. The obsession with having big and firm breasts, narrow waists and shapely legs drives vast numbers of women in the West to go on starvation diets. One and a half million women in the West are known to have their breasts artificially inflated through surgery. American friends tell me that losing weight is such a national obsession that you cannot talk to a woman for any length of time without the conversation veering round to calories and diets. Many women become anorexic in their anxiety to stay trim and get sick because they cannot eat. Others who cannot resist eating their fill, learn the art of vomiting soon after each meal so that they are able to eat with abandon without putting on any weight.

For years, magazines like *Femina* and *Eve's Weekly* (the latter is now defunct) have been trying to propagate these and other western obsessions among Indian women but so far, their influence has been confined to a very tiny section among the urban elite. Eating disorders and plastic surgery are relatively unheard of in our country. But if the euphoria over beauty contests keeps spreading at this pace, fuelled by interested sections of the mass media, women in India are in for a lot of trouble.

So far, our notion of beauty in women is unhealthy mainly in our tendency to consider dark skin a sign of ugliness. A heavy premium is put on women being 'fair skinned'. (In this respect Indians are no less racist than some white-skinned westerners). My friend, Surabhi Sheth, a Sanskrit scholar, confirms that the bias in favour of fair skin abounds in Indian literature. A *gaurvarna* is associated with *prakash* (light) and *saundarya* (beauty). There are also caste dimensions to the preference. Brahmins are associated with white skin, the Kshatriyas with red (valour), Vaishyas with yellow skin and Shudras with black. While fair skin was traditionally prized for its association with *saundarya,* during colonial rule it acquired a new connotation—that of power. That perhaps explains the fascination Indians have had with the Nehru family. Since they were almost as fair as Europeans, they were treated as though they were natural born rulers. I am convinced that Indira Gandhi would not have been so valourized despite having pursued many harmful policies, had she been dark-skinned.

A dark-skinned girl is often treated as the ugly duckling of the family and finds it tough going in the marriage market. Skin-whitening creams that promise a 'fair and lovely' complexion are as sought after as anti-wrinkle creams in the West. The premium that most Indians put on a fair complexion in women is indeed weird considering that the majority of us are rather brown-skinned, if not dark. However, in most other respects, I find traditional Indian ways of looking at beauty far more balanced and healthy.

For instance, in India, we are not tyrannized by the pressure to stay trim. If I put on some weight, most of my friends and family are likely to tell me that I'm looking healthy. Likewise, whenever I have lost a few kilos, I am constantly besieged with queries like: 'Have you been ill? Why are you looking so pulled down?' As long as a woman is not outright obese, a plump look is associated with being happy and healthy. Most parents actively discourage their daughters from going on diets to lose weight. In fact, if a woman does not put on weight after marriage, it is seen as a sign of a stressful marriage. It is widely believed that if a woman is happy in marriage, 'her body should fill out' (*sharir bhar jana chahiye*). Even film heroines in India are almost never skinny—unlike most Hollywood stars who have to have a lean and starved look in order to be considered right for glamorous roles. Our film stars would be considered plump and many even outrightly fat, by western standards. But in India, heroines like Meena Kumari, Nargis, Asha Parekh, Hema Malini, and Mala Sinha among the older generation were never rejected simply because they grew fat with age. Even among the younger generation, Sridevi, Juhi Chawla and many others have fairly plump bodies. But that does not prevent them from being considered attractive. Most Indians like them for their 'healthy' look.

The *Didi/Amma* Advantage

Unlike in the West, where women's youth is highly valued and old age dreaded, women in India are respected and taken far more seriously as they begin to get older. An Indian woman's position in the family is enhanced and she comes to acquire much greater bargaining power as she advances in age. As young wives, women in India do not have it so good. They are expected to be subservient to the elders in the family and are not allowed much autonomy. However, as they become mothers and grandmothers, they often emerge as authority figures in the family. That is why, by and large, Indian women do not dread ageing as do western women. Perhaps that explains the absence of anti-wrinkle creams in the Indian market—though there are dozens of brands of 'Fair and Lovely' creams floating around.

In public places, an older woman with grey hair is unlikely to be treated shabbily. The social norm is to extend 'mother-like' respect to such a woman. If you are not old enough to be treated in a mother-like fashion you will be addressed as a sister. *Behenji* is one of the most common forms of respectfully addressing a woman in many parts of India.

Some western feminists find the Indian obsession with respecting women as mothers and sisters offensive and an expression of denying women their selfhood. That is really missing the point altogether, for this ideology provides women a way out of the sex object trap and gives them opportunities to deal with men in a range of close relationships without having to be constantly viewed as sex objects. Thus, there is much less pressure on women to be forever sexually attractive to men. The ideology of glorifying motherhood has a major plus point in that men, even after they grow up, are expected to be reverential to their mothers. While society often condones a man behaving badly with his wife, a man being rude or nasty to his mother is socially looked down upon.

Bowing before a mother's commands and obeying her wishes is considered the appropriate behaviour for sons even after they are married. A dutiful son is held up as a social ideal. In western culture, such a man is likely to be laughed at. He would be seen as abnormal, needing to 'become a man' and told that he needs to see a psychiatrist for being tied to his mother's apron strings. Not so in India. It is popularly believed that you don't have to worship any God, as long as you serve your mother in a worshipful fashion. It is considered better than divine worship.

This can lead to major problems for the daughter-in-law if the mother is not wise about exercising her influence and authority, or if the son ignores his wife's needs. It also often means that Indian men are awkward as husbands, especially with young wives. That is perhaps why most Indian women start early at moulding themselves into matriarchs, often, in the process, undermining their role as attractive sex partners.

Likewise, women as older sisters, aunts and even grandmothers can exercise a great deal of power and influence over men who are expected to assume responsibility for and behave respectfully towards women in these roles. You don't have to be a real blood brother or nephew for that. Neighbourhood boys are expected to behave in a brotherly fashion towards girls of that area who can legitimately expect that they will come to her help if the girl is being harassed by someone. It is the very opposite in western culture, where men in their roles as brothers, sons and nephews can be both awkward and unwilling to take responsibility, and cringe at the idea of having a woman tell them what to do. Indian men tend to be rather soft and sentimental about these relationships and are used to being nagged and ordered around by women relatives.

Of innumerable such instances from my own experience, I shall cite just one. A few months ago, I was walking down to the local chemist in Lajpat Nagar when I saw a man on a two-wheeler scooter, suddenly fall down with a thud on the road. I rushed to help thinking he had been hit by a passing vehicle, but that was not the case. He had fallen from his scooter because he was dead drunk. With the help of nearby shopkeepers, we removed him from the road and made him sit on the pavement. I lifted his scooter, parked it on the side, took out the ignition keys, and told him that I was not going to allow him to drive home in that condition, and that we would send him home in an auto rickshaw. His first response was to start yelling at me in a drunken rage: 'Who the hell are you to stop me? How dare you keep my scooter back?' I calmly replied: 'Your older sister who doesn't want to see you dead in a road accident.' Though, I wasn't sure I was actually older than him, even in that drunken state, his tone changed. From then on he began pleading and apologizing, begging me to let him go home with his vehicle. In the meantime, nearly twenty-five people, some passers-by and neighbours, had collected around us, and they all supported me in preventing him from driving home in that drunken state. He was still too drunk to realize that I meant business. So, he kept pleading and arguing—though no longer in the earlier insulting tone. Now it was, *'Didi*, please let me go. I promise I will never drink again!' Some men of the locality wanted to hand him over to the police. When I resisted, saying they would only beat up the fellow and steal whatever money he was carrying, they began to hit the drunken man saying only a sound thrashing would teach him a lesson. I put myself between them and the drunkard and asked them to stop beating him up. This got them enraged and once again I was rudely confronted with: 'Who do you think you are? Supercop?' All I had to say with folded hands was: 'No, I am your neighbourhood sister, pleading with you not to beat up a man who is already in such a humiliating position.' That instantly calmed them down. They parked the scooter in a courtyard to ensure its safety and told the drunk man that he had to do as I told him and come back to collect his scooter when sober. Finally, a local shopkeeper offered to drive the man to his house in his car provided *'didi'* came along. The next morning, the man returned for his scooter not only profusely apologetic for what had happened but equally thankful to his *'didi'* for having taken care of him the previous night.

I find this *'didi', 'amma', 'mausi'* role far more advantageous for women because not only do men listen to a woman more respectfully once she establishes this kind of an equation with them, but it also saves her from being sexually harassed or being treated as a sex object. I have often been successful in thwarting unwanted sexual advances and flirtation by male friends or colleagues by beginning to address them as so and so 'bhaiya' or even 'beta' even if the man is not actually young enough to be a son to me. This didi/amma advantage does not work as well on the over-westernized men. Age, in fact, lends tremendous advantage to women in India, and that is why many women learn to use this advantage rather than to hide their age.

Through Male Eyes

In western culture, by contrast, as women grow older, they become more pitiable. Their husbands often start sniffing around for younger women. The concept of equality and women's rights has brought with it easy access to divorce. But in the ultimate analysis, high divorce rates and breakdowns of marriage do not go in favour of women, one reason being that as they advance in years, they find it harder and harder to find marriage partners, since men seem to prefer, and many are able to get, younger women. The notion that women must remain attractive sex partners forever, puts an enormously unrealistic burden on western women, many of whom go to ridiculous lengths to stay young and trim because in roles other than sex partners they get much less attention from men.

In the West, even after the feminists made beauty contests less respectable among the elite, women continue to be under tremendous pressure to be sexually interesting to men and try to mould their bodies to be copies of models in fashion magazines. Most western fashions, designed mostly by men, emphasize sexual provocativeness in women's clothing. By contrast, in cultures like India's, a woman might even jeopardize her chances of marriage by dressing up provocatively. While the system of family-arranged marriages in India has many drawbacks, there are several advantages to it, including the fact that a woman's chances for marriage are not largely dependent on whether or not men find her sexually attractive, as happens in the West, where self-arranged marriages are the norm. Since the entire family takes an active part in selecting a bride in India, a woman is expected to be pleasing to a vast range of people and not just one man. This plays an important role in ensuring that popular norms of beauty are not entirely male-defined, as in the West.

The relative stability of marriage and of family life in India frees women from the pressure to stay forever young and wrinkle-free.

Especially in a joint family setup, the stability of the marriage is to a large extent decided by how well a woman manages to gets along with the various members of her husband's family—his mother, brothers, sisters, aunts and uncles. For these people, her youthful good looks are of subsidiary importance and other human qualities far more valued. A woman who gets along with the rest of the family has some support against being deserted by her husband because the rest of the family would join in to keep the man on a leash. The stigma attached to divorced men may not be as strong as it is for women, but it is sufficiently strong to make a majority of men learn to make the effort required to keep their marriages intact, even when they do not get along with their wives or feel attracted to other women.

It is this relative confidence, that her marriage will last, whether or not a woman stays youthful and attractive enough to satisfy her husband's sexual fantasies, that allows women in cultures like ours to age more gracefully, rather than live in mortal dread of wrinkles, grey hair, sagging breasts and bulging waistlines. Women in India do not need to waste quite as much time in being seductive to men and can invest far more energy into building other relationships, especially with other women.

If the culture of beauty contests takes root in India, it will erode some of the areas of strength traditionally available to women in India. It brings in vicious forms of competitiveness among women and makes them self-hating as they get excessively self-involved and begin to look upon other women as rivals and competitors, desperate for a certain kind of male attention. It makes them more and more unidimensional creatures who are more easily manipulated by men because they see themselves mostly through the eyes of men. While millions of men indulge in sexual fantasies about Sushmita and Aishwarya, I cannot imagine young men wishing they had them as a sister or too many fathers/mothers being anxious to have them as daughters. They tend to provoke only two kinds of responses: sexual excitement in men and envy, or even hostility, among women. In my experience, a woman who only invites envy or hostility among other women becomes a very insecure person despite all the adulation she may get from men.

XIV

Love and Marriage

Feminists and other radicals often project the system of arranged marriages as one of the key factors leading to women's suppression in India. This view derives from the West, which recognizes two supposedly polar opposite forms of marriage—'love marriage' versus 'arranged marriage'. 'Love marriages' are assumed to be superior because they are supposedly based on romance, understanding, and mutual love—they are said to facilitate compatibility. In 'love marriages' the persons concerned are supposed to have married out of idealistic considerations while arranged marriages are assumed to be based on materialistic considerations, where parents and family dominate and deny individual choice to the young people. Consequently, family-arranged marriages are believed to be lacklustre and loveless. It is assumed that in arranged marriages compatibility rarely exists because the couple are denied the opportunity to discover areas of common interests and base their life together on mutual understanding. Moving away from family-arranged marriages towards love marriages is seen as an essential step towards building a better life for women. To it the social reformers add another favourite *mantra*—dowryless marriages as proof that money and status considerations play no role in determining the choice of one's life partner. The two together—that is, a dowryless love marriage—is projected as the route to a happy married life.

Does experience bear this out? From what I have seen of them, 'love marriages' compel me to conclude that most of them are not based on love and often end up being as big a bore or fiasco as many arranged marriages. Among the numerous cases I know, I have found that often there is nothing more than a fleeting sexual attraction which does not last beyond the honeymoon period. And then the marriage is as loveless or even worse than a bad arranged marriage. Nor have

First published in *Manushi*, No. 80, Jan–Feb 1994.

I found any evidence that material considerations do not play as important a role in people's choice when they decide to 'fall in love' with someone with a view to matrimony.

An American friend tells me his married aunt who was seeking a rich suitable husband spent many months going through women's obituaries to identify widowers as potential husbands. Her *modus operandi* was simple: she would go through the daily newspaper and note dowi the funeral details of married women, then go to the funeral and try to make contact with the widower. If she found him attractive and rich, she pretended she was a friend of his dead wife. This is how she targeted eligible men in the hope that one of her encounters would lead to marriage. The social and economic status of the man would be carefully surveyed before he was put on her hit list. This may well appear as a rather far fetched example but falling in love with someone is often based on considerations not very different from those that decide marriages arranged by families.

The romance industry (films, novels) in the West tries to convince us that love is something that happens involuntarily—hence you 'fall in' and 'out of love'. But even their own romance churners keep women's emotional aspirations neatly pigeon-holed. The *Mills* and *Boon* Barbara Cartland heroines make sure the man they 'fall in love' with is tall, dark, handsome, well-educated and from a rich, if not aristocratic family.

My colleague Giri Deshingkar tells me an amusing story of the time he worked as a pool typist in England. Like most Indian men, he never wore a wedding ring. Mistaking him as an eligible bachelor, his female colleagues showered him with attention and competed with each other in wooing him. However, as soon as they got to know through a chance remark that he was already married, they dropped him like a hot brick. No more teas and coffees and other gestures of attention. Suddenly, he became invisible for them. They would not hesitate to discuss their boyfriends and love affairs in his presence. He found them absolutely cynical in their calculation of who they were going to select as a target for loving attention. The experience cured him of all naive notions about love and romance.

This does not surprise me because I have seen these calculations at work at close quarters. For instance, during my university days, I found most of my fellow Mirandians from an English-speaking elite background determined to 'fall in love' with a Stephanian and would not 'stoop' to have a relationship with a man from Khalsa or Rao Tula

Ram College, because those were considered low status institutions, where people from ordinary middle-class backgrounds went to study. The additional qualification they looked for was that the man's family own a house in one of south Delhi's posh colonies. Thus men from colonies such as Jor Bagh, Golf Links or Sundar Nagar were much sought after. Likewise, sons of senior bureaucrats, ambassadors, and top industrialists could have the choicest pick among the beauties and cuties of Miranda House. But a man whose father was a small shopkeeper in Kamla Nagar or a clerk in a government office stood no chance, no matter how bright or decent he might be. I witnessed several instances of my fellow students ditching a man they had been having an affair with for years, as soon as someone from a wealthier background appeared on the scene. Often, they would not even bother to hide the crassness of their calculations; a friend conveniently 'fell out of love' with her boyfriend who owned a motorbike in favour of someone who had a car to take her out on dates.

While many of my friends would have scoffed at the idea of their parents 'arranging' for them to meet a man with a view to matrimony, they were only too eager to go to parties arranged by Stephanians so that they could pick boyfriends. In western campuses young people eagerly read notices of 'Mixers' in order to find future mates.

Men do precisely what women do about 'falling in love'. They take family status, who among her family are 'green card' holders, and other such material considerations into account before they take the plunge.

While men and women may be somewhat more adventurous when choosing someone for a mere sexual affair, the same people tend to become far more 'rational' in their calculations when 'falling in love' is meant to be a prelude to marriage.

In the 1950s, a study which is considered a classic on factors that determine love and marriage in America showed that it was easy to statistically predict the characteristics of the person a man or a woman is likely to fall in love with and marry. Three major factors that have a great influence on who a person falls in love with are: proximity, opportunity, and similarity. Thus it is no coincidence that most whites marry whites and that rich people marry among themselves even in a 'free' society like America where marriages are self-contracted. Why then are we surprised if most Brahmins marry within the Brahmin fold or Jats and Mahars do likewise in family contracted marriages?

Whatever the form of marriage, the motivations and calculations that go into it are fairly simple. Desire for regular sex, economic security, enhancement of one's social status, and the desire to have children, all play a role in both kinds of marriages. Therefore, instead of describing them as 'love' marriages, it is more appropriate to call them self-arranged marriages. Love, in the sense of caring for another person, may even be altogether absent in these marriages. Therefore, I feel, the term, 'love marriage' needs to be restricted to those marriages where people actually have a loving respect for each other and where there is continuing satisfaction and joy in togetherness.

Self-Arranged Marriages

Critics of the family-arranged marriage system in India have rightly focused on how prospective brides are humiliated by being endlessly displayed for approval when marriages are being negotiated by families. The ritual of *ladki dikhana*, with the inevitable rejections women (now even men) often undergo before being selected, does indeed make the whole process extremely stressful.

However, women do not really escape the pressures of displaying and parading themselves in cultures where they are expected to have self-arranged marriages. Witness the amount of effort a young woman in western societies has to put in to look attractive enough to hook eligible young men. One gets the feeling they are on constant self display as opposed to the periodic displays in family-arranged marriages. Western women have to diet to stay trim since it is not fashionable nowadays to be fat, get artificial padding for their breasts (1.5 million American women are reported to have gone through silicon surgery to get their breasts reshaped or enlarged), try to get their complexion to glow, if not with real health, at least with a cosmetic blush. They must also learn how to be viewed as 'attractive' and seductive to men, how to be a witty conversationalist as well as an ego-booster—in short, to become the kind of appendage a man would feel proud to have around him. Needless to say, not all women manage to do all of the above though most drive themselves crazy trying. Western women have to compete hard with each other in order to hook a partner. And once having found him, they have to be alert to prevent other women from snatching him. So fierce is the pressure to keep off other grabbing females that in many cases if a woman is divorced or single she is unlikely to be invited over to a married friend's house at a gathering of couples lest she try to grab someone else's husband.

The humiliations western women have to go through, having first to grab a man, and then to devise strategies to keep other women off him, is in many ways much worse than what a woman in parent-arranged marriages has to go through. She does not have to chase and hook men all by herself. Her father, her brother, her uncles and aunts and the entire *kunba* (kinship group) join together to hunt for a man. In that sense the woman concerned does not have to carry the burden of finding a husband all alone. And given the relative stability of marriage among communities where families take a lot of interest in keeping the marriage going, a woman is not so paranoid about her husband abandoning her in favour of a more attractive woman. Consequently, Indian women are not as desperate as their western counterparts to look for ever youthful, trim and sexually attractive marriage partners.

'Love' Marriage of Sunita

Let us take a few examples of 'love marriage' without dowry and see if women fare much better in them.

When Sunita* was sixteen years old and still in school she fell in love with Vinay who was then more than twice her age. She belonged to a well-off business family but was not well-educated herself. Vinay lived in her neighbourhood and had by then had a number of affairs. When her affair was discovered by Sunita's family, they were upset and tried to dissuade her from marrying Vinay because he was not particularly respected in the neighbourhood on account of his some-what wayward life. However, Sunita thought his 'love' for her would change things and determined to marry him against her family's wishes. Vinay's family was not too happy with the alliance because they saw Sunita as irresponsible and silly and too young to handle a marriage with someone like Vinay.

However, the two insisted and much against parental opposition eloped with a view to pressuring their parents into agreeing to the marriage. Both the families felt humiliated and blamed each other. Sunita's parents gave no dowry because they did not feel responsible for this marriage, nor did Vinay's family make an issue of it. But they felt very angry when the two of them came to live with them because Vinay could not afford to set up a separate household. Their marriage seemed okay for a while but swiftly began to deteriorate due to Vinay's drinking and compulsive womanizing. In the meantime, they had three children. As the children began to grow, Vinay became more and more irresponsible.

He would not even give her enough money for housekeeping, the children's education and other needs. If she objected to his drinking and sexual escapades, he would beat her up. Soon thrashing her became a regular event. In the meantime, he got involved with a divorced woman and this affair began to take the form of regular cohabitation. The more Sunita objected, the more she got beaten. Since she had not been trained for a job nor was she well-educated enough to pick up skills easily, she had to go back and seek financial help from her own father and brothers, in addition to the help she got from her mother-in-law, whose house provided Sunita and her children a home.

Thus, the very people Sunita had defied in marrying Vinay ended up providing her the wherewithal for survival when her 'love marriage' failed her. However, whatever little financial help came to Sunita from her natal family came more as a favour and as charity than as a right, even though she did not get her traditional due in the form of dowry. Her sisters, whose marriages were settled by their parents, all got handsome dowries and have fairly comfortable marriages, married as they are into wealthy families. Sunita's husband was not as financially well-off as her own father. Now she is the poorest of all her sisters and brothers and is virtually living on their charity, as well as that of her-in-laws.

By forsaking her dowry she has not gained anything—certainly not the right to a share in her father's property. For years, the hostility of her father and brothers to her self-arranged marriage prevented her from approaching them for help when her marriage began to crack up, because they would retaliate with: 'It is your own doing. Why come and cry on our shoulder now?' Her sisters would get expensive gifts on festivals and other occasions, but not Sunita. What hurts Sunita most is that her sisters' wedding anniversaries are celebrated with much fanfare. But the day of her wedding feels like a day of mourning. Neither of the two families want to remember that day for it brings back painful memories of humiliation and let-down.

Over the years, as her marriage deteriorated and she was on the verge of destitution, a small trickle of help began to flow towards her. Compare her situation with that of her two sisters. Had their husbands gone wrong, their parents along with other relatives could try and exercise a measure of influence on their husbands because of family bonds that come to be built in a family-arranged marriage. Since Sunita's father felt free to treat her self-chosen husband with contempt even when her marriage was fairly happy in the early years, the two families never built any bonds—nor can her parents claim any rights over him.

Falling Out of Love

Or take the case of Santavna. She was in her mid-twenties when she met Rajesh who was then a young university student struggling to make a living as an artist. Santavna was well-placed in a private company. Though she came from a lower-middle class family and was not highly educated, by her hard work she got a good job and began to rise rapidly in her profession. She was and continues to be a good-looking woman. Rajesh initiated a love affair with her, though he knew she was eight years older than him. In those days, he was poor and struggling and she provided him financial, as well as emotional and physical sustenance. However, his fortunes changed swiftly as he entered the world of journalism and made a successful career. With such rapid upward mobility, his social world also changed dramatically. He then began a series of extramarital affairs. In the early years, he was defensive about them and would keep protesting that his love was reserved exclusively for his wife. I was shown a number of letters of this type he wrote to his wife during the early years of surreptitious and guilt-ridden love affairs.

But as he became more and more successful, he had many more young and glamorous women available for affairs. Tension at home increased and led to crisis after crisis. Finally, he moved out of his house, abandoned his wife and two kids and began living separately, in all likelihood with another woman. Moving out was no big sacrifice because the organization he worked for provided him the house. Soon after, he changed to a still better paying job and asked his previous employers to use whatever means they thought necessary to get his wife to vacate the house. She does own a flat in her own name, so she won't be homeless. But being abandoned by her husband has left her emotionally shattered. Recently, he filed a case for divorce. Today, her salary is much less than his. It is certainly not enough to enable her and her two children to maintain their previous standard of living. Rajesh has made no arrangements for child support so far. It is unlikely that the wife can get anything more than a pittance as maintenance allowance for their children through the court.

The most distressing aspect of the breakdown of their 'love' marriage is the vicious and nasty manner in which he goes around defaming his own wife. I heard both their versions. Both had a lot of charges against each other but comparing their accounts one got the distinct impression that his was exaggerated and in parts even untruthful. He knew he was behaving irresponsibly and had to justify it by painting her as a monster and a whore. Her being eight years older than him was repeatedly mentioned, as though that fact alone justified his wanting to get rid of his wife. The same woman to whom he had written innumerable love letters, swearing life-long loyalty and begging her to have patience with him, to never reject him even if he made lapses because he depended on her more than on anyone else, had now become so offensive that he refuses to even talk to her on the phone. His office staff have instructions that they are not to let her in if she ever comes to see him. Since this is a new job, he has been able to justify his weird behaviour by telling people in the office that she is a vicious monster who will beat him up if they let her in at all. Since this was a self-arranged marriage, the two families have little or no contact. Thus, there are no family members who can temporarily act as communication channels between the husband and wife and help them sort out this crisis.

Fear of 'Love' Marriages

The westernized modernists insist that marriage ought to be a matter between two individuals, that interference by families makes it diffi-cult for the couple to build a close understanding. Hence, they romanticize marriages carried out in defiance of families. Parental opposition is invariably seen as proof of their authoritarian conserva-tism. This is frequently the case. However, fairly often, it turns out that young people are making choices that are impetuous and based on no more than a flush of sexual passion, which does not carry a marriage very far.

The possibility of meeting with Sunita's or Santavna's fate is what keeps a lot of young women from wanting to have self-arranged marriages without the consent or participation of their parents. Almost all of my women students in the college I teach in, told me that they would prefer family-arranged marriages. They would say something like,

At our age, we can easily make a mistake in judgement. Men behave very differently when they are courting a woman and change in unexpected ways when they become husbands. In any case, we can get to know *only* the man by dating him. But when our parents arrange a marriage they look into the family background and culture as well. If they arrange the marriage they take some of the responsibility if things go wrong. But if we marry against their wishes, who will we turn to for support, in case the marriage does not work?

For years I took such statements to be a sign of a woman's low self-confidence and proof of mental slavery. It is only when dealing with cases of women undergoing marital maltreatment that I began to see that many of those who went in for self-arranged marriages did not necessarily fare better. Often they ended up worse off, especially those women who burnt all their bridges with their families during a love affair.

The Eyewitness-MARG opinion poll conducted with 1,715 adults in the five metropolitan cities reported that 74 per cent of women and an almost equal proportion of men believe that arranged marriages are more likely to succeed than love marriages (*Sunday* magazine 9–15 January 1994). Almost 80 per cent of the respondents felt that a young recently married couple—if they had a choice—should live with their parents. That these opinions are not a mindless hangover of 'tradition' becomes evident as they report that over 90 per cent of the same respondents believed that men should help with household chores, and 80 per cent believed that, if they had one daughter and one son, they would leave an equal amount to each in any will that they made. These poll results are supportive of some of my impressions gathered from talking to numerous young women, including my own students, as to why most young women are not very enamoured with 'love' marriages.

While the presence of a large number of family-members rejoicing in the marriage can add to the couple's joy and strengthen their bonds with each other, the lack of parental support and effective communication between the two families, leaving the couple to their own devices, can threaten the well-being of a marriage.

If a family-arranged marriage threatens to fall apart, dozens of people will try to put in the effort to piece it together. However, in cultures where marriage is considered an individual affair, its tensions and breakdowns are by and large left to the concerned couple to sort out all by themselves. That is perhaps an important reason why the rate of marriage breakdown is much higher in such cultures.

Most women in India feel far more vulnerable if they cannot count on their parents or brothers to come to their help at times of crisis. In almost all the cases of marital abuse that have come to *Manushi* in the last 15 years, women have come to seek help along with their brothers, sisters, aunts, uncles or a range of other relatives. The parental house is almost always the only shelter they can count on if thrown out of their husband's home.

Not that adequate amounts of family support come to all those women who go in for family-arranged marriages. Few parents are willing to take their daughters back if they want to leave abusive marriages. But most families do intervene and offer emotional and psychological support, and even some financial support, if the daughter is in touble. This is an important factor which makes most Indian women desire active parental participation in their marriage.

While women are far more vulnerable if they lose the support of their parents, men too run considerable risks if their self-contracted marriage estranges them from their own family. I give, as an example, one of the saddest cases I have witnessed closely. Ajay was a happily married, highly-placed executive in a private firm and came from a very wealthy, propertied family. He started an affair with a woman colleague (let's call her Kavita) who came from an ordinary lower-middle class family. Kavita was already married to someone with whom she had first had a long affair. But since Ajay was 'superior' in every material way, it did not take long for Kavita to fall out of love with her first husband. When Ajay's wife discovered the affair, she was so hurt that in a fit of anger she packed up her suitcases and left for her parental home with her daughter. Kavita immediately moved in with Ajay, thus foreclosing the possibility of a rapprochement between Ajay and his wife. Meanwhile Ajay and Kavita filed for divorce from their respective spouses and had a week-long celebration projecting their union as a grand triumph of 'liberated' love over traditional bonds.

Ajay's parents were so angry at his irresponsible behaviour towards his first wife and child that they refused to make peace with his second wife who they saw as a scheming home-wrecker who had married their son for his property rather than love. This sudden estrangement from all his family made him take to liquor. He became an addict. This affected his job and he began to slide downhill professionally. In the meantime, Kavita started her own garment export business with Ajay's money and through his contacts it began to flourish in no time. Consequently, she had no time for Ajay or even their child. Along with her success came a string of extramarital affairs.

As their career graphs moved in opposite directions, Ajay became more and more resentful of Kavita's success and would often get violent when he found her with other men. The combination of too much drinking and constant fights at home made him emotionally imbalanced and he became mentally depressed. In revenge, he started having affairs with other women but that only made him more unstable. For a while, he found someone he grew very closely attached to but the woman left him saying she found it too painful to have an affair with a married man. Kavita refuses to divorce Ajay. Unlike her first husband, Ajay has huge properties in his name. Therefore, she says she will not leave him till he transfers most of his property to her name. The two go around calling each other the filthiest of names, their marriage not only loveless but full of hatred for each other. Ajay now feels that his wife is only waiting for him to die so that she can take over his property. At this moment of grave crisis, he has neither the sympathy nor the support of his father (his mother is dead) or other family-members because they never forgave him for his second marriage and think he deserves his fate. His isolation and failure in marriage have made him a total wreck.

Marital Compatibility

In the West, almost all marriages are self-contracted. Yet, there is no dearth of marital violence and abuse in those marriages. In fact, many women in the West get beaten not just by husbands, but as often by their lovers or boyfriends. But the problem is not just due to a certain number of husbands turning abusive resulting in breakdown of marriages. Equally often, marriages break down because of mutual incompatibility even when neither of the two spouses is guilty of abuse. Compatibility is a sort of miracle; it rarely happens spontaneously. More often, people have to work hard and patiently to understand each other's requirements and try to meet at least to some extent each other's highest priority mutual expectations.

Compatibility comes more easily if people respect each other's family and cultural backgrounds and are both willing to participate in them as part of mutual give and take. Not too long ago, a young woman came to seek my help in deciding about her marriage. She was very maladjusted with her parents and wanted to escape living with them. During her college days, she began an affair with someone from Orissa whereas her family came from Uttar Pradesh. She was confused about whether to marry him or not because while she thought she liked him, she did not like his family background. But she went ahead with the marriage anyway thinking his family would be living in far away Orissa and would have no chance to encroach upon their married life. However, trouble started in the first month of their marriage. When his family came to Delhi to attend the wedding, they stayed with the couple for a few weeks. She could not tolerate the way they talked, the way they ate, nor anything else in the family culture. Soon she began to resent that her husband shared the culture of his family in many intimate ways. She found his food habits offensive and his involvement with certain prayers and rituals unacceptable, among many other things. The more she tried to wean him away from them, the more his family traits began to assert themselves vigorously. Within seven months, she was talking of divorce.

A woman runs the risk of marring merely her own life if she makes a wrong choice of a husband. But if a man brings in a wife who does not get along with her marital family, he risks destroying the peace and well-being of his entire natal family. The entry of a new daughter-in-law is like blood transfusion. If the donor's blood group does not match the recipient's, the recipient could end up dead. The groom's family often has to cope with enormous stress to make space for a new member whose loyalty cannot be counted upon and who could easily cause irreparable splits in her marital family.

Family Pressures

My impression is that it takes much more than two people to make a good marriage. Overbearing parents on either side can indeed make married life difficult for a young couple and often women have to put up with a great deal of maltreatment at the hands of their in-laws. But more solidly enduring and happy marriages are almost always those where the families on both sides genuinely join together to celebrate their coming together and invest a lot of effort and emotion in making the marriage work. Very few people have the emotional and other resources required to make a happy marriage all on their own. Two people locked up with each other in a nuclear family having to meet with varied expectations inevitably generate too much heat and soon tend to suffocate each other. The proximity of other family members takes a lot of the load off. They can act as a glue, especially during times of crisis. In cultures where marriage is considered an internal affair of the couple with no responsibility taken by families on either side for the continuation and well-being of the marriage, breakdown in marriages is more frequent.

There is also the negative side. In communities where families consider it their responsibility to prevent divorce as far as possible women do very often get to be victims of vicious pressures against breaking out of abusive marriages. Among several communities in India, a divorced woman is viewed with contempt and parents often force their daughters to keep their marriages going, no matter what the cost. Consequently, many end up committing suicide or getting murdered because they are unable to walk out of abusive marriages. Many more have to learn to live a life of humiliation and even suffer routine beatings and other forms of torture. However, in such cultures, divorced men get to be viewed with some suspicion and are somewhat stigmatized. (In the Eyewitness-MARG survey 88% of the men and 86% of the women said that they would stay together for the sake of children even if their marriage did not work).

In family-arranged marriages, few parents are interested in marrying their young daughter to a divorced man, unless he is willing to marry a woman from a much poorer family (so that the family escapes having to pay dowry) or marry a divorced woman or widow. In India relatively few men resort to divorce even when they are unhappy in marriage. The stigma attached to divorce for men, if not as great as for women, is at least substantial enough to get them to try somewhat to control themselves. They know that they cannot get away with having a series of divorces, as they do in the West, and yet find a young, beautiful bride 30 years their junior. But this is only true for marriage within tight-knit communities, where the two families have effective ways of checking on each other's background. There is no dearth of instances nowadays in which parents fail to investigate the groom's background and end up marrying their daughters to men who have beaten or even murdered the first wife. My impression is that this is happening more among groups who are marrying beyond their kinship groups through matrimonial advertisements or professional marriage brokers.

Inter-Community Marriages

Hollywood-Bollywood propaganda tells us that passionate romance is the foundation of a real marriage; according to these myth makers, marriage is and ought to be an affair between two individuals. Marriages between people who defy caste, class, community and other prevalent norms are seen as demonstrating thereby their true love for each other and are glorified. This is not only over-simplistic but highly erroneous.

Our crusades against social inequality and communal prejudices are one thing. The ingredients that make for a good marriage are quite another. A married couple is more likely to have a stable marriage if the spouses can take 90 per cent of things for granted and have to work at adjustment in no more than 10 per cent of the areas of mutual living. The film *Ek Duje ke Liye* type of situation is very likely to spell disaster in real life. The hero and the heroine come from very different regional and linguistic groups. They don't even understand each other's languages and communicate mostly through sign or body language—yet are shown as willing to die for each other. In real life this may make for a brief sexual affair, but not a good marriage. The latter depends more on how well people understand and appreciate each other's language, culture, food habits personal nuances and quirks, and get along and win respect from each other's family. If the income gap is too large and the standards of living of the two families dramatically different, the couple are likely to find it much harder to adjust to each other.

The willing participation of the groom's family is very often crucial to the well-being of a marriage especially if the couple lives in a joint family with the groom's parents. But even if the couple is to live in a nuclear family after marriage, the support of her in-laws will help a woman keep her husband disciplined and domesticated. Most of my friends who have happy and secure marriages get along with their in-laws so well that they are confident that if their husbands were to behave irresponsibly or start extramarital affairs, their in-laws would not only side with the daughter in-law but also pressurize the man to behave better and in some cases go as far as to ask the son to quit the house.

Safety Measures for Women

I am not against self-arranged marriages but I feel they have a poor track record despite pompous claims about their superiority. A self-arranged marriage cannot arrogate to itself the nomenclature of a love marriage unless it endures with love. My own experience of the world tells me that marriages in which the two people concerned genuinely love and respect each other, marriages which slowly grow in the direction of mutual understanding, are very rare even among groups and cultures who believe in the superiority of self-arranged marriages.

The outcome of marriage depends on how realistic the calculations have been. For instance, a family may arrange the marriage of their daughter with a man settled in the USA in the hope of providing better life opportunities to the daughter. But if they have not been responsible enough to inquire carefully into the family, personal and professional history of the man, they could end up seriously jeopardizing their daughter's well-being. He may have boasted of being a computer scientist but could turn out to be a low paid cab driver or a guard in New York. He could well be living with or married to an American woman and take the Indian wife to be no more than a domestic servant or a camouflage to please his parents. He could in addition be a drunkard given to violent bouts of temper. His being so far away from India would isolate the young wife from all sources of support and thus make her far more vulnerable than if she were married in the same city as her parents.

Another case at the other end of the spectrum could end up just as disastrously if the woman concerned makes wrong calculations. Let's say a young student in an American University decides to arrange her marriage with a fellow student setting out to be a doctor. Through the years that her husband is studying to become a doctor, she works hard at a low or moderately paying job to support the family. When he becomes a doctor she decides to leave her job and have a baby. In a few years, he becomes successful, whereas she has become economically dependent on him. At this point, he finds a lot of young and attractive women willing to fall at his feet and he decides to 'fall in love' with one of them, divorces his wife and remarries a much younger woman. The wife is left at a time when she needs a marriage partner most. All she can hope to do is to get some kind of a financial settlement after lengthy legal proceedings. But that is not a substitute for a secure family.

I am by no means advocating that family-arranged marriages are 'superior' to self-arranged marriages but merely trying to point out that the superiority claimed by the votaries of the so-called love marriage system is not evident when one looks at the quality of the relationship in most self-arranged marriages. It is wrong to assume that simply because the two people supposedly 'chose' each other, they will have a better, more egalitarian marriage.

To me the outcome of marriage is more important than the mode of selecting one's partner. If women continue to get beaten and abused by their self-chosen husbands then there is reason to believe they are not chosing sensibly. In my own social circle, I find too many disastrous self-arranged marriages to put them on a higher pedestal compared to family arranged marriages. Moreover, if 'choice' is to be the all important factor in defining these things then let us not look down upon those who 'choose' to have family-arranged marriages. However, the assumption is that those who go in for family-arranged marriages are backward, not fully conscious of their rights.

I am not arguing that in the interest of stability people must go in for family-arranged marriages. Undoubtedly, there are numerous situations whereby family elders do take an altogether unreasonable position; defiance of their tyranny then becomes inevitable, even desirable. Parents can often go wrong in their judgements. Parents must take into account their children's best interests and preferences if they are to play a positive role. In fact, if a family-arranged marriage is forced on an unwilling person, I would be dead against it and would extend all help to such a person to enable her or him to resist parental tyranny, as *Manushi* has done many a time over these years.

The factors that decide the fate of women in marriage are:

- Whether the woman has independent means of survival. If she is absolutely dependent on her husband's goodwill for survival, she is more likely to have to lead a submissive life than if she is economically self-sufficient.
- Whether or not her husband is willing and equipped to take on the responsibility that goes with having a family.
- Whether or not a woman's in-laws welcome her coming into the family and how eager they are to make it work.
- How well the two families get along with and respect each other.
- Whether or not there are social restraints through family and community control on men's behaviour. In societies where men can get away with beating wives or abandoning them in favour of

younger women, women tend to live in insecurity. However, in communities where a man who treats his wife badly is looked down upon and finds it harder to find another wife because of social stigma, men are more likely to behave with a measure of responsibility.

- The ready availability of other women even after a man is known to have maltreated his wife tilts the balance against women. If men can easily find younger women as they grow older while women cannot as readily find marriage partners when they are older or divorced, the balance will inevitably tilt in favour of men irrespective of whether marriages in that culture are self-arranged or parent-arranged.

- Whether or not her parents are willing to support her emotionally and financially if she is facing an abusive marriage. Most important of all is whether her parents are willing to give her the share due to her in their property and in the parental home. In communities where parents' expectation concerning a daughter is that only her *arthi* (funeral pyre) should come out of her husband's house, women have to cope with a lot of insecurity.

We have to devise ways to tilt family support more in favour of women rather than seeking 'freedom' by alienating oneself from this crucial source of support over romanticizing self-arranged marriages and insisting on individual choice in marriage as an end in itself rather than as one means to more stable, dignified and egalitarian marriages.

NOTE

*All the names are fictitous but the situations described are real with a few details changed to ensure anonymity.

XV

Women, Sex and Marriage
Restraint as a Feminine Strategy

Though sexuality is considered an innate human drive, its expression varies in different cultures. Patterns of sexual behaviour in a society are outgrowths of an entire cultural ethos. The same sexual behaviour can acquire substantially different meanings and consequences in different societies.

Most societies have tried to regulate sexuality by placing it firmly within the marriage and kinship structure. However, in societies which evolved male-dominated forms of family, marriage became an instrument of control over women's sexuality. In the West, Engels preceded the feminists in critiquing the double standards of sexual morality inherent in such male-dominated family structures. He saw the destruction of the patriarchal family as a necessary step towards freeing women from men's control.

For the nineteenth century and early-twentieth century feminists, the right to education and the right to vote were the primary issues. It was only after the advent of cheap, effective and readily available contraceptives for the mass of women in the West that the feminist movement began to seriously engage with the idea of sexual liberation. The possibility of separation of women's sexuality from reproduction made it easier for women to assert their own sexuality. This phase witnessed not only perceptive analyses and radical insights into the power play behind the sexual aspects of man-woman relationships, but also ideological challenges to the cultural ideals of women's sexual purity, virginity, and lifelong sexual loyalty to a husband.

Efforts to promote sexual liberation in the contemporary West were accompanied by a very high rate of breakdown of marriages and families, especially since simultaneously many of the legal and religious bars against divorce were removed. At the same time, subjective expectations of marriage became more and more exaggerated.

*First Published in *Manushi*, No. 99, March–April 1997.

In the West, marriage is not just expected to provide economic and social security for raising children, but also sexual compatibility, continual orgasmic delight and romantic excitement. Walking out of marriage in search of more exciting liaisons is no longer only a male prerogative. Women frequently exercise this option. However, even though the ideal of lifelong sexual loyalty in marriage is no longer assumed in the West, the majority of believers in sexual liberation expect a new form of sexual commitment—serial monogamy. For whatever duration that a couple are together, the new morality assumes that they will refrain from sexual involvement with others. Marriages and even non-marital relationships often flounder if either partner discovers the other having clandestine sexual affairs.

While western women have begun to be more sexually assertive, many find they are not necessarily sexually fulfilled. A German feminist friend of mine who was an enthusiastic participant in the heady days of their sexual revolution once described in vivid detail to me how she came out of that experience bruised, hurt, and confused. This is how she summed up her experience: 'I now think we were buggered not just physically but also mentally and ended up feeling used by men.' Today, she feels that free sex without any emotional commitment suits men much more than women because it allows men easy access to any number of women without taking on any responsibility.

In my own social circle, I find that men who propound sexual liberation to women tend to be far more exploitative than the supposedly traditional men. They flaunt ultra-feminist rhetoric and the ideology of sexual liberation mostly as a device to intellectually seduce women into being sexually available at their pleasure. When a woman resists such advances, she often gets responses like: 'I had no idea that you are such a prude. I took you to be a liberated woman,' implying thereby that a sexually 'liberated' woman loses the right that even some prostitutes have—the right to say 'No'.

While many feminists might disagree about the negative fall-outs of sexual revolution in the West, there is little doubt that the resultant instability in life within the nuclear family causes havoc for the children. The breakdown of the patriarchal family has not yet led to more egalitarian and secure family structures. Rather, it has contributed to the atomization of society into a loose collection of self-obsessed individuals. Consequently, kinship and other human relations have become very fragile.

Sex and Liberation

This seems to be an important reason why most Indian women do not seem very enamoured of the idea of sexual liberation as it came to be understood and practised in the West. Feminism in the West came as an offshoot of individualism—the doctrine which holds that the interests of the individual should take precedence over the interests of the social group, family, or the state. However, in India, despite the cultural diversity among its various social, caste, and religious groups, there is a pervasive belief shared equally by men and women that individual rights must be strengthened not by pitching yourself against or isolating yourself from family and community, but rather by having your rights recognized within it. For individual rights to be meaningful, they have to be respected by those with whom you are close, rather than being asserted in a way that estranges you from them. The vast majority of Indian men and women grow up to believe that the interests of the family are primary and take precedence over individual interests.

Therefore, even our idea of the place of sex in life is very different from those of western women due to widely differing cultural values and philosophies. Children, the extended family and *biradari* continue to be the main anchoring points in our lives. Individual freedom is given far lower priority.

Many Indian women are unwilling to remarry after a divorce or widowhood if they already have children even if there is no family opposition to remarriage. They demonstrate enormous resilience and resolve in bringing up children on their own while snubbing sexual advances from men or their family's offers to get them remarried.

This self-denial is based on a fairly astute understanding of the risks involved in this culture in pursuing intimate male companionship at the cost of other valuable relations, and a careful calculation of their children's long term well-being. Women in our society seem to consider sexual deprivation as far less painful than being estranged from their children and family.

Since, in our culture, people (both men and women) who sacrifice their self-interest for others are given far more respect and reverence than those who pursue their own pleasure without taking the concerns of others into account, the idea of voluntary renunciation in pursuit of a higher goal or for the interest of others continues to have a profound hold on our imagination. For instance, an elder brother who remained unmarried for many years because he chose to put all his energy into ensuring that his younger siblings got well-settled in life would be an object of veneration in his community and family. Similarly, a man who refuses to remarry after his wife's death so that his children do not have to deal with the insecurity and risks that come with having a step-mother is treated with special respect in his entire social circle.

The Power of Celibacy

This self-denial no doubt takes a heavy toll and cannot be unduly romanticized as, for instance, Mahatma Gandhi often did. He saw 'voluntary enlightened widowhood' as a great 'social asset' and believed that 'a real Hindu widow is a treasure. She is one of the gifts of Hinduism to humanity'.[1] Gandhi's belief that a Hindu widow had 'learnt to find happiness in suffering, had accepted suffering as sacred....'[2] sounds horribly cruel given the privations many Indian widows have to suffer. However, he did not have a different yardstick for men. He wanted men to emulate the same ideal: 'Hinduism will remain imperfect as long as men do not accept suffering' as many widows did and, like them 'withdraw their interest from the pleasures of life.'[3]

Celibacy, as a voluntary option, seldom gets treated respectably in the West because the West has, by and large, succumbed to the theory that sexual abstinence is an unhealthy aberration which leads to unhealthy neuroses and a disoriented personality. Abstinence is undoubtedly harmful when it is due to external repression. However, when it is voluntary and purposeful it can often be liberating. In India, people have special respect for those who can live satisfactory lives without the need for sex. We are still heavily steeped in the old Indian tradition which holds that voluntary sexual abstinence bestows extraordinary powers on human beings. Indian mythology is full of stories of sages who went so far in *tapasya* that Indira's throne in the heavens would start shaking. The gods would then send some exceedingly attractive *apsara* to lure him and disrupt his *tapasya*. Those few who successfully resisted the sexual lure achieved *mokhsa* and a status higher than gods.

In the twentieth century we have the example of Mahatma Gandhi who tried to transcend his sexuality in order to make it contribute to forging the powerful, modern political weapon of *satyagraha*. His sexual abstinence was part of a larger *tapasya* through which he attempted to discipline his life for devotion to the cause of freeing India from political slavery. His rigorous austerity, various fasts and dietary experiments, vows of silence, and giving up material possessions were essential components of his *tapasya*. He believed that the spiritual force of even one fully formed *satyagrahi* could set right the world's wrongs.[4]

It is not just rishi-munis and mahatmas who practise rigorous *tapasya* with *brahmacharya* as an essential component in order to acquire powers greater than gods, but even ordinary men and women living a life of voluntary sexual abstinence come to be highly respected. Such women tend to be treated as a special category, are subjected to much less scrutiny and restrictions, and tend to get much greater respect from men provided they don't show signs of sexual frustration.

Many of the most revered women in Indian religious history opted out of sexual relations altogether, as the lives of Mirabai, Mahadevi Akka, Lal Ded and many others attest.[5] They are treated as virtual goddesses.

In India, men are trained to fear the wrath of non-consort Goddess figures like Durga, Chandi and Vaishno Devi. While Sita and Parvati invoke reverence, Durga invokes fear and awe. She is the great saviour from worldly adversity. 'Herself unassailable and hard to approach' but someone to whom men also turn for protection. Similarly, a woman who rises above being sexually accessible, consort of none, nor in search of a consort, tends to command tremendous awe and reverence.

Gurbachan Kaur's life-story is a good example. She is now 85 years old and has lived all her life in a small village town of Punjab called Samrala. Her father, Mann Singh was a farmer who had two sons and two daughters, one of whom died early. Gurbachan was married at the age of 16 to an army doctor who died within four months of their wedding without consummating their marriage. Gurbachan's family tried to get her remarried but she firmly refused, saying had married life been fated for her, then her husband would not have met with such an early death. She lived an extremely disciplined life. Seeing her take on such a tough resolve, her father transferred some land in her name and began to put the family finances and other decisions under her charge because he did not want her to live like a dependent on her brothers. He would proudly tell everyone that his daughter was stronger and more capable than any men. She became the virtual head of the family even in her father's lifetime.

The power balance in her family came to be tilted in her favour not just because of the special measures her father took but also because of her own very extraordinary qualities. I got her life-story from her niece who told me that even their kids and grandchildren revere her in the same fashion that her father and brothers did. She is the power centre and decision-maker for her entire extended family. It is she who has the final say in selecting grooms and brides even for her grand nieces and nephews. No financial decisions are taken in the joint family without her sanction and approval.

Her relatives say that she is held in such reverence because

she never tells lies, she is open and forthright, doesn't keep grudges in her heart, does not badmouth anyone and is a genuine well-wisher of everyone she knows. Whenever someone is in trouble she is the first one to go and help them and expects virtually nothing in return. Even her sisters in-law and their daughters in-law are devoted to her.

To quote her niece:

She has lived such a rigorous life of *japa-tapa* that our entire community treats her as a woman with a touch of divinity—a virtual goddess. Whenever she goes to the bazaar even local shopkeepers say 'we got *devi's darshan* today'.

However, her niece Devinder Kaur, who gave this account to me, emphasized that the starting point for this turn around of the power equation in the family began because she invoked great awe and respect from her father and brothers by demonstrating extraordinary self-discipline, especially in sexual matters. Lapses in this regard would have undoubtedly washed away all the credit she got for her other qualities.

It is noteworthy that a woman like Gurbachan Kaur could acquire such special powers and clout in rural Pujab which has a very repressive culture for women and in a community which does not today subscribe to the goddess tradition on account of their conversion to Sikhism. In the West, a woman like Gurbachan Kaur would be an object of ridicule and contempt as in Auden's famous poem, Miss Gee. Our culture has the remarkable ability to provide special space and respect for women who voluntarily opt out of the sexual, marital role.

Peripheralizing Sex

Even in the life of married ordinary women, making sex a contingent relationship works as a very effective strategy in carving out a space of respect and honour for them within their communities. I illustrate this strategy by sharing with you glimpses from the lives of some women I have known closely. They have told me their stories in many versions over a period of time. I may well be accused of being overly anecdotal and drawing conclusions from too few instances. But my perceptions are influenced not just by the lives and experiences of the women I describe below, but also by closely observing the lives of a good number of other women I have gotten to know closely over the years. The life-stories I have chosen as illustrations are fairly typical and representative of a wide spectrum of Indian women's concerns, calculations, and aspirations.

Let me begin with the example of my friend Razia, a Muslim woman in her mid 40s employed as a college teacher. She is respected by most of those who know her because of her quiet dignity and generous temperament. She was widowed after eight years of what was a very happy marriage to a medical doctor. He not only earned well but treated her with love and affection and took great delight in providing her with all possible comforts, even luxuries. His sudden death from a heart attack more than 14 years ago came as a big blow. She had to put herself together after this in order to bring up two small kids, depending on her own much smaller income. Their standard of living fell dramatically. Her in-laws turned her out of her marital home and she had to fight hard to secure even a portion of her husband's own property since her in-laws wanted to grab it all.

Even though she comes from a Muslim community which does not frown upon remarriage of women, she resolutely turned down all attempts to get her remarried. Considering that she was in her early 30s at the time of her husband's death, her natal family was worried as to how she would manage alone. But she was clear: while remarriage would get her a husband, for her children a step-father could never be a substitute for the father they had lost. If anything, they would feel even more insecure.

After being pushed out of her in-laws' home, she moved in with her own natal family so that her brothers, father and other family could give her and the children a sense of security. This is how she explains her choice:

My husband was such an ideal husband—one could not ask for better. That is why I kept his name connected to mine after his death. Had I remarried, I would be known as somebody else's wife. Whatever tasks he left incomplete, I have tried to fulfil those. However, even if I had not been lucky enough to marry such a good man, I still would have done the same. After children come, your target in life is their well-being and future—not just your own fulfillment. Unless you are willing to sacrifice you own self-interest, you will never be held up as an example to others.

She says sexual abstinence did not pose such a major problem because she has kept her connection with her husband very strong: 'He is never apart from me even for a moment. So I cannot even imagine the thought of another man in my life. The idea of sex was buried forever when I decided I was not going to remarry.' She explains that even while her emotional tie with him remains unshakeable, her strength comes from the fact that she has a very deep involvement with her numerous relatives especially parents, brothers and their wives, sisters, nephews, and nieces with whom she lives in a very large joint family. 'With each of these people I have a very strong bond', she says.

She is proud of the fact that her family holds her up as an example. They respect her for having performed her responsibility so well despite such odds. Even her colleagues hold her in high esteem for her resolute commitment. She has a specially close relationship with her teenage children and is convinced that this kind of closeness would not have been possible with a step-father in the house. She exudes enormous confidence in both her son and daughter: 'They would never do anything to hurt me or refuse me anything I asked of them.'

Rejecting Male Norms

This kind of resilience is frequently maintained even in cases where the husband is alive but blatantly disloyal to his marriage—as Maya's life shows. Maya works as a domestic in several homes in one of the south Delhi colonies. I have known her for years. She is an exceptionally attractive woman but not at all self-conscious about it. This is not to say she is sexually repressed—just that she never uses her charm for flirtations.

She comes from what is considered a lower caste south Indian community which, unlike many upper-caste north Indian communities, does not treat women's body and sexuality as a matter of shame. They celebrate it through various rituals. One of the most beautiful is the ritual to celebrate a girl's first menses.

A couple of years ago, Maya joyfully came to invite me to a 'party'. When I asked her what was the occasion, she happily answered:

Ladki ki khushi hui hai (my daughter's happiness has come). The celebration was a big affair. Sugandha, her daughter, after being given an oil and turmeric bath, was decked out like a bride, with a new brocade saree, flowers in her hair, new gold jewellery and all the traditional decorations on her body. Various relatives brought gifts—utensils, sarees, earrings, toiletry and what not. It was almost as big a celebration as a marriage; Sugandha was taken in a procession through their entire neighbourhood to the joyous beating of drums and dancing. This was followed by a whole series of rituals involving rice, coconuts and fruit to symbolize fertility. It all ended with a big feast for the whole community.

Even though Maya does not come from a sexually repressed tradition, yet her notion of female sexuality includes a very high degree of self-restraint. To her that is an essential component of self-respect. When I first got to know Maya about a decade ago, she would occasionally tell me about how her husband beat her. At that time, he was heavily addicted to liquor and spent a big part of family earnings on his drinking. For years, he worked as a casual labourer but has now got a regular job with the railways involving unskilled, manual work. He has a roving eye and has had numerous sexual affairs.

His extramarital affairs started from the early years of their marriage when they were living in a Tamil Nadu village. She first became aware of his affairs when she was eight months pregnant with their first child. The same pattern continued even after his children started growing up; in fact, even after he became a grandfather. Over the years, a good part of his income was spent on his various lovers and mistresses. For instance, in recent years he was stationed in a town in Haryana where he kept a regular mistress on whom he spent a good part of his earnings. Maya was both angry and hurt and had many fights with him over it. He would justify his actions by saying that since he was away from home, he needed a woman to cook for him and could not do without regular sex.

When he used to come home drunk and beat her up, she would refuse to cook for him for days on end. Some years ago, she unilaterally decided to abstain from having sex with her husband. She says she neither enjoys sex anymore nor does she feel obliged to provide it to him as a marital duty since he procures it from outside. I asked if he forced her every now and then. On those rare occasions, she says she gets sick and has terrible abdominal pains. On occasion, she had › to be taken to a doctor and had to miss work for several days. Seeing her reaction to forced sex he has learnt to keep away from her.

Her physical reaction seems a clear statement of emotional rejection. The message is: 'I don't really need you either financially or physically. I am with you mainly because of my children. It is you who need me more than I need you.'

She often tells me proudly how whenever he is unwell he rushes to her. It is she who has nursed him back to health through many an illnesses and helped him get over his addiction to liquor. He realizes her worth because none of his mistresses ever provided him with care during difficult times.

No matter how angry and hurt she has been with him over his infidelity, Maya has refrained from letting her children know about their father's proclivities (except recently when she told her married daughter about it). She feels the kids would have stopped respecting their father if they knew of all his doings. That would only harm the children and do her no good. Similarly, she feels she would never consider breaking off her marriage because that would not only make her children unhappy, but also have a negative effect on their marriage chances, especially those of her daughters.

Over the years she has resigned herself to his extramarital relationships, but gets particularly upset if he does it in ways that are likely to expose him before his children. On a few occasions, when she found him sneaking into a neighbouring woman's hut at night after everyone was asleep, she really gave hell to both him and the woman concerned. Apart from the personal humiliation his infidelity causes her, she feels outraged that he is not careful to hide it from his own young children, though in many other respects he is a good and caring father. Her expectations:

All I want is that he should live at home, return after work at a respectable hour, have his food and go to sleep. He should not pick up quarrels or give me trouble. All I want is peace in the house. I don't want any *pyar vyar* (love). I know he cannot do without screwing around and he knows I don't want to have sex with him. As long as both of us stick to keeping a peaceful home for our children, he can sleep around with whoever he likes; but when he returns home, I don't let him enter the house without a bath, be it summer or winter, so that all the filth he gathers when outside is not brought inside the house.

When I asked her whether she would ever consider having a relationship with another man, she looked at me in total disbelief, saying: 'Why would I behave as stupidly as men behave?' She is truly proud of her unconditional resolve not to mess around with men regardless of what her husband does. It is not as if she is afraid of retaliating in other matters. But, for her, having sexual relations outside marriage amounts to losing her own dignity.

Sometimes her views initially seem contradictory and confusing. For instance, she will start off by explaining her unilateral commitment to her marriage by saying,

For a woman, her husband is like a god. No matter how he behaves she is not supposed to stray. She must stay chaste and steadfast. I, too, touch his feet and pray that my *thali (mangalsutra)* stays around my neck till the day I die. Whether he is good or bad, he is after all my god.

When I remind her how I have heard her abuse him, heard her tell me about her fights with him and how she refused to cook for him or talk to him, her answer is disarming. Pointing to the statues of Ganesh and Krishna in my house, she says:

But I fight with and abuse those gods as well. When both my brothers were taken away (one was murdered over a land dispute and another committed suicide in recent years) I cursed God endlessly. I said to him—may you also experience being orphaned like me. [She was deeply attached to both her brothers and grieves a lot over their deaths]. I fight with God a lot for giving me so many troubles even though I am a firm believer.

When I ask her why it is that real god-like behaviour is not expected of her husband if she is expected to revere him like a god, I get a response so irreverent, it turns the whole concept of Sati-Savitri on its head. Maya is no Sati Anasuya who will carry her leper husband on her back to a prostitute's house at his bidding. She has learnt to cope with his irresponsible behaviour because she has a very low opinion of men in general: 'Men are like dogs. The will go around sniffing in every gutter. (*Char nali moonh maar ke hi aayega*).' It is part of her coping strategy that she can think of her husband as a god and at the same time call him a dog almost in the same breath. As a 'god' she accepts her relative helplessness before him as also the need to accept him for what he is, as one does with gods. But in describing him as a dog she seems to be saying that far from being superior to her, she thinks of him as a species much lower than herself and, hence, has very low expectations from him.

Usually, when a woman says her husband is her god, it is assumed that she is a mental slave, soaked in unhealthy tradition. However, when you probe deeper, it becomes clear that most women use this rhetoric as a way to anchor their loyalties to their marriages, not because they really believe that their husbands are infallible or deserve unconditional obedience.

Recently, when he broke off from his latest mistress, her response was equally cynical:

How long can a monkey go on eating tamarind? *(Bandar kitne din khatta khayega?)* He is bound to come down on his own. However, when a monkey is climbing up a tamarind tree and you call him down and say, don't do that, this fruit is no good for you, the monkey will get even more excited and climb still higher. But if you let him be, he soon rushes down when the sour tamarind hurts his teeth.

Even while Maya has a lot of complaints against her husband, she is proud of the fact that her husband trusts her and believes in her integrity completely. She tells of many women in her neighbourhood who are beaten up by suspicious husbands when they see their wives talking to other men. But in Maya's case, no matter what time she returns home, no matter who she is seen talking to, no matter what a gossip-monger might say, her husband never doubts her fidelity—a position more secure than even Sita's. Thus, she has him on a permanent guilt trip. He has never been able to maintain his sexual fidelity in their marriage. But she stays faithful unconditionally—not as a favour to him, but because her sense of dignity does not allow her to stoop to his irresponsible, undignified ways or to play the game by his norms. She despises his norms and his lack of self-restraint and, therefore, will not stoop to his level.

I don't see this resilience as that of someone trapped in an unhealthy patriarchal ideology. I see this as an attempt by a woman steeped in her cultural ethos to define her own sexual mores as a demonstration that she is not living by male-defined standards. Over the years, she has been able to tilt the scales more and more in her favour. She has been able to persuade her husband to give up drinking. And she is proud of the respect she commands. For instance, she says that when she gets angry and scolds him or even abuses him, he usually listens quietly. In recent years, his violence against her has decreased considerably. She gives him hell if he lifts his hand on her.

Maya's deliberate underplaying of her role as a wife and emphasis on her role as a mother is a strategy Indian women commonly use. They often move in the direction of suspending the sexual dimension of their relationship with their husbands, while retaining the marriage, thus ensuring a measure of security in the outside world and providing a stable family life for their children.

Maya lives in a dangerous and poor slum. It is infested with drug peddlers, sundry criminals, bootleggers, and prostitutes. Her status as a married woman provides her a measure of security and safety in this unsafe atmosphere. Yet, so unsafe is the atmosphere that in the hot summer months she dare not sleep out in the open with her young daughters. They huddle up in their *jhuggi* lest some *goondas* set upon her or her daughters. But she is never sexually harassed by any of the men in her community. I asked her why. Maya's answer was revealing: 'They only go after the loose women. They dare not make a pass at me because they know I will give them hell.' Not too long ago I witnessed what she meant. A railway employee lives nearby her hut. Maya and some other women take their regular supply of water from his courtyard tap. One day he made a pass at her and suggested she become his mistress. She picked up a broom lying nearby and threatened to beat him if he dared cast another dirty glance in her direction. The man never dared again.

Learning to Say 'No'

There is a lot more talk these days of the need to affirm of women's sexuality. However, in my view, the key to a dignified life for women is learning to say 'No' to sex when it comes on humiliating terms. Those who do not know when to reject sex end up far more messed up than those who can do without sex when it is available only as part of an unsatisfactory relationship.

Here is an example from a friend's life who went though years of severe battering by her husband. Describing her predicament, in those years she told me,

One of he most humiliating things about our relationship was that I would not resist sex with him even after he had beaten me black and blue. I got to hate myself when I found that after giving me a brutal beating along with awful verbal abuse, he would come to me for sex. As soon as he touched me to arouse me I would find myself going wet. I know he despised me for being so easy to manipulate and for desiring sex on any terms, but I still could not refuse him.

She also told me that it took her so many long years to break out of that abusive marriage in large part due to her being afraid that she could not live without regular sex. After she broke out of her marriage, living without regular sex has been her most serious problem, leading to one unsatisfactory affair after another.

Disciplining Husbands

While most women in India do not seem to find it hard to subordinate their sexual needs in order to enhance the well-being of their children, too many men think providing a stable home for him and the children is primarily a woman's responsibility and that men ought to be free for occasional fun. But it is hard for them to realize the point when this little bit of fun on the side begins to threaten the stability of their marriage. Maya, despite all her self-restraint, was unable to build a happy conjugal life for herself. But many women I know have been successful in building stable marriages by maintaining very strict self-discipline as a strategy for keeping their men on a tight leash.

My friend Reena explains the subtleties of this game very matter-of-factly. Her marriage is one of the best I know. She comes from an educated and well-connected middle-class Punjabi family. She married a man of her choice, a high-ranking bureaucrat climbing up the professional ladder very rapidly. Theirs is a relationship of mutual trust and respect. But she, too, feels she has to work hard to ensure that she plays an active role in defining the norms of their marriage.

Reena is well-aware that a man of Deepak's status, power, and good looks would attract any number of women ready for short-term or long-term affairs. She is also aware that he likes the company of attractive women. With his job requiring him to travel frequently, anything could happen to jeopardize her marriage. But she has kept Deepak disciplined by imposing a very strict discipline on herself. For instance, she refuses to drink alcohol, even though she admits she enjoys the experience, simply because she wants to keep control over Deepak's drinking. She feels men tend to use drunkenness as an excuse for many of their indiscretions. When they go to parties together, she refuses to dance with anyone other than Deepak. Even though she does not forbid Deepak from dancing with other women, she knows her refraining from dancing with anyone else makes Deepak feel guilty and rush back to her after a dance. It is not that she considers western dancing immoral. She simply recognizes its potential threat for it provides an opportunity for male-female closeness in a manner that may become the prelude to sexual involvement. Close physical proximity creates a whole chain reaction which, in her view, is better kept under check from the start. Even when they went to live in Europe for several years she did not change the rules for herself, even at the cost of being considered a prude.

Committed as she is to her marriage, Deepak, and their happy family, she says openly that she sees her own sexual restraint as a device for keeping her husband under check because he, like most men, might stray when tempted. She has already had a heartbreaking experience early in life. She was deeply in love with one of her childhood friends. The relationship was built over ten to twelve years and she believed he was as committed to it as she was. After his engineering degree he got a job in the US. Before he left, they got engaged. He was expected to come back, get married and take her with him. However, within no time he got involved with some American woman and broke off the engagement rather crudely, leaving her in a severe emotional trauma. Her opinion of men is not very high even though she has a very good relationship with her husband: 'Men are the same everywhere. They have few scruples. Society stays sane only when women set the rules.' She too, like Maya (in almost the same words), says that even if her husband began having affairs, she would not stoop to having affairs of her own. She is certain that his guilt would make him so miserable, he could not continue with it for long without breaking down himself.

I am not holding up Reena or Maya as role models but simply showing how women's strategies for building a stable family life often make sexual needs subservient to other requirements women consider more important.

Children as Allies

Promila comes from a fairly well-off middle-class family from Punjab. At the age of 19 she was married into the Batra family who run a business in the walled city of Delhi.

Soon after her marriage, Promila came to know that her husband, was involved with and had wanted to marry some other woman before their marriage, and that he was still continuing his relationship with that woman.

About three years after her marriage, Dinesh started a business independent from his father's and began to make a lot of money. Whereas earlier the couple used to get no more than Rs 200 as pocket money from her father-in-law, Dinesh was now earning Rs 15,000–

20,000 per day. With that came bad company—gambling, liquor and drugs. By now Promila had given birth to a son and a daughter. He began spending the money as swiftly as it was earned. If Promilla resisted Dinesh's ways, she would be thrashed and abused. For years she tried to help Dinesh get treatment for his addiction. But as soon as he would return from the hospital and meet his old buddies, he would go back to his old habits. In the early years, Promila tried to get her parents to intervene, and to get other relatives to put pressure on her husband. When none of that worked, she finally simply refused to let Dinesh into the flat. She told her parents-in-law, who live on the ground floor of the same house, that their son was their responsibility while her priority was to protect her two children from the influence of such an irresponsible father.

Promila is in the prime of her life. She is 35 and good looking. Since her husband's health and mental balance have been completely lost because of excessive drug abuse, he is no longer able to run his business. She gets an allowance of Rs 5,000 from her in-laws to run the house but that is not sufficient to meet the needs of her two growing children. Some three to four years ago, she met a man at a hospital she had taken her husband to for treatment. They became friends and he adopted her as a sister and eventually offered her a business partnership even though she had no previous experience. She was provided with a company car and a handsome, regular income. This upset both her husband and her in-laws. They began to accuse her of carrying on an affair with her 'bhaiyya'. She stoutly denies all such charges and insists she would 'never do such a thing'. I, for one, could not see why, if she so desired, she would deny herself a relationship with a man who had been so supportive of her and helped her back on her feet again. Undoubtedly, she is emotionally attached to him, but insists her feelings are 'sisterly'.

Her reasoning for ruling out a romantic or sexual involvement with the man is: 'My children will not respect me if I do such a thing'. But doesn't she need sex and all that goes with a man-woman relationship—especially considering that the relationship with her husband broke down more than a decade ago when she was in her early twenties and that since then beatings, fights and character assassination have constituted her conjugal life? Her firm answer:

My children need emotional security more than I need sex or romance. They already have no respect or trust in their father. If they lose their respect for me, if they stop feeling secure with me, they will have no emotional anchor left.'

Indeed both her children are devoted to her. Even though they are only in their teens, they are beginning to form a protective ring around their mother to defend her from her husband and in-laws. It is indeed likely that if she were to become sexually involved with another man or get remarried, she could not count upon her children as her strongest allies—an alliance likely to be much stronger and last longer than her relationships with her own parents and brothers.

Mothers vs Wives

Most Indian women, even when their marriages are good, depend much more on their children for emotional sustenance than they do on their husbands. They recognize that to enter into a sexual relation with a man is to enter into a power relation. Relationships with children are considered far more dependable, enduring, and fulfilling. This may be related to the fact that while as a wife, a woman is expected to serve and surrender, as a mother she is allowed the right to both nurture and dominate and is supposed to be venerated unconditionally. She can expect obedience, love, and *seva* (service) from her children, especially sons, even after they grow up. Unconditional giving brings in its own ample rewards. In her role as a mother, she is culturally far more glorified.

As Sudhir Kakar puts it in his discussion on the Ram-Sita relationship: for an Indian woman, motherhood brings not only personal fulfilment but is an event in which

the culture confirms her status as a renewer of the race, and extends to her a respect and consideration which were not accorded to her as a mere wife.... it is through their children's instrumentality that the injustice done to the mothers is redressed and they assume their rightful place as queens.[6]

This theme recurs in many Indian legends and tales:

Thus Ram repents and is ready to take Sita back from her exile in the forest after he sees his sons for the first time. Dushyanta remembers and accepts Shakuntala as his legitimate wife after he comes face to face with his infant son.[7]

Even though not all present day Indian women succeed in getting their rightful due with the help of their young children, Indian women are frequently able to rely on their children after they grow up to settle scores with husbands or in-laws who may have maltreated them during the early years of marriage. Without doubt

a Hindu woman's 'motherliness' ...is a relatively more inclusive element of her identity formation than it is among western women. Given her early training and ideals of femininity held up to her, motherhood does not have connotations of cultural imposition or a confinement in an isolating role.[8]

That is why, when necessary, she is often able to suppress many of her other needs as a woman, especially her sexual needs, without there being too many harmful effects on her personality.

Opting for Sexual Freedom

In direct contrast to Maya and Promila is Sunanda. She lives in a *basti* (neighbourhood) similar to Maya's but is from a north Indian community. She also works as a domestic in one of the south Delhi colonies. Though much younger than Maya, she looks wasted and rather disoriented. I came to know her some 15 years ago when she was in her early twenties. She was then a very vivacious and attractive woman. At that time, she was married to someone who beat her frequently. Many of their quarrels would start over her not being at home when he returned in the evening and his suspicion that she flirted with other men. One day, she left her two-year-old daughter and ran away with a truck-driver from another community. However, the beatings did not stop in her new home—if anything, they increased. This man encouraged her to join him in drinking because he told her sex was much more fun when both partners drop their inhibitions under the influence of liquor. Within the first year of their living together he squandered the money she had saved over the years in the form of some gold jewellery. She got into the liquor habit willingly because she says she had never before enjoyed sex as much as she did with this boisterous truck-driver. Even his beatings seemed less hurtful because he was not as sexually dull as her first husband.

However, when she was in an advanced stage of pregnancy and found it difficult to have sex, he became enraged, beat her up and forced her to submit regardless of how painful intercourse was for her. His reasoning was: 'I brought you here for fun, not to produce babies.' On several nights during the last months of her pregnancy, her would bring another woman into their *jhuggi*—often a prostitute—get drunk with her, abuse or even beat up Sunanda for protesting, and have sex with the other woman right in front of Sunanda.

Perhaps due to all the beatings and stress she gave birth to a premature baby girl who died within days of delivery. Since Sunanda was too weak for boisterous sex and unable to work and earn money, her truck-driver lover beat her out of his house. She returned to her *biradari's basti* (kinfolk's neighbourhood) but had nowhere to live.

Her husband had in the meantime married another woman. Her widowed mother in the village could not support her. In any case, going back to the village would mean living without a source of income. Neither of her two brothers were willing to keep her in their homes because she had 'shamed' the family by running away with a man of another community. Her sisters-in-law were both hostile and abusive, but one of them agreed to give her temporary shelter when she offered her the one pair of gold earrings she had left and the promise of Rs 250 a month from what she earned.

But now she was treated as a freely available woman by the men in the *basti*. She had three affairs in quick succession which caused nasty fights with her brothers and their wives. Finally, she moved in with one of the notorious *goondas* of the *basti* who had a wife and family, but also had the money to maintain her as a mistress and provide her with a separate *jhuggi*. But for him it wasn't just a sexual partnership. He made her join his very flourishing business of brewing illicit liquor. He required that she agree to make herself occasionally available to the local policemen as a sexual bribe. If she protested, he beat her up saying that she is hardly a Sita-Savitri to be acting so coy. Today, she in one of the most hated women in the *basti*. Since many of their husbands have regular dealings with her on account of her involvement in the liquor business, the women of the *basti* are very hostile to her and have big abusive battles with her.

Women vs Women

Women who are promiscuous provoke fear and hostility in other women rather then inspire them as symbols of freedom. That is because most women live in fear of their men straying: 'Men are men. They will always run after sex' is how they describe men's tendency towards promiscuity over which they can exercise only limited control. But married women fear and despise those women who make it easy for their men to be promiscuous by being easily available. Among my own women friends, the few who behave in sexually liberated ways—that is those who are willing to have sex whenever and with whichever man they feel attracted to, or have no qualms about having sexual affairs with any number of men—are generally hated by other women in their social circle for good reasons. They have jeopardized many a marriage and stable relationship.

Interestingly, I have also observed that almost all of the sexually liberated women I know are fiercely jealous and aggressive when it comes to the man they are currently involved with—for however long or short a period their attachment lasts. Women who consider being sexually attractive to men a very high priority in life, tend to be fiercely competitive and very mistrustful of other women. One of my close woman friends, who has had countless affairs with engaged and married men takes no time to drop a female friend if she finds the man she is currently interested in is paying the slightest bit of attention to her friend. I personally have been able to retain her friendship only by making sure that I avoid meeting her in the company of men she is interested in. On the few occasions we have met in the presence of any of her current boyfriends, she has been so jumpy and nervous, I have had to put in all the effort at my command to remain totally focused on her, while avoiding conversation with her male companion so she could be assured that I was not competing with her for his attention. Despite all of this effort, her insecurity remains strong. She speaks of other women, especially if they are young and attractive, in the most disparaging terms and trusts virtually none of her female friends and acquaintances.

Relationships of trust between women are not possible if a woman cannot trust other women to respect her marriage or romantic relationship. A woman cannot have close relationships with other women if she cannot feel secure that at least her own friends or sisters will not steal her husband or boyfriend. If women are forever insecure about each other, if they are forever competing for male sexual attention, they are bound to hate and mistrust each other. This makes them self-hating as women, more dependent on men and, hence, more vulnerable.

This is not just true in a relatively conservative society like ours, but is even more true in the supposedly sexually liberated societies. My American friends tell me that, usually, as soon as a woman's marriage breaks down, her social circle shrinks dramatically. Most of her married friends and acquaintances will exclude her from their social gatherings because they are afraid that she will try to grab one of their husbands. Single women find it hard to have a close social relationship with married couples and are expected to socialize mostly among singles where they are free to pick and choose partners without jeopardizing other women's marriages.

Among my friends who were sexually 'liberated' there is not one who has built a satisfactory personal life. I recall two cases in particular. During my university days my friend Smita was the most westernized and unconventional of us all in every respect. She had spent a good part of her student years in Europe. An extremely good hearted and generous friend, she believed sexual desire was no different from physical hunger and, therefore, you should have sex whenever you feel the urge and with whomever you felt attracted to. She was one of the few women I knew who was perfectly honest and open about it and had the courage to proposition a man in so many words, whenever she felt sexually attracted to him. A number of our fellow students had sexual relations with her for brief periods. She was neither possessive nor wished to be 'possessed' by any one man. But over the years I saw her become embittered over the fact that many of her male friends used her as a stop-gap between one steady affair and another, or someone to have a little bit of free fun with till they found someone in whom they were really interested. Even though most of her friends—male and female—liked her for her honesty, she could see she was not taken seriously and that the men she got involved with did not really respect her. By the time she began to feel the need for a steady and stable emotional relationship and became dissatisfied with casual sexual encounters, none of the men in her vast social circle were willing to consider her as a fit candidate for an enduring relationship. She is today, far from being an inspiring symbol of liberated womanhood. Most of her friends feel sympathy and pity for her.

Competing with Men

Equally pathetic has been the case of my friend, Veena. She married Rakesh after a fairly long courtship and affair. Both of them were part of university left radical circles and resolved to have a marriage which did not tie either of them down. In the early years of her marriage, Veena found it a very heady idea that both of them could exercise the freedom to have relationships outside marriage. However, when she gave birth to two children in quick succession, the relationship began to change dramatically. While Veena was stuck in the house nursing babies, Rakesh continued to have his flings. Now it began to hurt. But if she protested she was given a high sounding sermon on her 'bourgeois' tendencies, of trying to treat another human being as property, and, on resenting his freedom. She had to learn 'not to feel jealous'. After much heartache and argument they came to an agreement that while they would keep the marriage going for their own sake, as well as for the sake of their children, neither of them would object to the other one having affairs. She really sees herself as another Simone de Beauvoir and claims hers is a good liberated marriage and they both understand each other.

During the next few years, Veena, too, went on a competitive binge and got involved with one man after another. But it became increasingly difficult for her to find meaningful relationships as she began to age. For one thing, only married men were available to pick and choose from. Because of this, most of them wanted only clandestine sex rather then open and free relationships for fear of their own wives finding out. However, for her husband there were no such limitations. He is a fabulous earner in a position of power working for a multinational. For a man of his status and good looks, getting young, unmarried women is no big deal. A touch of silver in his hair only adds to his glamour whereas Veena, who has greyed and become fat, has found that it has become harder and harder for her to get men interested in her. The more interest she shows in men, the more they play hard to get. She is forever on the lookout for a meaningful relationship. Apart from wanting an emotional anchor, she wants a man she can claim to be in love with just to prove to her husband that she can also succeed at this game. But it is becoming harder and harder to win. Now, I constantly hear her complain that while Rakesh continues to have 'a good time', she is condemned to repeated rejections and sexual frustration.

A Losing Game

I am convinced that women cannot win if they play the game by men's rules. Men's capacity for irresponsible sex is relatively unlimited partly because nature has made it possible for men to escape most of the possible consequences of sexual encounters. Moreover, as power relations go in today's world, men, especially if they are rich and in positions of power, can easily get young women for sex or for marriage. However, in most cultures and societies, women find it harder and harder to get men sexually interested in them once they are past their youth. This is one of the reasons it is much more in women's long-term interests to bring about a measure of sexual restraint in men, to teach them to take emotional responsibility for their sexual partners, rather than for women to adopt a competitive approach emulating men's casual approach to sex. The 'I am free to have sex with who I please, when I please' approach may sound radical and liberating in theory, but in actual fact it works out to be patently harmful for women in the long run, especially after the birth of children.

Women in a nuclear family set-up have found it particularly hard raising children in the absence of stable relationships with the men who have fathered those children. Even in the West where remarriage and step-parents are so frequent as to be routine, there is glaring evidence that children become resentful, insecure and even traumatized when they see their parents have multiple sexual relations or bring home new sexual partners in close succession, especially since fierce nuclearization of the family has denied them the nurturance and support of grandparents, aunts, uncles and other relatives.

Stable family life plays a far more important role in the healthy development and well-being of children than material luxuries. In a nuclear family set up, no matter how much the two parents care for their children, they cannot provide emotional security to them if their own relationship is not stable, if either or both of them are carrying on affairs outside of their marriage, and if both of them feel they are free (or ought to be free) to walk out of their marriage as and when they please. Sexual loyalty and restraint are indeed a precondition for the stability of a nuclear family.

Extended Family Buffers

It is perhaps only in matrilineal communities with their complex extended family system that women have been able to exercise a large measure of sexual freedom without having disastrous consequences for children. For instance, in the *marumkakuttayam* system which prevailed in Kerala till a few decades ago, women stayed with their own families even after entering into a marriage or regular sexual relationship with a man. A husband merely had visiting rights in the wife's family home. Children belonged to the matrilineal joint family called the *tarwad* and enjoyed inalienable inheritance rights in the mother's *tarwad*.

A woman was free to terminate her relationship with her husband/lover any time she pleased by merely placing his slippers outside the door as a symbol that she wanted him out of her life. The brother-sister relationship was far more important than the conjugal tie on account of the siblings being members of the same *tarwad*. Consequently, maternal uncles played a far more important role in the lives of children than their own father. In such a large extended family, children got emotional security and nurturance from a large variety of relatives and were not so dependent on their biological parents, least of all their fathers, as in a nuclear family. Therefore, the comings and goings of men in their mother's life were not a source of much disturbance and anxiety for the children.

This is not to project the *marumakkattayam* system as an ideal to be nostalgically revived. It had many problems of its own. For example, this arrangement of visiting husbands could not have been very fair on Namboodri women who lived in patrilineal families, while their men were free to have relations with Nair women and raise parallel families with them while taking little responsibility for the latter. I give this example merely to point out that exercising sexual freedom in a nuclear family set-up causes far greater damage to children, as well as to women's emotional stability, whereas certain kinds of extended families act as buffers.

However, too many of the votaries of women's liberation seem simultaneously enamoured with nuclear families and the supremacy of the conjugal tie, to the exclusion of other relationships. They see any kind of extended family situation, including those that provided valuable support to women, as an encroachment on their personal freedom.

Nuclear families may look liberating on the surface but they put an excessively heavy load on women for the raising of children and maintaining a stable family life. In societies where the man-woman relationship and the nuclear family have come to occupy the central place in people's personal and emotional lives, at the expense of other relationships, women's emotional lives tend to become far more fragile and exercising sexual, as well as other types of freedom becomes a high risk venture.

By contrast, supposedly traditional Indian women rooted in the extended family tend to be far more resilient because they do not put all their energy into being sexually attractive to men. Thus, they avoid letting men play too large a role in determining their self-view. Consequently, they seem to have a stronger sense of self-definition, as well as of the special requirements of womanhood. They can more easily cope with emotional incompatibility and other kinds of stress in their conjugal relationship because they invest their emotions across a whole range of relationships within the family—parents, in-laws, sisters, brothers, nieces and nephews, and especially, among their own children who usually occupy a far more important place in their considerations than husbands. Since today, most women live in patrilineal families, which demand of women sexual loyalty and restraint as a pre-condition for a stable family life, they try to stick to the rules of the game far more determinedly than men.

It is over simplistic to interpret their opting for sexual restraint merely as proof of their subjugation to 'patriarchal norms' as is often done in feminist literature. I see it as an effective though costly strategy to win over the sympathy and support of the rest of the family, especially their children, which can by their disapproval of men's irresponsible sexual behaviour exercise a large measure of restraint on them, thereby bringing about a slow but definite shift in the power balance somewhat in a woman's direction. This is not my idea of an ideal situation if we subject it to the test of attaining full freedom and equality for women. But then we are not living in an ideal world.

The names and some details regarding the people mentioned in this article have been changed to ensure anonymity.

REFERENCES

1. Mahatma Gandhi, *Collected Works, Vol. XIII*, p. 314.
2. Mahatma Gandhi, *Collected Works, Vol. XXVII*, p. 307 and p. 309.
3. Ibid.
4. For a fuller analysis see *Gandhi and Women*, Madhu Kishwar, *Manushi* Prakashan, 1986.
5. For detailed discussion of this issue, see *Women Bhakt Poets, Manushi* Prakashan, January–June 1989.
6. *The Inner World*, Oxford University Press, 1978, p. 79.
7. Ibid.
8. Ibid.

XVI

Yes to Sita, No to Ram!
The Continuing Popularity of Sita in India

I wish to clarify at the outset that I am going to focus primarily on the Sita of popular imagination rather than the Sita of Tulsi, Balmiki or any other textual or oral version of the *Ramayan*. Therefore, I deliberately refrain from detailed textual analysis. I have focused on how her life is interpreted and sought to be emulated in today's context.

However, there is no escaping the fact that in north India the Sita of popular imagination has been deeply influenced by the Sita of *Ramcharit Manas* by Tulsi. In most other versions of the *Ramayan*, close companionship and joyful togetherness of the couple are the most prominent features of the Ram-Sita relationship rather than her self-effacing devotion and loyalty which have become the hallmark of the modern day stereotype of Sita. The medieval *Ramayan* of Tulsi marks the transition from Ram and Sita being presented as an ideal couple to projecting each of them as an ideal man and woman respectively.

As a *maryada purushottam*, Ram's conjugal life has to be sacrificed at the altar of 'higher' duties. Sita is now portrayed in a highly focused manner as an ideal wife who acts as the moral anchor in a marriage, and stays unswerving in her loyalty and righteousness no matter how ill-matched be her husband's response. The power of the ideal wife archetype in Tulsi's *Ramayan* overshadows the happy conjugal life of the couple prior to Ram's rejection of Sita.

The Sita image indeed lends itself to diverse appeals which is perhaps why it has continued to hold sway over the minds of the

*This article has been extracted from a longer paper presented at a conference organized in January 1996, at the School of Oriental and African Studies in London.

I am grateful to my friend Berny and my colleague Dhirubhai Sheth for their helpful comments and suggestions on an earlier draft of this paper.

First published in *Manushi*, No. 98, Jan–Feb 1997.

people of India over the centuries. For instance, in a study carried out in Uttar Pradesh, 500 boys and 360 girls between the ages of nine and twenty two years were asked to select the ideal woman from a list of twenty four names of gods, goddesses, heroes, and heroines of history. Sita was seen as the ideal woman by an overwhelming proportion of the respondents. There were no age or sex differences.[1] That was a 1957 survey. However, Sita continues to command similar reverence even today, even among modern educated people in India. This paper is a preliminary exploration into why Sita continues to exercise such a powerful grip on popular imagination, especially among women.

A Slavish Wife?

I grew up thinking of Sita as a much wronged woman—a slavish wife without a mind of her own. And precisely for that reason she was not for me a symbol of inspiration, but a warning. She was all that I did not want to be. I naively believed she deserved her fate for being so weak and submissive. It was not as though I were deliberately and consciously rejecting Sita as an ideal. Fortunately, she was never held up as an example for me and, therefore, she did not seem an important reference point—positive or negative—in my life. Sita forced herself on my consciousness only after I began working on *Manushi*. The articles and poems that came to us, especially those for the Hindi edition, showed an obsessive involvement with Sita and her fire ordeal (*agnipariksha*).

My impression is that 80 to 90 per cent of the poems that came to us for the Hindi version of *Manushi*, and at least half of those for English *Manushi*, revolved around the mythological Sita, or the writer as a contemporary Sita, with a focus on her steadfast resolve, her suffering, or her rebellion. Sita loomed large in the lives of these women, whether they were asserting their moral strength or rebelling against what they had come to see as the unreasonable demands of society or family. Either way Sita was the point of reference—an ideal they emulated or rejected. I was very puzzled by this obsession, and even began to get impatient with the harangues of our modern day Sitas.

And then came the biggest surprise of all. The first poem I ever wrote was in Hindi, and was entitled, *Agnipariksha*. I give some extracts in a rough translation:

I too have given agnipariksha,
Not one—but many
Everyday, a new one.
However, this agnipariksha
Is not to prove myself worthy of this or that Ram
But to make myself
Worthy of freedom.
Every day your envious, dirty looks
Reduced me to ashes
And everyday, like a Phoenix, I arose again
Out of my own ashes ... ...
Who is Ram to reject me?
I have rejected that entire society
Which has converted
Homes into prisons.

Not just myself, but even my former colleague, Ruth Vanita, who is from a Christian family, wrote many a poem around the Sita theme. Her poetry collection of recent has several poems that revolve around the Sita symbol. It took a long time, but eventually I became conscious that this obsession with Sita needs to be understood more sensitively than I was hitherto prepared for. Therefore, I began to ask this question fairly regularly of various men and women I met over the years: who do they hold up as an example of the ideal man and ideal woman? Young girls tend to name public figures like Rani Lakshmibai of Jhansi, Indira Gandhi, and Mother Teresa as their ideals. But those already married or on the threshold of marriage very frequently mention Sita as their ideal (barring the few who are avowedly feminist). At this point of their life, the distinction between an ideal woman and an ideal wife seems to often get blurred in the minds of women. That includes not just women of my mother or grandmother's generations but even young college-going girls—not just those in small towns and villages, but also those in metropolitan cities like Delhi.

Even among my students in the Delhi University college where I teach, Sita invariably crops up as their notion of an ideal woman. She is frequently the first choice if you ask someone to name a symbol of an ideal wife. When I ask women why they find this ideal still relevant, the most common response is that the example Sita sets will always remain relevant, even though they may themselves not be able to completely live up to it. This failure they attribute to their living in *kalyug*. They feel that in today's debased world it is difficult to measure up to such high standards. However, most women add that they do try to live up to the Sita ideal to the best of their ability, while making some adjustments keeping present day circumstances in view.

Importance of Being Sita

Since I don't have the space to quote extensively from the large number and variety of interviews I have done on the subject, I merely give the gist of what emerged out of these interviews.

It is a common sentiment among Indian women (and men) that the ideals set in bygone ages are still valid and worth emulating, though they admit few people manage to do so in today's world. This attitude contrasts sharply with the popular western view that assumes that people in by-gone ages were less knowledgeable, were far less aware and conscious of their rights and dignity, had fewer options, and therefore were less evolved as human beings. This linear view of human society makes the past something to be studied and kept in museums but is not expected to encroach upon the supposedly superior wisdom of the present generation. In India, on the other hand, Ram and Sita are not seen as remote figures out of a distant past to be dismissed lightly just because we are living in a different age and have evolved different lifestyles. They are living role models seen as having set standards so superior that they are hard to emulate for those living in our more 'corrupt' age, the *kalyug*.

I quote from a few select interviews among the scores I have collected over the years to illustrate how strong is the sentiment of condemnation of Ram's behaviour even by those who are otherwise deeply enmeshed in religious tradition. Most of these women come from fairly traditional families. Surubhi comes from a Brahmin family of Ram devotees but on this one aspect she is unsparing: Ram sounds like a raving lunatic when he subjects Sita to that nasty harangue about her not being pure enough for him on account of her having spent a year in Ravana's captivity. He loses both his reason and his dignity in the process. How dare he have even suggested the first *agnipariksha*? He is supposed to be *antaryami*. Then how come he doesn't know and understand that Sita is above suspicion? In his obsession to be considered an ideal king, he didn't at all think of a wife like Sita who was wholly devoted to him, who was utterly flawless. Even such a woman he humiliated and forsook.

Pratibha works as a typist in an office. Ram is the *Ishta Devta* of her Brahmin family. Yet she is strong in her criticism of Ram. According to her, 'Sita should have understood Ram's real character that he has a worm of mistrust in his mind when he asked her for the first *agnipariksha*. His abandoning her in a state of pregnancy can only be called cruelty and foolishness even though Tulsi tried covering up for this one flaw of Ram's which definitely lowers his *maryada* and image in the eyes of people. Yet people aren't willing to condone the injustice done to her. Balmiki had projected Ram's behaviour as uncouth and unbecoming because he had given shelter to Sita and understood her pain. But Tulsi was too far removed to know what she went through, therefore, he tries to exonerate Ram and make him appear all-perfect. But nobody is fooled by such a cover up.'

Sheila, who works as a domestic servant in south Delhi had this to say: 'What can you say of a man like him who cruelly drove away, *khaded diya* that Sati Savitri? He really tortured his wife. Pretending to be so good and pious before the world but treating his wife with such injustice. Quite a few men are like that. In their attempt to appear goody-goody to outsiders, they destroy their own families. Sita Mata was *Shakti* incarnate, so Mother Earth took her to her bosom. But ordinary women like me can only commit suicide when faced with a husband like Ram.'

Meena, the wife of a senior government official is very religious-minded but says: 'Ram is not my idea of a god I like to pray to. I find him too goody-goody, too enamoured with wanting to be considered an ideal at the cost of putting others into trouble. I know too many men like that. They won't say no to anyone—their mother or father. But they cause havoc all around, because they won't take a stand on anything but try to please everyone. I am not impressed by such pious trouble-makers.'

Poonam, a college teacher, expresses her disapproval thus: 'I feel his aggression towards Sita in their first meeting after *Ravana Vaddh* is typical of male behaviour whereby everytime a man feels inadequate in some way or the other—in valour or even in sexual prowess—he covers up his adequacy by counter-aggression. Ram had not only failed to protect Sita but had to seek the help of monkeys and bears to knock out Ravana's army. He daren't take on Ravana one-on-one… and, therefore, takes his frustration out on that helpless woman. Tulsi deliberately underplayed Ram's injustice to Sita by making it appear that Ram banished only the shadow of Sita. Ram is both cruel and foolish in his treatment of Sita. I fail to see why they call him *maryada purushottam* when he doesn't understand the elementary *maryada* expected of a husband.'

Rama, a Sanskrit teacher, admits to having Sita as the role model for herself. Yet she says: 'I can't stand men of Ram variety who daren't take a stand and hide under the garb of public opinion. He dare not admit that he had unworthy doubts about Sita. Instead he pretends he abandoned Sita to appease his *praja*. I call it cowardice. He should have the guts to at least take responsibility for his own actions rather than blame his *praja* for his unworthy deeds.'

Saroj, who runs a small home-based beauty parlour believes she is a pious Hindu rooted in her tradition. But Ram is not her ideal of a worthy God: 'So enamoured was Ram with the idea of being considered an ideal king that he did not treat even a wife like Sita with elementary consideration. I feel nauseated at Ram's behaviour every time I read those sections of *Ramayana* depicting Ram's injustice to Sita. But then she scores over him finally by appealing to Mother Earth to put her beyond the reach of such an ungrateful husband. It amounted to saying: 'I am not taking any more shit.' But she does it with such grace and dignity that he is left lamenting and grieving like a maniac.'

My interviews indicate that Indian women are not endorsing female slavery when they mention Sita as their ideal. Sita is not perceived as being a mindless creature who meekly suffers maltreatment at the hands of her husband without complaining. Nor does accepting Sita as an ideal mean endorsing a husband's right to behave unreasonably and a wife's duty to bear insults graciously. She is seen as a person whose sense of *dharma* is superior to and more awe-inspiring than that of Ram—someone who puts even *maryada purushottam* Ram—the most perfect of men—to shame. She is the darling of Kaushalya, her mother-in-law, who constantly mourns Sita's absence from Ayodhya. She worries about her more than she does for her son Ram. As the *bahu* of Avadh, she is everyone's dream of an ideal, loving daughter-in-law. To the people of Mithila, she is far more divine and worthy of reverence than Ram.

Her father-in-law, Dashrath, and her three brothers-in-law dote on her. Ram has at least some enemies like Bali who feel wronged and cheated by him. Ram can become angry and act the role of an avenger. Sita is love and forgiveness incarnate and has no ill feelings even for those who torture her in Ravan's captivity.

In many folk songs, even Lakshman, the forever obedient and devoted brother of Ram, takes Sita's side against his own brother when Ram decides to banish Sita. In one particular folk song, he argues with Ram: 'How can I abandon a *bhabhi* such as Sita who is like food for the hungry and clothes for the naked? She is like a cool drink of water for the thirsty. She is now in full term of pregnancy. How can I cast her away at your command?' (Singh, 1986)[2] He is in such pain at having to obey and carry out such an unjust command of his king and elder brother that he does not dare disclose the true intent of their trip to the forest. Squirming with shame, he leaves her there on a false pretence.

She is a woman who even the gods revere, a woman who refuses to accept her husband's tyranny even while she remains steadfast in her love for him and loyalty to him to the very end. People commonly perceive Sita's steadfastness as a sign of emotional strength and not slavery, because she refuses to forsake her *dharma* even though Ram forsook his *dharma* as a husband. Most women (and even men) I have spoken to on the subject refer to her as a 'flawless' person, overlooking even those episodes where she acts unreasonably (e.g., her humiliating Lakshman with crude allegations about his intentions towards her), whereas Ram is seen as possessing a major flaw in his otherwise respect-worthy character because of the way he behaved towards his wife and children.

When Gods go Wrong

Hindus talk of Ram and Sita, Shiv and Parvati and sundry other gods in very human ways and feel no hesitation in passing moral judgement on them. Very few Hindu men or women justify those actions of these deities which they consider wrong or immoral by contemporaneously upheld standards of morality. In other words, gods and goddesses are expected to live up to the expectations of fair play demanded by their present day worshippers. Their praiseworthy actions are neatly sifted from those where the gods fail to uphold *dharmic* conduct. Such criticism and condemnation is not seen as a sign of being irreligious or irreverent but as an acknowledgement that even gods are not perfect or infallible. This provides a far greater sense of freedom and volition to individuals within the Hindu faith than in religions where god's commandments are to be unconditionally obeyed and the god is upheld as a symbol of infallibility.

Sita's offer of *agnipariksha* and her coming out of it unscathed is by and large seen not as an act of supine surrender to the whims of an unreasonable husband but as an act of defiance that challenges her husband's aspersions, as a means of showing him to be so flawed in his judgement that the gods have to come and pull up Ram for his foolishness. Unlike Draupadi, she does not call upon them for help. Their help comes unsolicited. She emerges as a woman that even *agni dev* (fire god)—who has the power to destroy everything he touches—dare not touch or harm. Thus, in popular perception Sita's *agnipariksha* is not put in the same category as the mandatory virginity test Diana had to go through in order to prove herself a suitable bride for Prince Charles, but rather as an act of supreme defiance on her part. It only underscores the point that Ram is emotionally unreliable and can be unjust in his dealings with Sita, that he behaved like a petty-minded, stupidly mistrustful, jealous husband and showed himself to be a slave to social opinion. Most women and men I interviewed felt he had no right to reject and humiliate her or to demand an *agnipariksha*.

Rejection of Ram

The refusal of Sita to go through a second *agnipariksha*—which Ram demands in addition to the first one that she had offered in defiance—has left a far deeper impact on the popular imagination. It is interpreted not as an act of self-annihilation but as a momentous but dignified rejection of Ram as a husband. It is noteworthy that Sita is considered the foremost of the *mahasatis* even though she rejected Ram's tyrannical demand of that final fire ordeal resolutely and refused to come back and live with him. It is he who is left grieving for her and is humbled and rejected by his own sons. Ram may not have rejected her as a wife but only as a queen in deference to social opinion, but Sita rejects him as a husband. In Kalidasa's *Raghuvansha*, after her banishment by Ram, Sita does not address Ram as *Aryaputra* (a term for husband that literally translates as son of my father-in-law) but refers to him as 'king' instead. For instance, when Lakshman comes to her with Ram's message, she conveys her rejection of him as her husband in the following words: 'Tell the king on my behalf that even after finding me pure after the fire ordeal he had in your presence, now you have chosen to leave me because of public slander. Do you think it is befitting the noble family in which you were born?' (Kalidasa)[3]

His rejection of Sita is almost universally condemned while her rejection of him is held up as an example of supreme dignity. By that act she emerges triumphant and supreme, and leaves a permanent stigma on Ram's name. I have never heard even one person, man or woman, suggest that Sita should have gone through the second fire-ordeal quietly and obediently and accepted life with her husband once again, though I often hear people say that Ram should not have rejected her in the first place.

Despite the Divorce

Ram may have forsaken Sita, but the power of popular sentiment has kept them united. Her name precedes Ram's in the popular greeting in north India: *Jai Siya Ram,* as also in several *bhajans* and chants. He is seen as incomplete without her. He stands alone only in the BJP's propaganda and posters. Otherwise he is never worshipped without his spouse. There is no Ram *mandir* without Sita by his side. However, there is at least one Sita mandir that I personally know of where Sita presides without Ram. I was introduced to it by the workers of Shetkari Sangathana. This is in Raveri village of Yeotmal district in Maharashtra. The people of the village and surrounding areas tell a moving story associated with the Sita *mandir* in the area, about how that temple came to be. When Sita was banished by Ram, she roamed from village to village as a homeless destitute. When she came to this particular village, she was in an advanced stage of pregnancy. She begged for food but the villagers, for some reason, did not oblige. She cursed the village, vowing that no *anaj* (grain) would ever grow in their fields. The villagers say that until the advent of hybrid wheat, for centuries, no wheat grew in their village, though plenty grew in neighbouring villages. The villagers all believe in Sita *mai's* curse. Her two sons were both said to have been born on the outskirts of the village, where a temple was built commemorating Sita mata's years of banishment.

Apologia for Ram

The injustice done to Sita seems to weigh very heavily on the collective conscience of men in India. Those few who try to find justifications for Ram's cruel behaviour towards Sita take pains to explain it in one of the following ways:

• Ram did it not because he personally doubted Sita but because of the demands of his *dharma* as a king; he knew she was innocent but he had to show his *praja* (subjects) that unlike his father, he was not a slave to a woman, that as a just *raja* he was willing to make any amount of personal sacrifices for them.

• It was an act of sacrifice for him as well. He suffered no less, and lived an ascetic life thereafter.

• He banished only the shadow of Sita. He kept the real Sita by his side all the time.

Shastri Pandurang V. Athavale's interpretation typifies the far-fetched *apologia* offered by those who wish to exonerate Ram. They even drag in the modern day holy cow of nationalism in an attempt to explain away his conduct:

What we have to remember is that it is was not Ram who abandoned Sita; in reality it was the king who abandoned the queen, in the performance of his duty. He had to choose between a family or a nation. Ram sacrificed his personal happiness for the national interests and Sita extended her full cooperation to Ram. To perform his duty as a king, Ram had sacrificed his queen, not his wife.... At the time of performing *Ashvamedha Yagna*, many requested Ram to marry another woman [which could be done according to the command of holy scriptures] Ram firmly replied to them: "In the heart of Ram there is a place for only one woman and that one is Sita."

Athavale is at pains to point out that Ram's abandonment of Sita was a symbol of the highest self-sacrifice.

Sita was dearer to Ram than his own life. He had never doubted the chastity of Sita ... For had it been so, he would not have kept by his side the golden image of Sita during the sacrificial rites [*Ashwamedha Yagna*]. (Athavale, 1976)[1]

However, even a passionate devotee of Ram like Shastri Pandurang finds it hard to give a totally clean chit to Ram:

Once Ram appeared callous, even cruel. Upon the death of Ravan, after the battle of Lanka, Sita extremely happy appears before Ram. Sternly Ram says to her, "I do not want you who has been looked at and touched by another person. You may go wherever you want to. You may go either to Bharat, Laxman, Shatrughan, or Vibhishan and stay with any of them." We do not know for what purpose he was so harsh, or what he intended to convey to Sita by these words, but it is equally certain that they were terrible words ... Even the people who heard Ram saying such bitter words wept. Everyone felt the bitterness of those words, the injustice that was done, but none dared to protest or plead.[5]

The most powerful indictment, however, comes from the people of Mithila, the region which is the parental homeland of Sita. We are told that Sita's being is part of the very consciousness of Mithila; she is all pervasive in the land, in the water, and in the air of Mithila. 'Her pain sits like a heavy stone on the hearts of Mithila's people.' (Khan, 1986)[6]

This sentiment comes through numerous folk songs of the region. An account of what the injustice done to Sita means to the people of Mithila is poignantly evident in several accounts by leading Hindi writers published in the form of a joint travelogue. This project was organized by the don of Hindu literature, Sacchidananda Vatsayayan, whereby a large group of Hindi writers travelled through the region connected with Sita's name starting from her birthplace Sitamarhi on to Janakpur, Ayodhya and ending their journey in Chitrakoot. The purpose of this project was to delve into the secret of why and how the *Ramayan*, the story of Ram and Janaki, and the locales associated with their names, have become part of people's consciousness and how it has influenced the value system of the educated, as well as the illiterate and defined their cultural identity (Singh, 1986).[7]

Sita is not just the daughter of Janak in this region but a daughter of all Mithila because, as the folk songs of this region testify, popular sentiment maintains that, had Raja Janak by chance not gone to plough the fields that particular day, someone else from any other *jati* might have gone and found her. In that case she would have become that person's daughter. Therefore, Sita is treated as a daughter of every household in Mithila. In Mithila, the entire village is considered as Sita's *naihar* (parental home) not just her actual father's abode (Khan, 1986).[8] Therefore, various folk songs show the entire people of Mithila grieving over Sita's fate.

In some folk songs women of different strata plead with their respective husbands to go and fetch her back to her home after her desertion by Ram. However, Sita in her pride and dignity refused to return and brought up her two sons all on her own. Various writers of this anthology describe how the dignity with which Sita suffered privations after Ram's painful rejection has remained alive in people's consciousness as if this injustice was undergone by their own daughter.

Even today, people of Mithila avoid marrying off their daughters in *Marg-Shish* because that is the month Sita got married. Even today, people of Mithila do not want to marry their daughters into families living in Avadh, in fact anywhere west of Mithila.

They repeatedly recite Sita's name in marriage songs but Ram's name is omitted. At the end of the song there is usually one line which says 'such like Sita was married into Raghukul [the family name of Ram]' (Dalmia, 1986).[9]

There is a beautiful folk song of Mithila quoted by Usha Kiran Khan in which a daughter tells her father what kind of a groom he should find for her. After describing various qualities she is looking for, the daughter advises her father: 'Go search in the north, go south, or get me a groom from the east. But don't go westward, O father, get me a groom from the north.' (Khan, 1986)[10]

This daughter of Mithila has a status higher than that of Ram in her own region. In various polemical songs, Ram is shown as inferior to Sita. (ibid)[11]. At the time of marriage Shiv Parvati songs are more popular than Sita songs. In this context, it is well worth remembering that Ram had to prove himself worthy of Sita before her father offered his daughter to him. This is how one of the folk songs of his region describes it:

Everyday Sita used to clean and smear cowdung in the temple courtyard. One day, her father Janak saw her lift the heavy *Shiv dhanush* (bow) with her left hand while smearing with her right hand the floor where the *dhanush* was kept. At that very moment, he vowed that he would marry his daughter only to such a man who had the valour to break that *dhanush* into nine pieces. Hence, the condition of *swayamvar* that Sita would only be given in marriage to a man who could demonstrate such exceptional strength.[12]

People of Mithila still believe that though Ram passed the initial test for winning her, he failed to prove a worthy husband.

Another writer, Shankar Dayal Singh, commented on how he sensed the all pervasive sentiment of anguish and pain in the collective consiousness of the people of this region at the injustice done to Sita. He goes on to say:

This region has taken a strange revenge in a silent way. From *pauranic* times, everywhere, in every village and small town (*kasba*) are found Shri Janaki mandirs where Ram and Lakshman are also present along with Janaki. But the temples are named after Sita as evidence that somewhere the pain of Sita is still hurting the folk consciousness as though saying: 'Ram, you made our Sita walk barefoot in the forests. Ravan challenged your manhood and forcibly abducted Sita. Though this mother of the universe (*jagjannani*) went through the fire-ordeal to prove her innocence, you abandoned her. Our daughter, our sister was treated thus by Ayodhya. But we are careful of our *maryada* (honour). That is why O Ram, we will keep your idol in the temple. We will even worship it, but the temple will be known in Sita's name.' That is why the whole area is littered with Shri Janaki mandirs. There are Sita legends attached to every spot, even trees and ponds. (Singh, 1986)[13]

Vatsayan comments on how in Chitrakoot people offered them leaves from a tree believed to be the one from which the abandoned Sita used to eat in order to still her hunger. What is the proof offered? The leaves tasted sour and if you drink water after chewing some, the water tasted sweet. So the lore has it that Sita *mai* used to drink water after filling her stomach with these leaves and that sweet aftertaste helped sustain her through days of destitution. Thus, her memory is kept alive in every aspect of the natural, as well as the cultural landscape of Mithila. As writer Lakshmi Kant Varma sums it up: 'Sita *sahanshilta* (quality of dignified tolerance) is written on every leaf of Balmiki Nagar'—the ashram where she spent her years of banishment (Varma, 1986).[14]

The Television Ram

Even in the rest of India, very few people endorse Ram's behaviour towards Sita. He has not been forgiven this injustice through all these centuries, despite his being a revered figure in most other ways. In this context, I am reminded of the time when Ramanand Sagar's *Ramayan* was being telecast over Doordarshan. As the story began approaching the point when Sita was supposed to undergo her *agnipariksha* the serial makers were flooded in advance with so many letters of protest against the depiction of Sita going through the fire ordeal that Sagar was forced to deviate from his text and show the *agnipariksha* to be a mock one. The TV Ram was made to clarify that he did not doubt Sita's chastity. Clearly, Ram's injustice to Sita has hung so heavily on the collective conscience of Indians that they are willing to demand that a sacred text be altered. In this new text, determined by contemporary devotees, *maryada purushottam*, Ram, was being ordered to behave better.

Disqualified Husband

The final rejection of Ram by Sita has come to acquire a much larger meaning in popular imagination than one woman's individual protest against the injustice done to her. It is a whole culture's rejection of Ram as a husband. For instance, people will say approvingly: 'He is a Ram-like son, a Ram-like brother, or a Ram-like king.' But they will never say as a mark of approval, 'He is a Ram-like husband.' To quote Shetkari Sangathana leader, Sharad Joshi: If Ram had not been smart enough to win Sita for a wife by his skill in stringing Shiv's bow, if instead Janak had decided to match their horoscopes and it had predicted that Sita would be abandoned by him, I doubt that Ram would have ever found a wife. No father would have consented to give his daughter to a man like Ram—his claims to godlike perfection notwithstanding. Most people I talked to echoed this sentiment: '*Ram honge bade admi par Sita ne kya sukh paya?*' (Ram may have been a great man, but what good did it do Sita?)

Thus, not just modern day Sitas but even traditional women and men reject Ram as an appropriate husband. Indian women's favourite husband has forever been Bhole Shiv Shankar—the innocent, the trusting, the all devoted spouse who allowed his wife to guide his life and his decisions. Unmarried women keep fasts on Monday, the day assigned for Lord Shiv and pray that they may be blessed with Parvati's good fortune. Shiv and Parvati are the most celebrated and happy couple in Hindu mythology, representing perfect joy in togetherness, including in their sexual union. Their mutual devotion, companionship and respect for each other are legendary. Shiv is not seen as a bossy husband demanding unconditional obedience but as one who respected his wife's wishes, even her trivial whims. To quote Devyani (a middle aged woman working as a domestic help in my neighbourhood): 'Bhole Shankar never caused pain to his wife. He would indulge every whim of hers. Only when a man behaves with such respect for his wife can you have a *sukhi grahsthi* (happy domestic life).'

It is significant that *pauranic* descriptions of Shiv show him as the least domesticated and the most rebellious of all the gods, one whose appearance and adventures border on the weird. He is so unlike a normal husband that Sati's father never forgives her for marrying Shiv. Yet Hindu women have selectively domesticated him for their purpose, emphasizing his devotion to Sati/Parvati, as well as the fact that he allowed his spouse an important role in influencing his decisions. At the same time these women conveniently overlook the many very prominent and contradictory aspects of his life and deeds.

Interestingly, Parvati is not just seen as a *grihalakshmi*, as someone whose reign is confined to the domestic sphere. She often also controls and guides Shiv's dealings with the outside world, constantly goading him to be more generous, compassionate and sensitive to the needs of his *bhakts*.

While there has been a lot of discussion and analysis of the demands put on women in the Hindu tradition—the sacrifices expected of ideal wives—we have failed to evaluate the demands put on an ideal husband. The Hindu tradition might valourize wives who put up with tyrannical husbands gracefully but it does not valourize unreasonable husbands. On the contrary, it places heavy demands on them and expects very high levels of sexual and emotional loyalty from them if they are to qualify as 'good husbands'. Shiv, for instance, is perceived as someone who cannot live without Parvati. He is said to have no desire for other women. He is supposed to have roamed around the world like a crazed being carrying Parvati's dead body on his shoulders after she jumped into the fire to protest against her father's insult to her husband. His *tandava* threatens to destroy the whole world and he rests only after he has brought her back to life. However, most women realize that a Shiv-like husband is not easy to get. Therefore, they need other strategies to make husbands act responsibly.

There are several practical reasons why Sita-like behaviour makes sense to Indian women. The outcome of marriage in India depends not just on the attitude of a husband but as much on the kind of relationship a woman has with her marital family and extended kinship group. If, like Sita, she commands respect and affection from the latter, she can frequently count on them to intervene on her behalf and keep her husband from straying, from behaving unreasonably. Similarly, once her children grow up, they can often play an effective role in protecting her from being needlessly bullied by her husband, and bring about a real change in the power equation in the family, because in India, children, especially sons, frequently continue living with their parents even after they are grown up. A woman can hope to get her marital relatives and her children to act in her favour only if she is seen as being more or less above reproach.

Most women realize that it is not easy to tie men down to domestic responsibility. You need a lot of social and familial controls on men in order to prevent them from extramarital affairs which can seriously jeopardize the stability of a marriage. Thus, they think it is best to avoid taking on the ways of men. To respond to a husband's unreasonableness or extramarital affairs by seeking a divorce or having an affair herself would only allow men further excuses to legitimize their irresponsible behaviour. Thus, it is a strategy to domesticate men, to minimize the risk of marriage breakdown and of having to be a single parent, with its consequent effect on children. A man breaking off with a Sita-like wife is likely to invite widespread disapproval in his social circle and is therefore, more likely to be kept under a measure of restraint, even if he has a tendency to stray.

While for women Sita represents an example of an ideal wife, for men she is Sita mata (*jagjannani*), not just the daughter of earth but Mother Earth herself who inspires awe and reverence. By shaping themselves in the Sita mould, women often manage to acquire enormous clout and power over their husbands and family.

REFERENCES

1. Sudhir Kakar, 1978, quoting from P. Pratap's unpublished thesis in *The Inner World*, Oxford University Press.
2. Vidya Bindu Singh, 1986, 'Sita Surujva ke Joti', in Sacchidananda Vatsayayan (ed.) *Jan, Janak, Janaki*, pp. 125–6 (New Delhi, Vatsal Foundation).
3. Kalidasa, *Raghuvamsha*, 14, 61.
4 Shastri Pandurang v. Athavale, 1976, *Balmiki Ramayana—A Study*, pp. 161–2 (Bombay, Satvichar Darshan Trust).
5. Ibid.
6. Usha Kiran Khan, 1986, 'Sita Janam Biroge Gel', in Sacchidananda Vatsayayan (ed.) *Jan, Janak, Janaki*, pp. 119 (New Delhi, Vatsal Foundation).
7. Karan Singh, 1986. Introduction in Sacchidananda Vatsayayan (ed.) *Jan, Janak, Janaki*.
8. Usha Kiran Khan, 1986, *Jan, Janak, Janaki*, pp. 120.
9. Ila Dalmia, 1986, 'Sita Samaropti Vaam Bhagam', in Sacchidananda Vatsayayan (ed.) *Jan, Janak, Janaki*, p. 32.
10. Usha Kiran Khan, 1986, p. 120.
11. Ibid. p. 121.
12. Vidya Bindu Singh, *Jan, Janak, Janaki*, p. 122.
13. Shankar Dayal Singh, 1986, 'Ek Gudgudi, Ek Vyathageet', in Sacchidananda Vatsayayan (ed.) *Jan, Janak, Janaki*, p. 53.
14. Lakshmi Kant Varma, 1986, 'Kabir Ki Do Samadhiyon Ke Beech', in Sacchidanada Vatsayayan (ed.) *Jan, Janak, Janaki*, p. 73.

XVII

Who Am I?
Living Identities vs Acquired Ones

Every human being is the product of many cross-cutting, multi-layered identities. For instance, a vital part of my identity is defined by my gender. But I am also (among other things) a daughter, a sister, a college teacher, a writer, a Punjabi, a Hindu, a resident of a particular neighbourhood, and citizen of India. Most identities (e.g., those based on nationality, religion, language) are acquired or mutable. A few are fixed and immutable, such as biological parentage. Identities based on native land, village, or locale where a person is born and reared are also fixed.

For the most part, people take these identity layers for granted and they find expression in their appropriate realms at different points of time. However, a group or person may begin to assert a particular identity with greater vigour if it provides greater access to power and opportunities, as happens with caste or gender-based job reservations. Alternately, a person begins to assign a high priority to a particular basic identity if she or he perceives it as threatened or suppressed, especially if that identity is essential to the person's personal, economic or social well-being. For instance, if the government implemented censorship laws that forbade me as a writer to publish and disseminate my work freely, I would be forced to give greater emphasis to my identity as a writer, and to devote a good deal of my time and efforts to fighting against the censors. This struggle may require working in alliances with other writers, though our other identities and commitments may have very little in common.

When I travel in South India, I become aware of my identity as a north Indian, because most people there do not understand the languages I speak, and as a result I feel handicapped. By contrast, I feel culturally much closer to and communicate much better with

*First published in *Manushi*, No. 94, May–June 1996.

Punjabis from Pakistan, even though they are citizens of a country that has a long history of enmity with India. I become acutely aware of my identity as an Indian only when I travel abroad, especially in the West, because of the frequent incidents of racial prejudice and cultural arrogance I routinely encounter there.

Similarly, I become conscious of my identity as a woman only on those few occasions when I am discriminated against or feel special disabilities on account of my gender, for example, when facing sexual harassment or discrimination in employment. Otherwise, my gender identity is only one of my multiple overlapping and cross-cutting identities which peacefully coexists with other identities.

If too many women appear to be imprisoned in their gender identity today, it is because of the disabilities society imposes on them due to their gender. For instance, motherhood, which is an enriching experience for many women and a key component of their self-identification often becomes a terrible burden for women under current societal pressures. Too often, young girls who are not yet ready for marriage are forced into marriage and early motherhood. Too many women cannot decide for themselves when and how many children to have. A woman denied control over her own body might even grow to hate her identity as a woman for want of any prospect of escape from her oppression.

Without these pressures, womanhood would be a far more enriching experience than manhood. Even with all the discrimination they face as females, most women express their identity in benign ways in comparison to men. Women are simply content to be and they show a great deal of flexibility and adaptation to the many social contexts that they participate in during their life cycle, without inordinate strain. Most men, on the other hand, feel compelled to assert one or the other of their competitive identities all the time. Consequently, men become far more aggressive and violence-prone; at the same time their unremitting need to prove themselves makes their egos more fragile and anxiety-ridden.

Without a Homeland

A woman may not be as anxiety-ridden about her ego, but her identity is often riddled with a sense of insecurity. This is because in patrilocal, patriarchal societies like ours, she is denied roots even in her parental family—the most primary identity-inculcating unit of society. For men in our society, their parental identity, as well as their roots to their place of birth and upbringing are immutable. But in the case of women these two immutable identities are sought to be systematically weakened, if not altogether erased, leading to a great deal of insecurity and sense of hapless dependence on men.

In most parts of India daughters are considered *paraya dhan* (an alien's wealth) and excluded from full membership of their natal families after marriage. They can be reduced to the status of refugees without the occurrence of a war or even a riot. At the time of marriage it is made very clear to daughters that henceforth their basic rights are being transferred to their husband's family. The bride's obligations to others will henceforth be determined by the heads of their marital family. She is uprooted as a necessary concomitant of marriage, as a necessary custom, and is transplanted into someone else's home, someone else's village or *mohalla*, and severed from her close kin and friends to live among strangers. She is expected to adopt her husband's family name to indicate her absorption into their family. These uprootings and changes of identity help make women far more adaptable, sensible, practical, less grandiose and pompous, and capable of handling pain, uncertainties and doubt more easily than men. However, the negative consequences of such cultural practices are far more devastating to their survival and well-being. It makes too many women end up feeling dependent and worthless in comparison to men.

In most communities, daughters are formally disinherited from parental property at the time of marriage. They only have the right to come as occasional guests to their parental home; they are not allowed to take up residence in that home as a full-fledged member of the family ever again. This makes them particularly vulnerable to abuse in their marital homes. Many cannot walk out of even violent and demeaning marriages simply because they have nowhere to go. They continue accepting maltreatment to avoid ending up back in their own parental homes, which after their brothers' marriages become *bhabhiyon wala ghar* (a house of sisters-in-law) and, therefore, really out of bounds.

Even in her marital home, her rights are fragile. In case of breakdown of her marriage, she can easily be turned out of that home. After all, it is her husband's natal home, not hers. This lack of basic rights in both her natal and marital home contributes enormously to making a woman experience perpetual insecurity, especially in those communities where a woman is kept from owning property in her own name. There is no United Nations High Commission for Refugees which can give disinherited women internationally recognized refugee status. No wonder so many of them emerge from their marital homes battered or even dead.

I believe that the primary responsibility for their plight rests with their parents and our peculiar family structure which seeks to erase the previous identity of a woman upon marriage in ways that destroy her sense of self. Very often this insecurity creates negative consequences in her marital home, generally at the cost of other women in the house. In an effort to establish a place for herself in her husband's home, a woman may make desperate efforts to push a mother-in-law out, or to make her *nanad* (sister-in-law) feel unwelcome and unwanted, even as a short-term guest, leave alone someone who comes for long-term shelter in times of crisis. Such are the perverse norms of our family system that women themselves end up playing an active, often even a belligerent role in rendering other women refugees without a shelter and dependent on men for protection.

While Sita did not become Mrs Ramchandra and continued to be called Janaki (daughter of Janak) and Maithili (daughter of Mithila), as well as a host of other names acknowledging her diverse identities, our modern day women are expected to transform overnight from being, for example a Miss Sehgal, into a Mrs Kapoor. Our colonial rulers introduced this culture and practice into India through bureaucratic procedures requiring a woman to identify herself through her father or husband's family name. We slavishly spread it because such a form of address for dependent women within the family, accords with our contemporary culture's desire to make women become identified as the wife of some man after her marriage, rather than to provide her the option of retaining her original identity of her natal home.

Many women write and ask us at *Manushi* whether after their marriage they can retain their maiden names, i.e., their father's surname. They are distressed at the thought that without any choice in the matter they would henceforth cease to have the identity they were given while growing up. While assuring them that legally there is nothing to prevent them from retaining their present name, I tell them the exercise is somewhat meaningless if other rights do not come with retaining their father's surname. For instance, I see little point in a woman sticking to her father's name if right of residence in that home and inheritance rights there are going to be denied to her. It amounts to *dhobi ka kutta, na ghar ka na ghat ka*—belonging neither here nor there. If she expects her husband and/or in-laws to provide a share in their inheritance, she may as well adopt their family name and strengthen her roots there. However, it is unrealistic to expect husbands and in-laws to unconditionally offer the new bride economic security if her own parents have systematically denied it to her. Therefore, women should prioritize securing and strengthening their rights in their parental home instead of pitching all their expectations of security on to the husband and in-laws.

I have come to firmly believe that for a woman, having a roof over her head which she can call her own is a key element for a secure identity. If those parents who can afford it would ensure this vital asset for their daughters instead of providing them with exorbitant dowries, women would not be as vulnerable to marital abuse and a sense of worthlessness in cases of marriage breakdown.

Havoc of Nationalism

On a personal note, there is only one level at which I have felt the pangs of an uprooted identity and being a refugee remains a permanent, inescapable predicament for me. No amount of effort on my part can change that. I am from a Punjabi family which was forcibly ejected from what is now Pakistan during the Partition of 1947. Even though it did not take too long for my family to settle down in Delhi, the city I was born in, it has been a constant source of annoyance and pain that whenever someone asks me 'Where are you from?', a simple but important question that is a key element in defining my identity, I have no real answer. My reply is something like an explanation of my uprooted status rather than an answer: 'My father is from Lahore, my mother from Peshawar and I was born in Delhi.'

I have never been comfortable calling myself a *Dilliwali*, but only a person born in Delhi, because the real *Dilliwalas* do not recognize me as one of them. One can easily become a New Yorker by simply being born there or living there for some time, but one cannot become an Andhraite by being born in Andhra. That has to do with our special rootedness in regional identities (among others) in the subcontinent. Neither can I claim to be Lahori or Peshawari.

However, I grew up yearning to see and visit Pakistan. Whenever in school they asked us to write an essay on the place we would like to visit most, my classmates would write about exotic foreign lands.

My essay always contained the desire to visit Pakistan—especially Lahore and Peshawar. Yet, twice when I briefly visited Lahore in recent years caused me immense emotional distress. I was supposedly in a foreign country but unlike visits to other foreign countries, it was not my Indian identity that asserted itself. I felt I was a Punjabi returned to her homeland which had been usurped by many who had no right to it. I was seething inside with unexpected rage which had never found an outlet all these years because for Hindus to yearn for their homeland in what is now called Pakistan is considered politically incorrect. I think Hindu refugees are perhaps among the few groups anywhere in the world who are denied the right to even yearn and mourn for the homeland they lost.

At the Pak-India Amity Forum that I attended in Lahore, my soul rose in revolt when I heard many a Pakistani delegate tell us self-righteously that they feared India because they felt Indians had not made peace with the idea of Pakistan—that we still harboured secret fantasies of *Akhand Bharat* (undivided India) and had imperialist designs on their *mulk* (nation). I certainly am not willing to make peace with a Partition which permanently robbed me of my regional identity, while driving millions of Hindus and Muslims from their homes through terror, violence, murder, rape, and plunder.

However, when I say that I don't accept the Partition, I don't advocate undoing it by another war. All I mean to say is that it was based on a false idea that Hindus and Muslims are not just two communities but separate irreconcilable nationalities. In fact, I consider most nationalistic identities to be dangerous and poisonous. They have caused enormous bloodshed all over the world, including the recent recrudescence of this poisonous creed in its birthplace, Europe, where ethnic cleansing is the new term for this worldwide murderous epidemic that has made hundreds of millions of people homeless in their own homelands. What happened in our subcontinent in 1947 is merely one instance of this European disease.

In the subcontinent, as long as Hindus and Muslims believed that they were two religious-cultural communities living and sharing a common soil, they could easily work out decent traditional norms for co-living on the basis of other common layers of identity such as language, village, and culture. The moment the virus of ethnic and secular nationalism invaded us from the West, religious differences began to be dragged into the realm of secular politics and came to be used as the basis of mobilizing communal monoliths. Thereafter, multi-layered identities were made subservient to this single, voracious identity and politicians could convince themselves that Muslims and Hindus were hostile monolithic communities incapable of peaceful co-existence. Millions were uprooted from their homes and the land they considered their own, lost friendships, old bonds, historical roots, traditions, neighbourhoods, memories, and much else that is irreplaceable. It is tragic that despite the experience of the Partition, we continue on the same disastrous path of making people refugees in their own country as is happening in Kashmir.

Women Carry the Load

In the ongoing conflict in the state of Jammu and Kashmir, a large number of innocent people have already been uprooted from their homes by the brute actions of the Indian armed forces, as well as the terror brigades of Islamic terrorists. The BJP-RSS wants to convince us that only Kashmiri Hindus have been driven out as refugees, whereas the sad reality is that the actions of the Indian government and Pakistani terrorists have caused many more Muslim families to flee Kashmir and seek refuge in safer places. In my own area of Lajpat Nagar, thousands of Kashmiri Muslim families have come as refugees, purchased houses and shops because business and normal life has been badly hit in the Kashmir valley.

There is something to be learnt from the fact that when Kashmiri men want to launch their *jehad* against the Indian government they cross the border to get arms training and weapons from Pakistan, but when they want to move to a safe place with their families to earn a livelihood, they come to Delhi and other cities of India. Pakistan obviously does not seem like an attractive destination for those Kashmiri Muslims seeking security for their families and businesses. Are women determining the latter choice—the choice of their refuge?

Coming and living in cities like Delhi at the height of anti-India insurgency in Kashmir, is an important statement of trust in the Indian people, even while the government of India is hated and mistrusted. Living in Delhi in Hindu majority neighbourhoods, they seem to feel no danger to their Kashmiri identity. However, living in Kashmir among fellow Kashmiris, they felt a serious threat to their Kashmiri identity because of the ham-handed manner in which the various governments at the Centre tried to instal puppet chief ministers in Jammu and Kashmir, eroding whatever little federalism that existed in our constitution. There was no religious or cultural persecution of

Kashmiris. In fact, several crumbs were thrown at them as 'concessions', but this one major political irritant became the basis of identity assertion which took on the form of a terrorist separatist movement.

Kashmiri women have suffered indignities and violence from both sides. There have been frequent reports of rape, molestation, and abduction of women by the Indian armed forces, as well as by Muslim terrorists. An important strategy of this *azadi* movement comes out clearly in the way it has tried to enslave women as a first step towards establishing the terrorists' writ. Kashmiri Muslim women who had no tradition of being pushed behind *burqas* have been threatened into wearing them; beauty parlours have been attacked, acid thrown on women wearing un-Islamic clothes or wearing make-up. The regime of terror has devastated the social and cultural life of Kashmiri Muslim women. It is ironic that whenever men get enamoured with a particular kind of identity assertion, women usually have to carry the burden of implementing it by taking on more restrictive ways of life and cultural markers like dress codes.

Modern western dress for Muslim men is no problem, but Kashmiri women have to wear *burqas* in order to prove that they are good Muslims. However, nothing is sadder to witness than the hostility some Kashmiri Muslim women now express towards Kashmiri Hindu women and vice versa, even when they are both refugees. Too often gender identity is voluntarily suppressed by women in favour of community identity when they feel that their group is under siege or attack. Their primary concern then becomes the safety of their children, men and homes. In this situation, they are often unable to empathize with the pain and suffering of women from the other community on the basis of their common gender identity. In fact, the divide is harsher because it is not of their making. Neither is the process of reconciliation in their hands. It is far easier for Advani and Shabir Shah to sit down and sort out their political differences than for Kashmiri Muslim women in Delhi to build bridges of communication with Kashmiri Hindu refugee women, as long as women allow men of their community to determine their relationships to other groups.

Acquiring New Identities

There is yet another systematic process of identity uprootment going on in our country which has special implications for women. Millions of men and women are being regularly ejected from the rural economy as destitutes because of the callous way in which our policy makers have both neglected and exploited agriculture. These destitutes come as economic refugees from our villages to do menial work in cities—rickshaw-pulling, stone-breaking on construction sites, rag-picking, working as domestic servants, and so on. Among landed families, women, old parents, and children are left behind to take care of the impoverished land, while men come to earn in cities. Thus family lives are disrupted, women are overburdened with impossible loads of work and responsibility and as a result lead emotionally insecure lives. While residing without their families in relatively anonymous communities in the cities their men might take second wives, or blow what they earn on liquor or, prostitution gambling.

Those who migrate to cities with their husbands don't fare much better, condemned as they are to live in unauthorized slums, patronized by *goondas* and criminal mafias who, in league with police and politicians keep the populace, especially women, in perpetual fear and insecurity.

In a small slum near my house, women are afraid to sleep out in the open even in hot summer months, when their windowless, non-ventilated little *jhuggis* are worse than ovens. Their skin breaks out in severe prickly heat and they spend nights without sleep, due to heat and lack of air. Denied space for any privacy for bathing or toilet, they get up at unearthly hours even in the cold winter months to bathe before anyone else is up. In these migrants' new lives their previous identities are erased—they merely become an anonymous mass of *jhuggiwali Madrasinein* or *Madrasi mayiyan* (domestic help from Madras)—never mind whether they are from Andhra or Kerala or other districts of Tamil Nadu. To many north Indians for whom these women do domestic labour, they are all *Madrasi log* (a generic term for anyone from south India) whose identity is derived from their perceived function—to clean middle-class homes and to wash their utensils for low wages. Otherwise, as far as the settled middle-class housewives are concerned, these women should disappear after their work is done and not dirty the city with their ugly *jhuggis* and what northerners perceive as their dirty living habits. It is sad to observe how quickly this soul-destroying treatment of people as 'objects of service' is internalized. Many begin to talk of fellow *jhuggi* dwellers in similar derogatory terms and refer to themselves as Madrasis, even if none of them are from Madras.

An important aspiration of this new identity group called *jhuggi* dwellers is to acquire ration cards and have their names included in the voters' list so they have proof that they are citizens of India, an identity which means little more than the simple assurance that if their *bastis* are bulldozed to the ground in one place, they will have the right to protest and demand of their local political *neta* who they vote for that they be settled elsewhere, or at least occupy another piece of unauthorized land. This ensures that they do not have to live in terror like another group of economic refugees who are not supposed to be on the voters' list. For example, illegal Muslim migrants from Bangladesh who live in constant fear of being forcibly deported. Bangladeshi migrant women often attempt to dress up like north Indian Hindu or Muslim women, take to wearing *bindis*, and desperately pick up a smattering of Hindustani so that they can pass as north Indians when they go garbage picking for a livelihood. When I see them trying to pretend that they don't know Bengali and generally avoid talking to strangers to escape detection, I wonder what this process of acquiring a fictitious identity along with fictitious ration cards does to their sense of personal identity.

The Willing Migrants

At the other end of the spectrum, we have the interesting example of Indians who went as migrants to wealthy western countries in search of better economic opportunities. Those who went to the US as poor unskilled migrants in low paying jobs invariably stayed close to their regional groups (e.g. Punjabi taxi drivers, Sikh farm workers on the American west coast, Gujarati newspaper kiosk owners) and chose to live in neighbourhoods that had many others from their region whose support they could count on. They spoke among themselves in their mother tongue and have remained close-knit communities who continued seeking brides for their sons from their own region and caste group in India.

The enormous effort they put in to ensure that their children marry spouses from families 'back home' is a way of reinforcing their cultural identity by bringing in fresh recruits. However, they often end up becoming more culturally rigid than their counterparts in India because they perceive change largely in terms of westernization and loss of cultural identity, while those living in India do not view themselves in danger of losing their identity when they adapt to changing times.

Many tragedies for young brides can result from these cultural mis-perceptions. A young Sikh or Gujarati woman seeking to marry a non-resident Indian (NRI) in the USA or Canada, hoping for a freer and more 'modern' lifestyle, often ends up in an NRI family who in the name of 'tradition' and retaining their cultural identity, impose far more repressive norms on her than anything she experienced in India.

On the other hand, those who migrated as highly skilled profes-sionals, such as doctors, scientists or engineers, tended to merge with the mainstream western culture. Until very recently, they chose to live in predominantly white middle-class neighbourhoods where their contact with members of their own community became minimal. Thus, often their children learned no other language but English and thereby became estranged not only from their respective regional cultures, but also from their own parents, who they see as repre-sentatives of that culture.

In recent years many among this group have become nervous about the loss of their cultural identity and have become easy prey to the substitute syndicated 'Indian' identity being offered by the RSS-VHP type of outfits. They too are now seeking to protect their Indian identity by encouraging, and often forcing their westernized kids to attend summer camps organized by RSS-VHP to pick up a smattering of knowledge of Indian religion and culture, almost like you learn a foreign language. But trying to acquire Gujarati or Tamilian culture through English language lectures and books is as absurd as learning to swim by reading books without getting into water. Cultural values are imbibed by living in that culture rather than 'learning' them by attending courses as you would learn to operate a computer or pick up a weekend hobby.

As part of keeping their Indian identity, the westernized NRI children are often expected to marry spouses imported from India—mostly found through newspaper advertisements instead of the tradi-tional community networks which many of them discarded long ago. This demand for arranged marriages with spouses from India leads to enormous inter-generational conflict and resentment, as well as stressful marriages. Their peer groups look down upon them for succumbing to this cultural pressure, so they feel estranged in both worlds. The self-given nomenclature ABCDs (American Born Con-fused *Desis*) appropriately sums up their predicament.

There is another interesting aspect to the NRI identity. During my various trips to western countries, I experience two kinds of responses to my presence in the house of fellow Indians. A frequent response is a barrage of contempt and condemnation of India: its bureaucratic corruption, filth, squalor, disease, the inefficiency of Indians, and so on. Many of their complaints are legitimate, though they are often not counterbalanced by an equal comprehension of the good things that come from belonging to diverse Indian cultures. For many of these NRIs, being Indian is merely thought of as being a cultural carrier of various negative qualities. I have often responded to these complaints by asking whether all these negative epithets apply to the complainants, as well. The question is usually evaded. The obsessive nature of these harangues would make me wonder why those who seemed well-settled in opulent foreign lands remain so obsessed with India and its problems. Why don't they simply ignore India if they find the country so annoying and hateful, especially since they live so far away from it? It took me years to figure out that no matter how 'well-adapted and adjusted' to western ways they become, even after they procure American or Canadian citizenship, most people around them do not let them forget that they are Indians, and that, too, in mostly negative ways.

For instance, the rare occasions the western media carry any news and features on India they tend to bolster the negative stereotype that most westerners have of India—bride burning, child marriage, communal riots, epidemics, corruption, and so on. No matter how westernized these Indians might be, for their western colleagues and neighbours they are representatives of a culture that the West considers somewhat 'uncivilized' and 'barbaric', or at least 'backward'. These are issues on which they are often questioned by their western colleagues and friends whenever India comes up in conversation. Hence, the Indian part of their identity is like a wound that never gets a chance to heal and which they are not allowed to forget or ignore as others are constantly rubbing salt into it. In defence, many respond by becoming even more aggressive in their criticisms of India than the westerners whose acceptance they seek. Others increasingly are becoming easy targets for the recruiting efforts of the various components of the Sangh Parivar in order to shore up their sense of self and their cultural identity.

The other common response I experience when I visit NRI homes is the expression of nostalgia for 'home' and India. They begin recounting the warmth they miss in social interaction, the richness of family life, neighbourhood ties, their mothers' food, their grandparents' affection, the family get-togethers, and easy walking in and out of people's homes without having to take prior appointments.

One such person, full of nostalgia, a successful doctor, gave me the most revealing answer when I asked her, 'What is it that comes to your mind when you think of India?' She said without a moment's hesitation: 'The faces of my father and mother.' She has a truly heart-warming closeness to her natal family. All year round she yearns for the few weeks she will get to spend with them in India. For her, each trip to India is like emotionally recharging her batteries and coming back rejuvenated. Even though in most other respects, her two sons are as American as the kids with whom they study and interact, she has been able to build for them a close relationship with their maternal grandparents, uncles, aunts, and cousins living in India. She is looking forward to the time when she can come back and live in India after her children are somewhat older. Neither she nor her Americanized children seem to feel obsessed by the filth and squalor to be seen in many parts of India. Instead, her children seem to feel lucky to be the recipients of a great deal of unconditional love and affection from a large number of Indian relatives and friends. For them being Indian is a positive identity—something that gives them an emotional richness not easily found in the USA.

By contrast, her husband hates going back to India and has mostly negative memories of it. On probing a bit more, I found that he doesn't have much fondness for or closeness with his family and has not maintained regular contact with them. In fact, he looks down upon most of his relatives as being uncultured and backward. I suspect a good proportion of these NRIs who hate their 'Indian' identity are likely to have more fragile emotional ties with their families, due to their own negative experiences of family life. They have deliberately distanced themselves from their relatives who they perceive as backward, envious and greedy for *firangi* gifts, rather than as sources of love and affection. Hence being Indian or Bihari or Tamilian does not bring memories they cherish, but a past that they have escaped for a more opulent and free lifestyle. Therefore, they are more prone to think of India in negative terms. However, those who are rooted in their family and have retained close friendships are not as obsessed with or demoralized by the political culture, even while the corruption and squalor bothers them no less.

Politically Acquired Identities

It is precisely the emotionally and culturally uprooted people who are most prone to seeking political identities. Let me illustrate this with an encounter I had with a young NRI of Tamilian origin. A couple of years ago, after a lecture at Columbia University in New York, a group of Indian students suggested that we continue the discussion over a cup of coffee. Having been away from India for a couple of weeks, I was a bit homesick and somewhat tired of having to constantly use English. Seeing myself in the midst of so many Indians, I slipped into intermixing Hindi sentences in our discussion. While most of them seemed perfectly comfortable at this switch, a young woman suddenly interrupted the conversation, rather rudely and burst out saying something like: 'This is what I hate about you north Indians—your Hindi chauvinism!' All of us were a bit taken aback at the vehemence of her interjection, including a couple of other south Indians present in the group. I apologized for assuming she understood Hindi. To my surprise she answered: 'I do understand your Hindi but why should you impose it on me, a Tamilian? In this respect, I am a real Tamil chauvinist.' This led us into an interesting exchange which, as I recollect vividly, went something like this:

When you say you are a Tamil chauvinist, what exactly do you mean?
What I mean is that I would never allow Hindi to be imposed as a national language on us Tamilians.

Do you read and write Tamil?
No, I never really studied Tamil. I can't really read Tamil books or periodicals.

What language do you speak at home with your parents?
Mostly English. But they do occasionally use bits of Tamil among themselves.

When do you ever get a chance to use Tamil?
Oh, when I visit my grandparents' home in Madras. My grandmother knows no English so I have to use whatever little Tamil I know to communicate with her. And then of course, one has to deal with servants in the house, as well as shopkeepers and hawkers in the street.

What happens after the death of your grandmother? Won't Tamil then become a language of servants and hawkers for you rather than a language of self-expression and interpersonal communication?
That is not the point! I am a great lover of Tamil and, therefore, won't allow Hindi to be imposed in Tamil Nadu.

But why does your love of Tamil get expressed only in terms of opposition to Hindi? Why not in using it? Or in reading the great classics of Tamil literature and seeing Tamil films? (She seemed to have never read a Tamil book and admitted that they did not have a single Tamil book in their home.) Why should English have so taken over even your domestic life if you so love Tamil? But English is both an international language and a link language for India.

Who does it link you with in India? Maybe 2 per cent of the educated elite? Can you communicate with a Maharashtrian farmer in English? Or a Gujarati fisherwoman? Even in Tamil Nadu itself, what status has Tamil got? A person who knows no English is not likely to get even a clerical job in Tamil Nadu, let alone a well-paid one.

Our conversation remained inconclusive because, to her mind learning Hindi was synonymous with political subjugation to north Indians while English carried no such stigma. I need to clarify that this attitude is not due to her living in New York; I have experienced similar hostility to Hindi and a servile fascination for English among educated elites based in Tamil Nadu. There were serious language riots in Tamil Nadu in the 1960s, accompanied by a fierce movement demanding secession from India when Hindi was sought to be introduced as a national link language. It was not as if Hindi was to substitute for Tamil as the regional language; it was only to take the place of English in inter-state communication. Nevertheless, the leaders of anti-Hindi agitation made it out as if Tamil identity was under attack.

That negative reaction remains alive even today, especially among the Tamil intelligentsia, who somehow see no threat from English to their Tamil identity—English which limits their communication with fellow Tamilians, as well as with the majority of Indians. English is much sought after by Tamil nationalists because it is the language of opportunities and upward social mobility for the few who manage to learn it, both within India and in the West. Hindi brings no such comparable advantage and, therefore, it is easy to despise it.

The absurdity of people being aggressive about their linguistic identity without really knowing their own language, or in a situation where English continues to dominate their lives, demonstrates how politically arrived at identities can become harmful. This generates needless conflicts when these identities are acquired for purposes beyond cultural integrity or when they are only asserted in a competitive spirit.

We would do well to remember that the most vigorous support for creating Khalistan came from Sikhs settled in North America and England, almost none of whom had or have any intentions of coming and living in Punjab, even if it should ever become Khalistan. Many of them are still pursuing their vision by financing American senators like Dan Burton in the hope that America can help them achieve Khalistan, since Sikhs in Punjab do not seem as enamoured with the idea and political violence is no longer commonplace in Punjab.

On the other side, it was some members of the NRI Hindu community, especially Punjabi Hindus, who responded to events like Indira Gandhi's assassination and Operation Bluestar in India with a complete boycott of the Sikh community. Despite their diverse regional ties, too many NRI Hindus began to act like a monolithic 'Hindu community' and stopped communicating with Sikhs, branding them all as anti-national. The Punjabi Hindus forgot they had more in common with Sikhs, on account of a shared culture, language and religion than Hindus from other regions.

In Punjab, even at the height of the Khalistan movement, no such animosity took complete hold and Hindus continued to interact with their Sikh neighbours, and in many cases got protection and support from them. What remains of the schism between Hindus and Sikhs is taking much longer to heal in North America than the Hindu-Sikh estrangement in Punjab and the rest of India.

Uni-dimensional Identities

The moment a person or a group begins to subjugate their multi-layered identities in favour of one particular identity, especially if that identity is acquired politically and asserted as a nationality primarily in opposition to some other group, rather than used for self expression and internal cultural bonding, it becomes a sure recipe for civil strife and inter-group enmity likely to tear any society asunder. In this regard it is quite revealing that those who lead such movements are often those who do not live at the centre of their community's cultural life. Rather, westernized, culturally uprooted, and alienated people such as Jinnah and Advani are more prone to playing this leadership role in this game of competitive zero sum identity assertion and denigration of other groups.

Had the super-Anglicized Jinnah lived a little longer after creating Pakistan, in all likelihood he would have migrated to London because Pakistan was created out of his obsession to be one-up on rival 'Hindu leaders', rather than to provide a real haven for Muslims. He certainly could not have survived the regime of military dictators and religious fundamentalists that he helped bring to power in the name of creating a land for the *pak* (pure). In the process he jeopardized the safety and well-being of millions of Muslims whose identity he claimed to safeguard from 'Hindu domination'.

Today, Indian Muslims, who make up 12 per cent of the population, are a vulnerable and mistrusted minority in India, whereas in the unpartitioned India, the 25 per cent Muslim community would have had tremendous bargaining power. The idea behind the Partition was that Muslims could not live in a Hindu-majority India. But the Partition devised by Jinnah left many more million Muslims living in India than could be absorbed in Pakistan, even after the near total ethnic cleansing of Hindus in territories that became Pakistan. Had leaders like Gandhi accepted the Jinnah world-view of identity assertion, many more millions of Muslims would have been uprooted and murdered as a tit-for-tat measure by Hindus.

It is no coincidence that the Urdu-speaking Muslims of India who were the most enthusiastic supporters of the demand for Pakistan are virtually at war with the nation-state of their own making, as also with other ethnic communities of Pakistan. They are still called *Mohajirs* (migrants), indicating that they continue to be treated as aliens and provoke a great deal of hostility in Pakistan. In the 1940s it was their Muslim identity which came to dominate all their other identities, leading to their demand for a Partition. Subsequently, in an all Muslim state, it is their identity as migrants from India which has pitched them in a murderous battle against other groups in Pakistan. As we see in Pakistan and in many other parts of the world, the process of ethnic cleansing is inherently unstable. Pakistan's Muslims soon came to preceive dangers to their own group from other Muslims with other criteria to establish additional diverse identities; Sindhis, Mohajirs, Baluchis, Punjabis, Shi'ites and Sunnis. This begins a never ending process of division. In India, BJP's *Hindutvavad* has led to far more aggressive assertion of caste identities among the Hindus.

Thus the Jinnah model of identity assertion ended up harming large sections of the Muslims no less than it harmed many Hindus. Unfortunately, this ideology of identity assertion has gained greater legitimacy among sections of the Hindu community, thanks to the politics of the Sangh Parivar. Their *Hindutva* campaign has hardly anything positive to offer Hindus because it is simply based on fear and hatred of Muslims.

For instance, while the VHP-RSS-BJP leaders delighted in pulling down the Babri Masjid in Ayodhya in the name of reclaiming the locale of a Ram Mandir supposedly destroyed by a Muslim invader, hardly any of them ever went to do *puja* or made any offerings in the various Ram Mandirs in Ayodhya—not even the Ram Janamsthan Mandir that existed adjacent to the Masjid. In fact, they destroyed ancient and sacred temples like Sita ki Rasoi in the process of pulling down the Babri Masjid. Their riotous behaviour after pulling down the mosque shows that they were not really inspired by *Rambhakti* but motivated by the desire to humiliate and harm the Muslims. That is why their Hindu nationalism has come to play a terribly divisive role in Indian politics. They exhort the Hindu community to be proud of their Hindu identity. *Garv se kaho hum Hindu hain* (Say with pride we are Hindus) is their slogan, but their hate campaigns fill many of us Hindus with shame. Their politics have polarized and fractured our polity in dangerous ways.

To conclude, whenever someone's assertion of identity is loaded with overblown praise for one's own group, and hatred for some other group, whenever competition and tit-for-tat become the real motivating factors in identity consolidation and political struggle in nations, whenever our leaders try to make us paranoid or aggressive *vis à vis* others in asserting a particular aspect of our identity (whether based on caste, religion, gender, language or religion), we should subject such ideas and leaders to thorough scrutiny and check out whether we are being manipulated into imagining dangers from others or is there a real objective basis for it. Such leaders are in all likelihood goading us towards harming others to achieve their own self-determined goals rather than protecting our legitimate interests. Such assertions lead to increasing fragmentation and civil strife without real benefit to anyone. And the moment we begin to succumb to hate propaganda against another group, it is important to pause and subject ourselves to a thorough self-examination. Why is our own sense of self so fragile that we need to fear and hate others merely because they are somewhat different from us? Predominance of negative ethnocentric sentiments against others is a sure sign of a fragile, fractured, and uprooted identity. Hatred of others is usually a sign of self-contempt. Those who really like themselves, are comfortable being themselves and are not prone to hatred and aggression towards others.

XVIII

A Horror of 'Isms'
Why I do not Call Myself a Feminist

I have a horror of 'isms' especially when they are attached to proper names.[†]

M.K. Gandhi

Ideologies can play an important role in uniting people to bring about and hasten social change; in providing inspiration symbols for an organized expression of discontent; and in helping make individual struggles collective. However, an ideology or 'ism' cannot merely be judged by the abstract ideals it claims to represent. It has to be judged primarily by what its self-professed followers do in its name, by the kind of politics that gets practised as a concerted manifestation of that ideology.

I refuse to be labelled a feminist not because I want to be identified by some other 'ism'. In a way it was a self-defence strategy.

My estrangement from feminism came first and foremost from seeing and experiencing what is being practised in its name in India. Having grown up in a very liberal and supportive environment, I have never experienced fear or pressure to conform to set expectations in my growing years. But, from the start feminist gatherings began to frighten me because those were places where the requirement that each woman tow the line was overwhelming. I could not cope with the intellectual regimentation demanded in the name of solidarity for the women's movement. There are, however other reasons also for my scepticism of all available 'isms'—including feminism.

I am using the term 'feminist establishment' to refer to an all-India coterie based mainly in the metropolitan cities which, while maintaining a variety of differences among themselves, acquired the power and the clout to interpret feminism and draw up agendas on behalf of all of India's women, that are more congruent with their own

First published in *Manushi*, No. 61, Nov–Dec 1990.
[†] Gandhi, M.K., *Collected Works*, Vol. LXXI, p. 323.

hopes, self interest, fears and aspirations than with those of most women. Their main support bases are international agencies. As recipients of large grants, they have been able to set up highly visible organizations possessing the wherewithal to act as a concerted lobby at the national level, as well as on the international conference circuit. However, since they have not built any constituency among the wider cross-section of Indian women, they can only make a weak claim to represent them. A good part of their lobbying efforts have helped them gain greater power and clout for themselves, *vis-à-vis* the government and visibility in the media. But they have been largely ineffectual on the basic issues crucial to the well-being of the over-whelming majority of Indian women.

Time-specific and Culture-specific 'Isms'

Broadly speaking there are two different kinds of ideologies or 'isms' which operate in political theory and practice. The first kind evolves under the pressure of specific challenges in a given society at a particular point of time. Often, it is identified with the name of a particular thinker or political leader, such as Marxism, Leninism, or Maoism. The original founders of such 'isms', even during their own lifetimes, were often extremely intolerant in their own ideas, organi-zations and movements. Many of them claimed infallibility for them-selves, and declared anyone who opposed them as enemies of the society. They often encouraged a great deal of violence and hatred towards those who refused to fall in line with them at each new decision point. Even so many of them brought about far reaching changes. However, when the movement dies down, or once it achieves some of its immediate aims, and usually after the original leader's death, the 'ism' ossifies. It is then used more as a ritual chant reduced to a set of deadening formulae by its votaries to justify their own actions which may or may not be the logical outcomes of the original ideology.

My problem with this kind of 'ism' is that while it may sometimes, for brief periods, play an important role in a creative upsurge of ideas and action, it becomes totally moribund once it is institutionalized at a later point as the final truth. What may have been a very creative idea or strategy in the course of the development of a movement, as enunciated by its leaders in response to a particular situation, often becomes a bizarre parody when used in a completely changed context.

Another effect of such ossification is that it encourages the common tendency to approach reality with a preconception of what it should be, and to justify the adherent's own actions by manipulating the ideological jargon instead of responding relevantly to the changing circumstances. A good example is the manner in which the Indian communists defined their hostile relationship to the Mahatma Gandhi led freedom movement, attacking Gandhi and his colleagues with a vocabulary and critique borrowed wholesale from Marx, Lenin and Stalin, who were fighting a different sets of opponents in a completely different context. Marx's own writings on India were totally off the mark because his factual information about India was inadequate and prejudiced. As a result the application of Marxism as a *mantra* in Indian politics has often, resulted in many a tragedy.

In recent years, for instance, the section of Marxist-Leninists which lent support to the terrorist brigades inspired by Bhindranwale in Punjab, justified their approach by claiming that this was a class struggle of the poor and lower-middle peasantry against the *kulak* farmers represented by the Akalis. Other Marxist-Leninists who opposed Bhindranwale's politics dismissed the urgent significance of the ethnic and political strife in Punjab and considered terrorism merely as a sign of false consciousness, deliberately promoted to destroy the potential of real class struggle.

Similarly, some leftists who wish to climb on the bandwagon of the new peasant movements have tried to bestow Marxist credentials on these movements, portraying them as anti-capitalist, even though these movements make no such claim. At the other end are those, who dismiss even the movements of poor and middle farmers as reflecting the interests of *kulaks* and capitalist farmers—again mindlessly borrowing the vocabulary used by Stalin and his followers to physically exterminate large sections of the Russian peasantry in the name of building socialism. These ideologues borrow that deadly vocabulary even though the permissible and actual landholding size in most parts of India and the government policies in agriculture make the emergence or existence of a class of *kulaks* virtually impossible. The original meaning of this ideologically-loaded term, divorced as it was from reality even in the Soviet Union, tends to be used to legitimize harmful statist controls on agriculture, thereby depressing agricultural production and farm incomes. This is a major cause for

India's poverty. These ideologists make little attempt to grapple with our social reality on its own terms, so enamoured are they with borrowed paradigms.

Isms founded by individuals who defined certain tenets in response to a specific situation in a particular society, at a particular time—like Marxism-Leninism and Maoism—are in crucial ways both time-specific and culture-specific. While certain elements of these 'isms' may be relevant at other times and places and may provide inspiration or warning but applying them as formulae in alien societies and at different points in time, most often proves counter-productive.

The second kind of 'ism' does not arise from one movement or an individual leader but often pervades many different movements in the form of a structuring idea or tendency. Some examples are anarchism, humanism and feminism. Feminism was an outgrowth of eighteenth-century humanist thought in Europe and America, reinforced by thinkers from many other schools of thought, such as utilitarianism and Marxism. This second type of 'ism' may not be as time-specific as the first, but it is often culture-specific.

Importance of an Independent Self-view

Anyone working for women's rights in India, irrespective of the nature of their work, is automatically assumed to be a conscious or unconscious feminist, and allowed no choice on this issue. Yet people working for peace and disarmament in the West are not assumed to be Gandhians, even though Gandhi is the most outstanding leader of modern times to have provided a philosophy and politics of non-violence, and led the most effective mass movement based on non-violent principles. The Green Movement in Germany, and the peace movements in the West in general, do not need to display more than a mild and patronizing interest in Gandhi, because westerners assume that they have the right to define their own self-image and choose their own terminology to describe themselves. But the same right is not granted to us, the hitherto colonized. We are labelled 'feminists' without so much as a by-our-leave, not only by western feminists but also by their counterparts in India. Many view my refusal to accept the label either as an act of betrayal or as a sign of insufficient ideological growth. I believe that accepting or rejecting labels is not a meaningless task. Being able to choose an appropriate name and definition for one's politics is an important aspect of evolving an independent self-view, provided the exercise is not merely restricted to ritual debates about labels.

The problem does not stop with carrying or not carrying the label 'feminist'. As products of the far more homogenized western culture, most feminists assume that women's aspirations the world over must be identical or at least similar, even while their specific problems may be somewhat different. They are often unable to understand or accept that a person's idea of a good life and their aspirations are closely related to what is valued in that particular society and culture.

Western feminism is an offshoot of individualism and liberalism. Individualism is an ideology which posits that the rights of the individual are the foundation of all human rights. They consider each individual ultimately responsible primarily to herself or himself. At the same time, most feminists view the state as the crucial agency for the protection of their individual rights. This ideology has played an important role in atomizing western societies so that people often have only the authority and support of the state (not even of their kinship group) to appeal to for protection of their rights when they are violated by others.

In India, most of us find it difficult to tune in to the extreme individualism that comes to us through feminism. For instance, most women here are unwilling to assert their rights in a way that estranges them not just from their family but also from their larger kinship group and community. They want to ensure that their rights are respected and acknowledged by their family and prefer to avoid asserting their rights in a way that isolates them from those they consider their own. This need not be interpreted as a sign of mental slavery to social opinion. Rather, it is an indication that for many of us life is a poor thing if our freedom inevitably cuts us off from our interdependence with others. In our culture both men and women are taught to value the interests of our families and not make our lives revolve around individual self-interest. Most feminists consider this world view a product of lower self-esteem even when a woman is not facing problems or oppression as a consequence of such beliefs.

Though I stand committed to pro-women politics, I resist the label of feminism because of the few in India who are aware of the word associate it blindly with the western women's movement. I have no quarrel with western feminism in its own context. In fact, I feel strengthened by the existence of women's movements in western as in eastern countries but I am not comfortable with being treated as a mindless prototype.

At the time we launched *Manushi* in 1978, I did not openly challenge being labelled feminist. But I resisted pressure that *Manushi* be called a feminist magazine. Some of us felt that if the magazine proclaimed that as its identification, large sections of potential readers would be alienated, the word feminism means nothing to most Indians, except a microscopic number of highly westernized, elite people. There are no equivalents in any of the Indian languages to the term 'feminism'. Neither its history nor its symbolism evokes any response whatsoever among the vast majority of Indian women. If anything, the term has acquired many negative connotations in recent years. It inevitably evokes associations with the women's movement in the West, which is known in India mostly through simplistic stereotypes. These stereotypes become an unnecessary burden because people's responses to our work are then based on prejudices concerning the current popular notions of western feminism.

Moreover, being labelled a feminist puts you in a tight box. People expect you to have no other concern, no other opinion, other than that of women's equality. We deliberately chose the subtitle, 'a journal about women and society' which, we felt, would indicate that *Manushi* is concerned not just with women's equality but with a whole range of social, political issues related to the protection of human rights of all the disadvantaged or discriminated groups in our society as the word *Manushi* (meaning humane) implies—while having a special emphasis on women's rights.

The avoidance of the label was not just restricted to the title or subtitle of the magazine. The term 'feminism' almost never appeared in any of my writings even in the early days of *Manushi*. For a while, a popular feminist symbol appeared in each copy, but that too was dropped as soon as we could arrange for artists to do special graphics for us.

Apart from serious ideological reservations, there were more practical reasons for refusing to call *Manushi* a feminist magazine. The use of the term 'feminist' does not reveal enough about those who use the term to describe themselves. It, of course, indicates in some way that they believe in women's equality, but so do many non-feminist political appellations. It is possible to be a Gandhian, a liberal, or a Marxist, or simply a decent human being to believe in women's equality with men. Experience has shown that those who call themselves feminists may disagree with each other on almost all possible issues, including the definition of women's rights and freedoms.

Before I consciously shed the label, I was often reproached by feminists, asking: 'How can you refuse to join the campaign on such and such issue if you are a feminist?' On many important issues concerning women, I often found myself differing more with current feminist opinion than with other political groups not claiming to be feminist. One way of resisting being dragged into issues taken up by some feminists on which I held a differing position was to learn to say:

I do not call myself a feminist, so I am not duty bound to endorse anything and everything that comes boasting that label. Let us discuss the concrete facts of the case and consider the pros and cons of the approach being proposed and find out if we share any common ground, instead of starting out by assuming an overall solidarity or agreement just because we all assume we are feminists.

Let me illustrate the point. Some feminists have campaigned and lobbied for more stringent legislation and tougher implementation of laws to deal with obscenity or the degrading portrayal of women. I have had serious reservations regarding their approach and could not make common cause with them on this issue, despite my abhorrence of insulting images of women. My reservations were not related to a lack of commitment to women's equality but to my mistrust of authoritarian measures for social reform and to attempts to arm our very corrupt and criminalized state machinery with even more repressive powers than it already has, in the name of curbing pornography. I find this a risky and unacceptable way of fighting for women's dignity. In this case, my commitment to freedom of expression assumed primacy.

Similarly, a number of feminists welcomed the death penalty for wife-murderers, or when it was included as part of the anti-sati law after the protests about the killing of Roop Kanwar. I continue to demand an end to capital punishment, no matter what the crime, based on my objection to the legitimation of killing by the state machinery, even when the pretext may be protection of women. Another conflict arose over the Muslim Women's Bill of 1986, where a supposedly feminist position became the pretext for a large section of opinion-makers to stir up anti-Muslim hysteria. This could only work to the detriment of Muslim women. For this reason, even Shah Bano decided to withdraw her case challenging provisions of Muslim personal law. In my view, one cannot be effective in strengthening the rights of women from minority communities unless both men and women within that community see you as their well-wisher.[1]

Thus, we have differed on virtually every issue as some of the essays in this book testify. The position one takes on various issues is not guided solely by considerations of women's equality—other considerations do come in, whether or not they are acknowledged. Therefore, I find that the use of feminism as a label does not guarantee anything. It does not provide sufficiently significant information about people's perspective. Someone calling herself or himself a feminist need not necessarily have better insights into women's predicament than those who do not. Many non-feminist thinkers and writers have made significant contributions to our thinking on women's issues. The use of the word does not even ensure that the person sporting that label is pro-women. I know many feminists who are far more women-hating than misogynist men. The fierce competitiveness among feminists, sometimes even among those within the same organization, or between different feminist organizations, is often more ferocious than the notorious rivalry between the *saas* and *bahu* in our family life.

During these years of editing *Manushi*, we have often received articles from women who called themselves feminists. Often, the writers assumed that merely by labelling their articles 'feminist' they were guaranteeing not only ideological correctness but also a superior grasp of the issues. However, my experience has taught me that those who flaunt their feminism and undertake self-conscious feminist writing may easily miss out on the complex dimensions of reality because of their obsession with being politically correct. In judging the worth of a piece of writing I have never tried to ascertain whether or not the writer is a feminist or an adherent of any other 'ism'. I find it more useful to ask: Does it make sense? Has the author got the facts of the situation right? Does the writing take into account the many-sided versions of a situation? Or does it oversimplify reality to fit it into a preconceived notion of what the situation ought to be? Will the proposed solution take into account the wishes and aspirations of those for whom it is meant? Will it lead the society towards more humane and egalitarian norms, and expand rather than further restrict the horizons of people's freedom?

Indian vs Western Feminism

Feminism in the West emerged as a powerful challenge to existing power structures and gender equations at the level of the family, the economy and the polity. When used in the western context, the word 'feminism' evokes many positive associations of nearly two centuries or more of struggle by courageous women who braved social attack, ridicule, ostracism and male wrath in order to press women's claim for equality at home, in the workplace, in education, politics, religion and culture. Women like Mary Wollstonecraft and Susan B. Anthony paid a heavy personal price for their struggle to win equal human rights for women. In helping achieve a certain degree of equality for women, and by expanding the space for their aspirations, feminists in western societies pushed their societies to become more democratic.

However, the word 'feminism' evokes no such positive connotations in India. This is not because the idea of women's rights and dignity are alien to our society. Far from it. We have a much longer history of individual women's assertiveness in India and a well-established tradition of making space for women whose aspirations take them in directions different from the stereotypical roles assigned to them. The tradition of goddess worship, of seeing the feminine as *shakti* (power) to be feared and revered, allows Indian society to be far more receptive to women's assertions and strengths, even while it practices very offensive forms of discrimination against women. Yet most of those men and women who fought valiant struggles for women's rights in India—at about the same time that feminists in Europe and America were waging their battles—did not feel the need to use the term 'feminism' for their ideas and work. They coined their own words in their respective languages to describe their purpose. Since, at times, men played an important, even leading role in women's rights movements in India, the struggle did not acquire the overtones of gender warfare as it did in the West where women faced fierce hostility from most politically active men in their endeavours to win equality. Hence, the nature and character of women's articulation of their problems and their chosen methods of struggle remained substantially different from those of the western feminist movements.

Today, we are living in an overall context of a highly imbalanced power equation, where the general flow of ideas and of labels is one way, from the West to the East. Consequently, feminism, as appropriated and defined by the West, has too often become a tool of cultural imperialism. The definitions, the terminology, the assumptions, the forms of struggle and institutions and even the issues are exported from the West and applied to our situation rather mindlessly. In recent years, it has become fashionable to talk of the distinct nature of Third World feminism. But observing it in operation, one finds it is no more than a stick used by Third World feminist establishment to beat up First World feminists, a way of trapping them through guilt into yielding more space and funds for Third World feminist leaders. The underlying assumptions and basic ideology remain essentially the same.

One fundamental problem with many of the ideologies emanating from the West, starting with Christianity, is that they adopt a proselytizing role. Their underlying assumption is that all those who refuse to be converted are steeped in ignorance or stupidity, that their lives cannot be satisfactory if they do not follow the role model provided by western society. In societies like India, we accept differences and diversity as a way of life and take it for granted that different social groups and communities are likely to have their own cultural preferences and ways of life. Feminists may not use the sword and other such methods used by Christian crusaders to seek converts, but they do tend to display missionary zeal in wanting to 'save souls' and tend to look down upon and be hostile to, or at least pity those not already converted—and even more so those unwilling to be converted. Like religious proselytizers they too believe in the importance of head counts of converts especially among the elite.

And since those who believe in exporting this ideology to other cultures are working mainly through western aid agencies, both secular and religious, they too have a lot of goodies to offer anyone who converts to feminism, learns to mouth the appropriate rhetoric and spread the message among others by becoming another proselytizer. Since proselytization has become such a lucrative profession they inevitably react with hostility to anyone resisting that label.

Most Indian feminists felt very angry and outraged at my refusal to be labelled a feminist. This is especially surprising since on most important questions the feminist establishment in India is hostile to and disapproving of the stands I take or the way I analyse issues. For me, disowning the label was essentially a way of saying: 'Since I do not share the feminist leadership's views, demands, methods of struggle and way of dealing with our society, I obviously do not qualify to be called a feminist.' I had imagined it would have caused a sense of relief among those who were forever upset at my writings and other political interventions. On the contrary, this made them even more hostile. It took me a long time to understand the reason for this. Anyone refusing to be counted as a convert seems to them to be challenging one of the basic tenets of the 'ism'—that it is the *only* route to progress for Indian women, that its tenets have universal applicability, that only feminists know how to stand up for the rights of women. By refusing the label, one is also challenging their right and power to make people fall in line with all their commands.

The dos and don'ts expected of feminists can be both oppressive and or absurd. I remember being seriously advised many years ago, by one of my feminist colleagues at *Manushi* not to wear any jewellery when attending an international feminist conference or else I would be looked down upon. My response was 'I would rather not attend any conference than subject myself to such regimentation and give up—something I enjoy doing.' This turned out to be a case of subjects being more loyal than the king because by then many western feminists had gotten over the hang-up of trying 'not to look feminine'. Feminists in India have devised their own dress code: ethnic hand-woven dresses are the expected norm; wearing synthetics is definitely out. Ethnic silver jewellery is appropriate; gold and diamonds are looked down upon. These demands could be laughed off as trivia—not so their role as the thought police, especially on issues of vital importance.

Culture of Intolerance

The excessive intolerance within the feminist establishment is related to the fact that women's issues in India have come to be dominated in the media, in government policy and in influential, public fora by those claiming to be socialist feminists. Since the days of Nehru and his daughter, socialism has been the avowed policy of the state and continues to hold powerful sway in India even after the break up of the Congress party's monopoly of power. For instance, a requirement introduced by Mrs Indira Gandhi into the Constitution was that every political organization has to swear by socialism, as a prerequisite for recognition by the Election Commission in order to qualify to fight elections as a party. This has not been changed even after the Sangh Parivar's rise to power. They too have learnt to mouth the same old statist slogans. Socialism enjoys tremendous political and social clout in our country despite the lack of any coherent ideological pro- gramme or practice that corresponds to the label; it is usually a term flaunted by some advocates of increased state power, who hope thereby to acquire greater power and riches in its name.

However, the Indian state, for all its inefficiency, corruption and venality, is not an 'intolerant' state—partly because it is too inefficient to be effectively authoritarian—but also because our society doesn't take well to dictators. However, our Marxist feminists and some of the left parties who still include Stalin among their ideological mentors bring a great deal of intolerance into the public, political domain. No matter how disastrous their politics prove for society, they remain convinced that history has bestowed on them the exclusive privilege of prescribing solutions to the world's problems simply because their chosen ideology tells them they alone can be right. Even when they change their position to suit political expediency and to catch up with the latest political fashions, they somehow think they can get away with pretending that they alone have remained consistent in their political wisdom. Such is their grip over their versions of political correctness, and so much is their nuisance value for any anyone who dares differ with them, that very few in the left spectrum dare chal- lenge their prescriptions.

Imported Labels

Sections of the women's movement in India have picked up not just the term 'feminist' from the West but also all of the norms, assump- tions and debates that emanate from it, as well as to some extent those that emerged from the polemics of the Russian revolutionaries. An interesting example of the fledgling movement in India being com- pelled to act as an echo of the supposedly more advanced movements in the West, is the way divisions were assumed to exist in India before organized feminist activity had taken shape here. When, in the late seventies, *Manushi* and a number of new women's groups began to emerge, certain self-appointed theoreticians immediately went about labelling different groups and individuals as belonging to one of three trends: bourgeois feminist, socialist feminist or radical feminist. Some of these self-appointed certificate-givers descended directly from the West; others, although 'natives' like us, were better grounded in the western women's movement debates than in the reality of women's lives here. I remember my bewilderment at the ferocity of the label warfare. Where did it descend from? Certainly not from any split in India on ideological lines. There were only a handful of groups and individuals working on women's issues. Most activists were women from upper middle-class families and, most of the groups had not crystallized organizationally or theoretically. No political action on any significant scale had yet been undertaken, and so hardly any meaningful dialogue over strategy and tactics had taken place. Yet, those mesmerized by the rhetoric of other movements tried to force us to assume the existence at that time not only of a major women's movement here, but also of major divisions within it. We were supposed to have split even before we got a real opportunity to get together to see or hear one another, let alone carry out a debate among ourselves.

These labels were not used as descriptions of the positions taken by individuals or groups or the work being done by them, but as epithets to condemn people you did not like, i.e., as good or bad character certificates. The label-givers assumed that the most respectable term was 'socialist feminist'. This was usually reserved for oneself and one's friends, as proof of one's correct political credentials. Those one did not like were condemned as 'bourgeois feminists' or 'radical feminists'. The utter absurdity of these ideological labels was evident. They have been used as sticks to beat people with, to stifle intellectual growth and enquiry, to frighten people from thinking things out for themselves, to bully them into blindly accepting formula-ridden politics and repeating meaningless *mantras,* and to subject them to slander if they resist.

Interestingly, *Manushi* was honoured, often at the same time, with all three epithets. I was called everything from radical feminist man-hater to bourgeois feminist to leftist extremist, even anarchist. Some of those who imagined themselves Marxists or Socialists called me 'bourgeois'. Some even descried me as a 'Gandhian reactionary'. Those using these labels were clearly not describing my politics. Realizing that this ideological 'ism' warfare was an unreal one, I chose not to enter into it. Instead, whenever accused of being a bourgeois feminist or whatever, I would ask the persons concerned to define the terms they were using and then to point out what in *Manushi's* work conformed to their definition. Not one of the label-givers I spoke to actually ended up accurately going through this exercise.

The labelling requirement distorts not only the present but even the past. I remember being viciously attacked in certain meetings of staunch feminists for presenting in a positive light the lives, protest and poetry of women like Mahadeviakka and Mirabai. This occurred much before the time that Bhakti and Sufi saints became politically fashionable among Marxists. They argued at that time that these women did not talk of women's independence and equality in the manner they ought to have, that they merely chose to substitute slavery to a husband by slavery to a god. In sum, they were inadequate as historical sources of inspiration for women because they could not be considered sufficiently feminist. However, in recent years after the left parties changed their stance towards select religious movements and it became fashionable to identify with Bhakti-Sufi movements, leftist feminists have also started bending themselves backwards to discover feminist streaks in women like Mirabai. Branding Mirabai as a feminist is as inappropriate as calling Gautam Buddha a Gandhian or Jesus Christ a civil libertarian.

This approach of evaluating our past is exceedingly naive. Looking for historical figures to match each and every momentary fashion of today's feminists in completely different circumstances is patently absurd. We need to understand the aspirations and nature of women's stirrings and protest in different epochs in the context of the dilemmas of their age, rather than impose our own aspirations on them. The past ought not to be studied either to seek justifications for our present day political inclinations, nor faulted for not having lived up to them, but rather viewed on its own terms, while being acknowledged as our inherited legacy.

Expected to be a Mirror Image

The use of the term 'feminism' and the resultant 'ism' warfare brought with it a host of other problems. Even in forms of organization, we were expected to live up to the standards, patterns or mythologies evolved by western feminists, and even to mimic many of the stances taken within the movement there. You had to pre-decide, for instance, whether you were going to walk hand in hand with, ahead of, or behind men. We were bullied to take a position on separatism simply because the issue had been the cause of a major controversy in the West. In the early years, there were occasions when certain feminists from the West who believed in totally excluding men from participating in women's movements threatened to launch a boycott against *Manushi* since it included articles and letters by men. At the other end of the spectrum, a section of those who considered themselves socialist feminists in India accused *Manushi* of being anti-men and also attempted to organize a boycott against it. During all these years, despite these pressures and attacks on us, we studiously avoided duplicating the postures and responses of factions within the western feminist movement on the issue of men's participation in the women's movement. It seemed as foolish to take an *a priori* position against men, as some separatist feminists insisted on doing, as it would be to insist, as a cardinal principle, on an unconditional alliance with men, as those who called themselves socialist feminists required of everyone. It made no sense to expect an undifferentiated response from all men—or from women for that matter. I felt that the actual responses of people, men and women, to the issues we advocated would provide a better indicator of whom to build meaningful alliances with. Thus, we neither shunned men on the basis of theoretically postulated confrontation, nor did we woo them insisting on a preconceived alliance. Partly as a consequence, *Manushi* has over the years received an unusual amount of support from numerous men with a variety of ideological orientations.

Similarly, it was assumed that we must work through what western feminists call 'non-hierarchical collectives' even if the experiment had not really worked in the West. I have an inherent mistrust of authoritarian structures. However, the particular notion of a 'collective' common within the feminist fold at that time and the unrealistic expectations that it created, proved to be a mistaken import from the West. In the early phase of *Manushi's* existence, we unwittingly used the term without being aware of its history in the western women's movement. At that point of time, we were confronted with the task of putting together a loose heterogeneous group of volunteers whose work commitment was often not sustained. With fluctuating attendance and very unequal work contributions, it was hard to say who among the volunteers would actually persevere and take up responsibility in a continuing way. We could not announce a fixed set of names as a core group, since none existed. Though we provisionally chose the term 'collective', we were eventually compelled to drop it because it became a liability. Nevertheless, the entire set of controversies aroused by the term in the West descended on us lock, stock and barrel. We were besieged by any number of self-appointed inspectors who arrived to examine the health of our collective. The idea of collectives was poorly thought out even in the West. Attempts to import a structure that in actuality functions only rarely and temporarily created bizarre results among Indian women's groups and led to many more splits and fractures among groups because feminist anger came to be directed much more at other feminists rather than societal forces of oppression they claimed to fight. The rhetoric of anti-authoritarian collectives often gets to be used as a weapon of attack, to settle personal scores, and vent one's resentment and jealousy against one's colleagues. *Manushi* continues to be attacked for having failed to be a proper collective even though I feel we have arrived at a far more workable formula—anyone who wishes to work for *Manushi* is welcome to do so without any qualifying criteria and can have a say in whatever area of work they choose to volunteer for, for whatever length of period they are active.

It is unfortunate that the import of ideology follows a pattern similar to that of other imports, for example, certain technologies, fashions and addictions. Many things known to be obsolete or unworkable and therefore discarded in the West, continue to be dumped in Third World countries. Likewise, ideas and institutions which have been discarded by major elements in the feminist movement in the West continue to be advocated here as appropriate feminist responses.

It is not just that issues and campaigns have been imported. There has also been an attempt to emotionally live through the responses of the women's movement in the West, even though the situations have been different in India. For example, while the feminist movement in the West did experience ridicule, and even outright hostility, especially in the mass media, feminists in India (as distinguished from the oppressed women they try to represent) have, by and large, been rather well treated. Often they even get disproportionate attention. The mainstream mass media has gone out of its way to offer fairly uncritical support to feminists and their work. The media created this space for feminists without resistance. Yet, the vocabulary used by feminists in India is nevertheless often one that is used by a persecuted movement. India's mass media is often portrayed as though it has responded with ridicule and hostility toward Indian feminists as have many sections of the western media toward their own women's movements. It is the same with regard to men's responses to women's issues. Women's organizations have received a lot of support from men. There have been virtually no instances of attack—physical or political—on account of feminist politics. Yet, feminist literature in India has rarely tried to acknowledge or analyse this difference in response. It continues to use the standard Western rhetoric in describing male responses to women's struggle.

The International Bandwagon

In the West, feminism undoubtedly played a liberating role for women. The differences between the impact there and here are due to the channels through which this ideology is today reaching Third World countries. In the West, feminism evolved from women's own struggles against oppressive power structures which excluded them from equal participation in many aspects of the economic, social and political life of their society—for example, denial of the right to vote or exclusion from universities and other professional institutions. As a result, an important component of western feminism has been a radical and anti-authoritarian thrust.

However, the bulk of Third World women were exposed to the ideology of western feminism at a stage when western feminists, after years of struggle, began succeeding in occupying a few positions of power and influence in various institutions, including in government, universities and a whole range of international agencies. Through western feminist pressure and influence more funds were made available for what came to be called women's projects as well as for women's studies programmes in universities, first in the West and later in the Third World countries. Thus, in India, new opportunities were made available for a small number of western-educated women who gravitated towards feminism. Being absorbed in international feminist circles brought upward mobility in jobs and careers, and invitations to international conferences and study programmes. This access to jobs, consultancies and grants, especially in universities and came international aid organizations came relatively easy for those calling themselves feminists as compared to those unversed in feminist rhetoric. This was contrary to the experiences of western feminists who had to struggle hard to find acceptance in their professions. Since feminism brought with it is certain amount of easy international mobility for many Third World feminists, the ideological domination of western feminism and the resultant importation of frequently inappropriate issues was absorbed uncritically. In this context, the use of vaguely radical anti-establishment rhetoric borrowed by Indian feminists from the early stages of the western feminist movement appears especially inappropriate considering their close alliance with the Indian bureaucracy through whom all the grants must be channeled.

This mindless importation of issues is most evident at many of the international conferences. Third World feminists are invited to such conferences with the expectation that they will join the campaign on whatever issues are currently fashionable in the West. Those who have resisted or expressed reservations are usually excluded. To give just one example: some years ago, I was invited to attend a conference on reproductive technologies to be held in Germany. However, since the invitation letter mentioned that those who attended the conference would be expected to campaign against the use of certain new forms of contraception and reproductive technologies being developed in the West, I wrote back saying that while I was willing to discuss these issues, I was not prepared to commit myself in advance because, on the basis of available information, I had not yet been convinced about the need to oppose all these reproductive technologies. I was summarily told that in that case they would cancel the invitation they had extended. It came as a relief because had I gone there, I would have faced enormous hostility for refusing to tow the line. A few such unpleasant experiences in the early years of *Manushi* taught me to stay away from those feminist conferences where fund donors and organizers had already pre-set both their agendas and their conclusions.

In most cases, Third World feminists end up becoming part of so-called international campaigns on the basis of having been sent materials that present only a partial picture of the issues. They are often without access to any sources of independent research and investigation, even when the issue requires careful study, interpretation and evaluation of specialized technical data. Their naive campaigns against virtually every new form of contraceptives being introduced in the market is one of many examples of how many Third World feminists take up cudgels on this or that issue without doing proper homework. Such campaigns are often launched without even finding out whether these methods are actually being used in India, and if so, how widespread is their use, leave alone the conducting of any careful evaluations within India to assess the negative side effects of these contraceptives in comparison to other available options. The opposition is mostly based on campaign material prepared in the

West, using data from some of the inconclusive studies available to feminists at that time. It seems foolish for us to set such a high priority on opposing contraceptives on the basis of their side effects, while we are not paying sufficient attention to higher priority issues, such as the millions of deaths being caused in India due to the unavailability of any kind of effective and safe contraceptives for the majority of women. Meanwhile the government had in the recent past continued pushing sterilization operations as the preferred method of contraception, performing them under extremely unsafe and unhygienic conditions, causing serious health problems and frequent deaths for untold numbers of poor women. Nevertheless, opposing new contraceptives remains a favourite issue among the feminist activists in India.

Often issues are picked up simply because funds are available to work on these issues while they are not available for other more pressing priorities. The dependence on funding agencies causes an undue emulation of the changing fashions in the West. Most of these campaigners are primarily accountable to their donors rather than to the fellow women living in the society they claim to serve. Their priorities and agendas are prone to change from year to year depending on the availability of targeted funds. The moment the UN declares for example, that next year is to be the year of the girl child, everyone gets busy planning seminars, writing, researching and making films on the girl child. The poor creature is forgotten as soon as a new priority is declared by donor agencies and the focus shifts to whatever else brings in the money. All these factors seriously inhibit and stunt the process of understanding the reality of women's lives in India where women's struggles have followed quite a different course. Consequently, feminist scholarship has often failed to provide an appropriate means of analysis. Its literature is subject to wide swings with every change in intellectual fashion in the West: structuralism to deconstructionism to post-modernism and now even postfeminism. The compass needle keeps swinging from one fad to the other, depending on what brings in easy grants, jobs, fellowships, conference invitations and media recognition—even as it often leads many feminists towards irrelevance and the use of such an esoteric vocabulary that those whose lives they are supposed to represent, construct, and deconstruct do not comprehend a word of it.

Western aid money has also brought about a shift from political movements for the redressal of political, social, and economic power imbalances to 'development projects'. The 'development' ideology was an innovation of the West, notably the US, to counter the spread of communist ideas in many Third World countries. It operates on the assumption that the poor are poor because they are backward and underdeveloped as human beings. Therefore, in the tradition of nineteenth century European missionaries and colonizers, the 'backward' people are to be 'developed' by advanced outsiders through raising their awareness level, as well as by means of small token doses of financial help provided for running special health projects, income generating projects, literacy projects, and—of course—development projects! A good part of feminist energy is today going into writing project proposals for grants and reports to funding agencies on their supposed progress. Curiously enough, the western agencies support the liberal use of leftist rhetoric by the feminists; thus, the illusion of great revolutionary activity is kept intact even while the projects they run for their funders are as different from 'revolutionary' activity as chalk is from cheese.

Since most self-proclaimed Indian feminists come from elite families, their appearing before aid agencies as supplicants applying for grants amounts to making a career out of displaying the misery of the poor women of India in international fora. This has created a great deal of mistrust of the feminist establishment in India. Many people believe that the feminist elite have developed a vested interest in the poverty and misery of Indian women. How else, people speculate, can you explain their vigorous opposition to economic reforms in India?

The feminist establishment considers it their creditworthy achievement, that they were able to project a unanimous agenda at the UN conference on women held in Beijing, opposing even our half-hearted programme of economic reforms that have timidly suggested the dismantling of only a few of the most pernicious statist controls on economic activities. Crippling restrictions and obstacles imposed on business and agriculture by the bureaucracy in India have wrecked the Indian economy and criminalized our polity. Yet, the feminist lobby in India wishes the state to retain and even enchance its monopoly on almost all sectors of the economy, as well as its draconian restrictions that deny all of us the right to try to earn a livelihood without being held hostage by the *sarkar*. The total opposition by leading feminist groups to even token dismantling of government controls shows that for all their pro-poor rhetoric they are essentially statists. (For a detailed discussion of this see my article, 'A Half Step

Forward, The Thwarting of Economic Reforms in India, *Manushi* 92–93, 1996)

By statism, I mean a world-view which subordinates civil society to the dictates of the state and its bureaucracy. Statists are those who believe in the government playing an over-arching, omnipresent role in controlling social and economic affairs because they do not trust ordinary people to behave sensibly, nor to have the innate capacity to resolve social conflicts amongst themselves without petitioning the *sarkar* to intervene. They believe that the state is the primary vehicle for societal engineering and that those in positions of state power ought to determine the organizational principles for the entire society. They seem convinced that if they can prevail upon the state to pass what they consider proper laws, people can be made to behave in ways approved by these self-appointed reformers and social engineers.

Thus, they borrow lock, stock and barrel from the agenda of the Nehruvian Congress and its pet child—the 'socialist' bureaucracy. State socialism may be discredited the world over and violently disowned by those who have lived under socialist dictators and suffered the tyranny of those systems. Strangely enough, its ideological hold among Indian feminists is still strong even though ritual repetition of its abstractly attractive principles has not brought about equality in any society. It has only assisted our bureaucrats, politicians and 'licensees' to find newer justifications for looting the country for personal gain.

It is understandable that our bureaucracy is feeling threatened by the prospect of losing its power as our economy sinks further and further under the dead weight of the corrupt and bloated government machinery and more people begin to demand that those governmental controls which have wrecked our economy be removed. Being aware of how discredited and mistrusted these *sarkari babus* are on account of the mess they have made of our country, they dare not fight their battle openly on their own behalf. With no one else willing to defend them, our bureaucrats have found another valuable ally in the feminist establishment, which has valiantly risen to their rescue by declaring a *jehad* against economic reforms. Their alliance with the bureaucracy should hardly come as a surprise, since for all their 'anti-government' rhetoric, the statist feminists depend on the *sarkar* for their very survival. Even when the feminist organizations in our country get their funds from various international donor agencies they require prior clearance and sanction by the government. This allows the bureaucracy to keep their political activity within approved parameters.

Most feminists that campaign against the dismantling of government controls on economic activity have focused obsessively on the need to prevent the entry of foreign capital and to snipper collaborations between Indian and foreign companies. Here an ethical issue is involved. If they think bringing in western money and intellectual know-how, is so harmful, they ought to start their campaign by refusing to apply for or accept grants for their political work from various western donor agencies. Or is it that our statist feminists want us to continue presenting ourselves before the world as beggars requiring endless doses of foreign aid rather than aspiring to become active participants in the world economy?

The Indian feminists' fascination for strong arm statist methods is apparent even when they are dealing with sensitive social issues and human relations. The characteristic feminist response to most social issues affecting women is to demand more and more strictly implemented stringent laws. The results in most cases, do not better women's lives but rather facilitate a whole spate of burdensome and harmful legislation which has put even more arbitrary powers in the hands of the police and government—powers that are routinely abused for both harassing people, as well as extracting bribes. More often than not, feminists tend to intervene in people's lives in the guise of attacking outsiders rather than as caring insiders. That is why they have failed to forge strong links with the civil society they wish to reform.

An important reason for *Manushi's* survival has been its ability to keep a deliberate distance from many of the preoccupations of Indian feminists as well as from the wars between various other 'isms' in India. This has paradoxically, led to genuine, mutually beneficial interaction with a much larger cross-section of people of many shades of opinion and won the support of a very large spectrum of people in India—from the left to the right and also with a large range of women activists doing admirable work in various parts of India.

Finally, all that I have written should not result in the reader concluding that I do not have a coherent world-view. I would like to see a world in which the means for a dignified life are available to all human beings equally, where the polity and economy are decentralized so that people have greater control over their own lives, where the diversity within and among groups and individuals is respected, and where tolerance and equality of rights and responsibilities are fostered at all levels.

I believe in a non-authoritarian politics of consensus and non-violence and my immediate political goals include: working to ensure the survival needs of all, especially of vulnerable groups; working for the accountability of government to the citizens with minimal state control over people's lives; ensuring social and political space to minority groups for the evolution of their identities; and moving towards the lessening of economic disparities. A primary motive in my life is working for women's equality and freedom in all areas of life.

In this, I have never felt any sense of loss or disadvantage in working without the support of an 'ism'. In fact, it gives me a much greater sense of freedom in trying to work out meaningful responses to our specific social situation, for I have to assume full responsibility for my political interventions. Nor do I enjoy the license to use the ritual variety? of this or that ideology as a substitute for sensible, workable and creative ideas to meet the challenges we face today.

NOTES

1. For a detailed analysis see my article 'Pro-Women or Anti-Muslim? The Shah Bano Controversy' in *Manushi*, No. 32, 1986. This and related articles on this theme are included in a book of my essays: *Religion at the Service of Nationalism*, Oxford University Press, 1998.